W9-COT-353

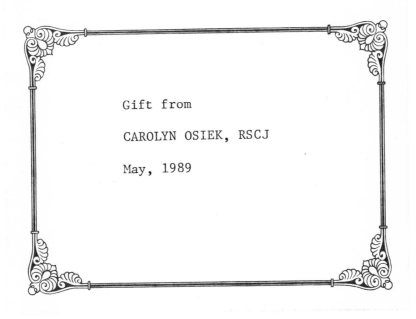

Gift from

CAROLYN OSIEK, RSCJ

May, 1989

JUDAISM

• THE EVOLUTION OF A FAITH •

by

PHILLIP SIGAL

Revised and Edited by

LILLIAN SIGAL

WILLIAM B. EERDMANS PUBLISHING COMPANY
GRAND RAPIDS, MICHIGAN

First published 1986 as *Judentum* by Kohlhammer, Stuttgart.

Library of Congress Cataloging-in-Publication Data

Sigal, Phillip.
  Judaism: the evolution of a faith / by Phillip Sigal;
revised and edited by Lillian Sigal.—Rev. ed. / Lillian Sigal.
    p.   cm.
  Bibliography: p. 307
  Includes index.
  ISBN 0-8028-0345-8
  1. Judaism—History.   I. Sigal, Lillian.   II. Title.
BM155.2.S47   1988
296'.09—dc19   88-21736
                                  CIP

Contents

Chapter Two • Judaism after the Babylonian Exile (ca. 400 B.C.E.-70 C.E.)

Chapter Four • The Medieval Era I: From Diaspora Goes Forth Torah

Chapter Five • The Medieval Era II: Philosophy and Mysticism

Chapter Six • Proto-Modernity: Renaissance and Reformation

Chapter Seven • The Modern and Contemporary Periods

CONTENTS

Preface

LILLIAN SIGAL

This book was originally written by my late husband, Phillip Sigal, as the distillation of a projected five-volume series entitled *The Emergence of Contemporary Judaism,* three volumes of which have been published. The distillation of that multivolume work was translated into German and published as a one-volume survey of Judaism entitled *Judentum.*[1] The present book is my revised and edited version of his original English manuscript of *Judentum,* to which I have added an appendix entitled "Images of Women in Judaism."

The basic approach of this book is both historical and thematic. It is historical in that it follows the chronological sequence of history from pre-Israelite days to the modern period. It is not, however, a history of the Jews, but rather an exposition of religious developments set in an historical pattern. The author emphasizes the continuity of the entire historical process. He therefore draws no dichotomy between the religion prior to the Babylonian exile and that of the period following it. By identifying the faith of the former period as "Proto-Judaism" and the religion of the latter period as "Judaism," he weaves the two together into one seamless tapestry. A major thread that winds its way through the labyrinth of complex events, personalities, and literature spanned by this book is the following thesis: Judaism has been and continues to be a dynamic and pluralistic religion with a common core of faith that has changed and adapted to the time, spirit, and conditions of the varying cultures and ages it has encountered.

The audience for which this book is intended are lay and clergy

---

1. *Judentum* (Stuttgart: Kohlhammer, 1986).

people of all faiths or people of no particular faith who seek a cogent account of the evolution of Judaism from its origins to the present. Readers interested in the Christian study of Judaism will find this work especially valuable, since its author, having been a rabbinic as well as a Christian Testament scholar, brings his unique expertise to the understanding of the relationship between Judaism and Christianity. He illuminates the Jewish matrix which gave birth to Christianity and explores both the tensions and the ongoing intellectual interchange between the two faiths.

It should be noted, however, that based on his research into the wide-ranging intertestamental and rabbinic literature of the milieu that spawned Christianity, the author presents his own original theory of the Pharisees (Chapter Three) in contrast to the standard one. For more detailed information concerning this theory and the author's other original insights into the nature of Judaism and Judeo-Christian studies, the reader is advised to consult his scholarly articles and books listed in the bibliography at the back of this book.[2]

Because of current interest in reclaiming women's participation in the development of culture and society, I have written and appended to this book a chapter on feminine images of God and on the evolving role of women in Judaism from biblical Eve to contemporary women rabbis.

The terms B.C.E. (Before the Common Era) and C.E. (the Common Era) are used in this text in lieu of B.C. (Before Christ) and A.D. (anno Domini—in the year of the Lord), respectively, in order to provide language that includes both the Christian and the non-Christian reader. Furthermore, the expressions "Jewish" or "Hebrew" Bible, Scriptures, or Testament (rather than "Old Testament") and "Christian" Bible, Scriptures, or Testament (rather than "New Testament") used in this volume are intended to acknowledge that the latter did not supersede the former, but that each is the sacred text of its respective faith. Other unfamiliar, technical, or foreign terms are either explained in the text or are included in the glossary at the back of this book.

The festivals are presented twice: Chapter One deals with their format in the Proto-Judaic period, and Chapter Eight discusses their development and theology from the postexilic era to the present.

To aid the reader further, a chronological table providing an over-

---

2. See especially *The Emergence of Contemporary Judaism*, I/1, and *The Halakah of Jesus of Nazareth According to the Gospel of Matthew*.

view of the major events of Jewish history as well as the corresponding highlights in both Christian and world history is available at the end of this text. Moreover, readers are encouraged to keep the Bible handy at all times to refer to biblical passages cited in the book. Actual quotations from the Jewish and Christian Scriptures are taken from the Jerusalem Bible, except where translated by the author.

I am indebted to numerous people for helping me prepare this manuscript. The following people have my deepest gratitude for their reading of chapters and useful comments: Dr. Donald Herman, Prof. David Huisman, Philip Jung, Sue Strimer Sweder, Dorothy Powell, Morris Kleiman, Rev. Thomas Toeller-Novak, and Rev. Claire Wolterstorff. I also offer special thanks to my daughter, Sabrina Sigal Falls, for her valuable suggestions and editorial assistance. Finally, I wish to acknowledge all my children—my daughters, Sharon and Sabrina, and my sons-in-law, David and Jim—for their love and encouragement while this work was in progress, and to dedicate this work to them and to my grandson, Michael.

Finally, I would like to pay tribute to my late husband, Phillip. Preparing this book for publication has been a labor of love. In his eulogy for him, Professor Jacob Petachowski said that Phillip was "'like a spring which wells up with ever-sustaining vigor' (Ab. 2:10-11), that is, bubbling with new ideas." As his partner in life, I was privileged to imbibe much wisdom from that spring, and in making this manuscript available to an English-speaking audience, I hope to keep his spring bubbling. I invite the reader to join me in drinking from it and in being thereby refreshed.

Preface

PHILLIP SIGAL

The task of portraying the entire range of Judaism in a brief volume is immense. Inevitably, justice will not be done to every period of its long development, to every theme of its theology, or to every branch of its *halakah* (religious practice). Nevertheless, I hope that these chapters will present a relatively adequate description of the Judaic religion. The student or scholar may pursue the suggested bibliography for further study and in-depth research into the profound areas of thought and practice only briefly surveyed here.

The task of writing this book, while I am engaged in a more comprehensive five-volume work on Judaism *(The Emergence of Contemporary Judaism)* and in my ongoing New Testament researches, has been gratifying and welcome. It has enabled me to formulate, if only briefly, some of the major theses and hypotheses that I have long aspired to read in the works of others but failed to discover there. I hope that I have put to rest some stereotypical ideas that recur in printed works on Judaism and have provided the reader with new and enriching insights.

Much of the material covering the ancient and medieval periods is based upon my previous studies published in *The Emergence of Contemporary Judaism,* Volumes I and II.[1] I wish, therefore, to express my sincerest appreciation to the publisher, Pickwick Press, and to Dikran Hadidian, the General Editor of the Pittsburgh Theological Monograph Series, of which those volumes constitute Numbers 12, 29, and 29a,

---

1. Vol. III, which deals with the 16th and 17th centuries, has been published posthumously. (See Bibliography.)

for their kind permission to use the material in this work. I wish also to thank the staff of the Calvin College Seminary Library, and especially the Theological Librarian Peter De Klerk, for all the courtesies shown me in my research in general, and specifically as these touched upon the execution of this book.

Finally, as in the case of all my previous books, I wish to take note of the fact that this work would not be possible without the understanding and encouragement of my wife, Dr. Lillian Sigal. My children have always been an inspiration to me in the quest for viable religion, and consequently, in the research for a way to articulate the Word that Judaism seeks to eternalize and concretize. I therefore dedicate this work to my three children, Sharon, Sabrina, and David.

As I complete this labor of love in the vineyard of the Lord I am thankful for the ability to have done so. With the psalmist I repeat,

> I will sing to Yhwh during my life,
> I will play for my God while yet I am.
> May my reflections be pleasing to him
> As I rejoice in Yhwh.

> Ps. 104:33-34

Symbols and Abbreviations

In general the abbreviations are the standard ones used by the Society of Biblical Literature.

JEWISH TESTAMENT

Gen.	Genesis
Exod.	Exodus
Lev.	Leviticus
Num.	Numbers
Deut.	Deuteronomy
Jgs.	Judges
1 and 2 Sam.	1 and 2 Samuel
1 and 2 Kgs.	1 and 2 Kings
Isa.	Isaiah
Jer.	Jeremiah
Ezek.	Ezekiel
Hos.	Hosea
Mic.	Micah
Zech.	Zechariah
Ps.	Psalms
Eccl.	Ecclesiastes (Kohelet or Qohelet)
Lam.	Lamentations
Dan.	Daniel
Neh.	Nehemiah

APOCRYPHA AND PSEUDEPIGRAPHA

Sir.	The Wisdom of Joshua ben Sirach (Ecclesiasticus)
En.	Enoch
Esdr.	Esdras
Jub.	Jubilees
Test. Benj.	Testament of Benjamin
Wisd.	The Book of Wisdom (Wisdom of Solomon)

CHRISTIAN TESTAMENT

Matt.	Matthew
Rom.	Romans
1 and 2 Cor.	1 and 2 Corinthians
Gal.	Galatians
Phil.	Philippians
1 Tim.	1 Timothy

PHILO

QG	*Questions on Genesis*
QE	*Questions on Exodus*

DEAD SEA SCROLLS

CD	Damascus (Zadokite) Document
1QS	Manual of Discipline

TARGUM

P. Targ.	Palestinian Targum

TALMUD

M.	Mishnah
T.	Tosefta
B.	Babylonian Talmud
P.	Palestinian Talmud
Ab.	Abot
Ab. R. Nat.	Abot de Rabbi Nathan
A.Z.	Aboda Zara
B. Mes.	Baba Mesia (or Metzia)
Ed.	Eduyyot
Git.	Gittin

Hor.	Horayot
Meg.	Megilla
Men.	Menahot
Naz.	Nazir
Nid.	Niddah
Qid.	Qiddushin
Rosh Hash.	Rosh Hashanah
San.	Sanhedrin
Shab.	Shabbat
Taan.	Taanit

MIDRASH

Lev. Rab.	Leviticus Rabbah

OTHER

Rab. (following name of book)	Rabbah
Gk.	Greek
Bib. Ant.	Biblical Antiquities of Pseudo-Philo
Thom.	Gospel of Thomas (Coptic)
M.T. Mel.	Mishnah Torah, Melakim (Kings) by Moses Maimonides
S.H.	*Sepher Hasidim*

JUDAISM

• THE EVOLUTION OF A FAITH •

Introduction
What Is Judaism?

I. FAITH AND FORM

Judaism and Jews, the latter more accurately called Judaists, elude definition. There never was, and there is not now, one Judaism; rather there have always been many Judaisms. Therefore, Judaism should be seen in all its complexity as the expression of a pluralistic theological and halakic system of a multinational religious association. Like every religion, Judaism possesses both essence and form. Its essence is its faith or doctrine, consisting of theology and spiritual aspirations. Its form is its halakah, incorporating guidelines for ethical conduct and sacred rituals that make its essence concrete.

A. Faith

Despite significant changes in the course of the evolution of Judaism, its primary doctrines recall the pristine theology of the ancient religion of Israel. These doctrines are monotheism, creation, covenant, election, revelation, and redemption. The meaning and ramifications of these principles of faith will be discussed in later chapters of this book, especially Chapters Five and Eight.

B. Form (Halakah)

Since the term *halakah* pervades this work and is central to understanding Judaism, and since its meaning is complex, it will be helpful to explain it in detail at the outset.

Halakah is the quintessential characteristic of Judaism. The great master of talmudic rabbinic literature, Louis Ginzberg, once described

1

halakah as "the really typical creation of our people." The word *halakah* is derived from the Hebrew verb *halak,* "to walk," signifying the way one lives, or norms of conduct. The foremost talmudist, Saul Lieberman, has indicated that halakah might be translated as "guideposts" to oberving the forms and norms of the tradition.

Halakah has been a long organic process found in both the Bible and rabbinic sources. Illustrative of this process are the Ten Commandments, which provided the halakah—rules of conduct—for the essence of the Judaic faith. But the interpretation of the Decalogue was put into the hands of human beings who elaborated it and gave it more specific application. For example, the fourth commandment declares, "Remember the sabbath day and keep it holy" (Exod. 20:8). The essence of the Sabbath is the commemoration of creation (Exod. 20:11) and the Exodus from Egypt (Deut. 5:15)—the theological affirmation of God as Creator and Redeemer. The pentateuchal halakah basically enjoins the Israelite to desist from work (Exod. 20:10) and from kindling fire (Exod. 35:3) on the Sabbath. There is scanty reference in the Pentateuch, however, to the form by which the Israelite was to observe the Sabbath. The rabbis therefore created halakah in the form of liturgy to help the Jew make the theology of the Sabbath concrete in ceremonies such as kiddush (a prayer recited over a cup of wine), lighting candles, and reciting grace.

Another example of halakah is circumcision, which is a sign of the covenant (Gen. 17:4). The particulars of the practice of circumcision as surgical act and as liturgical process constitute the forms by which the concept of covenant is expressed. Some other themes embodied in halakic norms are marriage, divorce, festivals, prayer, and dietary practices.

The word *halakah* is often loosely translated as "law," but this is neither accurate nor adequate. The rabbinic usage of the term cannot be considered an equivalent of what we call "law" in Western civilization, for there are inherent differences between halakah and other law systems. Foremost among these is that halakah, from the beginning, was not a fixed or standardized legal system supported by the authority of an autonomous state and reinforced by a judicial system free to administer penalties in the same way as, for example, was Roman law. Halakah evolved unsystematically over a long period of history, and multiple halakic approaches evolved simultaneously. Thus the people had options from which to choose their observance of the halakah. The diversity that obtained was true not only of ritual but also of civil halakah. Furthermore, as a widespread diaspora, Jewish communities were all autonomous, each pursuing its own halakic ends. The diversification of halakic decisions down through the centuries influenced different communities to perform diversified practices. No scholar saw himself as a dissenter; each thought his decision to be as divinely ordained as the others and equally binding. Thus, halakah was never monolithic, but rather represented multiform approaches.

Halakah has been the instrument by which Judaism has expressed its theology and morality. It is the "way" to reach the ideals of the faith embodied in both ritual and ethical behavior, which spiritualizes the life of the Jew. Moreover, halakah is a living, dynamic process, which in differing times and places seeks to make viable an eternal essence in a temporal setting.

II. PLURALISM AND EVOLUTION

Pluralism has characterized Judaism since its beginnings as the religion of Israel. Discrepancies within the earliest biblical documents attest to varying traditions, all of which were preserved. Different groups that practiced these traditions claimed equal legitimacy with other groups, or asserted a more aggressive piety and denied legitimacy to others. Both the pluralistic and evolving stages of the faith were kept in the final editing of the Jewish Scriptures. Thus, understanding the practice and faith of Judaism requires focusing on these phenomena: pluralism and evolution. Pluralism resulted in diversity of religious practice. More than one legitimate option was current at any given time. The evolutionary aspect was a consequence of Judaism's development over long spans of time and wide geographic areas, and of its flourishing as a separate religious system within dominant societies and cultures. Judaism arose within the variegated ancient Near Eastern pagan cultures and acculturated to them by absorbing their influences. Its development reflects its adaptation to Hellenism, Christianity, Islam, and what is presently called Western civilization. In turn, Judaism influenced the societies in which Jews lived. But our concern is with the emergence and development of the Judaic faith itself, and for this purpose we must be alert both to the changes that resulted from its periodic acculturation and to the continuity of its theology and halakah.

III. THE MIXED COMPOSITION OF JEWS

Judaism is an ancient and complex religion. It has been perceived narrowly as the faith of a particular people sequentially called Israel, Judah, Jews, and lately both Jews and Israelis. Contrary to some popular notions, however, it is not really a national religion, and its adherents are not properly a nation. It is incorrect to equate "Israelite" with "Israeli," or theological "Israel," as used in Judaic liturgy, with the contemporary term "Israel."

Although Judaism has not appeared to possess the multinational dimensions of either Christianity or Islam, in a very real sense it is equally multinational. People of every race and of most nations of the world have been and are adherents of Judaism.

Mixed marriage and intermarriage, or, more technically, exogamy, have occurred in Judaism with great frequency since its earliest days. Therefore, neither the Israelites nor the Judeans have constituted an unalloyed ethnic strain. The ancient Israelites, for example, believed that even at the most crucial moment of their redemptive history they incorporated an *ereb rab*, a multitude of disparate ethnic varieties who became integrated with Israel at the time of the Exodus from Egypt (Exod. 12:38). Moreover, after the Exodus the substantial branch of the people who settled in the northern part of Canaan was descended from Ephraim, offspring of Joseph and his Egyptian wife Asenath (Gen. 41:50-52).

The biblical traditions reflecting exogamy in Judaism attest to a multiethnic development from its beginnings among the Arameans to the early monarchy. These traditions indicate that into this Aramean strain came not only Egyptians, but also Canaanites through Simeon (Gen. 46:10) and through Judah's relationship with Tamar (Gen. 38:1-30); Midianites through Moses (Exod. 2:16-22); and even Moabites (despite or prior to the ban at Deut. 23:4); Gibeonites; Jebusites; Jerahmeelites; Kenites, a strange brand of non-Israelite Hebrews; Philistines; and Phoenicians, all adequately documented in Scripture. Exogamy was practiced not only by the common people, but by Levites and priests (Ezra 9:1-2), and also, since the days of David, by royal families, many of whom married foreign women, as exemplified in the extreme by Solomon (1 Kgs. 11:1-2).

The period of Ezra and Nehemiah, after the return of the exiled Jews to Judah from Babylonia, witnessed a severe ban on exogamy. This ban became the norm in Judaism until modern times. Simultaneously with the ban, however, the institution of *gerut,* proselytism, developed, facilitating the admission of non-Jewish spouses into Judaism by the rites of conversion. In this way, people of manifold racial, ethnic, and national origins continued to enter Judaism. And, as is the case with Christianity, the proselyte entered a faith community and not a nation or an ethnic group.

In the light of these biblical and postbiblical intimations, it is a fantasy of pseudoscientific anthropology to suggest that there is or ever was a specific Israelite or Jewish ethnic strain. From its very inception, Israel was a theological entity—a federation of tribes based upon a common faith. This common faith, not blood kinship, was the test of belonging to the people of God. Even in modern times, many of the inhabitants of the state of Israel who are of the Judaic faith belong to a broad variety of European and Oriental ethnic strains. Furthermore, many members of the Jewish faith who live all around the globe are similarly descended from diverse ethnic groups. They are acculturated to non-Judaic cultural forms while preserving a profession of one or another variety of Judaism.

Chapter One
Proto-Judaism (ca. 2000-400 B.C.E.)

I. WHAT IS PROTO-JUDAISM?

One cannot give the precise date of the origins of Judaism, since historical verification of the biblical account of its beginnings is still unavailable. In this book the term *Proto-Judaism* will be used for the earliest form of the religion that emerged from this shadowy era and came to be called Judaism.[1] Thus Proto-Judaism refers to the religion that existed from ca. 2000 to ca. 400 B.C.E., and the term Judaism designates the faith after 400 B.C.E., following the Babylonian exile.

II. THEORIES OF ORIGINS

A. The *Apiru* (or *Habiru*)

Scholars have long debated whether the *Apiru*, a group of people widespread in the Near East between 2000 and 1200 B.C.E., were the Hebrews who eventually were known as Israel. In general, the *Apiru* represented a social class of outcasts uprooted from their native lands. This group of dispossessed people has been identified with the Israelites because their alien status resembled that of the Israelites during their sojourn in Egypt, and because of the etymological relationship between the words *Apiru* and *Ibri* (Hebrew).[2]

---

1. See the Comparative Chronological Table. A term used interchangeably with "Proto-Judaism" in this book is the "religion of Israel."
2. The relation between *Apiru*/*Habiru* and "Hebrew" has been much de-

B. The Hyksos

Some scholars have proposed a connection between the Hebrews who became Israelites and the easterners whom the Egyptians called *Hyksos* ("rulers of foreign countries" or "shepherd kings"). The Hyksos, a mixed group many of whom were Semites, settled in Egypt in the 17th century B.C.E., coming there in flight from famine and eventually gaining hegemony over the land. Their movement to the land of the Nile corresponds with the migration of the Hebrews to Egypt during a drought in Canaan. Furthermore, the rule of the Hyksos in Egypt parallels the political ascension of Joseph, grandson of Abraham, founder of the religion of Israel. It is conceivable that the pharaoh of Joseph's period welcomed the Hebrews to his kingdom because he was one of the Hyksos and a Semite like themselves. When the Hyksos were overthrown, the new Egyptian monarch, regarding the Hebrews as consorts of the Hyksos and therefore enemies, proceeded to enslave them.

C. Biblical Traditions

Biblical Israel viewed its origin in two ascending stages. The first stage was the original call to Abram (Abraham) by God: "Leave your country, your family, and your father's house, for the land I will show you. I will make you a great nation" (Gen. 12:1-2). The second stage was the Exodus from Egypt, climaxing in the revelation of God's commandments at Sinai, which transformed a tribal association into a holy, covenanted people. This miraculous and mysterious encounter with God was understood as the natural outcome of the original call to Abram. The two stages—the call of Abram and the experience at Sinai—were seen as sequential in the editing of Israel's sacred Scriptures, but at one time they might have been two separate accounts of the origins of two diverse branches of Israel. Indeed, there may have been three accounts of origins: Abram's call, the Exodus tradition, and the Sinai tradition.

---

bated; see, e.g., M. Greenberg, *The Hab/piru* (New Haven: Yale University Press, 1955); B. J. Beitzel, "Habiru," in *The International Standard Bible Encyclopedia*, II (Grand Rapids: Eerdmans, 1982), 586-90; M. C. Astour, "Habiru," in *The Interpreter's Dictionary of the Bible, Supplementary Volume* (Nashville: Abingdon, 1976), pp. 382-85.

III. A SURVEY OF PROTO-JUDAISM

A. The Patriarchal Period

1. Introduction

The patriarchal period covers the lives of the patriarchs—Abraham, Isaac, and Jacob—the founding fathers of the monotheistic faith that evolved into what is called Judaism. Although any dating of the origins of Israel is precarious, scholars generally date the setting for the biblical stories about the patriarchs between 2000 and 1600 B.C.E. The dating of Abraham may be changed to an earlier time when the recent archeological finds at Ebla, Syria, are studied and put into perspective.[3]

The Judaism that has come down to the contemporary world avers that Abram was the originator of the faith, and that God entered into an agreement with Abram called a covenant. According to the terms of the covenant, God promised the land of Canaan to Abram's descendants (Gen. 15:18), and the covenant was renewed through Isaac and Jacob as an eternal one. The book of Exodus recalls the covenant with the patriarchs and indicates that redemption was also an aspect of it when God says to Moses: "I made my covenant with them [Abraham, Isaac, and Jacob] . . . and have remembered my covenant. [Therefore] . . . I will free you of the burdens which the Egyptians lay on you" (Exod. 6:4-6).

2. Abraham (Abram)

According to the biblical narrative, God calls Abram in Haran (Gen. 12:1-3). In response to God's summons, Abram journeys to Shechem in northern Canaan and builds an altar at an ancient pagan grove—a dramatic symbol that the new faith would supplant the old one. Afterward he travels throughout the country building altars to God in different places. Due to famine in Canaan (12:10), foreshadowing the descent into Egyptian slavery, Abram goes down to Egypt. God brings him forth in safety (12:11-20), prefiguring the Exodus redemption.

---

3. The significance of the finds at Ebla (Tell Mardikh) will surely be great, though they are already debated. See C. Barmant and M. Weitzman, *Ebla: A Revelation in Archaeology* (New York: Times Books, 1979); P. Craigie, *Ugarit and the Old Testament* (Grand Rapids: Eerdmans, 1983), pp. 91-98; W. S. LaSor, "Tell Mardikh," in *The International Standard Bible Encyclopedia,* IV (Grand Rapids: Eerdmans, 1988), 750-58.

God then enters the covenant with Abram in a profound mystical experience, which anticipates the awesome event of God's covenant with the people of Israel at Sinai.

Abram believed in one God, *el elyon* (God Most High), who was the Creator (14:22). Abram further believed that God was just in His dealings with human beings, as is evident in the story of Sodom and Gomorrah. According to this story, Abraham begs God to spare these wicked cities from destruction for the sake of its innocent inhabitants: "Will the judge of the whole earth not administer justice?" (18:25). God's concern for justice in the story reveals that the earliest conception of Israelite monotheism already harbored a penetrating sense of divine compassion which precludes the suffering of the innocent. Brought together here, at their most primitive level, are the love of God and the love of fellow human beings, which emerge as the twofold love command: "You shall love Yahweh your God" (Deut. 6:5) and "You must love your neighbor as yourself" (Lev. 19:18).

3. Isaac

God renews the promise He gave to Abraham with his son Isaac (Gen. 26:2-5). Central to the career of Isaac is the story of the *aqedah,* the binding of Isaac. God tests Abraham's faith by asking him to sacrifice Isaac upon an altar. Just as Abraham lifts the knife, an angel of God prevents him from killing his son and substitutes a ram in his place (22:1-19). Although Isaac's life is spared in the biblical account, tradition has epitomized Isaac as a righteous sufferer who atones vicariously for the sins of others. It is conceivable that at one time the oral tradition, from which the biblical writer received the story of the *aqedah,* contained another version which appears in postbiblical midrashic literature. In these midrashic accounts, Isaac dies as an expiatory sacrifice and is resurrected.[4] Two concepts of Judaic theology emerge from the story of the *aqedah:* vicarious atonement and the suffering of the righteous. Both are impenetrable mysteries, and both are illustrated by the prophetic portion of the Bible that speaks of a suffering servant of *Yhwh* (Isa. 53).

4. Jacob

Jacob receives the promise given to his father, Isaac (Gen. 28:13-15).

---

4. Shalom Spiegel, *The Last Trial,* trans. Judah Goldin (Philadelphia: Jewish Publication Society, 1967).

The Bible presents Jacob as a quiet dweller of tents in his youth. Born after his twin Esau, he deceives both his brother and father in order to gain Esau's birthright, which entitled Esau to be the spiritual heir of Isaac. To be worthy of succeeding his father, Jacob must undergo a profound conversion experience. This transformation takes place during a mysterious encounter between Jacob and a celestial being (32:25-32). Jacob wrestles with the divine visitor, triumphs over him, and emerges with a new personality more spiritually suitable for the next bearer of the covenant. Jacob is renamed "Israel," the champion or prince of God. His new name signifies a change in both character and status and implies that as Israel he is now the repository of blessing. Eventually, his name Israel is given to the people who adhere to God's covenant, and the names of his sons, in turn, are attributed to the twelve tribes of Israel.

B. The Mosaic Period

1. Introduction

Israel believed in God's covenant with Abraham, renewed through Isaac and Jacob, and that its history originated in the experiential opposites of bondage and redemption. Israel believed, however, that the actual source of its religion—the Torah—did not come into full force until the entire redeemed people stood at Sinai under the leadership of Moses.

The sequence of biblical salvation theology, then, is as follows: God creates the world, makes a covenant with Abraham, and transmits it to Isaac and Jacob. During a period of drought, Jacob's descendants settle in Egypt upon the invitation of the pharaoh, who views with favor Jacob's son Joseph—the savior of Egypt from famine. After the death of Joseph, a new pharaoh arises, who imposes hard labor upon the Israelites and, in escalating fashion, threatens further tribulations. Providentially, Moses is born and prepared for his divinely appointed task. God hears the groaning of Israel and begins to fulfill the covenant. Salvation history takes its course and leads inexorably to the Exodus from Egypt.

There is presently only one known reference outside the Bible to the name Israel. It is found on the famous "Israel stele," on which is inscribed a poetic eulogy of Pharaoh Merneptah, dating to the end of the 13th century B.C.E. The boast on this commemorative stone that "Israel is laid waste, his seed is not" was evidently wishful hyperbole.

In any case, the evidence on the stele is not decisive for the Israelite Exodus.[5]

2. Moses

The biographical data of the biblical account of Moses are not yet attested elsewhere by independent literary tradition or archeology. It would be natural, however, that such a man as Moses had a biographer who would recount the mystery of the master, and that Moses would have left notes with disciples. These notes probably later formed part of the revised and updated Pentateuch, thus giving some credibility to the concept of "the Torah of Moses." A well-known scholar has written, "If Moses did not exist, we should have to invent him."[6] Suffice it to affirm that this book is written from the premise that Moses lived, that he led out of Egypt whatever elements of Israel were there and chose to depart, and that he mediated the extraordinary experience they shared at Sinai.

In all the documents that compose the Pentateuch, Moses, the redeemer, is the commanding personality, transmitter of divine teaching, and mediator of the divine will. A mystique surrounds his birth (Exod. 2) and encompasses his death (Deut. 34:5-6). When he ascends Mt. Sinai, he is enveloped in the divine cloud that descends to bear him aloft to heaven (Exod. 24:15-18). For forty days and forty nights he remains closeted with God within the cloud, which is divinity itself. There he becomes transfigured—enveloped by a radiance—so that he no longer is the same human Moses (Exod. 34:28ff.). He is declared to be God's servant with whom God speaks "face to face . . . [who has seen] the form of Yahweh" (Num. 12:7-8). Moses is said to have possessed the divine spirit so abundantly that God took some from him with which to endow others (Num. 11:17). It is Moses, not God, who fills Joshua with the spirit of wisdom (Deut. 34:9), so that others are really secondary vessels deriving the holy spirit from Moses himself. Accordingly, Moses stands in the stead of God, unique in his face-to-face relationship with God (Deut. 34:10).

---

5. For a translation of this stele, see *Ancient Near Eastern Texts Relating to the Old Testament,* ed. J. B. Pritchard, 3rd ed. (Princeton: Princeton University Press, 1969), pp. 376-78.

6. Though many have repeated this saying, it apparently originated with N. Söderblom, *Das Werden des Gottesglaubens* (Leipzig: 1916), p. 310. For a similar statement, see J. Bright, *A History of Israel,* 3rd ed. (Philadelphia: Westminster, 1981), p. 127.

Moses looms up in the Pentateuch as a more-than-human figure, a view that becomes even more pronounced in the Hellenistic, Rabbinic, and Samaritan traditions. So awesome is the figure of Moses that Israel is said to have "believed" in him, or had faith in him as in God (Exod. 14:31). And yet, even Moses was not believed to have received all knowledge in its absolute sense. Like other human beings, he too was confronted by ultimate inaccessible mystery, as recorded later in the Babylonian Talmud (Rosh Hash. 21b). Human beings can apprehend certain insights; other matters are metaphysical and metahistorical secrets available only to God (Deut. 29:29).

Aside from his fundamental role as prophet and savior, Moses was, for all intents and purposes, a major founder, transmitter, and mediator of the religion of Israel, in the same sense as Zarathustra was of Zoroastrianism, Muhammad was of Islam, and from one perspective perhaps, as Paul (somewhat more than Jesus) was of Christianity.

3. The Mosaic Religion

Most of the basic theological doctrines of later Judaism emerged from the Mosaic era or earlier. The Hebrew Scriptures are replete with the teachings of Moses concerning monotheism, election, revelation, and redemption.[7] This theology is largely reflected in a cultic creed proclaimed at the festival of firstfruits, which scholars agree is archaic (Deut. 26:5-10). Furthermore, a consensus of scholarly opinion advocates a Mosaic date for the Decalogue, which incorporates the monotheistic idea, the doctrine of creation, the Sabbath, and the foundations of the entire moral order of Western Judeo-Christian civilization.

Despite the insistence of Moses upon absolute monotheism, Joshua still admonishes Israel for imperfect adherence to monotheism. This situation mirrors the great struggle for religious integrity evident throughout Israel's history. Imperfect adherence, however, should not be reason to deny Israel's monotheism, at least in the sense that Israel was to recognize only one God, even if competitors were believed to exist. The Israelite prohibition of all images, the dissociation of *Yhwh* from all elements of nature, and the stress upon God's role as sole creator make the Israelite idea of God wholly unlike other ideas of God in the ancient Mediterranean and Near Eastern world.

In summary, the Mosaic religion contains both beliefs and practices. The beliefs include the doctrines of monotheism, creation, elec-

---

7. These doctrines will be elaborated upon in Chapters Five and Eight.

tion, revelation, and redemption, and a powerful advocacy of the moral imperative as found in the Decalogue and in many passages from Exodus through Deuteronomy. The practices encompass circumcision, the Sabbath and holy days, sacrifices, and a system of taboos related to purity and impurity. Much ambiguity is present in the early biblical conception of God, but this ambiguity continues throughout the history of Judaism and challenges theological ingenuity to this day. Biblical tradition teaches of a God who is loving, forgiving, and chastising (Exod. 34:6-7), and is not only creator of that which is good (Gen. 1:31) but also the source of evil (Isa. 45:7).[8] At times God appears in vindictive, demonic posture, and at other times as a compassionate parent. God is simultaneously like a mother who comforts her child (Isa. 66:13) and like a warrior who crushes his foes (Exod. 15:7). God appears in human form (Gen. 18:1-2), and throughout biblical literature transcends human nature as a cosmic power that is not subject to the ravages of matter or the limitations of time and space. These ambiguities highlight the uniting of clashing traditions into a common sacred Scripture to serve the conflicting needs of a federation of diverse groups. They may lead to inability at any time to comprehend fully the mystery of life and death and the suffering of the innocent, but they serve as a permanent caution to those who would seek a monolithic theology in the ancient religion of Israel.

C. The Period of the Judges

After the death of Moses, Joshua receives the mantle of leadership and conducts Israel into the Promised Land. He conquers Canaan and distributes the land among the tribes of Israel. In his old age, at the northern sanctuary of Shechem, Joshua recites a history of Israel which brings together the sequence of the call of Abraham, the mission of Moses, the Exodus, and the miracle of the crossing of the Sea of Reeds. Here Joshua performs the role of a second Moses as mediator of a renewal of the covenant. Joshua's covenant renewal affirms that Israel believed in Abrahamic-Mosaic origins and in a two-sided doctrine of election and redemption. These ideas are taught later as doctrine by such early prophets as Hosea (11:1; 13:4) and Amos (2:10; 3:1).

---

8. The original Hebrew of Isa. 45:7, which the Jerusalem Bible translates as "calamity," is the word *ra,* which the author translates as "evil" (as does, e.g., Sheldon Blank in *Prophetic Faith in Isaiah* [Detroit: Wayne State University, 1967], p. 113).

Furthermore, the prolific body of halakah that applies to daily life, encompassing large segments of civil and criminal law and ritual that stretch from Exodus 19:1 to Numbers 10:10 and to Deuteronomy, exhibit a strong connection with Moses.

At this stage of their history, Israel takes the form of an amphictyony, a confederacy of twelve tribes loosely bound together by a common religious obligation and a central sanctuary. The bond that unites them is not political. These tribes, who trace their ancestry to the twelve sons of Jacob/Israel, are a theocratic community uniting during military emergencies under the leadership of a judge. The term *judge* during this period is not used in a legal sense, but rather has the broader meaning of "a ruler." The judges are charismatic saviors to whom the Israelite tribes turn for deliverance from foreign oppression. Examples of this kind of heroic leader are Deborah, Gideon, Jephthah, and Samson, whose exploits are recounted in the book of Judges.

D. The Period of the Monarchy

Rivalry between the tribes of the North and the South for primacy becomes a great source of tension which prevails throughout their common history in the land. A second source of tension is the problem of establishing a political order to supplant the religious federation. The last judge of Israel, Samuel, warns the people of the dire ramifications of a central monarchy. But the people insist that they want a king so that they may be "like the other nations" (1 Sam. 8:5). Whether this was part of the design for a "kingdom of priests and a holy people" (Exod. 19:6) is the core of the historical enigma of Israel. In any event, Samuel accedes to the will of the people and anoints Saul as first king. David follows Saul and succeeds in uniting the northern and southern tribes and centralizes the religious cult in Jerusalem. His son, King Solomon, builds a great temple that is venerated by those who regard it as a significant center of religious life, but also opposed by those who view it as a Canaanite-Phoenician monument to the pagan territorialized religion.[9] As the pagan notion of state and crown submerges the tribal federation, the territorialized, centralized cult tends to suppress the older idea of an unconfined God and localist spiritual authority. This suppression becomes a long-term ambiguity in the his-

---

9. See Roland de Vaux, *Ancient Israel*, II (New York: McGraw-Hill, 1965), 329-30. De Vaux documents opposition to the temple in ancient Israel that existed simultaneously with a strong positive attitude toward it.

tory of Israel until after the fall of the Temple in 70 C.E. At the time, Rabbinic Judaism triumphs and establishes the supremacy of local autonomy, and, like the canonical prophets, affirms a geography-free concept of worship.

The political unity forged by David lasts less than a century. Solomon's oppressive taxes and policy of forced labor exacerbate the dormant North-South tensions of the past, and upon his death the northern tribes of Israel secede. Nevertheless, the historic religious federation does not wholly come apart. Israelites now look to their own sanctuaries at Shechem, Bethel, and Dan, rather than to Jerusalem. But North and South continue to share a basic theology—northerners even continue to worship at Jerusalem. Israel and Judah, as the northern and southern tribes are now called respectively, practice a cult and believe in doctrines that relate to their God *Yhwh,* centered in various shrines, including Samaria, Bethel, and Jerusalem. Considering that the Pentateuch reflects a composite of both northern and southern traditions, it is clear that the two separate entities have much religious belief and practice in common. Judah looks with disfavor upon sacrifices outside of Jerusalem, but this is basically of little moment. If the place and the priestly hierarchy differ, and if there are breaches in the ideal practice of *Yhwhism,* the basic cultic rites are held in common. Similarly, the prophetic literature of North and South evidences a common ethical tradition, even if it also exposes consistent violations in both Israel and Judah of the ideal behavior expected of the covenant people. Although North and South are politically alienated from one another, the two, at times, share the conviction of being branches of the covenant people, and, at times, each believes it is the only truly elected people.

The northern kingdom of Israel, after a succession of dynasties, falls to the empire of Assyria in 721 B.C.E. Nevertheless, Proto-Judaism survives in the southern kingdom of Judah, albeit riddled with religious syncretism by merging the pagan rites of its neighbors with its own. In 621 B.C.E. King Josiah initiates a religious reform, which attempts to eradicate these pagan elements and purify the worship of *Yhwh.* However, Judah succumbs to Babylonia, successor empire to Assyria, in 587 B.C.E., and Jerusalem and the Temple are destroyed. The people of Judah are led into Babylonian captivity, which is ended by the Persian king Cyrus, conqueror of Babylonia. Cyrus permits the exiled Jews to return to Jerusalem, where, under the political leadership of Nehemiah and the spiritual leadership of Ezra, they begin to rebuild the Temple and a religious reformation takes place. The era of Proto-

Judaism draws to a close under the spiritual aegis of Ezra and evolves into the faith called Judaism that will be explored in the remaining chapters of this book.

Having surveyed the history of Judaism from Abraham to Ezra, this chapter now concludes with a discussion of the sacrificial cult, sacred days, and spiritual leadership of the Proto-Judaic period.

IV. THE SACRIFICIAL CULT

A. Sanctuaries and Shrines

Under this heading we will examine the places and mode of worship that obtained during the Proto-Judaic stage of the evolution of Judaism.

The traditions that purport to describe Israel's earliest cultic life tell of a portable tent that housed an "ark" or cabinet in which reposed the two tablets of stone on which were inscribed the Decalogue. Outside the tent stood an altar where animal offerings were brought for sacrifice and expiatory blood rituals were performed. The functionaries who assembled, dismantled, guarded, and transported the tent and its appurtenances were the Levites *(lewiyim)*, while the priests *(kohanim)* conducted the cult, assisted also by Levites who participated in the musical accompaniment.

Israelite history long witnessed a struggle between localism and centralization: the basic human thrust for greater convenience and independence of shrines and cultic options versus a governmental push for centralized control of religious life that enhanced state and clergy power. The anti-monarchical posture reflected in 1 Samuel 8 is an echo of the drive for religious individuation. Ultimately, the Davidic monarchy's choice of Jerusalem created a mystique of centralization, but in reality not even in Judah was Jerusalem the exclusive place of worship, except for brief periods. None of the kings of Judah was either willing or able to abolish the *bamot* (rural altars or "high places"; singular *bamah*) or idolatrous images, except for Hezekiah (2 Kgs. 18:2-5) and Josiah (23:4-6), both of whom enjoyed a little success. It is clear that the priests functioned at *bamot* until Josiah eliminated them (23:8ff.), even at *bamot* within earshot of Jerusalem's temple, dating to Solomon's apostasy to the pagan gods Ashtoret (Astarte), Chemosh, and Milcom (23:13). Josiah's reformation spread into the north, where he eliminated the *bamah* at Bethel (v. 15) and all the *bamot* of Syria (v. 19), where he savagely slaughtered the northern priests upon their own altars. But he died at the hands of Pharaoh Neco at Megiddo (ca. 609 B.C.E.), and his successor, Jehoahaz, immediately restored the old customs.

B. Sacrifices

Although the Bible does not provide a systematic theological understanding of the sacrificial ritual, certain inferences may be made from biblical sources that point to three underlying concepts regarding the Israelites' obligation to God: (1) to offer the yield of human beings, animals, and land; (2) to express gratitude to God; and (3) to seek reconciliation with God. Apparently the first premise of the cult was that all things belonged to God, and therefore the individual should surrender the first of his yield, whether human, animal, or vegetable. Only upon gratefully sharing with God did the individual have the right to partake of it. In Israelite times, however, whatever its origin, the male child who was the yield of the first opening of the human womb, the *peter rehem,* was no longer subjected to the altar, but was to be redeemed (Exod. 13:14). An animal was accepted as surrogate for the human firstborn. Here we have one more instance, which was probably true for all animal offerings, where the animal was the vicarious atonement for the human being. This kind of atonement was unique in Israel, for some of Israel's neighbors offered their firstborn upon altars, and the worship of Molech was fueled by child sacrifice long into Israelite times.

The various sacrifices enumerated in biblical sources, in addition to this firstborn surrogate, were preceded by the *pesah* (or pesach) (Exod. 12). The name of this offering is etymologically connected with the word that denoted the sacred dance around the altar (1 Kgs. 18:26). It may have been an annual offering when the dance in honor of the moon was conducted—a monthly liturgical rite still preserved in leaps upward, symbolically toward the moon, by certain groups that in modern times style themselves Orthodox. But it was reinterpreted to relate to God's leap, or defense of the doors of the Israelites in Egypt, and became the blood atonement which saved the Israelites from the angel of destruction.

Aside from the *pesah,* the cultic roster included the *olah,* a whole burnt offering, all of which "ascended" (the verb *alah* means "to go up") to God in smoke; *shelamim,* conciliatory offerings denoting renewed communion with God; *todah,* a thanksgiving offering; *nedabah,* a freewill offering denoting pious devotion; *neder,* a vow offering; *hatat* and *asham,* expiatory and guilt or reparation offerings; *minhah,* a vegetable offering; *lehem hapanim,* the Bread of the Presence arranged upon the table in the sanctuary; and *qetoret,* incense (from the verb *qatar,* "to go up in smoke"). In addition, blood and fat were offered, both of which were considered life-giving. There were also various sacrifices accompanying ablutions after childbirth, disease, sexual emissions, and the like, and those expressing gratitude, expiation, and reconciliation. Furthermore, there was an array of Sabbath and holy day offerings, celebrated in processions with accompanying singers and musical instruments, aside from the twice-daily *tamid* (perpetual burnt offerings).

Great similarities existed between the Israelite cult and that of its pagan neighbors. Terminology used in the Canaanite and Israelite cults was quite similar, as we know, for instance, from Ras Shamra texts. Perhaps even the underlying theology of vicarious expiatory offering as a means to reconciliation and renewal with the deity was similar. In such offerings, the whole or part of the offering was burned on the altar, and blood was sprinkled upon both altar and donor to signify the coming together of donor and god. Eating of the sacrifice in a sacred meal symbolized the reconciliation of the donor and deity, and blood sprinkled upon the altar in expiatory rites symbolized that the person's life was restored to him. But while such theories, rites, and terminology might have been widespread, Israel differed from its pagan neighbors in its consistent thrust toward a monotheistic faith. Israelite theory early transcended the notion of making the yield of human, animal, and land excessive by offering a portion or a surrogate to God, and went beyond the concept of vicarious atonement. It included the more spiritually sensitive concept of gratitude for blessing, as, for example, in the recital of formulaic texts at Deuteronomy 26:1-11.

In summary, during the preexilic period the Israelites worshiped *Yhwh* primarily by offering sacrifices mediated by priests who were assisted by Levites. Their sanctuary, at first, was a portable table that was supplanted by a permanent temple in Jerusalem and various shrines and altars outside the Holy City. Eventually synagogues, whose mode of worship was prayer rather than sacrifice, arose and functioned simultaneously with the theoretically centralized sacrificial system in Jerusalem. The rise of the synagogue, which became the institution of localism par excellence, will be discussed in greater detail in Chapter Two.

V. THE SACRED DAYS

A. Introduction

It is not possible in this limited work to expound upon the nature of the various technically complex calendars used through the centuries of the early history of Israel and Judah. Both the solar and lunar calendars were in vogue alternatively and contemporaneously among variegated segments of the two peoples. What is of importance for our purposes is to summarize the roster of sacred days as found in the Pentateuch, for it is these which became the permanent legacy of Judaism.[10] The days to be discussed below have undergone transformation both conceptually and in ritual observance, and in some instances, because of varying liturgical calendars, the days were not celebrated on the same day among all groups within Judaism. In addition to the fact that certain sacred days listed in the Pentateuch underwent decisive redesign, for instance, "the first day of the seventh month" (Lev. 23:24), in later times new festivals were added, and some of these did not become universally consecrated among all sections of Judaism.

The full theological significance these days assume in Judaism will be discussed below in the exposition of Rabbinic Judaism. It is during the Rabbinic period that this theology takes on its permanent historical nature, when priesthood, central sanctuary, and cult have been swept away by the vicissitudes of history. After the destruction of the Temple in 70 C.E., "postbiblical Judaism" takes on full significance with the emergence of the new spiritual leadership historically known as the rabbinate.

Several different parts of the Pentateuch provide rosters of the sacred days, most notably Exodus 23:14-19; 34:18-26; Leviticus 23; Numbers 28:9-29; Deuteronomy 16:1-17. The roster at Leviticus 23 is the most comprehensive, because it is the formal priestly liturgical document that obtained in the cult.

B. The New Moon (Rosh Hodesh)

Rosh Hodesh is listed in the roster of festivals and their sacrificial rites at Numbers 28:11ff. It appears that this New Moon festival was a time of feasting and enjoyment during which normal gainful occupations were suspended (1 Sam. 20:24ff.). Since the sacrifices of Rosh Hodesh

---

10. For more discussion of the sacred days see Chapter Eight.

are even more numerous than those of the Sabbath, in all likelihood this monthly festival was originally of greater significance, and was probably an old Israelite practice which was changed in the evolution of Judaism. Although suppressed and submerged because of its association with pagan lunar worship, Rosh Hodesh demonstrates the endurance of popular religion, for despite its pagan associations the rabbis were unable to uproot it, but instead placed it under halakic control. They arranged a New Moon liturgy to be recited on the day itself, and a special sanctification liturgy for Saturday night following the appearance of the new moon.

C. The Sabbath (Shabbat)

The sacred days included the weekly Sabbath, the seventh day of a seven-day cycle, in which every male and female Israelite-Judahite, the animals, servants, and resident strangers were not to engage in their regular occupations (Exod. 23:12). This comprehensive inclusion of all elements of the community in Sabbath observance is to be taken in tandem with Exodus 20:10, which details the same notion even more explicitly, and is undoubtedly to be understood as an expansion or *midrash* of an originally brief Sabbath commandment at Exodus 20:8. In what may be the earliest of rosters (23:14-19), the Sabbath precedes the listing of sacred days and is actually apart from it, because the Sabbath alone is included in the Sinaitic revelation and thus takes on a very special position in the religious life of Israel. The Sabbath alone is considered "a sign of the covenant" (31:12-17). What we cannot know from any of the Sabbath statements is whether the Sabbath was observed before the Egyptian experience, precisely what the nature of Sabbath "rest" was to be, and the explicit definition of *melakah* (work) from which the believer was to abstain.[11] Only a few particulars are given in different contexts, including a prohibition on agricultural labor (34:21), the kindling of fire (35:3), and by implication, on the gathering of firewood on the Sabbath (Num. 15:32-36). Allusions in the writings of some of the preexilic and postexilic preaching prophets provide a few other imprecise details from which inferences are made (e.g., Amos 8:5; Jer. 17:21-27), and the book of Nehemiah expands the Sabbath restrictions with a degree of authority (13:15-22). The book of Jubilees (2:27; 50:8, 12) and the Dead Sea Scrolls (CD 10:14–11:18) provide an expanded list of prohibitions observed among some segments of ancient, pre-Rabbinic Judah, but these must all remain for discussion below.

D. Passover (Pesach)

This festival is called by two names: *Pesach* (or *Pesah*) and *Hag Hamatzot*. The Hebrew word *pesah* denotes the "Paschal lamb" (Exod. 12:3-6, 13) that was to be offered on the fourteenth day of the first month of the year. *Hag Hamatzot* designates the "festival of the unleavened bread" (12:14-15) to be observed for seven days, beginning with the fifteenth day of the first month (Lev. 23:5). The springtime festival, known as Passover, possibly was the product of the merging of two separate ancient festivals: (1) the Paschal feast, a relic of a primitive atonement rite, and (2) the matza festival, representing a thanksgiving celebration for the harvest.

The Pesach and matzot celebrations commemorate the redemption of Israel from Egypt. There is no real agricultural or mythic reminiscence left in the Pentateuch regardless of how these festivals originated in pre-Israelite times. Passover in Judaism is inextricably bound up with the doctrines of election, redemption, and revelation. The redemption from Egyptian bondage takes place as fulfillment of the promise that was part of the covenant. When God summons Moses from the burning bush, God is identified as "the God of Abraham, the God of Isaac, and the God of Jacob" (Exod. 3:6), and recalls his pledge to bring his elected people to a "land where milk and honey flow" (3:8). The redemption, so central to the Pesach festival, is also consummated by the revelation at Sinai and the giving of the Decalogue.

Pesach, Shabuot (or Shabbuoth), and Sukkot (or Sukkoth) are known as the "pilgrimage festivals" because of the biblical requirement that pilgrimages to the sanctuary be made at those crucial junctures in the agricultural calendar. They were times of harvest, and gifts of first products were to be presented to the priests. In time, these nature-oriented sacred days were historicized by connecting them with the redemption from Egypt (Pesach and Sukkot) and with the revelation at Sinai (Shabuot).

E. The Omer Day

The Omer Day begins a fifty-day cycle between Pesach and Shabuot. As far as can be determined from Leviticus 23, there is no set date for the offering of the firstfruit grain. The Torah prescribes that when the

---

11. For a discussion of the concept of *melakah,* see Phillip Sigal, "Toward a Renewal of Sabbath Halakah," *Judaism* 1 (1982), 77-81.

harvest is gathered (23:10), an omer (the first sheaf) of the spring grain should be brought to the priest, and that "on the day after the Sabbath" the priest is to wave it, lift it up, and consecrate it before the Lord (v. 11). At that time, an *olah* (a whole burnt offering) and supplementary offerings are to be brought before the Lord (vv. 12-13), after which the new grain is permitted as food (v. 14).

F. Pentecost (Shabuot)

From the Day of the Omer, seven Sabbaths are to be counted, and on the morrow of the seventh Sabbath—the fiftieth day—a grain offering along with other offerings is brought before the Lord (Lev. 23:15-20). This fiftieth day is then declared a holy convocation and is called "the day of firstfruits," or *Hag Habikkurim* (Num. 28:26) and "the Feast of Weeks," or *Hag Hashabuot* (Deut. 16:10). At a later time, the Judaic sages proclaimed Pentecost as "the time of the giving of the Torah," thus transforming it from an agricultural festival to one that celebrated an historic event central to the redemptive history of Judaism.

G. The First Day of the Seventh Month (Rosh Hashanah)

This sacred day was to be "proclaimed with trumpet call" (Lev. 23:24), namely, by blowing the ram's horn to mark it as a holy convocation. It is the source for the festival later discussed in the Rabbinic literature that is known as the New Year (Rosh Hashanah), which celebrates the day of creation and the theme of repentance, and which inaugurates ten days of penitence climaxing in the Day of Atonement (Yom Kippur).

Some scholars suggest that the preexilic Psalms 93–100, which highlight the doctrines of God as Creator, as King, and as Judge, provide a relic of Rosh Hashanah liturgy. This view would imply that a New Year festival celebrating the same concepts and theological constructs as are found in Rabbinic Judaism was already in place in the religion of Israel, or Proto-Judaism.

One might conjecture that the fact that the Torah does not name the festival as a New Year reflects the historical circumstance that the New Year was celebrated in spring with the matza festival, but that other influences in Israel pressed for the adoption of the Mesopotamian autumnal New Year. Should this conjecture prove valid, Rosh Hashanah offers another example of the tension of diversity underlying the development of Judaism. It further illustrates the pluralism inherent in a faith which long endured struggle over whether to adopt the solar or lunar calendar, and whether to see the beginning of all things in the spring, with the reawakening of nature, or at the autumn equinox, as was done in some Mesopotamian centers.

The theology of this day will be more fully presented in Chapter Eight below. What can be noted here is that in Nehemiah it appears to have been a joyous festival celebrated at home, and that at its public convocation a special feature was the reading of the Torah (Neh. 8:2-9).

H. The Day of Atonement (Yom Kippur)

The Day of Atonement (Lev. 16; 23:27-32; Num. 29:7-11) was designed to be a day of "afflicting" or "humbling" oneself, occurring on the tenth day of the seventh month. The sacrificial ritual, abstention from *melakah* (work), and the process of self-affliction or self-abasement prescribed for this festival were for the purpose of personal atonement (Lev. 23:28). Although there is no explicit connection between the first day of the seventh month and the tenth day in the Torah, it is quite likely that just as there was such an interrelated ten-day period in the Babylonian New Year festival, Israel observed the ten days in an interconnected way long before Rabbinic Judaism arose. There is no explicit mention of a requirement to fast on Yom Kippur. This is apparently the product of later exegesis of the term *weinnitem,* "you shall afflict (or humble) yourselves."

I. The Festival of Booths (Sukkot)

This is a seven-day festival also referred to as the Festival of Ingathering *(Hag Haasiph).* It is considered one of the pilgrimage festivals along with Pesach and Shabuot (Exod. 23:14, 17; 34:23; Deut. 16:16).

Whatever Sukkot may have been originally, whether a primitive New Year festival or strictly a thanksgiving harvest festival, Israel attached to it both historical and social importance. In Israel's general reorientation of its inherited pagan festivals it changed the focus of its observance from nature to history in the ongoing process of retheologizing the sacred days. Thus, we hear specifically (in what may actually be a later addendum to the sacred day roster at Lev. 23) that, in addition to the agriculturally oriented ritual in which four basic species of the land are carried before the Lord, the people are to dwell in booths for seven days, as an historic remembrance that Israelites dwelt in booths when they left Egypt. In this way, a purely agricultural festival began to undergo a transformation into an historic commemoration of a vital theological doctrine: the Exodus from Egypt as a saving event of divine redemption.

The new social emphasis that was parallel to the social passion of the preaching prophets was then referred to at Deuteronomy 16:14, where Sukkot was enhanced by the explicit ordinance to include all of the underprivileged classes in the great festival.

J. The Eighth Day of Assembly (Shemini Atzeret)

The Eighth Day of Assembly follows the seven days of Sukkot and is designated an *atzeret*. The Septuagint reads *exodion* for *atzeret,* interpreting it in the same sense of "the end of the festival," the last day of the festival, or literally, "the going out of the festival." Not until the Hellenistic period did the term *atzeret* attach itself to *pentekoste,* "the fiftieth-day festival" of Shabuot, although it had long been used for the seventh day of Passover (Deut. 16:8). In all festival usages the Hebrew term *atzeret* probably signifies "a detention," from its root *'tzr,* which means "restrain" or "detain," and in this sense has the significance of detaining the people at the sanctuary, from which it has taken on the conventional English meaning of a "solemn assembly." The Greek translators, however, in using *exodion,* understood the term either to refer to the final day of a festive period, or to imply that the festival is a celebration of the Exodus from Egypt. This was self-evident at Passover, but even in reference to Sukkot, once the historicization of the festival linking it to the redemption from Egypt was in place (Lev. 23:42ff.), the later Greek translator could justifiably use the term *exodion* (23:36). No particular significance is attached to Shemini Atzeret in Scripture, and it is not listed in the rosters of Exodus and Deuteronomy.

K. Final Comments

Variegated rosters for the holy days remained intact in the Pentateuch despite their discrepancies, because the final editor sought to reconcile North and South as well as priestly, lay-sage, and preaching-prophet circles in one great ecumenical design. The significance of the rosters is in the fact that they point to the preexilic existence of all of the sacred and semi-sacred days, exhibiting a rhythm to the sacred year. This rhythm corresponded to the rhythm of nature, but was already being recast into a mold that attributed historical significance to them. Just as at one time a long process of change transformed fertility rites into ceremonials of gratitude for God's blessings, so too a continuing process transformed the celebration of God's blessings in nature into celebrations of the manifestation of God in history. This transition from a nature-oriented theology to an historicizing theology was imperceptible and is still in process. Illustrative of the process whereby holy days were historicized is the Sabbath. Originally the celebration of creation, the Sabbath was changed into a commemoration of the redemption from Egypt as well as creation, thus linking the cosmic role of the creator to redemptive history. In this way too, the pilgrimage festivals—Pesach, Shabuot, and Sukkot—went through their agricultural phase to become moments of historical awareness. This process never touched "the first day of the seventh month" or Yom Kippur. In due course, these two sacred days became elevated to a special status. The former, the "day of memorial blowing," became the awesome Rosh Hashanah, the New Year Day. Transformed into a day of repentance and of judgment, Rosh Hashanah inaugurated a ten-day period climaxing in the Day of Atonement, when the faithful expiated their sins by humbling themselves and when the Lord redeemed them.

In sum, we have here an interesting rhythm and symmetry. Each day of the week is a God-given occasion for atonement, and the seventh day crowns the week. Rosh Hodesh occurs once a month and begins the four-week cycles of seven days with their Sabbaths. As the first day of the first month initiates the first half of the year and at one time must have been notable, so the first day of the seventh month inaugurates the second half of the year. On the tenth day of the first month the Paschal lamb is prepared (Exod. 12:3), a ritual originally bound up with atonement rites; so too the tenth day of the seventh month is devoted to atonement rites. Pesach and Sukkot maintain the symmetry of seven-day festivals occurring at identical positions in the first and seventh months respectively. Shabuot appears to break the symmetry, as does Shemini Atzeret. But the likelihood is that the latter of these festivals is misplaced in the Torah's rosters, and was originally also the concluding day of a seven-week period from Sukkot, as Shabuot is of a seven-week period from Passover.

In later times new festivals were introduced, among them most prominently the Festival of Rededication (Hanukkah or Hanukah), the Feast of Lots (Purim), and Rejoicing with the Torah (Simhat [or Simchas] Torah). These will be discussed in Chapter Eight.

VI. THE SPIRITUAL LEADERS

Three figures shared the spiritual leadership of ancient Israel: the priest *(kohen)*, the prophet *(nabi)*, and the sage *(hakam)*. All three were responsible for the transmission of torah and, in their respective circles, were teachers and role models for the populace to emulate.

A. The Priest *(Kohen)*

The priest attended the altar and supervised the cult of the religion of Israel. In later historical times, as Israelite religion moved toward becoming Judaism, the priest *(kohen)* filled many functions: guarding the sanctuary; teaching; offering oracles; supervising ordeals; and conducting all the sacerdotal rites related to the offering of sacrifices, including slaughtering and dividing the animal, burning incense, applying perfumes, and sprinkling blood.

Biblical narratives are silent on the evolution of the priesthood, but they do reflect conflict concerning which functions were to be priestly and which Levitical, and concerning the rivalry between the rural and Jerusalem royal priesthood. As the office of priest evolved into its formal postexilic structure, the priest was expected to comply with extensive restrictions on his behavior. He was obliged to engage in frequent purifications, and his freedom of marriage was curtailed. The Bible reflects a mass of detailed provisions, indicated above, designed for the priest. None of these, except for teaching, applied later to the emergent rabbi, although the latter did embody the role of the priest when he superseded all three biblical figures: priest, prophet, and sage.

B. The Prophet *(Nabi)*

The *nabi,* who has made an historic impact on the pages of Scripture, was a "prophet" in the pristine sense of the Greek word *prophetes,* "one who speaks forth," or "one who serves as a preacher." The *nabi* was not the oracular functionary engaged by the state who performed at a given shrine and served the needs of the reigning sovereign. The message of the celebrated "prophets" of Scripture consisted of a mix of chastisement of Israel's and Judah's sinfulness, pronouncement of divine judgment, call for repentance, hope of reconciliation between the people and God, and concomitant announcement of redemption for the remnant. The last was to be an event or experience known as the "Day of the Lord," the "end-time," or the *eschaton,* which in the course of history became identified with a messiah figure and as the messianic era. All of this theology was deeply pervaded by a profound sense of indignation over the suffering of the disadvantaged classes of society and a social passion to correct the wrongs, relieve the oppression, and eliminate the evils that afflict society. When we speak of the "prophets of Israel" in the classical sense, we generally have reference to the remarkable figures who are either mentioned at length in Scripture (such as Samuel, Nathan, Elijah, and Elisha), or who have had writings ascribed to them (such as Isaiah, the anonymous Deutero-Isaiah, Jeremiah, Ezekiel, and Hosea).

The prophets are variously charismatic and workers of miracles (Elijah), overcome by mystical experiences (Ezekiel), reluctant to preach (Amos), and charged as guilty of near-treason in the eyes of the establishment (Jeremiah). Sometimes one individual exhibits two or more of these characteristics, and sometimes he exhibits none of them. But all the prophets have in common the core of their message. The typical preachers denounce idolatry as adultery and attack ritualistic hypocrisy, moral deception, and pietistic perversity. They are opposed to all forms of social and economic degeneration prevalent in the societies of Israel and Judah, such as conspicuous consumption, wasteful luxury of the rich, oppression of the poor, judicial corruption, avarice, and flamboyant reveling and lust. Although other ancient Near Eastern societies had prophets—Balaam (Num. 22–24) is a paradigm of these—the function and careers of the classical biblical preachers is far different from those of other Near Eastern types, including the cultic and royal prophets of Israel and Judah.

The classical preachers opposed the kings, and this dissident pattern is evident in their predecessors from Samuel through Nathan to Elijah. The preaching prophets were also independent of the priestly establishment and were opposed to the prophets who served both king and priest. They denounced those whom they called prophets, while denying that they themselves were prophets. When Amaziah, priest of Bethel, refers to Amos as a *hozeh,* a seer, Amos denies that he is one of those paid professionals who offer oracular responses on the basis of divination or vision: "I was no prophet, neither did I belong to any of the brotherhoods of prophets" (Amos 7:14). This refusal to identify oneself as a "prophet" was endemic to the great biblical preachers. Just as Amos expresses an anti-prophet view early in the history of this classical preaching type, Zechariah, toward the end of the period, indicates a similar antagonism (Zech. 13:2-6). The classical prophets were virtually leaders of alternative teaching and worship centers that coexisted with the central priestly-sacrificial cult in Jerusalem. This reality was at the heart of the serious conflict between such people as Amos and Amaziah (Amos 7:10-17) in early times and continues over the centuries, as is evident in the conflict between Jeremiah and Pashhur (Jer. 20:1-6).

The verbs "to go" and "to send" in a variety of forms are so pervasive in the accounts of the preachers' experiences that it is clear they are in their own minds "apostles," messengers, selected by God for a given period and a particular mission. The message of every apostle ultimately holds forth promise of redemption, and the redeemed world is seen to be a place of abundance, harmony, and universal peace when

> these will hammer their swords into plowshares,
> their spears into sickles.
> Nation will not lift sword against nation,
> there will be no more training for war.

(Isa. 2:4)

Along with the message of peace is the comcomitant emphasis upon love. God's will is for love, not cultic exercises (Hos. 6:6; Mic. 6:6-8).

In addition to these humanistic ideals, out of this early preaching of an eschaton, an end-time, came two significant theological elements. The first was the theme of apocalypse, the second the doctrine of resurrection. The apostles of peace gave us a picture of the end-time as an awesome era which will be punctuated by cosmic upheavals, including earthquakes, fiery storms, the trembling of the heavens, bloody and vengeful war, and the advent of God. They taught that this cataclysmic time will be followed by the resurrection of the dead. It must be noted here that, contrary to much scholarship on the subject, I concur with the scholarly opinion that the idea of resurrection was present in Israelite-Judean religion. As a matter of fact, the notion of resurrection was already so well understood in earliest times that Hosea used it as a metaphor (6:2).

Thus, not only did the classical apostolic prophets preach ethics, but they also taught Judaic theology. Moreover, they became the source of important perceptions about ritual which have helped shape Judaism through millennia. They underlined ritual integrity, underscored ritual limitation, and encouraged the heterogeneity of practice by themselves offering an alternative system. But in addition to these three aspects of the faith—ethics, theology, and ritual—these preachers, most notably

Ezekiel, became the foundation for an entirely different dimension of faith, the realm of mysticism. Both prophetic apocalyptic passages and mystical experiences of deity that Ezekiel reported inspired later movements. With the opening chapter of his experience of the throne-chariot, for example, Ezekiel had a major impact on all later Judaic mysticism.

In many ways, therefore, if the classical apostolic preachers were not utterly original, they were truly radical in seeking to return to the roots of faith and covenant. They were intrepid in their willingness to confront king and state, priest and temple, prophet and oracle. But they were in a general way theologically conservative, teaching the traditional doctrines: monotheism; God as creator, redeemer, and source of revelation; the election of Israel-Judah; the desirability of repentance; eschatological judgment; forgiveness and atonement; and the resurrection of the dead.

If these men (and women, as at 2 Kgs. 22:14-20) were ultimately failures in that they did not recall Israel to God, they left an enduring legacy. Not only did their theology and ethics, including their vision of human welfare and universal peace, become deeply rooted in all Western religion, but for Judaism in particular they became the paradigms of the right to dissent, criticism of dead ritual, reluctance to centralize religious authority, and disdain for a hereditary hierarchical priesthood. Their charismatic, independent leadership was transformed into the meritocracy of the rabbinate which superseded the priestly aristocracy.

C. The Sage *(Hakam)*

The term *hakam* is synonymous with the terms *zaqen* (elder) and *sopher* (scribe). When Jeremiah preached that God would do to Jerusalem what he had done to Shiloh (Jer. 26), he was defended against the wrath of priest and prophet by certain "elders" (26:17). A confederate of these pro-Jeremiah elders in the royal court saved Jeremiah from death (v. 24). Here we have an example of the tension between the prophet-priest-state establishment on the one hand and the classical preachers on the other. But here too we get a glimpse of the fact that the preachers spoke for others as well, and that these others represented another segment in public life. They were the *zeqenim,* or "elders," leaders of government and opinion who dissented from conventional policy. Among these elders were *sopherim,* or "scribes," a class of scholastics who were government functionaries, experts on

29

texts and repositories of tradition. Such a scribe was Shaphan, the father of Jeremiah's benefactor (2 Kgs. 22:8). The scribes and their associates, the elders, were the leaders of dissident groups who were alienated from the syncretistic worship that prevailed in Jerusalem down through the centuries. These were not separatists such as the Rechabites, but constituted a newly emerging alternative spiritual leadership. Some of this group taught in non-priestly schools, and out of these circles developed the Wisdom literature (see Chapter Two). This group produced Ezra and the postexilic religious elements that evolved into a wide spectrum of sects and into proto-Rabbinism.

Chapter Two

Judaism after the Babylonian Exile (ca. 400 B.C.E.-70 C.E.)

I. INTRODUCTION:
FROM PROTO-JUDAISM TO JUDAISM

As discussed in Chapter One, the early form of Judaism prior to the Babylonian exile is here called "Proto-Judaism." The premise of this chapter is that after the Babylonian exile, beginning with the fourth century B.C.E., Judaism was basically the same faith that existed at the time of the destruction of Jerusalem in 587 B.C.E., and that it essentially continued the tradition of the Hebrew Scriptures. Furthermore, that which scholars call "late Judaism," or "Rabbinic Judaism," has its origins and evolution in the period of Israel's monarchy and even earlier. Proto-Judaism/Judaism never ceased evolving and changing. The quintessential theological doctrines, ethical principles, and rituals were present from the dim beginnings of Israel's odyssey. Moreover, in certain dissenting circles of preaching prophets and court scribes we have the germ of the later rabbinate, and in the persistence of local shrines and prayer gatherings the embryo of the synagogue movement.

In the fifth to fourth centuries B.C.E., Ezra and Nehemiah brought about a religious renewal. Prior to this renewal, the biblical faith cannot be said to have had a name which can be verified in primary sources. Only after postexilic Judah became the successor state to the old northern kingdom of Israel and the southern kingdom of Judah, and after it laid sole claim to preserving the older Yahwistic religion and Mosaic tradition, is it proper to refer to this religion as "Judaism."

II. EZRA

The fifth century B.C.E. saw the religion of Judah and Jerusalem in low estate. This is clearly evidenced in the biblical writings of the prophet Malachi and of Nehemiah. Ezra came to Jerusalem, and being equipped for the task because he was a "*sopher,* fluent in the Torah of Moses" (Ezra 7:1-10), he undertook to establish as authoritative both the law of God and the law of the Persian king (7:25ff.).

A careful reading of the activity of Ezra indicates that he set in motion radical transitional forces. He marks a watershed in the history of Judaism. First, the recognition of the equal validity of the secular, gentile law alongside the precepts of Judaism ultimately led to the famous formulation, "The sovereign law is the law," and made it possible for Jesus to declare, "Render unto Caesar what is Caesar's." This position taken by Ezra enabled Judaism down through history to recognize a law foreign to itself and made possible continuous adjustment and adaptation. The obverse of this proposition was that Jews generally were given a special status within the larger empires in which they resided (Persian, Greek, and Roman), and were free to exclude the worship of any imperial gods from their temple, although they accepted sacrifices sent by the gentile king and offered sacrifices in his honor. This Persian concession to Judaism was continued by Antiochus III of the Seleucid regime and ultimately by the Roman empire. In a new form it was administered in medieval Europe, where the Jewish community was given a degree of autonomy to live by its own civil precepts that virtually made it a state within a state.

Ezra had no greater concrete authority than later *sopherim* and proto-rabbis, however, and could achieve whatever he did only because the governors assisted his community (Ezra 8:36). He was not armed with an "episcopal" power drawing potency within Judaism, and was neither a "proto-exilarch" nor anything similar to a papal figure; nor was he the first "chief rabbi" in Judaism. Such a centralized, hierarchical authoritarian office did not exist, and was never indigenous to Judaism. Even the "exilarch" of later times in Babylonia wielded only certain aspects of secular power while rabbis continued to decide halakah independently. And only to the extent that "chief rabbis" are granted power by secular authorities, as in modern Israel, can they wield such authority over other rabbis. Such rabbinical authority of one rabbi over another is not indigenous to Judaism. Only when Nehemiah came to Jerusalem, armed with the power of the office of governor, could Ezra's program be successfully inaugurated.

This Ezraic program included the stabilization of a synagogue liturgical form, as seen in Nehemiah 8. Here, in rudimentary form, is the earliest description of the section of the regular holy day liturgy related to the reading of the Torah. After these prayerful rites, the reader (in this case Ezra) and his assistants read, translated, and explained the scroll (Neh. 8:1-8).

Ezra here enacted the role of the earliest proto-rabbi. He was called a *sopher,* which is a term synonymous with *hakam* from the old Judean royal court usage. The *hakamim* of the Persian-Hellenistic era also evolved into the proto-rabbis and ultimately, after 70 C.E., into the ordained rabbis. Ezra is a prototype. He is an academic authority and a spiritual leader of a congregation in an assembly at worship. He conveys the holy Word. But he does not act in the role of a priest—he offers no sacrifices, he performs no libations, blood sprinklings, or other rites. The assembly is not covenantal, but merely a congregation at holy worship.

Thus, in Ezra 7 and Nehemiah 8 we witness the first stirrings of new institutions arising before our very eyes: the synagogue and the rabbinate. The synagogue already existed, but only now does it take on formal legitimacy. The rabbinate is yet to evolve, but here as a proto-rabbinic prefiguration it begins to function outside the biblical institution of prophet-preacher and wisdom teacher.

Although Ezra is a central figure in this radical metamorphosis of Judaism, he is not mentioned in Ben Sira's paean to the postexilic leaders (Sir. 49:11-13). Ezra is also not mentioned when Nehemiah is praised at 2 Maccabees 1:18; 2:13. This is because Ezra was singularly ineffective. His mission had to be taken over by Nehemiah, who as governor enforced the Ezraic program. In his paean, Ben Sira hails success: Zerubbabel and Joshua rebuilt the Temple; Nehemiah restored the walls of Jerusalem—symbols of the reconstitution of the Judean church-state glory. Followers of Ezra, however, understood the profound significance of his life, and so we find already prior to the rabbinic literature that Ezra is enshrined in the apocryphal 2 Esdras as a prophet-seer who is granted a celestial vision and tour and is exalted to the status of an associate of the messiah. But if he is exalted to be an associate of the messiah at the eschaton, he is also accorded a similar role to that of the first messiah or redeemer figure, Moses (2 Esdr.

14:19-48). He is commissioned to spend forty days virtually as a second Moses. Inspired by the Holy Spirit, he dictates ninety-four books to his assistants. He is told to reveal twenty-four, which undoubtedly refer to the five books of Moses, Joshua, Judges, Samuel (both books counted as one), Kings (both counted as one), Isaiah, Jeremiah, Ezekiel, the Twelve (counted as one), and eleven books of the third division of the Hebrew Bible, the Ketubim or Writings. He is told to withhold the other seventy from the common people and to transmit their content only to the wise. Thus we have here an Ezra who is a second Moses, revealer and teacher of God's Word, and a source of the esoteric apocalyptic wisdom. This Ezraic tradition undoubtedly developed as a counterforce to the tradition that elevated Nehemiah, and finds itself fully expressed in rabbinic literature.

III. NEHEMIAH

Nehemiah was not the model of the *sopher*-proto-rabbi that Ezra was. He was a pietist who acted with vigor to enforce stringent halakah and compelled the community through a covenant to bind itself to a revived fidelity to God's Word as Nehemiah understood it. As Persian governor of Judea, he had the necessary means to institute the religious retrenchment sought by postexilic preachers like Malachi and attempted by Ezra. This retrenchment is reflected in the dissolution of marriages between the people of Israel and foreigners (Ezra 9), and in the promise of the Israelites, "We will not give our daughters to the nations of the lands nor take their daughters for our sons" (Neh. 10:30). Nehemiah indicates that all classes of Judeans, "separated from the people of the lands," formed a covenant community to obey the Torah of God given by Moses, the servant of God (Neh. 10:29ff.). This community became the prototype of future "new covenant" communities like that of Qumran and those of the early Christians. It also became the prototype of the *haburot* of Pharisaic provenance, in which members covenanted with each other to obey certain rigorous practices.[1] Thus, while Ezra became the prototype of the proto-rabbi, Nehemiah became the prototype of the pietist-separatist figure who set an ex-

---

1. My view of the Pharisees is a nonconventional interpretation that regards this group as pietistic separatists. See Chapter Three below for more detailed discussion.

ample for the Pharisaic-Essene complex that arose during the second century B.C.E.

Despite Nehemiah's efforts, strong currents existed against the Ezraic-Nehemian program. While Nehemiah enforced the Ezraic program, for some reason Ezra was not among the signers of the covenant. We will never know from our present literature whether Ezra had the same kind of reservations about Nehemiah's method as the proto-rabbis had about that of the Pharisees. And so the currents of opposition to Nehemiah may have included not only Samaritans and certain priestly and prophetic circles (Neh. 6:12-14), but also likeminded people who nevertheless rejected the pietistic-separatistic approach to the regeneration of Judaism. In the evolving opposition, therefore, we may see the beginnings of several conflicting movements: the Sadducees, the followers of the later proto-rabbis, and the broad mass of the people, the *ammey haaretz,* who cannot be categorized in any of the so-called sects of later times.

IV. THE RISE OF THE SYNAGOGUE

The synagogue had its origin in the conflict between the prophets and the priestly establishment and offered an alternative worship system. The institution is clearly foreshadowed in the story of the woman of Shunem, when she prepares to seek the prophet Elisha to revive her child who has died suddenly. Unaware of the purpose of her journey to "the man of God," her husband asks why she is going that day, since "it is not New Moon or sabbath" (2 Kgs. 4:23). Implicit in the husband's question is the notion that people customarily gathered at the prophet's home on Sabbaths and New Moons, presumably for religious inspiration, study, and prayer. Apparently, the prophets offered their homes as meeting houses, and out of this alternative spiritual experience arose what was later termed the *synagoge* in Greek.

It is clear from Nehemiah 8 that the gathering of an assembly on the first day of the seventh month (later denominated Rosh Hashanah) was nothing new to Judeans, for they gather as a matter of course, not because a new practice is ordained. They are accustomed to gathering in assembly because their Torah already contained such provision (Lev. 23:24; Num. 29:1). Ezra brings the scroll because this system of prayer and study at such gatherings is already several centuries old.

Ezra, however, introduces a new procedure. The holy man was wont to sit (Ezra 8:1; 14:1), but Ezra introduces the custom of standing upon a dais, surrounded by other liturgical assistants, thus establishing that prayer gatherings are the equivalent of the priestly-Levitical sacred worship. The scroll is raised to the full view of the people and they rise. Ezra then recites a *berakah,* a formula of praise, and the people respond "amen," evincing the prayer-posture of the time— raising their arms and bowing and prostrating themselves. Here we find the earliest synagogue rite, but we note also that it is still under the control of priests and Levites. The great lay breakthrough, in which non-priests conduct the worship ritual, is still in the future. We thus find that the alternative system of worship to that of the Jerusalem Temple began to be formalized, and that it was only a matter of time before it would transcend the sacrificial system and supplant it.

V. A BASIC PORTRAIT OF JUDAISM CA. 400 B.C.E.

The present Masoretic text of Nehemiah provides a basic portrait of the essence of Judaism ca. 400 B.C.E. It may be assumed that this Judaism came through the fourth century B.C.E., but it should not be assumed that this was a monolithic faith to which all who styled themselves Judeans or Judahites adhered in a uniform way. As indicated above, many points of view coexisted. After the emergence of Rabbinic Judaism to a dominant position, those who were responsible in some official way for transmitting the literature of faith handed down the biblical literature as we know it. But one should remember that many people during the fourth and third centuries B.C.E. did follow norms, beliefs, and attitudes present in other literature that circulated then, but which we no longer have. Similarly, during the Hellenistic period, from the third century B.C.E. to the first century C.E., the books we call "apocryphal" circulated, and they provided acceptable standards for many even though they were not admitted to the authoritative collection of Scripture we call the "canon."

Bearing in mind this reservation, we may extrapolate from Nehemiah 9 a basic outline of at least that version of Judaism which was held by later generations to represent best the historically evolved tradition. Nehemiah 9 has a prayer-psalm which affirms the divine role in history and ascribes Israel's historic sufferings to Israel's repeated apostasies. But it also embodies a primary source for the theology of the fourth century B.C.E.:

1. God is Creator (v. 6)
2. God selected Abraham and entered into a covenant with him (vv. 7-8)
3. God redeemed Israel from Egypt miraculously (vv. 9-12)
4. God's revelation at Sinai was mediated by Moses (vv. 13-14)
5. God ordained the Sabbath (v. 14)
6. God's attributes are grace, compassion, love, and patience (vv. 27-33).

Important in this profile of Judaism is the confession that Israel's suffering is retribution for Israel's rebellion, that Israel had either killed or ignored God's chosen prophets whom God had sent to exhort them to repentance, and that God's loving grace will be extended to the undeserving.

Since this psalm refers to the suffering that Israel has endured since the coming of Assyria (v. 32) and refers to the people being "slaves in the land" (v. 36), it must pertain to a time before that of Nehemiah. It is of the same genre as the poems in Lamentations, and may be seen as a liturgical composition prepared after the destruction of Jerusalem in 587 B.C.E. It therefore attests to the continuity between preexilic and postexilic Judaism. That some of the lines no longer apply to the post-Nehemian condition does not invalidate this view, for the nature of liturgical compositions is to become fossilized and to be used long after the specific historical context may no longer apply. This adaptation continues in synagogal liturgy, which still uses penitential prayers that grew out of medieval expulsions or massacres and no longer express the condition of the Jews. The underlying theological justification for the use of such liturgical compositions is that the devout relate to the past vertically, think of suffering communities horizontally, or simply understand the prayers in some broad symbolic sense.

The liturgical assembly at Nehemiah 9 is not accompanied by sacrifices. It therefore highlights the notion that such congregational worship in a proto-synagogue, unrelated to the Temple cult, was a matter of accepted form during the fifth century B.C.E. In this proto-synagogue, as in the old prophetic meeting houses, teaching and worship were conducted. A "school of Ezra" undoubtedly flourished as a precursor of the later proto-rabbinic schools of Shammai and Hillel, which in turn were merely continuations of the *bet midrash* (study hall) presided over by men like Ben Sira, the wisdom teacher who authored the apocryphal book Ecclesiasticus (or Sirach).

VI. THE VARIETIES OF JUDAIC RELIGIOUS EXPERIENCE

A. Introduction

As indicated above, to delineate a form of Judaism prevalent ca. 400 B.C.E. is not to imply that there existed either a monolithic "orthodoxy" or a consensus which can be termed "normative." Contrary to the frequent occurrence of the term *normative* in the writings of many contemporary scholars since it was coined by George Foote Moore early in the twentieth century, there has never been a "normative" Judaism. Rather there has always been an emergent variety of literary works that have articulated a wide diversity of religious experience within broad parameters.

A careful reading of the history of Judaism will yield at least three reasonable axioms. First, the development or the separation of a branch of Judaism into an entirely new religion is rare. Second, halakic diversification may produce a new denomination but not a new religion. Third, theological variety along with variegated practices, even ideas and rites considered heresy by some, is tolerated. These axioms are as evident in the first century as they are in the twentieth. The current state of our knowledge makes it impossible to determine precisely how many differentiated schools of thought or denominations existed within Judaism during the period under discussion. Certainly the prevalence of virtually hundreds of Protestant groups today, all of which are considered Christian, should teach us that the separation of groups into different houses of worship, their use of a slightly different liturgy, or even their observance of different holy days and sacraments does not preclude their being of the same religion. This is no less true of contemporary Judaism (to be discussed in Chapter Seven below). This Judaism presently consists of at least six major groupings, each of which—especially the Hasidic—is easily subdividable into many more varieties of religious experience. One cannot limit contemporary Judaism to the following denominations: Hasidism, non-Hasidic Ultra-Orthodoxy, Conservatism, Reform, and Reconstructionism. If one were a modern-day Josephus writing rather peremptorily about religious movements, one could easily distort the picture, as he did when he wrote of only three groupings in the first century C.E.—the Pharisees, Sadducees, and Essenes—adding casually "and a Fourth Philosophy." Actually, the Essenes constituted a branch of the broader Pharisaic movement. One might similarly oversimplify that there are today traditionalists and modernists, subsuming all forms of Hasidism and orthodoxy under "traditionalism," and under "modernism" all forms of Judaism that recognize the legitimacy of revision and advocate contemporary authority over a theoretical divine authority frozen in revelation. But this categorization would distort history and the current realities. Amidst all that these groups hold in common there are also significant differences that deserve greater recognition.

Similarly, for the period now under discussion, often historians not adequately attuned to theological nuances view the mass of Jews as subscribing more or less to a common Judaism, and look upon the evidence for variety as something in the nature of peripheral sectarianism or heresy, in the modern pejorative connotation of that word. But an accurate understanding of Judaism would yield other results. Despite all the beliefs and practices that the various factions and schools within Judaism held in common, which demonstrated a semblance of homogeneity, their differences were significant enough to give rise to separate denominations. In some cases these denominations, although Judaic, practiced exclusion of Jews, and sometimes one claimed over against all others to be the only true Israel, the saved remnant foretold by the canonical preachers.

Both heteropraxis (varied practice) and heterodoxy (varied belief) are evident. Asceticism and monasticism were seen as the way of the righteous by one group, while these virtues were eschewed by another. Some paid meticulous attention to purity practices, and others believed that disregarding such practices did not exclude them from being God's people. For example, the *ammey haaretz* may have been lax in their purity practices, tithing, and other rituals of Judaism, but they were possibly representative of the majority population and remained total Jews, their salvation never in question. It appears that after the rise of Christianity and the ascendancy of rabbinic Yabneh, when certain ritual observances were emphasized, some rabbis looked askance upon the *ammey haaretz* for laxity in wearing fringes on the corners of their garments or phylacteries, for failing to recite the Shema twice a day or to place mezuzot on their doorposts, and for ignoring the study of Torah. But their salvation was not denied. Those who felt comfortable as *ammey haaretz* grouped together in their own synagogues (M. Ab. 3:14), thus forming what we would today call an independent denomination. The negative judgment rendered by rabbinic literature on these synagogues does not indicate anything more than the reality that rabbinic literature survived. It in no way proves the exclusion of the *ammey haaretz* from salvation. If they were unfortunate enough to die on the same day as one who was either a sage or a sage's disciple, class distinction dictated that their burial had to be delayed until the other's was completed. But their right to burial in the Jewish cemetery and to all normal burial procedures was not questioned.

In the conventional discussions of postexilic Judaism, much attention is focused upon so-called Pharisees as the originators of a phenomenon called "normative" Judaism, which allegedly finds its ultimate expression in Rabbinic Judaism. Essenism is seen as something apart from Pharisaism and is now identified with the Qumranites whose legacy is found in the Dead Sea Scrolls. Sadducees are dismissed as having been overwhelmed by the destruction of Jerusalem and the termination of the biblical priesthood. But all of this analysis is oversimplified. What has been said about the *ammey haaretz* should caution us that broad masses of Jews were not Pharisees. Furthermore, because we do not have their literature, we have no idea at all who the Sadducees really were. We know of Boethusians and Morning Bathers—religious fellowships that were private associations within or without the Pharisaic complex. We are aware of individuals called *hakamim*, whom I refer to as proto-rabbis. These were at odds with Pharisees and Sadducees alike, were contemptuous of *ammey haaretz*, and may or may not have belonged to a religious fellowship. They spoke of earlier pietists but were not among them, and referred to Morning Bathers but were not among them. They spoke of *minim*, perhaps having reference in later times to those of Gnostic tendencies, but in all probability generally denoting Christian Jews who appear in the third or early fourth decade of the first century. There were, moreover, extreme Hellenistic allegorists, who rejected ritual observance, and extreme literalists, both of whom were criticized by Philo, the Alexandrian Hellenistic Jewish philosopher. Additionally, there were those like Philo who were traditional, ritually observant allegorists. There were also Samaritans, Therapeutae (much like Essenes), Galileans, and probably some unknown sects.

In evaluations such as the foregoing, however, it is important not to be anachronistic. Some groups referred to in the literature of the second century C.E. may not have origins as early as the fourth century B.C.E. But it is clear that from the earliest postexilic years extensive differentiation took place in Judaism, and there should be no doubt that the newly emerging groups had antecedents in preexilic Judaism and in the pristine religion of Israel. Thus, for example, it can be assumed that the pietism of the Hasidim had antecedents in the Rechabites and other Nazirite groups known in preexilic literature. But new socio-economic and political phenomena also gave rise to new religious phenomena. One example of this interaction is the Hellenistic encounter.

When varieties of Judaic religious expression from 400 B.C.E. to 70 C.E. are examined in this chapter, an effort is made to include those literary traditions and streams of thought of which we have a modicum of knowledge and a reasonable amount of literature. Adhering to this objective, our discussion will be limited to the Wisdom literature, the Hellenistic literature, the apocryphal works, and the Dead Sea Scrolls. We will also examine the major denominational groupings subsumed under Hellenistic Judaism, Pharisaism (including Essenes and Qumranites), Samaritanism, proto-Rabbinism, and early Christianity.

B. The Wisdom Tradition

Collections of poems, hymns, theological and philosophical discourses, and wise sayings or pragmatic maxims on the right way to live in books we have come to call Wisdom literature enlarged Israel's sacred literature and expanded its theological horizons. This literature consists of the books of Proverbs, Job, Ecclesiastes (also called Koheleth or Qohelet), certain select Psalms in Jewish canonical Scripture, and a variety of other ancient Jewish works called "Apocrypha" and "Pseudepigrapha," which were excluded from the canon of Scripture as determined in the second century C.E. Among the Apocrypha and Pseudepigrapha are the writings of Ben Sira, Tobit, 2 Esdras, the Letter of Aristeas, the Wisdom of Solomon, 4 Maccabees, part of Baruch, and the didactic poem Pseudo-Phocylides. Other Near Eastern countries such as Egypt, Syro-Phoenicia, and Mesopotamia had "wisdom schools," and Israelite-Judean wisdom had much in common with them. Although in his earlier biblical form the wisdom teacher never rises to the same prominence of spiritual leader as the priest or prophet, his role ultimately transcends theirs, and as he moves upward from being the *sopher* and *hakam* (scholastic and sage), and as the prophet disappears and the priest loses credibility, the wisdom teacher emerges as the proto-rabbi. He then incorporates into his person the charisma and the functions of prophet and priest along with those of the *hakam*.

A special feature of the Wisdom tradition that undoubtedly had its influence in conjunction with Hellenism and could have led to the broader vistas of some elements within Rabbinic Judaism and Christianity was the newly emerging sense of universality. Wisdom's emphasis upon duty to fellow human beings is not particularized to members of a given race, nation, tribe, or religion. It does not specify an Israelite or Judean, but speaks of *adam,* a generic term for "human being" or "person."

The wisdom teachers saw their teaching as divinely inspired. This idea is as old as the Davidic monarchy, when Ahithophel's advice was regarded as a "word of God" (2 Sam. 16:23). Wisdom was considered a "breath of the Almighty" by the author of Job (32:7ff.). At Ezra 7:26, the advice of the elders is equated with the Torah of the priest and the vision of the prophet. The sage and elder are sometimes synonymous with the scribe in certain respects, and the first two terms are later used for the personage of the rabbi.

Wisdom teachings, therefore, have to be seen equally with those of prophetic literature as constituting legitimate sources of theology, although they were not accorded the same halakic status as the Torah of Moses. Since wisdom teachers had this self-perception, it was only natural that they would expound on such matters as retribution, theodicy, and eschatology. Both Pentateuch and prophetic writings drew a causal link between sin and suffering, and righteousness and well-being. Yet confronting this conventional theology was the reality of the suffering of the righteous and the apparent well-being of the wicked. Sometime later the author of Job agonized over the impenetrable mysteries of the human condition. But it is clear that the underlying premise of Job is a rejection of the conventional notion that there is a nexus between sin and suffering. The author eschews the possibility of theodicy (justification of God in the face of evil). The author's real contribution to theology is his poignant expression of profound faith when confronting suffering: "I know my Redeemer lives" (19:25ff.). Faith expressed in the power of endurance does not offer a theodicy; it makes suffering and the absence of theodicy bearable, and allows for human-divine reconciliation. It appears, therefore, that this element of Wisdom literature contributed to an understanding of the existential human condition and made it possible to be liberated from a self-deceptive philosophy of suffering as retribution for personal evil. The Jobean view of suffering, however, does not imply that the doctrine of collective responsibility in which the people of God suffer national catastrophe was wholly superseded. The opposing doctrines of theological individuality and collectivity continued throughout Judaism. Diametrically opposed ideas have always existed within the faith.

Of special importance in the Wisdom tradition is the writing and the person of Joshua (Jesus) ben Sira, author of the book frequently called Ecclesiasticus, or the Wisdom of Sirach. Ben Sira, self-described as a *sopher,* presided over a *bet midrash* (study hall, or even a "research institute"). He taught that people enjoy free will and are therefore capable of choosing the good. He denounced empty ritualism and equated economic oppression with homicide, demanding, along with professed homage to God, concern for the poor and other underprivileged groups in society. Ben Sira identified personified Wisdom with the Torah of Moses and stressed the independence of the *sopher* who teaches, counsels, and instructs in that Wisdom/Torah. In so doing, he in effect accorded to the *hakam* a divine right for presenting "interpretative Torah," or what was the burgeoning, emerging proto-rabbinic halakah.

Ben Sira's reference to the creation of the world as one of beauty, order, and purpose, and as including the eternity of matter (44:22-25), is a Greek and a somewhat more scientific approach to this concept than the one found in the Hebrew Scriptures. In Ben Sira's writing, we find evidence that Hellenism pervaded Palestinian Judaism to the extent that even a conservative admirer of the ideal Jerusalem priesthood was also on the road to acculturation. But Ben Sira, unlike Ecclesiastes, kept his Hellenism reined in. He was concerned about those who go too far. Like a Nehemian separatist, he warned the pious against intellectual and social intercourse with apostates. Thus, despite his acculturated intellectualism, he was unwittingly a forerunner of the pietistic-separatistic groups, of which we have a paradigm in the community of Qumran. Yet, despite this conservative streak and his prefiguration of the whole proto-rabbinic movement, he was sufficiently under suspicion of Hellenism to be excluded from the canon.

Ben Sira was the product of a process of major transformation in the Judaism of the third century B.C.E. He represented a variety of views that were adopted by differing and even mutually antagonistic factions. Some of his views became identified with Sadducees, but he was not a Sadducee, for he believed and taught ideas rejected by those whom we know as Sadducees. Those whom we call Pharisees seem to have upheld some of his views, especially his opposition to mingling with apostates. But he was not a Pharisee. His theology appeared to conform to much of what we know as Rabbinism, but this may simply be biblical theology filtered through Ben Sira's pen. All we can be certain of is that Ben Sira was a sage, or *sopher* in its earlier sense, synonymous with *hakam;* a teacher in the *bet midrash;* a master to disciples; in a very real sense, the first proto-rabbi known to us by name, but not so recorded in the rabbinic literature.

C. Hellenistic Judaism

1. Introduction

In this segment, we will be concerned with the interaction between Judaism and Greek or Hellenistic culture and religion. For our purposes, the Hellenistic period begins with the impact of Greek culture from the time of Alexander the Great's occupation of Palestine in 332 B.C.E. until the ascension of the Roman emperor Augustus in 27 B.C.E. The influences of Greek culture upon Judaism, however, had actually begun earlier than the fourth century B.C.E. and persisted as late as the talmudic era, into the third and fourth centuries C.E.

Judaism and Hellenism were two separate cultural complexes, but this dichotomy should not be overstated or oversimplified. Before 300 B.C.E., Jews in Antioch were already apparently participating in Hellenistic culture, when Seleucus I subsidized those who had to purchase their own oil for anointment during gymnastic games, because the halakah forbade the use of the regular pagan oil. Perhaps we have here an early symbol of Hellenistic acculturation going hand in hand with the preservation of religious traditions.

Hellenism was a complex phenomenon that infused all areas of life: political, social, economic, technological, cultural, and religious. Hellenization was a process in which elements of Greek thought were generally strained through the Near Eastern and, for our purposes, the Judaic filter.

Little is known of the period from 400 to 200 B.C.E. Contrary to historians who surmise that little change took place in Judaism during that period, however, it must be averred that radical change was indeed experienced, although the process by which it occurred is as yet not clearly perceived. What is known is only that by 200 B.C.E. a Judaism aspiring to acculturation was struggling with a Judaism fending off all Hellenization—the struggle oversimplified in conventional histories as "Hellenism versus Judaism." The struggle, however, was really one of ultraditionalism (Hasidism) against acculturation (Hellenization). Furthermore, Hellenization was no more apostasy than similar processes of acculturation in more recent periods, such as nineteenth-century Germany or twentieth-century America. As was seen in the case of Ben Sira, and in the Jews of Antioch, one could be an acculturated traditionalist. In addition, persistent notions of an ancient kinship between Judah and Sparta circulated with reports of claims made by the Spartan king Areus (308 B.C.E.-265 B.C.E.) that Spartans were descended from Abraham. Coincidental with that reign, Greek culture was so deeply ingrained among Jews that the necessity to translate the Pentateuch into Greek became urgent.

Hellenistic cities were characterized by patron gods who were worshiped in a great annual festival called the *panegyris*. This festival included music, poetry, drama, dance, and athletic games, and attracted the Oriental peoples among whom the Greeks now settled, including the Jews. As these state festivals engaged excessively in king-worship, however, the Near Eastern people were alienated from them. At the same time, the Greeks were reluctant to adopt the Eastern gods. In time, the two religious tracks began to converge, and in a persistent syncretistic movement their deities were fused into composites.

Some Jews were attracted to elements of this syncretism. Possibly the "Hellenists," as they were called, were willing to identify the Judaic Deity with Dionysus, who was identified with Sabazios (the Thracian Zeus)—a term misconstrued as Tzebaot (also spelled Sabaoth, an epithet for Yahweh). For opponents of Hellenism, the recognition of Dionysus by Jews was comparable to the earlier Israelites' worship of the Canaanite god Baal, which the prophets denounced intensely. These opponents were characterized as Hasidim, pious ones.

Internecine quarrels between the Hellenists and the Hasidim often broke out over the priesthood. The Hellenistic high priest who favored the establishment in Jerusalem of a *gymnasium* and *ephebeum*[2]—chief symbols of acculturation in recreation, education, and general lifestyle—was rejected by those who claimed the legitimacy of another priestly line and the illegitimacy of Hellenizing Jerusalem. It must be underscored, however, that while many of the symbols of Hellenism constituted outward signs that a significant new direction was being taken, they did not presage or affirm apostasy. Even the wearing of the *petasos,* the broad-brimmed felt hat of Hermes, was not a fundamental theological breach. Nor was the practice of *epispasm,* concealing the circumcision by drawing the foreskin over it, necessarily an act of apostasy, but rather an effort to minimize differences in an ambience where nudity was the general practice. The Hellenists were seeking to

---

2. A *gymnasium* was a place where physical exercises were practiced. An *ephebeum* was a school in which young men were trained in exercise games.

"Hellenize" Judaism in much the same way as it has been "Anglicized" or "Americanized" in the twentieth century. But conservative opponents—traditionalists, or, as they were termed, Hasidim—opposed these forms of acculturation as steps to apostasy, just as the orthodox argued similarly against the Judaic reformation of the eighteenth and nineteenth centuries in central and western Europe and in North America.

2. The Maccabean Rebellion

Space does not permit here a review of the historical circumstances that brought together socioeconomic and political realities with the religious tensions between the Hellenists and the Hasidim which erupted into the Maccabean revolt and shaped the subsequent Hasmonean dynasty. In brief, the Maccabees' uprising was related to the attempts of Antiochus IV Epiphanes, Seleucid king of Syria, to suppress Judaism and to impose Greek religious practices throughout Judea. He ordered the cessation of the cult in the temple as then conducted, of the celebration of the Sabbath and holy days, and of circumcision. Furthermore, he imposed upon the Jews the offering of swine on altars—a special feature of Dionysiac ritual—as well as other ritually unfit animals.

Under the leadership of the priest Mattathias and his five sons, a Jewish rebellion against the oppressive decrees of Antiochus broke out in 167 B.C.E. After the death of Mattathias, the leadership of the rebellion passed on to his son Judas, surnamed "Maccabeus" (probably from the Aramaic word *maqqaba,* meaning "hammer"). Although Mattathias was a descendant of the Hasmonean family, his sons, as well as those who followed Judah, were popularly called "Maccabees."

The Maccabees achieved victory over the Syrians in 164 B.C.E. They liberated Jerusalem, purified the Temple, and reconsecrated the Temple to the worship of the God of Israel in an eight-day celebration, which became an annual festival in Judaism called Hanukkah (or Chanukah), meaning "dedication."

Hellenism constituted a great challenge of accommodation and acculturation to Judaism, a challenge which continued into talmudic times. The Maccabean rebellion was an immediate response to a moment of crisis. The proscriptions of Antiochus placed Palestinian Judaism in jeopardy. The Maccabean revolt was designed not against Hellenism but against paganism superimposed upon Judaism. There is no way to determine whether the Maccabees were at least moderate

Hellenists or traditionalists. If one were to judge by the Hasmoneans who ruled Judea after 140 B.C.E., one might say they were Hellenists, and rode to victory on the backs of the Hasidim, who did not understand the true nationalistic motives of the Hasmoneans until after the liberation of the Temple in 164 B.C.E. Hellenization was an attempt to reorient Judaism toward universalism and reflected once more the oldest tensions of Israel: centralist religious hegemony versus diversity; particularism versus universalism; and separatism versus openness to cultural intercourse.

The Hellenization of Judaism took place in both the diaspora and in Palestine, albeit to a lesser degree in the latter. In the diaspora it was most prolifically manifested in Alexandria, Egypt, from 200 B.C.E. to 50 C.E., although Jews resided all around Hellenized Syria and Asia Minor, and their communities were affected by Greek language, literature, philosophy, and religion. Everywhere it became necessary for Judaic sages to help their coreligionists adapt the Torah to the Hellenistic ambience, and later to Greco-Roman society. The result of this effort was an independently evolving midrash and halakah in Greek-speaking regions, of which the works of Philo are an outstanding illustration.

3. Hellenism in Palestine

Jews in the diaspora encountered the same Hellenistic influences as Jews in Palestine (Judea, Samaria, and Galilee) and in Jerusalem itself. A foremost illustration of this development is seen in the work of the Hellenistic historian Eupolemus, who was Judah the Maccabee's ambassador to Rome. The early Christian figures Eusebius and Clement of Alexandria credited Eupolemus with the notion that Moses was the first wise man, thus setting him above the famous seven wise men who were believed to have originated civilization. According to Eupolemus, Moses was the first person to establish a social order based upon constitutional law.

Other Hellenistic writers outdid Eupolemus. They discovered that it was Abraham who even earlier had transmitted civilization. As early as 2000 B.C.E., the idea circulated that biblical Enoch, known to Greeks as Atlas, learned all the secrets of heaven and earth from the angels. This esoteric knowledge he transmitted to Abraham, who in turn taught wisdom to the Phoenicians and to Egyptian priests at Heliopolis. Whether the teacher of civilization was Abraham or Moses, it was Judaism which these writers saw as the source of the world's wisdom.

Further evidence of Hellenistic thought making its way early through Palestine is reflected in such writings as Ecclesiastes and Ecclesiasticus, and in the Greek fragments among the Dead Sea Scrolls at Qumran.

4. Hellenism in Alexandria

In Alexandria one witnesses the earliest laboratory in Judaic acculturation in which a vast community preserves its ancestral religious tradition in the vernacular of a society which does not share that tradition, and under the impact of alien cultural influences. The *Letter of Aristeas,* a work whose date is not definitively set but is certainly from the second century B.C.E., is a sample of Hellenized Judaic religious writing prior to Philo (ca. 20 B.C.E.-50 C.E.). Undoubtedly Aristeas draws on earlier Judaic Hellenistic writers, in which rationales are offered for Judaic observances by allegorizing and philosophizing about them. For example, Aristeas justifies details of the dietary practices in which certain birds are forbidden by claiming they are wild and carnivorous, procuring their food through violence. Not eating these birds presumably teaches the Jew to eschew oppression. Similarly, he explains *tefillin* (or *tephillin,* phylacteries) as representing symbols that assist the faithful in calling God to constant day-long remembrance in order to avert sin. His affirmative discussion of such ritual symbols as tefillin, mezuzot (the encapsulated pentateuchal passages affixed to a doorpost), and zizit (fringes worn on the edges of garments) indicates that these ritual objects and their rites were part of Hellenistic diaspora Judaism.

References in the Letter of Aristeas, even if their chronological exactitude is open to question, leave us with a realization that it was credible to the writer's audience that Greek translations of at least sections of Scripture circulated during the fourth century B.C.E., and that Greek poets, historians, and philosophers had access to them. This situation inevitably makes us ponder the possible reality behind ancient Judaic claims that Greek philosophers were influenced by Judaism. It also opens the way to the plausibility of the reverse, that as early as the fourth century B.C.E., if not before, Judaic writers might have come into contact with Greek sources. This possibility further reinforces the notion that what the Maccabees were rebelling against was not a long-standing Hellenistic tradition taking root in Judaism, but rather Syro-Phoenician syncretism with Judaism.

The precise chronology of the process that led to the presently known Greek Bible, conventionally referred to as the Septuagint, is not clear. It is apparent that there was a long-standing tradition that some sort of Greek translation of some extent of Scripture was made during the reign of Ptolemy II, ca. 250 B.C.E. This Greek translation of the Hebrew Scriptures, whether in its entirety or in part, had a significant influence upon Jews and gentiles alike, and contributed to the conversion of gentiles to Judaism and ultimately to the development of early Christianity. Circulating in a variety of versions, the Greek translation of the Hebrew Bible was the theological baggage brought into the early Church. This variety of versions is reflected in the Christian Bible and, along with the Aramaic targums (translations), constitutes the reason why quotations from the Hebrew Testament in the Christian Testament frequently vary from the Hebrew text, and even in some cases from one Gospel to another.

The Greek Bible also contained works not included in the Hebrew Bible. These works later came to be known as "Apocrypha" and "Pseudepigrapha," and will be discussed separately below.

5. Philo Judaeus of Alexandria

Philo Judaeus of Alexandria was near the close of this long Hellenistic tradition in Judaism, and in a certain sense he expresses its fullest development. His work represents a highly ethicized fusion of Judaism with Hellenistic philosophy and culture. While he writes felicitous Greek, his work is rooted in Judaic tradition. He transmits much *aggadah* (or *haggadah,* legend) in his biographies of biblical figures, as well as in other writings, and conveys halakah in *The Special Laws* and in *The Decalogue,* among other works. Philo exhibits the rational approach of a philosopher, but also reveals that he was equally a mystic, introducing at times the sense of the sacramental in his discussion of the festivals. In *The Special Laws,* he expounds upon almost the entire range of Judaism by referring to numerous themes under the rubric of each of the Ten Commandments. In all, Philo expatiates upon psychology, ethics, history, politics, philosophy, halakah, and theology, from both a rational and a mystical view.

Scholars have differed over Philo's facility with Hebrew and his knowledge of Palestinian halakah, but space does not permit special treatment of this problem here.[3] Suffice it to say that the weight of evi-

---

3. For further discussion of the conflicting scholarly opinions on this issue see my *Emergence of Contemporary Judaism,* I/1, 314 and 362n.99.

dence indicates that Philo was steeped in the halakah of his time and wrote the first comprehensive and encyclopedic interpretation of halakah since the postexilic publication of the Torah. Those scholars who have rejected Philo as a knowledgeable proto-rabbinic scholar have missed the essential Philo.

Evidence is available for journeys by proto-rabbis to Alexandria before the existence of Philo. There is no reason to doubt that just as they must have lectured in the Alexandrian synagogues they also brought back speculations and interpretations of Alexandrian sages to Jerusalem. In addition to this logic, the knowledge exhibited in Palestinian literary sources of conditions or of science in Alexandria points to the interaction between the two centers. Thus Philo could have built upon Palestinian learning included in his Alexandrian background. Philo's own description of synagogue study sessions, of unwritten law and custom, and his reference to his midrashic method all attest to a situation in Alexandria that paralleled that of proto-rabbinic Jerusalem in style, method, and content. He indicates that in the Egyptian synagogues men of "special experience" (proto-rabbis) lecture, and subsumes the content under the typical rabbinic rubrics of "duty to God . . . duty to men." Just as the proto-rabbis and their rabbinic successors believed that whatever they extracted from the Torah by exegesis should be considered as having been revealed in the Torah and as carrying the significance of divine revelation, Philo argued that there are unwritten laws and customs which are "in the laws themselves."

Philo may be understood as a representative of a school of thought much like certain proto-rabbis typified in the early first century and before, and as rabbis later articulated in both Palestine and Babylonia. A school advocates a position, and sometimes one school of thought becomes predominant for a period. A modern analogy may be seen, for example, in the role of Tübingen in Christian Testament studies. Thus Philo approached Scripture from both an allegorical and a literal point of view. He discussed two other schools of thought in Alexandria, the one emphasizing a literal approach to Scripture, the other a radical allegorical one; he rejected both, though he lauded both methodologies. He opined that while the literalists were amiss in refusing to allegorize and philosophize in order to give contemporary meaning to the prescribed rituals in the Torah, the radical allegorists, who dispensed with the requirement to observe the rites physically, were in error. This synthesis of the allegorical and the literal approaches to observance proliferates in his major work on Judaic religious practice, *The Special Laws,* as well as in his other writings.

An example of Philo's views may be offered from his discussion of the dietary practices, which continue to be a source of tension in the twentieth century. Philo explains all of the practices by offering ethical and humanitarian connotations, but unlike radical allegorists who would be content to adopt the concepts without the actual practice, Philo advocates the practice of these dietary prescriptions. Yet in comparing the dietary practices of the twentieth century, as observed by those who consider themselves Orthodox, with those recorded by Philo, we find no reference in Philo to the vast complex of detailed practices related to the mixing of dairy and meat products or to utensils and vessels. Philo can therefore be seen to represent an older tradition when meat and dairy could be cooked and eaten together. This older tradition continues to be evident in Galilean Palestine as late as the second century, and even later in Babylonia.

The question as to when certain Palestinian proto-rabbis began to interpret "you must not boil a kid in its mother's milk" (Exod. 23:19; 34:26; Deut. 14:21) to apply to all mixing of dairy and meat products is unanswerable in our present state of knowledge. Similarly, the process by which it became universal practice in later centuries, until abandoned by the Reform movement in the nineteenth century and modified by the Conservative movement in the twentieth century, cannot currently be ascertained. An old view did exist that boiling and eating milk and meat together was prohibited (P. Targ. to Exod. 23:19), but this view obviously did not take on universal authority. Philo still expatiates on Exodus 23:19 as referring to a literal boiling of the calf in its own mother's milk.

While various scholars enumerate Philo's basic theology as encompassing different numbers of tenets, it is my view that his basic theology encompasses ten fundamental principles: (1) the eternal existence of God; (2) monotheism; (3) divine providence; (4) the divine creation of the world; (5) the unity of the world, there being no matter that does not constitute part of this world; (6) the revelation of the Torah to Moses; (7) the eternity of the Torah; (8) immortality; (9) both free will and grace granted by God; and (10) the messianic idea. Space does not permit elaboration of the influences of Pythagoras, Plato, Aristotle, the Stoics, or the Skeptics on Philo, and the extent to which

Philo critiques Epicurus and other philosophical schools such as the "Atomists."[4] Nevertheless, what is meaningful is that Philo's writings are clearly permeated by a loyalty to Torah and by the view that God's self-revelation to Israel in the Torah is the highest form of *nomos* (law).

In many ways, Philo's discussions of aspects of Judaism are relevant to contemporary Judaism. For example, as has been noted in the Introduction above, there has been much disagreement regarding the definition of "Jew" and "Judaism" as related to race, nationality, peoplehood, nation, or religion. This debate has been current since the eighteenth century. The whole matter has in recent decades been complicated by the rise of the State of Israel. In searching Philo we encounter his reference to Jews as a nation, seeing them as such by virtue of the historical reality that the practitioners of Judaism functioned as a separate nation in Palestine for centuries. But in his more reasoned statement on the nature of the polity by which Judaism functions, he sees the Jews as constituting an *ekklesia,* an "assembly" in the sense of "church" or "synagogue." He defines them quite naturally as a "holy polity" *(hiera politeia).* Drawing upon the scriptural phrase frequently used in reference to Israelites and Judeans, *qahal Yhwh,* translated in the Greek Bible as *ekklesia kyriou,* "the assembly of the Lord," he defines Jews all over the world as a universal *ekklesia,* or in his phrase, *ekklesias tes hieras,* "a holy congregation."

Philo's interest in numbers and his intensive allegorical discussion—the elements in his writings which are aggadic as opposed to halakic—all point to an aspect of mysticism that combined with his rationalism to complete the nature of the scholar. Not only does he deal with Scripture by using rich symbolism, but he is carried away by profound mysticism. To bridge the gap between the Uncreated God and God's mundane creation, Philo offers the *logos,* "the word" or divine reason. The *logos* is essentially a newer Hellenistic reformulation of Wisdom literature's term for "wisdom," *hokmah,* which is comparable to the Greek *sophia.* Philo's concept of *logos* as divinity immanent in the world is the counterpart to the divine agent of creation called *hokmah* in apocryphal writings. As his mystical flights have Philo soaring higher and higher, *logos* becomes the only real image of God created by God (*QG* II, 62), God's firstborn son, second to God, and indeed ultimately a second God. The *logos* becomes the backbone of the

---

4. For a fuller discussion of these influences see my *Emergence of Contemporary Judaism,* I/1, 320 and 370nn.123 and 124.

Christianity of John, and explains why, from the time of Justin Martyr and later in the works of Clement of Alexandria, Origen, and Ambrose, Philo becomes a major influence. Undoubtedly, because some of these became the premises of Christianity, they led to rabbinic abandonment of Philo's writings.

Philo's concept of the "mystical marriages" of biblical men of great virtue and his mystical flights with the life and death of Moses attest to the interesting synthesis of the rational and nonrational tendencies that existed within the one scholar. It is also with Philo's views of Moses that we encounter a Christian-like presentation in Judaism prior to the advent of Christianity. Utilizing Hellenistic mystical analogies, Philo sees Moses in terms similar to those in Hermetic literature (the literature of the cult of Hermes). According to Philo, Moses experienced a second birth by the Father of all, "a divine birth . . . from the ether and without a body" (*QE* 46). In effect, however, Philo rejected the pagan mysteries as based upon false deities and heroes. It is ironic that his virtual Judaic chauvinism did not have an impact on Judaism, while he apparently never heard of Jesus, around whom was soon centered a new Judaic faith rooted in his own theology.

D. The Apocrypha

1. Definition of Apocrypha

Long before the impact of Hellenism, other widespread permanent influences upon Judaism came from Babylonian, Persian Zoroastrian, and Egyptian wisdom literatures. This material contained apocalyptic visions with cosmic eschatological events that combined with Greek materials, which were all synthesized in the emerging Judaic literature. Some of this apocalyptic literature, along with related halakic and historical material, found its way into fragments embedded in the Bible, in proto-rabbinic literature, and in other rabbinic materials, such as the midrashim, but the bulk of it was kept outside the formal parameters of what became Judaism's collection of sacred Scripture. Consequently, this group of writings was later named *Apocrypha,* from the Greek verb *apokrypto,* "to hide from," and also "to obscure." It took on a dual meaning of something hidden as well as something hard to understand. In point of fact, these writings were simply set aside as "extraneous" writings, and the rabbinic term used to describe them was either *siphrey hitzonim,* "extraneous books," or *siphrey minim,* "the books of sectarians." Often, perhaps pointedly, the latter term referred specifically to Christian writings, since the term *min* was the usual epithet for a Christian Jew.

A major apocryphal work was Ecclesiasticus, written by Ben Sira. The interesting views of this sage have already been discussed earlier within the context of Wisdom literature, and will not be repeated here. At this juncture I will focus upon a serious halakic rival to the Pentateuch, the Book of Jubilees, and on the apocalyptic literature as a whole, almost all of which, with the exception, for example, of some fragments especially prominent in Ezekiel, Isaiah, and Daniel, is confined to the apocryphal and pseudepigraphal material.

2. The Book of Jubilees

Consideration of the halakic content of Jubilees, a midrashic rewrite of Genesis and Exodus 1–14, is indispensable to a study of the evolution of Judaism. It illustrates the "strict constructionist" approach in interpreting Scripture by one point of view during the period between Ezra and the rise of Rabbinism, a view that was countered by those who advocated a "loose constructionist" orientation. Another way to describe these basic positions is to refer to the former as conservative and to the latter as liberal, but such terms can be misleading. The hallmark of Jubilees is its agreement with the ideology and halakah of Qumran (the community of the Dead Sea Scrolls), with some apparent exceptions, which is characteristically strict, as opposed to the more flexible proto-rabbinic halakah. Undoubtedly, its disagreement with proto-rabbinic halakah, and its advocacy of the solar calendar, were the major reasons that the rabbis who fixed the so-called canon did not include Jubilees in it.

The date of Jubilees cannot be decided with certainty, but I tend to date it early, its earliest edition being ca. 190 B.C.E. and its latest editing ca. 160 B.C.E. The book includes a polemic against the growing Hellenization movement within Judaism and alludes to the Alexandrian allegorists, who argued against performing the mitzvot literally.

The book contains superficial hints of predestination, a doctrine which is also evident at Qumran (1QS 3:15-17). These hints are found in verses that stress that Moses received a full revelation of all of history (Jub. 1:3, 26). Nevertheless, it is clear that the author holds open the opportunity for repentance and forgiveness, and the possibilities of free will and choice (Jub. 5:13-16; 21:25; etc.). Other characteristic doctrines of Judaism are present in the book, and thus it cannot be argued that it is in some way "heretical." The book includes teachings on eschatology, which encompass the idea of a period of tribulation followed by the end-time restoration and reconciliation of Israel to its land and its God; the renewal of the cosmos; and a last judgment followed by eternal bliss for the righteous. While there is no explicit statement of resurrection, there is of immortality, this immortality being a post-eschatological phenomenon and therefore quite related to spiritualized ideas of resurrection.

Angelology and demonology in Jubilees are far more developed than in the canonical books. In contrast with later rabbinic views that trace themselves to Daniel (10:12; 12:1), Jubilees denies that angels govern the destiny of Israel, stressing rather that Israel is subject to God alone (Jub. 15:32), much the same as Paul later rejected any role for angels in the destiny of the Church.

Scholars have examined Jubilees and the Pentateuch and found many discrepancies, which reinforces the notion that the book was designed to replace Ezra's version of the Torah of Moses with an even stricter one. Its major difference is in affirming the sun alone, rather than the moon and the sun as in Genesis, as setting the holy days of Judaism. Festivals are traced to origins other than those given in the Pentateuch, and Jubilees contains four "days of remembrance" in contrast to the Pentateuch's one. Even the Day of Atonement is explained differently here than in the Pentateuch, its origin being attributed to Joseph's having been sold by his brothers, the eponyms of the twelve tribes, on the tenth day of the seventh month, thus requiring an annual ritual of atonement by all their progeny into perpetuity. Furthermore, in Jubilees, Pentecost is related to God's covenants with Noah and Abraham.

Despite the points of contact between Jubilees and Qumran, there are differences, chiefly in the highly developed messianic idea. A two-messiah theory obtains at Qumran, while Jubilees makes no explicit mention of such a concept. Another major distinction is Jubilees' death penalty for Sabbath violation, absent from Qumran. But perhaps most important is that Jubilees addresses itself to the entire people of Israel, while the Qumran literature serves the purposes of a separatist elect-elitist community. It must therefore be concluded that although the people of Qumran found reinforcement in Jubilees and used it as an ally against Hellenization, Jubilees was not a Qumranite document. Jubilees was also not a Hasidic document, for Hasidim did not contradict the Torah; and it was not an Essene document, conforming not at all to Essene practices. It was neither Sadducean nor so-called

Pharisaic, for it preceded both of these groups and neither of these groups would contradict the Torah. It was obviously not a Hellenistic document, for it polemicized against the Hellenization of Judaism.

Where did Jubilees arise? Undoubtedly Jubilees is living evidence of a wide variety of factions among Jews, some of whom had affinities with others, sharing doctrine and halakah and differing at one and the same time. A host of groups dissented from the so-called establishment, the official priestly religion of Jerusalem, and Jubilees represents a literary product of one such movement. This unnameable movement shared doctrines or halakah with apocalyptic groups and with Qumran. Its rigid conservatism, a tendency most evident in its Sabbath halakah and in its insistence on the literal *lex talionis* ("the law of retaliation," of "an eye for an eye") illustrates the dichotomy between some movements and the proto-rabbinic movement. The latter reflected more liberal and flexible tendencies, exemplified by the work and views of a contemporary of Jubilees, Yosi ben Yoezer, whose school of thought ultimately emerged predominant in Rabbinism.

3. Apocalyptic Literature

The term *apocalypse* is derived from the Greek *apokalypsis,* "revelation." This is a genre of literature which purports to disclose secret, divine knowledge. It includes celestial visits by famous personalities, such as Enoch, who impart mystical teachings about historical ultimates. The writings contain descriptions of cosmic upheaval to come, numerical symbolism, cryptic language, and religious enthusiasm. They teach a view of history as consisting of two ages: the present historical world and the future metahistorical world, which is the age to come or eternity. Frequently the message is conveyed in parables; people are sometimes represented by animals; and events are symbolized by occurrences in nature.

Since apocalyptic literature is designed to detail the end-time experience, it also includes the teachings concerning individual and cosmic last judgment, immortality, resurrection, and the redemptive or so-called messianic age. The apocalyptists generally taught a form of predestination, in which the birth, development, and decline of all nations was predetermined by God since pre-creation. To deal with this cyclical aspect of history and to discover the time of the final unfolding of God's plan to terminate history, the literature is much given to the calculation of time cycles and calendrical projections, a process later common in millenarianism, a movement which emphasized the division of history into thousand-year cycles.

It is in apocalyptic literature that the term *son of man* first arises in a very special sense related to eschatological expectation. In Daniel it emerges from its simpler meaning evident in Ezekiel, where it can be translated "man," or "sir," to signify a transcendent, supramundane individual or a personification of the corporate body of saints. In the book of Enoch the "son of man" more clearly becomes a preexistent, divine, messianic figure (1 En. 46:3-4; 48:3; 49:2; etc.). It is in this sense that early Christianity applied the term to Jesus.

The belief in the afterlife develops more broadly in apocalyptic literature. It is clearly from these sources, rather than simply from biblical sources, that the complex of afterlife beliefs in Rabbinic Judaism should be traced. The oldest biblical faith certainly included a concept of life after death, in which in some indescribable manner the human continues a shadowy form of existence in a place called *Sheol*, the Pit, or *Abaddon*, deep beneath either the earth or the cosmic ocean. But individuals sought more than this vague afterlife. They yearned for fellowship with God and vindication for undeserved suffering in this world. The belief in a shadowy existence was only a small step from an affirmation of a spiritual existence that follows death, and consequently of a doctrine of nonphysical immortality. Such gropings for immortality and also for resurrection begin to surface at Job 14:13-15; Isaiah 26:29; and Daniel 12:2.

With these stirrings of faith in an immortal life of bliss for the righteous arise the notions of heaven and hell. These notions are nurtured in apocalyptic literature in a manner hitherto unknown in biblical works. It is not always clear whether the punishment of the soul takes place after death or after final judgment. Nor is it always certain whether *Gehenna*, where punishment ensues, is subterrestrial; or whether *Gan Eden* (Garden of Eden, Paradise), where reward is received, is in heaven. These ambiguities were never settled and continued on into rabbinic literature and throughout the history of Judaism. Similarly, it is difficult to ascertain whether resurrection is to take place on this earth, or on a recreated earth; whether it precedes the age to come, or is to constitute that age; whether it is heavenly and spiritual, or part of a real this-worldly messianic kingdom; whether it is only for the righteous (Dan. 12:2), or for all human beings (Test. Benj. 10:8).

In sum, we have biblical and postexilic Judaism, including the apocryphal apocalyptic literature, providing intimations of heaven, hell, immortality, final judgment, and resurrection, but not a definitive uniformity of doctrine. This lack of uniformity is a further reflection of one of the theses of this work, that diversity is the hallmark of Judaism, and that far from an orthodoxy ever imposing itself upon Judaism, the nature of Judaism is best understood as interrelated heterodoxies. Biblical Israel had notions concerning life after death. These were fused with Mesopotamian, Persian, and Syro-Phoenician ideas, and ultimately took the form that is found in Rabbinic and medieval Judaism.

E. The Dead Sea Scrolls

1. Qumran

It was noted at the beginning of this chapter that Judaism between 400 B.C.E. and 70 C.E. experienced an emergent variety of literary works that articulated a wide diversity of religious experience within Judaic parameters. We have now briefly glimpsed the contributions made to the evolution of Judaism by the Wisdom literature, by the Hellenistic literature, especially as represented by Philo of Alexandria, and by the apocryphal writings, at least as sampled in Ben Sira, Jubilees, and the apocalyptic books. Another group of apocryphal or extraneous writings in Judaism were the many works we now know as the Dead Sea Scrolls, attributed to an ancient community at Qumran.

This literature was found in a series of caves near the western shore of the Dead Sea at Wadi Qumran. Among the works indigenous to the pietistic monastic community at Qumran were also found all of the books of the Hebrew Testament, except Esther, and many of the apocryphal works, including the apocalyptic writings, especially Jubilees and Enoch. Commentaries to biblical works were found, and these were given the epithet *pesher,* although essentially they are of the same genre as proto-rabbinic and rabbinic midrash. Perhaps one of the most important discoveries was the Temple Scroll, which, like Jubilees, was another alternative Torah containing more stringent halakah than that of contemporary proto-Rabbinism.

Who were the people of Qumran? This is a major question regarding which much speculation persists. Related to this question are three others: How valid is the consensus of modern scholarship that defines Qumranites and Essenes? The second is, What is the relationship, if any, of the Qumranites to the Pharisees? And what is the connection between Pharisaism and Rabbinism?

On the one hand, since I do not agree that we can identify the people of Qumran explicitly as any one of the known groups of ancient Judaism, I prefer to call them Qumranites. On the other hand, I do believe they were part of a vast complex of groups or movements, all of whom can be subsumed under the rubric "Pharisees." Among the Pharisees were also the Essenes, the Therapeutae of whom Philo speaks, and other undesignated pietistic, zealous, and separatistic religious sects or movements. The actual community that arose at Qumran was an offshoot of the Hasidim who had joined the Maccabean rebellion in 167 B.C.E., but withdrew from support of the Hasmoneans in two stages: the first after the liberation of the Temple in 164 B.C.E., and the second after the continuation and expansion of the war in 160 B.C.E. The Hasidim who withdrew were undoubtedly soon branded *Perushim*, pietists or separatists, or more emphatically pietistic separatists.

When the Jerusalem priesthood was usurped by the illegitimate Hasmonean line, and when Simon the Hasmonean assumed the title "Prince of the People," suggesting a drive for monarchy which would be a usurpation of the Davidic throne, some of the more ardent Hasidim and *Perushim* (Pharisees) organized the ascetic-monastic new-covenant community at Qumran. Hereafter they considered themselves the true Israel, the "sons of light," and the Jerusalem establishment was seen as "the sons of darkness." These zealous "Pharisees" produced what we call the Dead Sea Scrolls, and ultimately, as many were absorbed into Rabbinism after 70 C.E., their stringent ritualism became part of Judaism. Others were drawn to Christian Judaism or Ebionism, and others yet to gentile Christianity. A segment remained sectarian, and some centuries later, along with other nonrabbinic and anti-rabbinic groups like Ebionites and Sadducees and perhaps remnants of ancient Israel residing in the far reaches of present-day Iran, some entered Islam, and the remainder surfaced in a new movement called Karaism.

During the second century B.C.E., however, and until the destruction of Qumran by the Romans during the war of 66-73 C.E., these people flourished as a separatist segment of the larger pietistic movement that included those whom we call Essenes and those whom we call Pharisees.

2. *The Religion of Qumran*

Primary for all who took the oath of covenant at Qumran was to obey the Torah of Moses. But the understanding of this Torah was to be in accord with how it was revealed to the "sons of Zadok" (1QS 1:3; 5:8-9). There was, therefore, wide agreement between Qumranites and other Jews, but also many differences. The differences manifested themselves largely in those elements of Judaism most susceptible to pietism: sexual and purity norms, and Sabbath and dietary observance. Unlike the literature that embodies the views of the proto-rabbinic contemporaries of the Qumranites, which included a variety of options for the fulfillment of the same mitzvah, the Qumran literature, with an air of infallibility, required the form of each practice to be in accord with one approach.

The inflexibility and stringency of Qumran halakah is well exemplified in its Sabbath halakah, as set forth mainly in the *Damascus Document* (CD 10:14–11:18). At the very outset it is clear that the Qumran community began its Sabbath much earlier than the conventional practice of opening the Sabbath at sunset or dark. While earlier halakah, expressed in both the Torah and in Deutero-Isaiah, provided for the non-Israelite to observe the Sabbath within the context of the faith community (Exod. 20:8-11; Deut. 5:12-15; Isa. 56:3-6), the pietists of Qumran excluded the gentile from all participation in the Sabbath. It is true that a gentile was not to be requested to do a task forbidden to a Jew by Qumran halakah (CD 11:2), which superficially would lead one to infer that the gentile was eligible to participate in Sabbath rest. But this prohibition did not include gentiles in Sabbath observance, as is evident from general Qumranite anti-gentilism and the caution not to spend the Sabbath in their midst (CD 11:14-15). Rather, the prohibition was simply one more stringency upon the part of the pietistic movement to enforce a Sabbath of utter quiescence.

The basic proto-rabbinic principle that *piqquah nephesh,* the saving of life, supersedes all Sabbath prohibitions, was not recognized at Qumran (CD 11:16-17), just as it was absent from Jubilees. It was at Qumran (CD 11:7-9) that the earlier prohibition against commercially transporting goods on the Sabbath (Jer. 17:21-27; Neh. 13:15ff.) became a prohibition against all carrying of any objects from one domain to another, even from one's house to the street. This extended prohibition ultimately entered Rabbinic Judaism, among many other such pietistic attitudes, in order to enable Rabbinism to consolidate its hold over those committed to this folk-piety.

Along with the Sabbath halakah, the Qumran community favored more restrictive practices in the areas of dietary traditions, purity customs, and domestic relations. The last area is evident in the cases of both polygamy and divorce. Furthermore, it is clear that the sect not only banned polygamy and divorce, contrary to the Torah, but also re-marriage after divorce, again contrary to the Torah (CD 4:20–5:1). The perplexed who might wonder how Qumranite pietists could go con-trary to the Torah should understand that in all versions of Judaism, to be beyond the Torah by pietistically forbidding what is permitted was meritorious. Permitting that which is forbidden was probably the radi-cal innovation of nonpietistic, that is, non-Pharisaic[5] proto-rabbinic and Rabbinic Judaism.

The liturgical cycle at Qumran was based upon the biblical twice-daily *olah* (the atoning burnt offering). However, the Qumranites' holy days were determined by the solar calendar rather than by the lunar, as at Jerusalem, and they added holy days to the biblical roster. The most serious difference between Jerusalem and Qumran was in the des-ignation of the day that Pentecost (Shabuot, the Festival of Weeks) was to be observed. This difference was due to their disagreement regard-ing the interpretation of Leviticus 23:11.

In the case of baptism, Qumran also varied from Jerusalem. While it included the various baptisms of purification, it also added a bap-tism of admission into the elect community. Christian baptism is un-doubtedly modeled after this particular rite of Qumran, except that added to the admission aspect of the rite was the forgiveness of sins. At Qumran, as in proto-rabbinic thought, atonement could not come from the water alone, but from repentance, the immersion in the water being merely an outward symbol of the inner transformation. One of the Qumran scrolls reads: "he is not sanctified by seas and rivers . . . as long as he rejects the statutes of God" (1QS 3:4-9; 5:13-14). This understanding of baptism is surely true in Christianity as well. Al-though forgiveness of sins is achieved by the grace that pours out upon the believer, John the Baptist also emphasized repentance.

It appears that a daily meal was taken at Qumran, presided over by a priest and possessing a sacramental character. It served as a pro-totype of the ultimate messianic banquet. Worship and meals were in minimum units of ten (1QS 6:3-8; CD 13:2), each quorum of ten pre-sided over by a priest. The units of tens operated in relays. While some slept, others prayed and others studied. Whether this quorum of ten was modeled after an earlier quorum of ten, or whether the rabbinic

---

5. Like my view of the Pharisees, my view of Qumran is an original, non-standard one, and is discussed in greater detail in Chapter Three below.

prayer quorum of ten, the *minyan* (M. Meg. 4:3; etc.), was ultimately modeled after the Qumran quorum cannot be ascertained.

The following doctrines were held at Qumran: an intense eschatological belief, which included "a day of vengeance" when evil will be destroyed; a two-messiah belief, which is not entirely clear; the re-creation of a new world; life eternal for the saints, the sons of light; and hell for the wicked, the sons of darkness. These doctrines are clearly expressed in a variety of places throughout the Scrolls and do not require documentation here.[6] Space here does not allow us to clarify the complexity of the Qumranic figure, the Teacher of Righteousness, but whatever else he was, he most certainly was their interpreter of mysteries and expounder of revelations.[7]

Just as some eschatological elements of the Scrolls, such as the messianic idea and the figure of the Teacher of Righteousness, are unclear, so too are other related elements, such as the doctrines of immortality and resurrection. But this lack of clarity is also found in both the Hebrew Scriptures and in rabbinic literature, and is due to the variety of religious experience that obtained in Judaism and the failure of the editors of the sacred writings to provide lucid expositions of all metaphysical questions. The Wisdom of Solomon (3:1-9) points to a belief in immortality, as Daniel (12:2) points to the doctrine of resurrection. These concepts were probably taken for granted as part of the faith of some Jews and therefore did not require special mention, though they were rejected by others, as resurrection was by the Sadducees.[8]

F. Samaritanism

Following the death of Solomon and the subsequent separation of the North (of Israel) from the South, the religion of Israel emerged in two forms. One was practiced in the southern kingdom of Judah and Jerusalem, the other in the northern kingdom of Israel. There were, of course, variations, but it is impossible to know precisely how the northern cult in Bethel or Samaria (Shomron) differed from that in Jerusalem. Furthermore, it is still not possible to ascertain to what extent the northern religion became even more diluted and syncretistic after the con-

---

6. See especially my *Emergence of Contemporary Judaism,* I/1, 307-10, 355 n. 72.

7. Ibid., pp. 308, 357 n. 74.

8. See Chapter Three below for discussion of Sadducees.

quest by Assyria, because we must rely upon Judean accounts and later Judean biases. The Samaritans, however, date their separation from the southern religion to as early as the eleventh century B.C.E., claiming that Eli, a son of Aaron's son Ithamar, usurped the priesthood, which belonged to the line of Eleazar, and that Eli abandoned the true sanctuary of Mt. Gerizim for that of Shiloh. The problem of when and why the final separation took place cannot be resolved.

A few suggestions might reasonably be made. On the one hand, since the Samaritans used some southern historical works, they could not have engaged in an irrevocable separation before 400 B.C.E. On the other hand, they did not include proto-rabbinic halakah in their observances and seemed already to be held in contempt during the first century C.E. They must have been separated before having had an opportunity to absorb proto-rabbinic elements prior to the rise of Christianity. In view of the presence of the institution we call "synagogue" in Samaritan religious life, it is clear that they had not yet broken away or been irrevocably excluded before the spread of that institution during the Persian and Hellenistic eras. Therefore it is fair to surmise that Samaritanism separated from Judaism sometime between 400 B.C.E. and the first century C.E. That this separation preceded the first century is clear from both the Christian Testament and the works of Josephus.

The foregoing discussion points to the separate development of Samaritanism precisely when other Judaic groups were individuating themselves. During the Hasmonean era, which saw the rise of Essenes, the ubiquitous *Perushim* (Pharisees), Sadducees, Qumran pietists, and other groups, the Samaritans were further alienated. The scenario must have been somewhat as follows. Solomon died in 922 B.C.E., and the southern and northern kingdoms went their own way. But after the conquest of the North in 721 B.C.E., Assyria moved pagan settlers into land vacated by Israelite refugees and deportees. Nevertheless, many remaining Israelites remained loyal to Yahweh and worshiped at Mt. Gerizim. These Israelite-Samaritans were called *shamrin* ("guardians," perhaps of the "true faith") or *shomronim* (2 Kgs. 17:29), and were not sundered from Jerusalem alone but also from the new transplanted pagans who inundated Samaria and are known in Greek as *Samaritai,* a name which later covered all of the northerners. The priestly cult did not function in Jerusalem and Judah during the Babylonian exile (587-538 B.C.E.). When Cyrus of Persia allowed the rebuilding of the Temple, priests probably saw that period as a good time to restore their control of the priesthood. They recognized that this meant renewing a relationship, indeed a dominant one, with Jerusalem. When they were rejected by Nehemiah, however, they in turn rejected any further legitimacy for Jerusalem. Since the Hasmoneans claimed descent from Phineas, son of Eleazar, John Hyrcanus decided to do away with their challenge to his legitimacy by destroying the Samaritan worship center in 128 B.C.E.

These Israelite-Samaritans, called *Kuthim* in rabbinic literature, never ceased to be "theological Israel," and while some rabbinic sources accused them of "gentilism" in some of their practices, they also conceded that they were "mostly like Israel" (Kuthim 1). Yet, later rabbis interdicted marriage with Samaritans (B. Qid. 75a). The Samaritans were not Sadducees who recognized Jerusalem. They were not Qumranites as a whole, for the Qumranites evinced no interest in Mt. Gerizim. Nevertheless, some adopted the type of pietism known of the Essenes and other *Perushim,* and were apparently present at Qumran. There is much ambivalence in rabbinic literature regarding the Samaritans, due to their development over a long span of time and under varying historical pressures. Thus, at times the Samaritan was classed as an *am haaretz,* who was certainly a Jew, distinct from the *nokri,* a gentile. At times the Samaritan was regarded not quite as a Jew, and at other times Jew enough to be part of the quorum of ten for Grace after Meals. There are also grounds in our extant literature to conclude that Samaritans, like Judeans, included Hasidim (Pietists) and were divided into a variety of sects.

The religion of the Samaritans was basically that of preexilic Israel, adhering to monotheism, the covenantal sign of circumcision, and loyalty to Torah, and greatly emphasizing the role of Moses. But the Samaritans had no spiritual interest in Jerusalem. They observed the Sabbath and the holy days, and had doctrines of creation, covenantal election, revelation, and the eschaton, including, for some, a belief in resurrection. As with the southern Judeans who gave their name to Judaism, the Samaritans developed a "postbiblical" expansion of their religion, comprising literature, liturgy, theology, and halakah or *hilluk.* They believed Moses deposited the holy ark at Mt. Gerizim, and they visited it on the three biblical pilgrimage festivals of Passover, Pentecost, and Tabernacles. The *hilluk* contains a wide assortment of Samaritan religious practice related to circumcision, the Sabbath, holy days, purity practices, dietary customs, domestic relations, and other life-cycle halakah bound up with birth, marriage, and death. In some instances, Samaritan *hilluk* evinces stringencies reminiscent of Jubilees and Qumran. Samaritanism and Judaism differ on the Decalogue. The first nine commandments of Judaism are so divided that they constitute only eight in Samaritanism; the commandment not to covet is their ninth; and their tenth is a commandment derived from Deuteronomy 27:3-8, ordaining Mt. Gerizim as the chosen place of God.

The assumption must be made that later Talmudic Rabbinism, which had expelled Christianity, brought the differentiation between Judaism and Samaritanism to completion by the fifth or sixth century. Subsequently Samaritans had interaction with the emergent new anti-rabbinic movement, Karaism, and the two groups exhibited mutual influences. Samaritans used a different calendar, which they claimed was bequeathed by Adam down through the generations to Moses, who taught it to Phineas, who in turn transmitted its mysteries to the priesthood of Mt. Gerizim. Consequently, Jews and Samaritans never observed holy days on the same days, and Samaritans, like Qumranites, always observed Pentecost on a Sunday. Like Jews, they did not mingle meat and dairy in their food practices. Unlike Jews, however, they did not observe such rituals as tefillin, which were a later post-Hasmonean proto-rabbinic innovation, when the irrevocable schism between Jews and Samaritans had taken place.

G. The Rise and Separation of Christianity

1. Introduction

Christianity, no less than Samaritanism or Qumranism, was at first a variety of Judaic faith. And as in the case of Samaritanism, the irrevocable separation of Christianity was initially the product of politics and not of theology. Ultimately, the doctrine of salvation centered in Jesus of Nazareth made it difficult for Christians (people who believed that Joshua of Nazareth was the promised redeemer figure, the anointed one, or Christ) to remain in the same synagogues with Jews who did not believe this doctrine. Nevertheless, a *modus vivendi* might have been found had not the national political issue created insurmountable obstacles and roused intense emotions between Christian and Jew. After almost two hundred years (64 B.C.E.-135 C.E.) of insurrection, civil war, rebellion, nationalist violence and terrorism, repression and oppression—all intertwined with apocalyptic messianic visions—those who went contrary to what was perceived to be "the national interest" were not appreciated. Thus Jews who were Christians and their pagan converts, who after the crucifixion of Jesus harbored an apolitical messianic faith, were inevitably due for rejection. The predominant segment of Rabbinic Judaism swamped the peace party of Yohanan ben Zakkai[9] and engaged in nationalist assertiveness between 80 and 130 C.E.

This nationalist assertiveness was new to the proto-rabbinic circles early in the first century, when Judas of Galilee, whom Josephus describes as a *sophistes* (a *hakam,* or proto-rabbi), organized extremists known in various manifestations by the most familiar terms, "zealots" *(sicarii)* and generically brigands *(lestai).* Josephus charges these extremists with all the calamities that ensue, and informs us that their major notion was that God alone is Lord and King over Israel, and that Judeans ought not to pay tribute to Caesar. That this was not a universal view is borne out in the famous episode recorded in the Synoptic Gospels in which Jesus ordered that one must obey what later literature calls the *hilkata demedinah* (the sovereign law of the land), and therefore one must render to Caesar what is rightfully his (Matt. 22:15-22 and Gospel parallels). The *Perushim* and Herodians, who sought to trap Jesus into self-incrimination as a rebel, were thereby astonished, for Jesus herewith indicated that his eschatological views were apolitical.

The nonmilitant position of Jesus was akin to that of the peace party led and represented by Yohanan ben Zakkai—an older contemporary of Jesus, founder of Rabbinism, and conceivably a colleague of Jesus in Galilee between 20 and 30 C.E. Yohanan's segment of the proto-rabbinic movement remained aloof from the rebellion of 66 C.E., as did Christian Jews.[10] It attempted to still the stormy waters of a new rising tide of militancy after 73 C.E. but failed. As it failed, the position of apolitical Christian Jews became precarious. When Yohanan was deposed as leader of the academy at Yabneh, the fate of Christian Judaism as a variant form of Judaism was sealed. The irony of this particular development is that the person behind the expulsion of Christians from the synagogue was Rabbi Gamaliel II, grandson of Ga-

---

9. See Chapter Three below for discussion of Yohanan ben Zakkai.

10. The adherents of the earliest Palestinian church which evolved into Ebionism should be termed "Christian Jews," and their faith "Christian Judaism," as opposed to the conventional forms, "Jewish Christians" and "Jewish Christianity." This terminology is preferable because for these people "Jew" and "Judaism" remained substantive, and "Christian" and "Christianity" played the role of modifier.

maliel I, who saved Peter from potential disaster before the Sanhedrin (Acts 5:34-35).

As indicated earlier, the first century witnessed a wide variety of *haereses,* factions within Palestinian and Greek-speaking diaspora Judaism. There were bound to be groups in the Parthian east of whom we know less. Some Jews in Persia were "Parthianized," as those in the west were "Hellenized," and some maintained stricter conceptions of tradition. For example, Eusebius mentions a group called Masbothei, and the Palestinian Talmud informs us that there were twenty-four branches of Judaism when the Temple was destroyed in 70 C.E. (P. San. 29c).

It is therefore no surprise to hear of another Judaic movement, this one convinced that the long-awaited redeemer figure had arrived in the person of Joshua of Nazareth, and subsequent to his crucifixion beginning to observe messianic liturgical rituals and new holy days in addition to those of their ancestral faith. The central article of belief of these Jews and of the pagans who joined them was that the Messiah (Gk. *Christos*) had come, and consequently they were denominated as "Christians."

A variety of messianic ideas, all in some way having grown partially from the Egyptian experience of Moses as prophet-redeemer and partially from the prophetic vision of the "day of the Lord," circulated in the first century C.E. Sometimes the idea included a Davidic dynast, sometimes an undesignated human political liberator, at times God Himself as the redeeming and liberating figure, occasionally the suffering and dying "servant of the Lord," and at times two messiahs. In general terms two basic messianic ideas held sway. The first, and predominant one, was a nationalist messianic idea in which a this-worldly restoration of the united kingdom of Judah and Israel would be followed by a great age of abundance and peace characterized by universal harmony in nature and humanity. The second was an apolitical belief in the spiritual regeneration of Israel (including Judah), accompanied by the advent of God's own sovereignty, or *malkut shamayim* (lit. "kingdom of heaven"). In both cases the apocalyptic visions of cosmic upheaval played a role—some saw the messianic age as a utopian period climaxing human history, and others saw it as a wholly metahistorical and metaphysical era. It was into this complex environment that John the Baptist and Jesus of Nazareth were born.

For a short while there were probably a John-circle and a Jesus-circle. Ultimately John's followers joined the Christian movement, which included John in its pantheon as Elijah *redivivus* (resurrected). Elijah was depicted as being of a priestly family (P. Targ. Lam. 4:22), as was John. Furthermore, a tradition known in the first century told that when Elijah returns to earth in a pre-messianic function he will die, as John must die (Bib. Ant. 48). John's main contribution, as far as we can presently ascertain, was his fusion of the Qumran admission baptism for fellow Jews and of the general Jewish proselyte baptism for pagans into a symbolic rite of both admission and cleansing from sin. The latter, however, was to be accompanied by actual repentance or transformation of one's character. John also emphasized the pietistic exercises of prayer and fasting. Jesus' disciples, however, noted that Jesus saw fasting as secondary. Quite probably, after John the Baptist's circle of disciples joined the Christian movement, fasting and other pietistic exercises grew in prominence in the new church.

Jesus' less ritualized and more ethicized approach to faith was ultimately supplanted by a new ritualism. The new rites replaced the old Judaic observances, seen by Paul to be obsolete in the post-messianic era, by a new form of Christianized ritual building upon the Judaic antecedents. Thus, for example, Christianity preserved a Lenten period of forty days, akin to the forty-day period of Judaic repentance (the first of the month of Elul to the tenth of the month of Tishri); it kept Pentecost, the fiftieth day from the resurrection, comparable to the Judaic celebration on the fiftieth day from the Exodus (the "resurrection" of the people); and it maintained the Passover in the form of the eucharist. Furthermore, especially the early liturgy was heavily Judaic in form and content.

2. Jesus of Nazareth

How did Jesus relate to the variety of religious expressions that were current in the first century C.E.? Jesus was not a Pharisee, for he rejected the separatism of the *Perushim* (Pharisees), like his older proto-rabbinic contemporary Hillel (M. Ab. 2:5), and he rejected the excessive pietism of their dietary and purity practices. This conflict is reflected in the Gospels. He was neither a member of the school of Hillel nor that of Shammai, as some apologists have suggested. He rejected the Jerusalem priesthood and the Sadducees, another conflict reflected in the Gospels. He eschewed all forms of violence and provocation, and disassociated himself from all branches of zealots, again reflected in the Gospels in the episode concerning paying taxes to Caesar. He was not truly an eschatological preacher of the extreme type, despite his occasional allusion to the cosmic end-time expectations. In my view Jesus was a charismatic teacher who preached and taught in a manner that exhibits a fusion of the biblical preaching-prophet and the emerging proto-rabbi. Eschatology was one element in his teaching. Like some other proto-rabbis, he was a faith healer and was capable of exorcism.[11]

Although persons of Christian faith will approach Jesus in a manner other than those scholars who do not share that faith, nothing is to be gained in our understanding of Jesus by failing to recognize that Jesus is to be perceived on two levels, that of the human ministry from birth to crucifixion, and as the Jesus of Christian faith, post-crucifixion. During his earthly ministry Jesus was a first-century charismatic proto-rabbi. A careful, objective reading of the Christian Testament reveals a Jesus who did not offer interpretations replacing the oral torah, and one who certainly did not abrogate the written Scripture. Like other proto-rabbinic figures of his time, Jesus provided *alternative* interpretations, *alternative* oral torah. He reached conclusions by a traditional hermeneutic (interpretative method), a process evident throughout the Christian Testament and rabbinic literature.

Conditions were right in first-century Galilee for a Jesus to grow into a proto-rabbinic type. Josephus describes a pre-66 C.E. Galilee loyal to the halakah, strict in its observance, and sometimes at variance with Jerusalem. The Galilee was also a center of aggadah (all non-halakic literary matter, including theology, history, folklore, homilies, etc.), and this included mystical vision and spiritual tension. His studies in aggadah prompted Jesus to investigate an apocalyptic movement like that of John the Baptist. According to Luke, he was already thirty years old (3:23), the same age the midrashic tradition believes Isaac was when Abraham offered him upon the altar. The similarity of age is more theological coalescence than accident. For, from the perspective of some theological circles at that time, both of these men were believed to have been born of the Spirit, and both were offered—the one upon an altar, the other upon the cross—as atonement for their people. More will be said of this point shortly. At this juncture it is important only to note that if Luke is correct, Jesus lived and studied in

---

11. For further discussion of my original and nonconventional ideas about Jesus and the Pharisees see my *Emergence of Contemporary Judaism*, I/1, chap. 7; and *The Halakah of Jesus of Nazareth According to the Gospel of Matthew*.

Galilee when sharp social conflicts multiplied, and where brigandage and political rebellion proliferated. Much of this turmoil was designed as messianic liberation. It is a special mark of Jesus' individuality that he was not absorbed into this political militancy, but rather preached a nonpolitical eschatology, just as his contemporary and neighbor, Yohanan ben Zakkai, formulated the tenets of a peace party that rejected the rebellion.

It is difficult to ascertain precisely what led up to it, but Jesus presented himself to John the Baptist for baptism, and in the process of undergoing the baptism he experienced a mystical phenomenon in which the heavens opened and the Spirit of God descended in the form of a dove, while a voice declared, "This is [or, you are] my beloved son in whom I take delight" (Matt. 3:16ff. and parallels). The unanimity concerning this experience in all four Gospels attests to a persistent tradition which had to be based upon reality. One can understand the "sonship" of Jesus in a variety of ways: as Israel's sonship, a special relationship in which the son is designated to fulfill a divine purpose (Exod. 4:22; 19:6); as a saintly person in the sight of God (implied at Wisd. 2:18); as the Davidic king (2 Sam. 7:14-16); and as the Hellenistic personification of the *logos,* the firstborn son of God (comparable to an emanation of deity known as the *Shekinah,* or Holy Spirit).

How are we to understand the sonship of Jesus as he believed it revealed to him at his baptism, when the Spirit of God descends upon him and a heavenly voice calls him, "my beloved son in whom I take delight" (Matt. 3:17)? This reference to Jesus in the Gospels closely corresponds to the following passage at Jubilees 17:16: "Abraham loves Isaac his son and delights in him above all things." It also echoes the description of the servant of God at Isaiah 42:1: "my chosen one in whom I take delight, I have placed my spirit upon him." Matthew 3:17 is to be understood as bringing together three themes: (1) the Holy Spirit, (2) Isaac's *aqedah* (the binding of Isaac, Gen. 22), and (3) the servant of *Yhwh* who suffers, dies, and atones. These three motifs are all joined at John 1:29-34, where Isaac is alluded to (Gen. 22:8) when Jesus is called the lamb. Jesus is here identified with Isaac, and, as is known from ancient tradition, just as Isaac had a mystical celestial vision at the moment of the binding, so Jesus experiences a vision. Just as Isaac, the atoning Son/Servant, received the Spirit and the assurance that his sacrifice will be perpetually redemptive for Israel, Jesus receives the Spirit which leads him to reenact the Isaac/Servant motif. The baptism therefore becomes the *aqedah*/crucifixion, and as Jesus thus becomes to God what Isaac was to Abraham, when the faithful enter into baptism they identify with the sacrifice. Thus Paul always stresses: baptism into the *death (aqedah)* of Jesus.[12]

Neither Paul nor any evangelist, nor any of the authors of the epistles of John or Peter, ever connects the baptism and passion experiences with a Hellenistic mystery cult, or with any Hellenistic philosophical circles. The phenomena are entirely understood within Judaism, and for Paul and other early church figures, such as Matthew or James, these concepts were in no way a departure from Judaism. They were Judaism in its new-age application. The alleged presence of anti-Judaism in the Christian Testament is no different from the acrimony of one group of Jews against another in modern times when caught up in serious religious controversy.

It is clear from the Christian Scriptures that the baptist movement and the Jesus movement did not leave Judaism. The earliest Christian experience was connected to the Jerusalem temple and the synagogues. Jesus' role was not clear to the disciples (Matt. 16:13-20; 22:41-45), and hence one can understand that it could not have been clear to the masses. Even if it was believed that he was "the anointed one," it is apparent that Jesus understood that designation as only metaphorical. He did not believe he was to be an anointed king, nor did he teach it. He did not see himself as an anointed priest. In his own eyes, he was neither the Davidic dynast nor the possible priestly messiah of Qumran. Immediately after Matthew informs us that Jesus accepted the designation *christos* (anointed one) from his disciples, he also informs us that "from that time on" (Matt. 16:21) Jesus taught about his conviction that he was to die and rise again. Peter was a more traditionalist believer, convinced that the redeemer was to be a Davidic dynast, a heroic political liberator. It was unthinkable in that theology to consider the death of the messiah. This attitude explains the exchange between Peter and Jesus (Matt. 16:22-23), in which Jesus rebukes Peter for having in mind human processes rather than divine ones. Then Jesus declares that the "son of man" is the equivalent of the redeemer figure, and that this coming of the son of man is something different from either a Davidic political liberation or the career of Jesus (Matt.

---

12. For discussion of midrashim that suggest parallels between the Isaac *aqedah* and Jesus and indicate that Abraham actually slew Isaac, who was subsequently resurrected, see Shalom Spiegel, *The Last Trial,* trans. Judah Goldin (Philadelphia: Jewish Publication Society, 1967).

16:24-28). In other words, although Jesus is here said to believe that the kingship of God is about to dawn, his death does not serve that purpose. His death serves the atoning purpose of Isaac's *aqedah*. The divine process must work itself out. The son of man is identified with the dying figure, but as the redeemer figure he will appear later (Matt. 17:9, 12).

This alternative messianic idea is not contrary to Judaism, but is manifestly one of the strands of faith current at that time. It binds together the servant motif and the son of man motif in the book of Daniel (Dan. 7:13). Originally the Danielic son of man was interpreted to be the elect people, "the people of the saints of the Most High," and ultimately came to signify an individual who becomes identified with the end-time redeemer figure. Thus Jesus is referred to allusively as "son of the Most High" (Luke 1:32).

Neither the disciples nor the crowds that listened to Jesus preach grasped that for Jesus the sonship revelation at his baptism signified an *aqedah* sonship pointing to his redemptive death, that the "messianic" function was metaphorical, for not by power but by his death would he redeem the people. It is no accident that the redactor (editor) of Matthew brought together Matthew 16:21-28 with the transfiguration scene (17:1-8), which bears this point out further. Moses and Elijah are eschatological figures in Judaism. Jesus is thus identified with both, neither of whom is a Davidic dynast, both of whom are believed to be eschatological teachers. Thus the statement by a voice at the transfiguration, "This is my son . . . listen to him" (Matt. 17:5), reinforces Jesus' role in this respect. Furthermore, the entire process of atonement, redemption, and the post-redemption new teaching is therefore a spiritual process, not to be confused with the Davidic political-liberator messianic idea. But it was at first confused, and although Jesus went deliberately from baptism to crucifixion in order to enact the process, those who opposed him were only conscious of seeking to prevent a messianic political and military debacle by having him executed for treason, the natural charge for the messianic claim which by their standards implied he would wear the Davidic dynastic crown in defiance of the Roman emperor. Jesus did not deny this function (Matt. 26:64), because he recognized it as the most assured way to fulfill his Isaac role, but he unequivocally concluded with his futuristic promise of the advent of the son of man.

There is no problem in Jesus' seeing himself as the Isaac *aqedah* and both as the Paschal lamb and son of God. Philo long before had written of Isaac as son of God, and the *aqedah* was believed, in some versions of the tradition, to have occurred at Passover. Isaac was the prototype of the Paschal lamb, and, from the standpoint of Christology, Jesus was the ultimate Paschal lamb. As Isaac's *aqedah* was a redemptive death for Israel, Jesus' crucifixion was the *aqedah* extended to the gentiles.

The foregoing discussion places Christology into its Judaic perspective and matrix. However, during Jesus' ministry the fact that he was not a Davidic political liberator, but rather a spiritual atoning redeemer, was not self-evident. As a charismatic preacher-teacher, Jesus functioned and thought similarly to all other proto-rabbinic figures of his time. Jesus differed in his halakah from the pietists, the Jerusalem priestly establishment, and from fellow proto-rabbis, as the latter also differed from each other and from other contemporary movements. Undoubtedly he frequently agreed with colleagues as well. At no time did Jesus attack the halakic system; rather, he was concerned with attacking hypocrisy or deficiency in humanitarian compassion. Thus Jesus never rejected the Sabbath tradition, as is surely evident when he taught, "If you do not observe the Sabbath as a Sabbath you will not see the Father" (Thom. 28). Jesus argued certain aspects of *Perushite* (Pharisaic) stringencies, and asserted the primacy of the love command, as did other proto-rabbis, but not against the Sabbath idea.

Jesus taught the observance of ritual as well as ethics. While his primary concern appears to have been the conduct of people in their relationship with other people, he also urged the observance of ritual (Matt. 23:23; Luke 11:42). Although it would be wrong to argue from silence, it is a fact that certain rituals are specified as having been either personally abandoned by Jesus or, with his concurrence, by his disciples. It can therefore be assumed that Jesus observed a good proportion of Judaic ritual of the time, such as the holy days, liturgy, and the dietary practices. It is apparent that Jesus did not abolish the dietary practices (despite Mark 7:19), or Peter would not have preserved them, as he testifies (Acts 10:14), nor would he require a revelation that they need no longer be observed (Acts 10:10-13; 11:4-9). We cannot even be certain that he issued a blanket cancellation of all purity practices, for all we can determine from Matthew 15 and Mark 7 is that he did not teach the need to wash the hands ritually before eating. There was, indeed, no halakic unanimity on this matter at that time nor for several centuries thereafter. That one need not wash was a view not unique to

Jesus. Other proto-rabbis rejected the requirement, and even for those who adopted it the particulars of the rite were not definitive.

The Gospels do not constitute punctilious biographies of Jesus and do not provide a careful description of his day-to-day religious life. He attended synagogue, participated in the public liturgy, and engaged in prayer. He declared the entire *nomos* (Torah in the sense of "religious practice") important, as he perceived the *nomos*. Like other proto-rabbis, he reserved the right to himself to declare what the halakah was, and when he used the powerful phrase *ego lego,* "I say unto you," he exercised a common proto-rabbinic prerogative.

When Jesus taught his version of Sabbath halakah—allowing healing, plucking grain, carrying, compounding a medicine, and lifting an animal out of a pit—he was simply extending the contemporary hermeneutic on the basis of the love command, as is clearly attested at Matthew 12:7, where Jesus cites Hosea in order to teach that God places love above cult. That which he permitted was forbidden by *pharisaioi* (Pharisees), the pietists, as we know from the Dead Sea Scrolls.

A study of the proto-rabbinic strata embedded in rabbinic literature, however, will indicate that outside of the Pharisaic-Qumran-Jubilees circles, other Jews had a variety of options which they were entitled to follow. For example, Qumran Sabbath halakah knows nothing of the principle found in rabbinic literature, that *piqquah nephesh doheh et hashabbat,* the saving of life supersedes the Sabbath, as does circumcision, and a variety of other necessary matters. Danger to life need not be overt and immediate, and even if it is doubtful that a fatality will ensue from a potential danger, the action may still be engaged in, and the Sabbath disregarded (M. Yoma 8:6). Space does not permit an analysis of Jesus' halakah here, but it is important in this connection to take note that what Jesus taught was not always an abrogation of prior teaching but an *alternative halakah,* a procedure many of his contemporaries among the proto-rabbis also practiced.[13] He appealed to the hermeneutical principles of the time, to *a fortiori (qal wehomer),* to analogy *(gezerah shawah),* and to texts in the Hebrew Scriptures. And although at times he might be proven to have abrogated a halakah, this right prevailed in proto-rabbinic circles, at least from the time of Yosi ben Yoezer (M. Ed. 8:4).

---

13. See my *Emergence of Contemporary Judaism,* I/1, 408-13; and my *Halakhah of Jesus of Nazareth according to the Gospel of Matthew.*

As one examines all the halakic verses of Jesus' teaching in the Gospels, one encounters a consistency of proto-rabbinic style and form. This consistency applies not only in Matthew, but in Luke, John, and Mark as well, except insofar as Mark has abbreviated the Judaic material and is less careful with it.[14] Jesus never conceded that he or his disciples were in violation of halakah. Like all proto-rabbis of the time, he vigorously maintained his own halakic prerogative. That such proto-rabbinic activity would lead to wide diversity and internal contradiction in the halakah, with varying options available to the people, was inevitable, and is evident in the rabbinic literature. In contrast, Jesus' opponents, the Pharisees, exhibit a monolithic tendency both in the Christian Scriptures and in the Qumran literature.

Jesus was excluded from the Judaic proto-rabbinic pantheon not because of anything he taught either in theology or in halakah. The absence of Jesus of Nazareth as a significant figure in Judaism was determined by the way he emerged in Christianity. At the beginning he was simply the rejected messiah. But the Christian challenge to Judaism would make it necessary to deal with him as a religious figure. During the second and third centuries, Judaic-Christian polemics proliferated. Additionally, as can be seen from the Epistle of Barnabas, the writings of the Apostolic Fathers and Justin Martyr, and finally Origen and Irenaeus, the doctrine of the incarnation and what might almost be termed the role of "second God" given by Philo to the *logos*, which became virtually the function of Jesus of Nazareth, precluded any positive affirmation of Jesus in Judaism.

It is necessary to examine the interplay of Hellenistic elements in the literature of the Apostle John with the Gnostic elements—now best known from the Nag Hammadi documents—with Paul's teaching and with the philosophical perspectives brought to this complex of material by second- and third-century church fathers. This task cannot be undertaken here, nor even summarized.[15] Suffice it to say that when Jesus was fully identified with the *logos* and began to share with God a position in church liturgy, Judaism turned away from any recognition of a potential role for him in the spiritual process. But on an entirely different level, from the perspective of the matrix out of which

---

14. The reader should be aware that I view the Gospel of Mark not as the first Gospel but as a condensation of an earlier Gospel.

15. See my *Emergence of Contemporary Judaism*, I/1, 321-26, 413-22, 426-31.

the Christology emerged and from a renewed understanding of Jesus the proto-rabbi, there should arise a new form of interreligious theological dialogue. This dialogue could lead toward a new perspective of the Jew Jesus of Nazareth, and a sophisticated empathy of the Jew for the Christology and of the Christian for Judaism's rejection of aspects of the Christology.

3. Paul of Tarsus

What emerges from what has been said of Jesus of Nazareth is that he was a proto-rabbi, fully immersed in his Judaism, and at no time removed from his faith. He did not consciously originate a new religion, and in his time and for some years after his death, all those who were won to his charisma remained within the synagogues. The same may be said of Paul, except that in his time there emerged rival synagogues consisting of Jews and pagans who became Christians and were no longer comfortable in traditional synagogues. But Paul's teaching was not antithetical to Judaism. Like Jesus before him, Paul, with all his arguments for "justification by faith," urged the "doing" or fulfillment of religious practices (Rom. 2:13), using the same terminology that Jesus used in the Sermon on the Mount and that James used, with serious attention to "the doing," "the hearing" not being sufficient. Romans 12 stands as a monument to Paul's thesis that spirituality is fulfilled in a life dedicated to right conduct.

Paul (or Saul, as he was originally called) was a proto-rabbinic disciple of Gamaliel I, a leading proto-rabbi in the first half of the first century. Paul studied in Jerusalem, and was certainly not an unlearned Hellenistic Jew. His midrash and hermeneutics, like those of Jesus, indicate his moorings in the proto-rabbinic and intertestamental era of Judaism. Paul was a rigorist, and, unlike his own mentor Gamaliel I, who saved Peter and his cohorts before the Sanhedrin (Acts 5:33-39), Paul engaged in harassment of Christians. Paul's rigorism, however, remained with him after his conversion to faith in Jesus. It is Paul's Pharisaic tendencies, to which he confesses, which placed their mark upon a variety of halakic stringencies that remained part of Christian polity to this day, especially in the Roman Catholic faith and in some Protestant groups. Among these are the preference for celibacy, opposition to divorce, and the subordination of women. In fundamentalist churches it is often Paul's theology which serves to succor such attitudes as the condemnation of the theory of evolution.

As a rigorous proto-rabbinic disciple, Paul underwent a mystical experience and became convinced that the crucified proto-rabbi of Nazareth was indeed son of God and the anointed one (Christ). From this time forth Paul became an apostle for Christianity and a leading preacher and teacher of the growing movement. But it is important to emphasize that all through his life the Christian movement was within the synagogue. Paul's contemporary, James, still refers to the Christian house of worship as a synagogue (2:2; a meaning circumvented by some translations with the word "meeting"). Even when they worship apart and the place is called *ekklesia* (assembly place), Paul considers the young movement as being "Israel." Paul's movement was one of many varieties of religious experience in Judaism, and a careful dissection of Paul's writings will show how he drew upon Jewish sources within that variety. These sources included apocryphal works, Philo, traditional Jerusalem-school teachings, Qumran materials, and halakic and apocalyptic works. He initiated original turns of phrase, framed new ideas, and created a new alternative within Judaism, based upon the advent and death of the *Christos*. Paul died decades before Christianity and Judaism were rent asunder. This schism was not the work of Paul or the result of his theology. Ultimately, it was not a theologically induced separation, but rather the product of an inevitable political collision between those who prepared for a third messianic war with Rome (after the war of 66-73 C.E. and the rebellion that swept the western diaspora during the reign of Trajan) and the Christians for whom the second messianic advent, the hoped-for *parousia,* did not signify political liberation.

Here it is only possible to summarize the major emphases in Paul's Judaic Christianity. Although Paul argued that the Torah *(nomos)* was no longer the instrument of salvation, this role having been fulfilled by the death of Jesus, he by no means abrogated the moral imperatives of the Torah. For Paul it remained vital that the adherents of those now called Israel remain under the command, no less than Israel always had been, to refrain from such vices as sexual immorality, usury, idolatry, witchcraft, hatred, envy, slander, drunkenness, dishonesty, murder, and sedition.

At times Paul's involvement in polemics with a variety of Christians, Christian Jews, and non-Christian Jews leads him to strong negative words about traditional Judaic observance, which have led some students of Paul to misinterpret him. But careful examination of these instances indicates that Paul has reference to the cultic or ritualistic aspects of the faith, and believes that their soteriological (salvational) value has been superseded by the death of Jesus. Paul's argument is never against living the life of righteousness through proper conduct (e.g., 2 Cor. 5:10); it is against the notion that proper conduct alone is sufficient for salvation, for obedience is never adequate. Paul emphasizes, as did his teachers in Jerusalem, that because there is a gap between God's expectation of the human being and the human being's ability to fulfill the expectation, there is a need for divine grace. Where Paul differs from his proto-rabbinic colleagues and teachers is in his belief that this grace is derived from faith in the death of Jesus as the atoning sacrifice for all. The Torah, therefore, does not cease to be a model for Christian conduct. It only ceases to be the valid sign for the covenant and the salvation of those who stand under the covenant. The new covenant of Israel is sealed in the death of Jesus.

Paul saw Jesus' death as expiatory in terms both of Isaac's *aqedah* and the Passover lamb. Paul knew of the targumic midrash that declared the origin of *olah* (daily burnt offering) in ancient Judaic worship to be a reminder to God of Isaac's self-sacrifice. Included as the beneficiaries of the *olah* rites are "the gentile and the Israelite, man and woman, female and male servant" (Lev. Rab. 2:11). We have here a remarkable parallel to Paul's famous words that in the salvational rite of baptism, that is, once one enters into the *aqedah* of Jesus, "there are no more distinctions between Jew and Greek, slave and free, male and female. . . . Merely by belonging to Christ you are the posterity of Abraham" (Gal. 3:28-29). Paul clearly adapted the midrash and "Christianized" it. But in addition to his allusions and references to Isaac typology, Paul saw the expiatory death of Jesus specifically in terms of the Paschal lamb as well (1 Cor. 5:7).

This emphasis upon the death of Jesus had further ramifications. It is this identification—of the going down into the water with the death and the emergence from the water with the resurrection—that enabled the believer to be free of the mitzvot, as a dead Jew who is resurrected would be exempt from them (B. Nid. 61b). Thus, Paul's theses of early Christian theology are basically Judaic, and under normal circumstances would have made only for differentiation within Judaism. That a wholly new religion resulted was not the product of Paul's thought, but of political events that intruded upon theological dispute. The Septuagint rendering of Psalm 88:6 (LXX 87:5), "among the dead, free" points to the idea in a pre-rabbinic and pre-Christian text that the dead were considered "free," and this was understood in early rabbinic tradition as Paul understood it—free of mitzvot (one's religious obligations)—as he made clear at Romans 7:1-6.

In those ways Paul applied Judaic eschatological ideas to the Christian experience. Death frees from mitzvot, from the obligation to fulfill cultic and soteriological (salvational) rites. Death is also a source of atonement. Death, in fact, is the conquest of sin, for in the life to come there is neither merit nor guilt (B. Shab. 151b).

Just as Paul did not teach the abrogation of the Torah, he did not teach the abrogation of God's covenant with Israel. Paul struggled with the status of Judaism in what he considered the messianic era. This intellectual and emotional struggle is evident in Romans 9–11. What Paul argued was not that Israel ceased to be the covenant people, but that it is not necessary to be of Israel "in the flesh," that is, either descended from a Jew or proselytized into Judaism and thereby part of "corporate Israel," in order to be "Israel." The pagan-turned-Christian was Israel, Paul argued. Thus the person of faith was Israel, and the person who did not believe in the atoning death and resurrection of Jesus was not Israel, even if he was a Jew. But this new definition did not signify the abrogation of the election of Israel, it merely argued that the election continued through those who became the children of Abraham through the promise. Paul was the first to advance a theory used later by the author of the Epistle of Barnabas, Justin, and other early Christian polemicists in a way that Paul might not have intended. They said the "elder" son of Genesis 25:23 is Israel in the flesh, "the natural children" (Rom. 9:8), and the "younger" whom he will serve, or to whom he will become subordinate, is the Israel constituting the Christian community. The distinction between Paul and his successors might be subtle, but Paul saw the unbroken continuation of the election, and not its abrogation. He did not see the Christian experience as the establishment of a "new" covenant in the sense of a different one with another people. For him the church was the "saved remnant," as Judah was the saved remnant when northern Israel was destroyed. Otherwise Paul hopelessly contradicted himself when he said that the free gifts and call of God are not repentable or revocable (Rom. 11:29). Romans 11 closes with a hymn which sums up Paul's struggle by confessing to the utter mystery of God's processes.

This brief sketch of Paul's proto-rabbinic Judaic approach must serve as a mere indicator. Throughout his letters Paul used proto-rabbinic hermeneutics, midrash, and halakic values. A careful reading of his letters shows how frequently he based his views on midrash of Scripture. He stressed the moral imperatives of his heritage; he adapted the Judaic theology of creation, revelation, election, redemption, resurrection, free will, judgment, and reward and punishment—all of which remain part of Christian theology. Paul reinterpreted basic aspects of the first-century tradition, to which he was heir and of which he was a student, to meet his conviction that followed his mystical experience on the road to Damascus. Considering the diversity of Judaism and the total absence of a centralized monolithic authority which had the power to enforce an orthodoxy, it cannot plausibly be argued that in the years 45-65 C.E. Paul's teaching would be considered either heretical or un-Jewish. In time, the main body of Christianity ceased to be Jewish, not because of Paul's theology or his alternative halakah, but because the church became predominantly gentile, and because the rabbis at Yabneh ca. 90-100 C.E. read even Christian Jews out of Judaism for political reasons.

4. James and Christian Judaism

Just as the Jerusalem priesthood and Temple enjoyed preeminence in Judaism, James and the Jerusalem church sought to assert hegemony over all Christians, including the predominantly gentile churches in the diaspora. This hegemony was not possible, however, and soon a two-track Christianity evolved, one for those born Jews and one for those born pagans. Nevertheless, the Epistle of James sought to assert the Judaic principle of the importance of "works" in the spiritual constellation. This emphasis became necessary because, as Paul attested, Paul's teachings were being distorted, and James must have been informed that Paul was teaching a libertine heresy in the diaspora.

It is not possible here to examine the scholarly evidence for the authenticity of James's letter, nor the critique which denies that James, the brother of Jesus, is the actual author of the epistle.[16] Suffice it to say that I accept this letter as the authentic work of James, the brother of Jesus, and as one of the earliest documents of the Christian Scriptures. A careful comparative study of the Epistle of James and Paul's letters will reveal that they were not so far apart, although James was under the impression that Paul had abandoned Judaism.

James emphasized the centrality of the love command in fulfilling the Torah, and one can see his views well reflected in Matthew. As one

---

16. See my *Emergence of Contemporary Judaism*, I/1, 424-25.

follows the Epistle of James verse by verse, one can discover many allusions to Qumran literature and to proto-rabbinic and rabbinic materials. Because his church believed that Jesus was the messiah who had come, it opposed war with Rome. James was martyred because he was a major symbol of dissension, and was responsible for a large segment of the community refusing to support unity of political purpose. When war came the Christian Jews refused to participate, and, like the peace party of Yohanan ben Zakkai which withdrew to Yabneh, the church withdrew to Pella. Ultimately this dissension led to their being sundered from the main trunk of Judaism. The pro-resistance segments who, after 73 C.E., continued to spoil for another round with Rome, deposed Yohanan ben Zakkai. Furthermore, they anathematized the Christian community by adding a prayer to the *amidah,* the core prayer of every liturgy, which invoked God's curse upon *notzrim* (Christians, followers of the one of Nazareth).

Nevertheless, the Judaic church continued to function in Jerusalem. It recognized James as its founder and patron saint. It saw in Paul the villain who turned Christian Judaism into a gentile religion. These Christian Jews had formed a body of messianic Jews within Judaism since the time of Jesus. They frequented the Temple and participated in the Judaic sacrificial cult. They insisted that when a pagan desires to become a Christian he must do so through Judaism, but they lost this argument to Paul. It was these early Christian Jews who developed the proto-Gospels, the letter of James, and the background material upon which was based the literature of the apostles John and Peter, including Revelation. Considering the Judaic nature of Paul's thought, one can say that the entire Christian Testament was a product of Jews reflecting Judaic tradition and values. Paul continued to be loyal to Jerusalem, despite his theological and halakic differences with James and his followers.

In time, however, the work of Peter, Paul, and John, in the western and eastern diasporas, resulted in a predominantly gentile church. This development had various ramifications. It reduced the importance of Judaism within Christianity and diminished the influence of Jerusalem. Since the Christian-Jewish mother church of Jerusalem no longer had spiritual sway over diaspora Christianity, and since it was discredited as treasonous and dangerous to the Judean community still seeking liberation from Rome, it was reduced to impotence. Judaic animosity led to its expulsion from Judaism, and mutual antagonism with gentile Christianity led to its reduction to the status of a heresy within

Christianity. Ultimately, diaspora Christian Judaism in Babylon, Cyrene, Egypt, Cyprus, and elsewhere suffered attrition as a consequence of both Jewish repression and Christian ostracism. In time, even in Jerusalem the Christian-Jewish church was supplanted by gentile Christianity, when Hadrian banned all Jews from Jerusalem after the rebellion of 132 C.E., and when Jerusalem was replaced by the new pagan city of Aelia Capitolina.

Christian Judaism continued to survive east of the Jordan River and south and east of the Dead Sea. It survived in the variegated sects known to patristic writers, most notably as Ebionites. The Christian-Jewish church of James predominated until 70 C.E., and while the significance of James is diminished in canonical Christian literature, the now-available Nag Hammadi literature highlights the major role he played. It is clear that some Christians believed Jesus first appeared to James, and that the disciples chose James as bishop. Although what became the mainstream of Christianity veered to Paul in the West and to John in the East, the Ebionites continued to look upon James as the legitimate leader of the church of Jesus. And among these Ebionites and other Christian Jews Judaic practices continued to flourish. For a while Philip the evangelist and others influenced the survival of Judaic elements in the East, a condition aided by the migration of Christian Jews through Caesarea to Ephesus and Hierapolis. The celebration of Easter on Passover is a major example of this survival. In time, however, all diaspora churches in the East assumed new theological motifs and abandoned Judaic practices. Nonetheless, Judaic influences survived in predominantly gentile Christian areas, as well as a Christian-Jewish movement which preserved its teachings, beliefs, and practices. This movement grew increasingly isolated from emergent "Catholic" Christianity in the fourth and fifth centuries.

Modern scholarship is still not certain what form the Christian-Jewish Gospel or Gospels took, and therefore what the particulars of their beliefs and observances might have been. Late first- and second-century apostolic literature is not of much help, although the Martyrdom of Polycarp does suggest that the seventh-day Sabbath was observed. Clement of Rome still reserves the epithet "holy scripture" for the Hebrew Scriptures, and encourages joyousness in the observance of the Torah (see 1 Clement 31:2; 35:2), and it is far from explicit in Clement's writings that he believed in the divine nature of Jesus. Pseudo-Clementine literature from the third century argues the validity of Judaic observances and identifies Paul with the famous heretic Simon Magus.

VI. THE VARIETIES OF JUDAIC RELIGIOUS EXPERIENCE

The foregoing discussion points, albeit summarily, to the complexity of Christianity during the first three centuries. Even within the expanding gentile Christianity there survived pockets of Judaic influence. The evidence shows a remarkable degree of Christian Judaism pervading the diaspora, even when it was not directly connected with the Jerusalem church. But the best-known and most studied form of Christian Judaism is that which is called Ebionism. Ebionites believed that Jesus was the human son of the sexual union of Joseph and Mary. Moreover, they regarded him as the last and the greatest of the prophets of Israel, who restored a corrupted Torah of Moses to its original state—a teaching much the same as Islam taught concerning Muhammad. Furthermore, Ebionites affirmed that Jesus was Moses *redivivus,* the Messiah or Christ—an idea related to the Samaritan conception of a last great Moses-like prophet, derived from Deuteronomy 18:15, 18.

The unbridgeable gulf that grew between what we call, only for convenience' sake, "Christian Judaism" and "gentile Christianity" grew slowly between 40 and 66 C.E., and escalated after 73 C.E. At the heart of the schism was the Christian Jewish perspective that Paul's teaching was antinomian (opposed to Judaic law), and that John's teaching of the incarnation of God's Word in Jesus of Nazareth was unacceptable. Ebionites continued the practice of circumcision; the rite of divorce; the observance of Passover and other pentateuchal holy days; certain purity practices, especially immersion after sexual relations; the seventh-day Sabbath; abstention from meat; and the use of unleavened bread, salt, and water for the eucharist, but not the use of wine. The rejection of wine and meat might have been rooted in a mourning symbolism for Jesus, as we read also of certain pietists rebuked by the early rabbis for rejecting wine and meat out of mourning for Jerusalem. Along with these Judaic elements, they observed the rites of baptism, the eucharist, and Sunday as the Lord's Day. Their possible connection with Pharisaism, that is, with Qumran or Essene antecedents, is reflected in their encouragement of celibacy and poverty, although this might just as well have been their independent practice of such pieties, just as other Encratites (ascetic sects) of that period were accustomed to prohibit animal food, alcoholic beverages, and sexual relations.

Here, in fact, we have a divergence between Christian Judaism and Rabbinic Judaism which is of some interest. Jesus reflects the proto-rabbinic milieu which shied away from Encratism, and is even charged by Pharisees—*Perushim*—with being hedonistic (Matt.

83

11:18-19; Luke 7:34), while Christian Judaism reflects the ascetic tendency of John the Baptist and James.

In the end, Rabbinic Judaism, based in the academy of Yabneh, suppressed and expelled Christian Judaism, and the majority, gentile Greco-Roman church suppressed and excommunicated Christian Judaism. Nevertheless, what was termed "Judaization" continued for centuries within the gentile diaspora church. Christians known as *Quartodecimans* observed Easter on the fourteenth of Nisan, the day when the Paschal lamb was offered; many frequented synagogues on the Sabbath and holy days and observed the dietary practices and circumcision. As late as 395, John Chrysostom inveighed against these practices. Ultimately, Christian Jews disappeared into Islam and Karaism. Perhaps some turned to Samaritan and Rabbinic Judaism and others made peace with gentile Christianity. But they had a strong and enduring influence upon historic Christianity and other movements such as the Gnostics, Mandeans, Manicheans, Nestorian Christianity, and Islam. There can be no doubt that the effort to uncover the Christian-Jewish strand in both Christianity and Judaism (witness the rise of many groups such as Messianic Jews, Hebrew Christians, Jews for Jesus, and the Christian search for roots), although still in its infancy, is evident today.

5. Jewish and Christian Liturgy

Judaic liturgical practices of the first century were very ancient, and because their origin was lost in the mist of the past, many elements were ascribed to the amorphous and little-understood body called "the men of the great synagogue." Paul, Peter, and John were heir to this liturgy and adapted it to Christian usage. Paul followed his proto-rabbinic teaching that the liturgy should contain *shebah* (Gk. *eulogia*, the glorification of God), *baqqashah* (*deesei*, petition), and *hodayah* (*eucharistia*, the giving of thanks), as well as teaching and preaching (1 Tim. 2:1; Phil. 4:6). Early Christians prayed in synagogues and adapted their twice-daily and thrice-daily worship order to the church. The wording of early Christian liturgy, as found in pseudo-Clementine literature, is Judaic in character. Thus, the eucharistic meal and grace after the meal, described in the Didache, are parallel to the Jewish kiddush, preceding a meal on a Sabbath or holy day, and *birkat hamazon*, the Grace after Meals. Like the *amidah*, recited at *shahrit, minhah*, and *maarib* (morning, afternoon, and evening worship) in Judaism, the Lord's Prayer was recited thrice daily.

The Lord's Prayer consists entirely of ideas current in Judaic theology and liturgy. But it is nevertheless to be regarded as an original prayer recited by Jesus. Its context was as a private prayer recited after the *amidah.* Contrary to much scholarship on the subject, it is not to be seen as an abridged *amidah,* and certainly not a revised kaddish. Unlike the *amidah,* although it contains praise *(shebah:* "May your name be hallowed") and petition *(baqqashah:* "give us this day our daily bread"), it does not contain a closing formula of thanks *(hodayah)* in all versions. But it is important to note that not all rabbinic prayers contained the thanks formula, and in those versions of the Lord's Prayer in which the closing doxology is included we have the third Judaic element, *hodayah,* a closing thanks or praise of God. Its wide divergence from the *amidah* is seen in its lack of the *berakah* formula. Many rabbinic prayers to be recited as private devotion, aside from, or in conclusion of, the *amidah,* lack the *berakah* formula. Therefore, the Lord's Prayer probably constitutes a sample offered by Jesus to the disciples of a closing private prayer at the end of the *amidah.*

The relationship between Jewish and Christian liturgy shows that the Judaic aspect of Christianity is deeply rooted, and allows for Christianity to be a proper subject of inquiry in any study of Judaism. Contemporary with the rise of Christianity, and prefigured by Jesus and Yohanan ben Zakkai in Galilee, there arose what we call Rabbinic Judaism. This was another tributary arising from the stream that began its flow at Sinai and has as yet not fulfilled its course. Both the rise of Christianity and the destruction of Jerusalem had immeasurable influence upon the new courses taken by Judaism, upon its structure, its ritual, and its programmatic emphasis.

H. Summary

The foregoing has described the evolution of Judaism from the religion of Israel to Rabbinism, how it acculturated to Hellenism and developed within its matrix a variety of forms that gave rise to a prolific literature and many competing as well as mutually supplementing groups. Political and military events led to the Roman conquest and the occupation of Palestine. Although the Jerusalem priesthood remained in power as the official custodian of the faith, however, a meritocracy arose with proto-rabbinic figures serving as the spiritual consultants and the teachers of the autonomous congregationalist movement embodied in the synagogue.

The destruction of Jerusalem by the Romans in 70 C.E. undoubtedly sent a traumatic shock wave through the Jews. But this shock did not cause Judaism to perish anymore than did the trauma of the Babylonian conquest in 587 B.C.E. The proto-rabbis, who were the scholars and spiritual leaders, had developed their function and calling since the days of Ezra. Most especially they had been growing prominent since the *bet midrash* (house of study) milieu described by Ben Sira. The early Hasmonean scholars, such as Yosi ben Yoezer, escalated this movement. In the first century, they were positioned to assume the role of prophet, priest, and sage. Moreover, the synagogue was prepared to replace the venerable Temple and its cult. Furthermore, ordination took the place of the prophetic call and priestly birth, and scholarship supplanted charisma and heredity. It is this new institution of synagogue and ordained scholar-sage that is historically known as Rabbinic Judaism.

Chapter Three

Rabbinism (Rabbinic Judaism)

I. THE FORMATION AND EVOLUTION OF RABBINISM

A. The Pharisees

It is difficult to trace all groupings within Judaism at the turn of the first century C.E., but in general the following groups are identifiable: the Jerusalem priesthood, a complex of pietistic and separatistic groups, moderate acculturated groups, and the amorphous mass of Jews called *ammey haaretz*. The ancient sources have preserved a few names of what are considered major groups such as Essenes, Thera-peutae, Hasidim, Pharisees, Sadducees, Morning-Bathers, and Boe-thusians, among others listed in rabbinic and patristic literature. But historians and theologians have singled out Pharisees and Sadducees in their discussions of pre-Rabbinic Judaism, and for the sake of historical convention I will follow that pattern, although I believe that neither the pattern nor the conventional linking of Pharisaism to Rabbinism is accurate.

The post-70 C.E. sages, who are called "rabbis," saw themselves as successors to a long line of *hakamim* going back to the third or fourth century B.C.E. and even to Ezra and Nehemiah. They normally contrasted themselves as *hakamim* with Sadducees. They never referred to themselves as part of a movement called *Perushim* (literally, "separatists," the Hebrew term for Pharisees), however; indeed, they were critical of *Perushim*. Thus their great predecessor, Hillel, taught *al tiphrosh min hatzibor,* "Do not separate yourself from the congregation" (M. Ab. 2:5), thus articulating the negative proto-rabbinic stance toward Pharisaism. The rabbis contrasted the *Perushim* with *ammey haaretz,* Sadducees, and Boethusians, and particular halakot (practices) of Rabbinism did have broad affinities with Pharisaism. However, the similarities between Rabbinism and Pharisaism were due to the fact that differing strands within the same religion naturally will have many aspects in common, even if their underlying presuppositions are different. Additionally, after 70 C.E. proto-Rabbinism imposed itself upon Pharisaism in order to secure its authority, and in turn absorbed its pietistic and more stringent elements. Josephus saw Pharisaism as the major movement in Judaism, not because it was coidentical with Rabbinism but because, as a Greek historian trying to present post-70 C.E. Judaism in the light of a Greek philosophical school, he found the term *Pharisaioi* near at hand and used it. For although the Pharisees were the stringent, separatist, and pietistic group before 70 C.E., when Rabbinism took over and absorbed them, in a sense they became the Establishment, and now Josephus could use their name as his leading school. But the rabbis never identified themselves as Pharisees, and Josephus never speaks of the rabbis or Rabbinism.

The result has been that, based upon Josephus, historians of Judaism have considered Pharisaism and Rabbinism as the same, whereas, in my view, they are separate phenomena. The Christian Testament, Philo, and Josephus give us a picture of *Essaioi-Pharisaioi* (Essenes-Pharisees); Jubilees and the Qumran literature give us a picture of Hasidim (pious ones) and, for lack of a better term, the Qumranite monastic movement, which was similar in character to the Essenes and Therapeutae. These portraits do not match the character of the proto-rabbis we know. These men were not members of a movement; they were individuals. For this reason it is *Pharisaioi* and not *sophistoi (hakamim,* sages) who are at odds with Jesus, the proto-rabbi. For this reason too, the Gospel of Luke's use of *nomikos* (expert at the *nomos*) generally distinguishes between a Pharisee and a proto-rabbi, and Jesus himself is called *didaskalos* (teacher), as would be a proto-rabbi, or even honorifically "rabbi" (Matt. 26:49). Moreover, the "scribes" are not a movement, but rather functionaries within every group.

The *Pharisaioi* were meticulous about ritual observance, especially in such matters as purity, dietary practices, the Sabbath, and tithing. They emphasized one mode of observance, insisting upon the correctness of their own. But rabbinic literature also reflects how from the earliest times the proto-rabbis offered options in observance. Proto-rabbis operated with a program of leniency and pragmatism, while *Pe-*

rushim were restrictive and pietistic, often ascetically oriented and sometimes monastically isolated. In sum, the *Pharisaioi* were very severe and did not govern their halakah by the love command as did the proto-rabbis.

B. The Sadducees

The origin of Sadducees or *Tzeduqim* (from *tzadaq*, "righteous") is cloaked in obscurity. There appears to be no serious reason, however, why credence should be denied to tradition. The tradition teaches that Zadok and Boethus, two disciples of the proto-rabbi Antigonus, dissented from their master and established two separate groups: Sadducees and Boethusians. Not possessing any of their literature, we cannot be certain of what they taught or of their similarities and differences. It appears that for the rabbis who edited the rabbinic literature containing a few reminiscences concerning these groups their names were interchangeable. They evidently shared cultic practices, denied an afterlife and resurrection, and both were opposed to *Perushim* (Ab. R. Nat. A, 5; B, 10).

This origin of Sadduceeism would place it early in the second century B.C.E., and would indicate that the name *Tzeduqim* has no reference to the priestly line of Zadok. Since they opposed *Perushim*, it is apparent that there were people already called such. The original Sadducees were contemporaries of Yosi ben Yoezer, and it seems plausible that these Sadducees spawned a new school of thought which permeated the later school of Shammai. The school of Shammai moved away from some of the Sadducean theological ideas, especially as related to life after death; probably like the Sadducees, however, it interpreted the halakah more tightly than, for example, the school of Hillel. The disciples of Simon the Righteous (M. Ab. 1:2) and Antigonus (M. Ab. 1:3) spawned the school of Hillel. Unfortunately, since Sadducean literature was either ignored or suppressed by Rabbinism so that it did not survive, we cannot demonstrate how the Sadducees exegeted Torah and which forms of post-pentateuchal halakah they practiced. It is logical to assume that all branches of Judaism held a considerable proportion of practices and customs in common while differing over details. Rabbinic reports of Sadducean views are fragmentary, and are conveyed in the context of polemic, thus hardly providing creditable evidence of Sadducean thought. But the Sadducees should in no sense be understood as "literalists" who did not depart from the Torah's text. They too had a post-pentateuchal halakah embodied in a book called *sepher gezeratah* (Book of Decisions), which was later abolished. Evidence of their oral torah is also found in the polemics recorded in rabbinic literature, even if it is not presented in a favorable light.

We cannot be certain what the Sadducees believed about revelation and the complex question of human authority. But it is plausible to assume that they differed with the amorphous complex of Pharisees and with proto-rabbis over the extent of lay authority. It appears from our sources, as sketchy as the evidence is, that the Sadducees supported priestly authority. It is for this reason that when priestly authority came to an end with the destruction of Jerusalem the Sadducees went out of existence.

C. Rabbinism

1. Yohanan ben Zakkai (73-132 C.E.)

The reformation of Ezra and Nehemiah established broad new restrictive guidelines in Judaic religious practice, especially in the areas of cult, Sabbath observance, and mixed marriage. This process highlights an extremely important aspect of Judaism pertinent to the entire evolution of the faith, which became normative in the movement we identify as "Rabbinism." I refer here to the supposition that by a process of progressive revelation, in which the Holy Spirit influences the human mind, the teachings of the sages can supersede the Torah even without a new revelation.

Who the spiritual leaders were between Nehemiah and Ben Sira or Simon the Righteous (early proto-rabbis) is obscure, for our knowledge of religious developments between 425 B.C.E. and 200 B.C.E. is meager. Nevertheless, from Ben Sira we can ascertain that new media were in their early stages of development. The ideal *hakam-sopher* described by Ben Sira gives us our first glimpse of a proto-rabbi ca. 200 B.C.E. (Sir. 39:1-11). He was a scholar and teacher who engaged in prayer, welcomed students without fees (a practice later continued by the school of Hillel), offered instruction, counseled, poured forth wisdom, and investigated obscure things. Ben Sira was thus the historical link between the biblical tradition and the new Rabbinism. He and Simon the Righteous were the real founders of proto-Rabbinism, which was later transformed into Rabbinic Judaism by Yohanan ben Zakkai's inauguration of formal ordination as "rabbis" for his disciples after 70 C.E.

Yohanan ben Zakkai was one of many men known to us by name, after Ben Sira, who were involved in the preservation of the teachings of an obscure group of scholars subsumed under the puzzling rubric of "men of the great assembly." Such a body probably met periodically as a synod to affirm evolving traditions or to innovate new practices in rapidly changing conditions such as transpired during the Hellenistic era. But such synods were not a regular central authority which imposed a discipline upon proto-rabbinic interpretation. Such synods no longer functioned, in any event, in early Rabbinism. The schools were autonomous, and independent scholars deliberated halakic questions arising from life's experiences and their studies. Each school had its followers, and there was no uniformity and no orthodoxy. This proto-rabbinic period prefigured the entire future history of Judaism in which local and contemporary authority held sway, and in which there was no so-called normative Judaism, as modern scholars have referred to it.

The rabbinic literature established proto-rabbinic authority as coming directly from God to Moses in a line of succession to the proto-rabbis of the first century B.C.E. (M. Ab. 1:1). The high priestly authority was superseded and transcended, with the only exception being the high priest Simon the Righteous, who, however, received special treatment, probably because it was believed that he was accompanied by the incarnate deity into the Holy of Holies (Lev. Rab. 21:12). By tracing their legitimacy to Simon, however, and ignoring the Hasmonean priesthood, the rabbis signified that their own legitimacy was after all derived from the priestly line along with the prophetic. Moreover, they claimed that this authority was through the last truly legitimate pre-Hasmonean priest, and that they thus embodied the role and authority of both the biblical priest and prophet. The chain of tradition thus redacted in rabbinic literature was a theological and halakic affirmation that the entire interpretative Torah is a legitimate supplement to the written Torah, for in the great synod of which Simon the Righteous was still a member, there also sat the biblical *kohen* (priest), *nabi* (prophet), and *hakam* (sage).

It was out of this succession that Yohanan ben Zakkai emerged. His authority was further enhanced by the assertion that he absorbed the teachings of both Shammai and Hillel and thus embodied the ripest of traditional wisdom (M. Ab. 2:9). His ordination was thus presented as being "catholic" in the sense of not representing only one major school of thought. Thus, legitimacy was given to Hillelite and Shammaite rabbis, and the way was opened to what in modern times is called "denominationalism." This diversity of view and legitimacy of alternative halakic decision making was later embodied in the persons of Rabbi Ishmael and Rabbi Akiba, and down through the centuries in other individuals and schools of thought.

There is no doubt, however, that Hillelite supremacy emerged, as a careful examination of the halakah shows. This fact is recorded in an anecdote of a *bat qol,* a heavenly "echo" (generically: "voice"), announcing that the halakah follows the decision of Bet (school of) Hillel (T. Ed. 2:3). But we also find that Bet (school of) Shammai placed no validity in a *bat qol* (T. Naz. 1:1), and such figures as Rabbi Gamaliel II, Rabbi Eliezer ben Hyrcanus, and Rabbi Ishmael persisted with Shammaite views.

Either when Jerusalem was destroyed in 70 C.E., or when the war against Rome ended in 73 C.E., the proto-rabbis of the school at Yabneh (Jamnia) appeared to be the only logical religious leaders to reform the shattered polity of Judaism. There was at Yabneh a peace party led by Yohanan ben Zakkai, and he and his disciples emerged as the core of the restoration. Yohanan virtually remodeled the covenant community of Israel from a nation back into an *ekklesia,* a religious assembly. He was, in a sense, engineering a truly radical restoration insofar as he took Judaism back to its origins as the heart of an Israelite amphictyony.

The major single contribution Yohanan made to Judaism was his introduction of formal ordination. This was a new form of *semikah,* the laying-on of hands which symbolized the transference of the Holy Spirit from master to disciple, the paradigm for which was the transmission of the Spirit from Moses to Joshua. This was the ultimate challenge to the hereditary priestly aristocracy, and brought its authority to a close. Yohanan created what is called the "rabbinate," a new authoritative body which possessed the democratic virtue of being a meritocracy in which a person did not hold authority by virtue of his birth to a priestly father, but by virtue of his knowledge and competence.

A second important contribution was Yohanan's insistence that certain rites previously practiced only in Jerusalem should be legitimate at Yabneh. He did not seek this prerogative for the sacrificial system. More important was his replacement of Jerusalem as the center of authority by the academy of Yabneh, with the implication that wherever there was an academy with recognized and ordained scholars there was authority. Consequently, a multiplicity of centers with equally legitimate authorities arose, resulting in a worldwide proliferation of Judaic intellectual excellence and the preservation of the diversity and heterogeneity of Judaic religious life. The scholars who presided over these schools and synagogues were ordained and given the title "rabbi," and this ordination signaled the birth of Rabbinic Judaism. Yohanan accomplished a historic reversal of the ancient heresy of Israel: he transformed a territorially centered nation and a central-Temple theology, dominated by a hereditary priesthood, into a universal faith.

2. Yabneh (73-132 C.E.)

Yohanan ben Zakkai and his Yabnean associates did nothing less than restate the theology of Judaism with Hosea 6:6 as their motto: "It is love I desire, not sacrifice." The sacrificial system and the priesthood were superseded, and sins were to be expiated by loving deeds and prayer. While the rabbis of Yabneh theoretically recognized the priesthood and the cult, they regarded it as in suspension, and perpetuated biblical institutions in their own persons. In place of the surrogate animal or vegetable offering, Jews now offered their prayers and loving deeds. Prayer worship was no longer a supplement to the true cult—it was the true cult. It was referred to as *abodah* (Sifre Deut. 41), the term normally used for the sacrificial system. Prayer was no longer a concession to the diaspora or to those in Palestine unable or unwilling to come to Jerusalem. It was now the God-ordained form for God's worship. For this reason Yabneh was the center of great liturgical development. Prayers of old were brought together, recast, and joined with newly composed prayers, and a fixed form of worship was arranged, although spontaneity was still encouraged (M. Ab. 2:18).

The core of Judaic public worship is the *amidah,* also known as the *tefillah.* Although most of its content was venerable, it was redacted and instituted in a formal way at Yabneh. The paragraphs connected with the profession of the monotheistic faith (the Shema) and paragraphs that affirm the doctrines of creation, revelation, and redemption were all pre-70 C.E., but were arranged in their current form at Yabneh. The true revolution at Yabneh was to require obligatory communal worship with a quorum of ten. On the one hand, this perpetuated the synagogue as a mandatory place of worship; on the other hand, each quorum was entitled to establish its own worship center and to consecrate it as a synagogue. The freedom to establish a synagogue wherever a quorum of ten obtained implied the permanent decentralization of worship, no longer to be seen as error or sin sporadically corrected by a virtuous king, but as a basic, enduring theological proposition.

It is not possible at this time to determine how much was achieved by Yohanan, and how much was actually carried forward later under Gamaliel II. It is clear that Yohanan set in motion the mechanism of consolidation and the restatement of Judaic theology. But Yohanan was ousted from leadership sometime between 80 and 90 C.E., when the Romans saw fit to bestow government-backed authority upon Gamaliel II, naming him Nasi (president or prince) at Yabneh. This erstwhile supporter of anti-Roman policies in the late 60s thus became presiding rabbi at Yabneh. Undoubtedly, as son and grandson of leading pre-war figures, he yearned for this leadership and led a coalition of anti-Yohanan forces to unseat the latter. This coalition consisted of former associates, and even disciples who resented Yohanan's anti-war posture. It included the priests who resented his anti-priestly stance and his persistence in "laicizing" Judaism. True, Yohanan only "retired" the priests and continued to offer them certain ceremonial honors which persist to this day among those who claim to be descended from ancient *kohanim,* in those groups that style themselves "Orthodox." Nevertheless, they resented what they regarded as his patronizing them and joined in the coalition against him. He allowed space for them in the liturgy of future expectation by including prayers for the restoration of the sacrificial system. But these prayers did not assuage the priests. By elevating Yabneh to a status nearly that of Jerusalem and the rabbis as the successor-priests, he incurred priestly animosity.

Not only priests opposed Yohanan's diminishing the centrality of Jerusalem. Surviving Sadducees and Boethusians also opposed both this and the escalation of proto-rabbinic interpretative Torah. They, as well as those who believed him to be soft on Christianity, aimed at his downfall. As soon as Gamaliel II assumed authority he moved against Christians, and sometime between 90 and 100 C.E. he had the *amidah* redacted to include a paragraph that invoked God's curse upon all sectarians including *notzrim,* Christians.[1] This change made it impossible for a Christian to pray in a synagogue. In addition, Gamaliel sent out letters for the expulsion of Christians from synagogues that led to the permanent fissure in Judaism between Rabbinic Judaism and Christianity.

---

1. This anti-Christian clause has long been removed from the *amidah.*

I. THE FORMATION AND EVOLUTION OF RABBINISM

It was during the reign of Gamaliel II that Rabbi Akiba (or Aqiba) was able to include a ban on extraneous writings, and that the belief in the doctrine of resurrection of the dead was suggested as a prerequisite for membership in theological Israel. These ideas, however, have never been enforced. Thus, despite having benefited from Sadducees in his rise to power, at the outset Gamaliel II excluded Sadducees, Boethusians, and others from Judaism, unless they professed the theological affirmations he required. This act hastened the disappearance of these sects but did not necessarily eliminate alternative faith.

Just as it is impossible to tell how much liturgical activity was achieved by Yohanan and how much by Gamaliel II, it is also impossible to determine to what extent Yohanan can be credited with the systematization of the Mishnah (a digest of halakah). A pre-70 C.E. body of mishnaic material existed, and undoubtedly Yohanan's disciples began to add to this prior to the accession of Gamaliel II. Rabbi Akiba and Rabbi Meir formed new collections building upon a "first Mishnah." Similarly, while working on collecting and digesting the postbiblical halakic material, the scholars at Yabneh made final decisions on what should constitute "sacred scripture" in Judaism. In this activity they excluded all books that we know as "intertestamental" or by the designations of "apocrypha" and "pseudepigrapha"; the Dead Sea Scrolls; and all those writings composed by members of the new Christian movement.

Gamaliel II's Yabneh became not only a center of prolific liturgical and halakic effort, but also an advocate of an inward turning by the Jewish community. The rabbis saw their generation as the surviving remnant which had to bring messianic redemption. Yohanan tried to forge an ecumenical community and defuse the opposition by reducing tension among Shammaites and Hillelites, incorporating halakic options of the pre-70 C.E. *Perushite* groups, and preserving Sadducean priestly prerogatives. But his successors saw Gnosticism, apocalypticism, and Christianity as superior dangers. Thus, at the turn of the century, the Yabnean scholars excluded the literature of these groups and the adherents of these movements, and the term *minim* (literally, "species") was attached to all those whom the rabbis regarded as deviational, aberrational, extraneous, or heretical. The major source of irritation to Gamaliel II was the Christian Jewish movement, and as noted, he saw to their exclusion. But these same rabbis also regarded the mass of unobservant *ammey haaretz* as a peril. It was in response both to the Christian challenge which eschewed the old ritual and to that of the *ammey haaretz* that the rabbis placed such a powerful emphasis upon ritualism, especially upon such distinctive symbols as tallit, tefillin, and mezuzot, and escalated Sabbath restrictiveness, proliferating forbidden activities in the style of the pietists of old.

II. THE INSTITUTIONS AND LITERATURE OF RABBINISM

A. The Synagogue

The origin of the synagogue is obscure, and documentable certainty is not available.[2] The earliest form, albeit much different from the synagogues we know from the talmudic era, is very ancient. Many people might have regarded the priestly-sacrificial cult as appearing too impersonal; others might have firmly objected to the frequent syncretism evident in the established Jerusalem cult. Such disparate "dissenters" would seek out a holy man to garner torah from him, and perhaps to join together in prayer. Thus it became customary to visit the home of an *ish elohim,* a man of God, on Sabbaths and New Moons (2 Kgs. 4:23). In time this type of meeting emerged as an alternative worship system. The effort of Hezekiah and Josiah to abolish local shrines and high places and compel all public worship to be conducted in Jerusalem, making local prayer and study gatherings more important, escalated the expansion of such an alternative worship system.

One cannot determine when the term *synagoge* came into use exclusively for a Jewish house of worship. Both this Greek word and its Hebrew parallel, *bet hakeneset,* mean simply a "place of assembly." As noted earlier, Israel constitutes an *edah* or a *qahal* (congregation, assembly), and both these words are rendered by *synagoge* in the Greek Bible (Num. 13:27; 15:15; cf. 14:5). But a place of worship is also known as *proseuche* in the Greek, a term which translates in Hebrew as *bet tephillah,* house of prayer (Isa. 56:7). *Proseuche* is a term also used frequently by Philo, Josephus, and Paul. To distinguish themselves from Jews, the Christians chose *ekklesia* (Acts 16:5) as a synonym for *synagoge* to denote their places of worship.

The alternative worship centers of monarchical times served as ready models for the deportees to Babylonia and refugees to Egypt and other diaspora centers after 597 B.C.E. This type of gathering influenced

---

2. See also "The Rise of the Synagogue" in Chapter Two.

the rise of *maamadot,* rotations of laypeople, after the resurgence of the priestly cult with the success of Nehemiah. These *maamadot* corresponded to the twenty-four rotations of priests at the Temple. The *maamadot* assembled in their towns and villages and sent representatives to Jerusalem to be present at the cultic exercises. In essence, this representation implied that the people at large were participating in the sacrificial rites. The source for this participation was traced to Numbers 28:2, which was taken to mean that the cult was not an exclusive prerogative of priests but that each individual was to offer his own sacrifice, even if only symbolically. These *maamadot,* in turn, spurred the expansion of the institution of the synagogue as we know it.

An early inscription informs us that the function of the synagogue was "for the reading of the Torah and inquiry into the commandments; furthermore, . . . for lodging of needy strangers."[3] Josephus and Philo emphasize Sabbath gatherings with teaching of torah as a major feature of the synagogue. The antiquity of buildings that housed such alternative worship centers is to be seen at Psalm 74:8, where the enemy burns *moadey el,* which must be translated "the meeting places of God." This text refers to the co-destruction of synagogues and Temple, either in 485 B.C.E. according to one theory, or more probably in 587 B.C.E. Similarly, the Christian Testament attests to the synagogue as a place of "reading Moses . . . from earliest generations" (Acts 15:21).

Rabbinic tradition elevated the sanctity of the synagogue in order to establish it as equally legitimate as a place of worship with the Jerusalem Temple. One was not to conduct oneself there in a disrespectful manner, nor to eat, drink, or sleep therein. The hospice and inn facilities were adjuncts to the sanctuary for these last purposes. The sacred literature was to be studied there, and prayer and preaching to be centered there. The building belonged to the corporate community. It was administered by appointed elders, but who did the appointing is not clear. Any layperson who was invited or volunteered was eligible to lead prayers or read Scripture before the congregation, the earliest evidence for which is at Luke 4:16-20. The person who saw that all things functioned was known as the *archisynagogos* in Greek, or *rosh hakeneset* in Hebrew; and he was assisted by a functionary called *hazan,* a term not to be confused with the modern *hazan* who serves

---

3. E. L. Sukenik, *The Ancient Synagogue of El Hammeh,* cited by John Bowker in *The Targums and Rabbinic Literature* (New York: Cambridge University Press, 1969), p. 11n.2.

as a chanter or cantor, but rather identified with the modern English term sexton. Other functionaries were collectors and distributors of alms. The rabbi did not yet serve as a synagogue functionary, but largely taught, made decisions in halakah, and probably served as a consultant on all religious matters. His time was generally occupied not by ministering to a congregation or community, a function that became more typical in later centuries. Rather, the rabbi was engaged, first, in making a living at some secular occupation, and second, in scholarship, academic deliberation, and service in various types of ecclesiastical tribunals.

The synagogue was a portable sanctuary. The destruction of the buildings or the scrolls could no longer profoundly affect the new non-territorial, synagogue-centered, study-oriented Judaism. New buildings and new scrolls and books could easily replace the old wherever Jews resided. Ten Jews constituted a congregation. No clergy and no clerical trappings were mandatory in the conduct of the liturgy. The religious process was so highly spiritualized that it was believed that wherever two or three gathered to speak words of Torah there the Shekinah (the Holy Spirit) was present (M. Ab. 3:3). The vicissitudes of centuries led frequently to simple synagogue structures. Nevertheless, synagogue structures were often lavishly decorated, emulated the finest of local architecture, and did not at all eschew art, even if sculptured figures were frowned upon. Archeology and historical studies have opened a new understanding of the ancient attitude toward art. This attitude was far more open than believed by some, who rely upon presuppositions derived from a misinterpretation of the second commandment ("You shall not make yourself a carved image") and a misunderstanding of how ancient Judaism read the second commandment.

B. The Scriptural Canon

The term *canon,* in its Greek form *kanon,* has been used only since the fourth century. It signified that books are eligible for public reading of Scripture in liturgical contexts. Such a term did not exist in Judaism, nor is there any definition given for its counterpart, *siphrey hizonim* ("extraneous books"). A book like Sirach was not included in sacred Scripture until the end of the first century; Ezekiel was debated at the same time; and Esther and Song of Songs were not included until the second century, and still debated in the third.

The first two divisions of sacred Scripture as we know it now—

the Pentateuch and the Prophets—were known and given special status as early as 200 B.C.E., as is evident from their listing by Ben Sira (Sir. 45:1-5; 46:1–49:13). Ben Sira's grandson, who translated his book into Greek ca. 130 B.C.E., refers to writings of the third division of Scripture known as Hagiographa, or Sacred Writings, thus attesting to the expansion of the acceptable works. The Alexandrian collection and the finds at Qumran indicate that some books designated later as "apocryphal" were included in sacred Scripture and were freely used.

There was no official collection of sacred writings before the middle of the second century, and such a collection was undoubtedly prompted by the serious challenge presented by the rise and expansion of Christianity.[4] We have no accurate knowledge of how the present collection was actually finalized. Some books were excluded because they were not pre-Maccabean, and Daniel was saved because it had an older Persian setting. Some books, such as Enoch, were excluded because they were used extensively by Christians, or had many affinities with Christian son-of-man views. Others, such as Jubilees, were excluded for being diametrically opposed to the halakah of Rabbinism; and still others were abandoned because they were either written in Greek or no Hebrew originals survived. The exclusion of the books of the Maccabees reflects the rabbinic opposition to the Hasmonean era and its excesses, and the rejection of the books of Qumran is a product of the halakic discrepancies, apocalyptic excess, and the basic opposition of Rabbinism to the sect because of its monastic separation.

The collection of sacred writings was later enlarged by the quasi-equality given to the classical rabbinic works: the Targums, the Mishnah, Tosefta, *tannaitic* and other midrashim, and the two Talmuds, to be discussed below. Like the synagogue, the literature was portable, and made vertical historical continuity of Judaism possible, as well as horizontal affinity in the religious thought of a worldwide denomination with widely scattered congregations. The term *torah* was extended to all teaching, research, and discussion of Judaism. In this way, synagogue and canon became two vital media of post-70 C.E. Judaism leading to a massive and enriching resurgence of the faith.

---

4. I disagree with the scholarly consensus that dates the fixing of the canon at Yabneh to ca. 90 C.E. Question raised about Ecclesiastes, Esther, and Song of Songs were still in dispute during the second and third centuries.

C. The Rabbinic Literature

1. Targum

Translation of a text from one language into another frequently results in *midrash,* the interpretation of that text. When the ancient Judean translated the Pentateuch, and later the Prophets and Writings, into Aramaic, or when the Alexandrian Jew translated these works into Greek, he was compelled to make certain choices of words or to construct phrases in a given way in order to make the Hebrew understandable in Aramaic or Greek. This need might often result in applying his notion of what the Hebrew language seeks to convey, rather than a literal translation of the original. Frequently it might result in the translator providing in the new language the current popular interpretation or the interpretation of a particular school regarding a word or phrase. A translation or a *targum,* therefore, whether the Greek one, known as the Septuagint, or the Aramaic ones, known as Onkelos or Pseudo-Jonathan, is not simply a translation. It is also a form of midrash, and can enlighten us regarding the interpretation of Scripture during the centuries before the rise of Christianity and Rabbinism.

The Aramaic Targum exemplifies other exegetical features as well. It seeks to remove theological problems which might not be comprehended by a popular audience hearing Scripture in the synagogue. It incorporates older traditions that might otherwise have disappeared, and sometimes represents a Hebrew text which is an ancient variant of the Masoretic text (the traditional text currently used by Jews).

A revealing diversity in halakah is found in the Onkelos and Palestinian targums to the injunction not to boil a kid in its mother's milk (Exod. 23:29; 34:26; Deut. 14:21). Onkelos forbids only the eating of flesh with milk, ignoring the Hebrew "boil," while the Palestinian targums include both boiling and eating the two (meat and dairy) together. Finally, rabbinic tradition prohibited boiling, eating, and deriving any benefit whatever from such a mixture. This diversity of halakic opinion is even more striking in that it reflects a major reinterpretation of Scripture. The targums reveal to us a transformation of a cultic prohibition into a dietary restraint. Since there is no hint of a new interpretation of the text in the Septuagint, it is evident that this halakic transformation took place after 250 B.C.E., probably originating among the Hasidim of early Hasmonean times or among their successors, the *Perushim*-Pharisees. The proto-rabbis, however, had not yet taken the prohibition to boil a kid in its mother's milk to the extreme conclusion we find in later rabbinic literature. Thus Rabbi Ishmael, in the first or second century, was still of the opinion of his proto-rabbinic mentors that the verse is cited three times in order to emphasize God's triple covenant with Israel (Exod. 24:7-8; Deut. 28:69; 29:11). In this way he still attached cultic, rather than dietary, significance to the verse.

Although the term *targum* is generally reserved generically for the Aramaic translations of the synagogue, the term can serve equally to describe the Septuagint. It is logical to assume that just as the targum tradition arose from the time of Ezra and Nehemiah, because of the need to enable the average person to understand Scripture in the vernacular in Palestine, Babylonia, and other eastern, Aramaic-speaking areas, so too it was necessary to apply this convenience to the Greek-speaking diaspora. A translation was given by a functionary called a *meturgeman* (translator, interpreter) during the synagogue scriptural reading. Since these targums were to be used in the synagogue during the scriptural reading, it became desirable for the authorities to establish a more-or-less officially recognized text. It is impossible at this time to determine how many such proto-official texts existed or who were their authors, just as it is difficult to pinpoint the texts that stand behind the Masoretic Hebrew Bible. Our Aramaic targums reveal a serious "synoptic problem" because no two targum texts are identical. In time, however, variant texts were suppressed and some texts became as official as the Masoretic text. Ultimately, the Greek text was not preserved by Judaism, because Greek-speaking Jews ceased to flourish, but three Aramaic targums were carefully transmitted.

The Aramaic targum texts that were preserved and published with Masoretic Bibles were Onkelos; Pseudo-Jonathan and Fragmentary Pseudo-Jonathan (also called Targum Yerushalmi and Fragmentary Targum or Palestinian Targum); and Neofiti I, a recently discovered manuscript which has enhanced our knowledge of the targumic literature.

2. Midrash

According to some scholars who favor dissection and atomization, Judaism contained five forms of scriptural exegesis: targum, midrash, *pesher,* typology, and allegory. These forms overlapped, however, and midrash, which was expository, contained allegory and typology, as did *pesher;* and as noted, targum was actually midrashic. In a very real sense, there is one genre, midrash, which encompasses many forms of exposition. The word *midrash,* from *darash,* signifies both the process of research, inquiry, and interpretation, and the results of the process embodied in a corpus of literature. The midrashic process is part of both halakah (practice, norms of conduct) and aggadah (nonhalakic matters of belief, history, homiletics, biography, folklore, etc.). Out of targum and midrash, as processes, grew the "oral torah," which should be referred to more accurately as "interpretative torah," for much of it was not oral.

Aggadah is expository material which illuminates a text but does not determine the meaning of texts related to practice, whether ritual or ethical. Aggadah seeks to inspire and edify. The midrashic "interpretative torah," which forms and regulates conduct, is halakah. But aggadah is found in midrashim primarily considered halakic, and halakah is found in midrashim denominated aggadic. The basic halakic midrashim are known as Mekilta, Sifra, and Sifre. These are considered *tannaitic* because they reflect the teachings of sages who lived and functioned betwen 200 B.C.E. and 200 C.E., and who have been historically named *tannaim.* These *tannaitic* midrashim are a basic reservoir containing early proto-rabbinic and late rabbinic halakah. In their present form they reflect the expository treatment of Scripture taught in the rabbinic schools of Rabbi Akiba and Rabbi Ishmael, of the second century, although much of the content is older.

The other midrashim, including such collections as Midrash Rabbah, Tanhuma, Pesikta de Rab Kahana, and Pesikta Rabbati, among others, are basically homiletical in character. They are collections of material for sermons, or the sermons themselves. Early and later material mingle together. There are also midrashim considered historical, such as Pirke de Rabbi Eliezer, which, although of later vintage, also contain early traditions and much mystical material. In all, there are over forty titles in the genre midrash, many of which are multivolumed. The massive nature of this literature not only makes it a formidable ocean to traverse, but also a vast source of much diverse halakic thought. Again, as in the case of the targums and the earlier and contemporary apocryphal and Qumran literature, it attests to the wide diversity of thought and practice in pre-Rabbinic and Rabbinic Judaism.

3. Mishnah

Since every word of Torah was deemed sacred, by extension the exposition of it was also deemed sacred. This meant that the text and its interpretation were to be transmitted with great care. Although much of this transmission was done orally in the classroom or wherever torah was taught, much of it was also written in notes taken by disciples or crib sheets prepared by teachers for presentation in session. It was regarded as a religious and ethical imperative for a scholar to "use the language of his teacher," that is, to be utterly accurate in the transmission of a text or tradition (M. Ed. 1:3). It was also important to cite a tradition in the name of one's teacher (M. Ab. 6:6), but not to give the names of one's teacher's predecessors who transmitted the same teaching. Thus, traditions reported in the name of any given scholar might be much older. Despite a widespread opposition to putting the material into writing, we read of the equally widespread existence of written sources, in both the field of aggadah and of halakah.

The *tanna* (plural: *tannaim*) was the repository of the texts, and he recited them before teachers and students. He was not necessarily a scholar, a photographic memory being more important than a brilliant mind. Since he was required to be able to recite accurately all the extant texts upon demand, a *tanna* literally had to be a walking textbook. Nevertheless, our sources reveal that talmudic rabbis often evoked alternative texts, thus indicating that a diversity of texts, as of ideas and halakah, existed in the various schools.

Out of the mass of expository material were formulated succinct halakic norms. These norms were discussed in the schools for an indefinite period. But some evidence indicates that even before the destruction of Jerusalem the schools of Shammai and Hillel made an effort to collect these norms in some thematic fashion, such as in the tractate Tamid. Later, at Yabneh, far more of an effort was put forth, and we know of collections that go by the name of the late first- and early second-century rabbi, Akiba. Akiba arranged a proto-Mishnah which was at the base of Rabbi Judah's Mishnah. The Mishnah as we have it, though credited to Rabbi Judah the Nasi at the end of the second century, is actually a later revision, which is evident from the fact that it includes teachings of sages who lived after Rabbi Judah.

The Mishnah is a collection of a number of separate documents that antedated it, as well as of small units of halakah previously not included in any collections. The halakic norms collected in this useful digest of halakah, or manual of reference, represent the thinking and teaching of the individuals who lived between the time of Ben Sira and Rabbi Judah the Nasi, 200 B.C.E.-200 C.E., and were now given the major role in shaping the development of Judaism for the future. This Mishnah is to be understood as a repository of halakah rather than a "code of law," which is evidenced, among other reasons, by its diversity of opinion on many subjects, all of them equally presented.

Rabbi Judah the Nasi sought to stabilize the textbook of interpretative torah used in the schools. His halakic digest was taken to Babylonia and also used as the basic text there. That this Palestinian work was acceptable in the increasingly self-assertive Babylonian schools is due to the fact that it had much Babylonian content, as will be discussed below. But stabilization of text did not lead to stabilization of halakah into a monolithic pattern. Rabbi Judah had himself indicated the desirability of options in halakah by incorporating variant halakic opinions into the body of his own work. Rabbi Judah's text, which was incorporated into the volumes of the Mishnah, was now recited by a *tanna* orally and discussed in the rabbinic schools. These discussions and interpretations of the Mishnah, along with those of the Tosefta (see below), evolved into the body of literature called the Talmud.

4. Tosefta

The term *tosefta* means "supplement." The material is similar in type and arrangement to the Mishnah and, like the Mishnah, is considered the product of *tannaitic* teachers. Its name derives from its function as supplementary halakic data, and is termed extraneous material *(beraita)* in the Talmud. This is owing to the fact that it is not included in the Mishnah. But it serves as alternative halakah. There are many unsatisfactory theories concerning its compilation, authorship, and date. It appears, however, that in comparative study of halakah, and sometimes also with halakic material in Philo, Tosefta represents an older halakah, although it is quite possible to argue that its date of compilation is later than that of the Mishnah. Tosefta is discussed in the two Talmuds—the Palestinian and Babylonian—just as Mishnah is, and is regarded in both as *beraita,* extraneous material.

5. The Two Talmuds

There are two Talmuds, both forged in the give-and-take of intellectual interchange centered on the Mishnah and Tosefta. The term *talmud* means "teaching," and in effect, as noted earlier, represents midrash on Mishnah and Tosefta. It serves a function similar to that of both the homiletical (or aggadic), and halakic midrashim. The Palestinian Talmud came to a close in Tiberias during the fourth century, comprising a compilation of materials developed in Caesarea and Sepphoris as well. It was not developed, compiled, or promulgated in Jerusalem, and for this reason the epithet "Yerushalmi" occasionally attached to it is incorrect. The Babylonian Talmud frequently refers to it as *talmud demaaraba,* "the talmud of the west." The Babylonian Talmud was concluded during the sixth century, and was a product of a variety of schools, including Sura, Nehardea, Pumbedita, and Nisibis, among others. Post-*tannaitic* teachers are termed *amoraim,* the term *amora* signifying "expositor." As a result of the ultimate predominance of the Babylonian *geonim* (later rabbinic heads of academies) from the seventh to the eleventh centuries, the Babylonian Talmud gained religious hegemony in Judaism. Although he was not the "editor" of the Babylonian Talmud, as often thought, Rabbi Ashi (d. 427) was probably a major collector of the material in his school, over which he presided for seventy years.

The word *gemara* is generally used as a synonym for talmud, and is applied to the discussions on the Mishnah text. But *gemara,* as some scholars have noted, might be derived from *gamar,* "to conclude," and signifies halakic conclusions, in contrast to the discussion leading up to the conclusions. In this sense it would be a synonym for halakah rather than talmud, which represents both the material of discussion and the corpus of literature composed of Mishnah and its talmud. A group of scholars who succeeded the *amoraim,* known as *saboraim* (reflectors or examiners), put the finishing touches upon the Babylonian Talmud which we possess, and expanded it in the process.

The two Talmuds are a monument to the massive effort of the early rabbis to continue the interpretative work they believed was started at Sinai, and the Talmuds partook of the nature of revelation. They are difficult to study and comprehend because of the need to master background material and because of their complex language, involving both Eastern and Western Aramaic, Greek and Latin loan-words, and a little Persian. Adding to the difficulty is the laconic manner in which the material is expressed, and the inchoate nature of how the material is collected. Despite all that has been written about the "editing" of the Talmuds, it is clear that neither one of these collections was edited in the modern sense of the word. Rather, a mass of material, often unrelated and out of context and sequence, was simply compiled. Since the discussions were centered on mishnaic verses, the collection was gathered in the thematic sequence of the Mishnah. But despite this appearance of a thematic arrangement, the material is far from coherent. In any discussion of a given theme one will find the interjection of other themes, sometimes loosely joined to the matter under discussion, and frequently merely part of a string of reminiscences in a stream of consciousness style. Complex halakic discussions might be interrupted by mystical concerns, punctuated by mundane table talk, and interlaced with aggadah.

The talmudic material grew in a wide variety of Palestinian and Babylonian schools, and it is therefore no surprise that mishnaic and Tosefta texts varied, and that more than one version of each of the Talmuds also circulated. Scholars of the two major centers exchanged visits and learning, and are therefore found mentioned in both Talmuds. Once the Talmuds were compiled and manuscripts began to reach the diaspora in North Africa, Italy, and elsewhere, these works were studied internationally, just as they were in the Babylonian and Palestinian schools. The Talmuds now took on the role of textbooks as once the Mishnah had, and their availability further democratized Judaic religious life. Babylonian scholars, who had access to the Mishnah and Tosefta earlier, had rejected Palestinian authority; and now scholars in Egypt, North Africa, Italy, Spain, and France were soon to reject Babylonian authority. Access to the sacred literature led to the renewed assertion of independence on the part of rabbis and their communities. Nevertheless, the long hegemony of the *geonim* and the popularity of the Babylonian Talmud resulted in medieval and early modern Judaism being shaped by the Babylonian interpretation of theology and practice.

Like the synagogue, the biblical canon, targums, midrashim, Mishnah, and Tosefta, the Talmuds became a vital medium for the preservation of Judaism. All of these media were a latter-day version of the portable sanctuary of the wilderness. They liberated theological Israel from a territorially centered and cultically oriented faith. The Talmuds became as significant as Scripture, and in the ongoing metamorphosis of Judaism, even through the twentieth century, change and innovation were measured against talmudic precedent.

D. Rabbinic Leadership in Babylonia

Little is known of Judaism's development in Babylonia, Mesopotamia, or Iran from the time of the conquest of Jerusalem in 587 B.C.E. to the second century C.E. What becomes evident by the second century is the existence of a widespread, populous Jewish community extending from the northern end of the Tigris-Euphrates plain to the southern tip of the Persian Gulf. But it is also apparent that as early as the beginning of the first century Babylonian studies advanced significantly, to the extent that Palestinian tradition is willing to assign a major role to a Babylonian, the famous but obscure Hillel. Tannaitic sources reveal exchange visits and interchange of halakic opinions, as well as clear influences of Babylonian scholars upon Palestinian halakah later incorporated in the Mishnah. The level of Babylonian studies and schools must have advanced considerably by the second century. Thus, just as Hillel is said to have replaced the obscure Palestinians, known as Bene Bathyra, in the proto-rabbinic leadership, so too did Rabbi Nathan of Babylonia depose the Palestinian Rabbi Simon ben Gamaliel II (B. Hor. 13b). The replacement of these Palestinian rabbis by their Babylonian counterparts not only reflects growing Babylonian assertiveness but also implies the desire to overthrow any effort to centralize authority in the hands of the Gamaliel dynasty and a Palestinian "Patriarch," as the office was called.

The Bar Kokhba War of 132-135 caused scholars to flee to Babylonia. Some of these returned to Palestine after the war and brought with them Babylonian views that were incorporated into Mishnah and Tosefta. Babylonian scholars often resided for some years in Palestine and influenced the thinking in the schools. A shift of leadership from Palestine to Babylonia began during the second century and was escalated by the publication and distribution of the Mishnah in the third. Babylonians already had their independent *hilkata* (halakah) and developed an independent Mishnah tradition. During the third century, Babylonian scholars moved into a position of supremacy, and ultimately, ca. 358, the Palestinians surrendered their last symbol of authority, the promulgation of the calendar, and issued a permanent computation which still determines the Judaic liturgical year. Babylonia now became spiritual parent to the diaspora for fifteen hundred years, although all of its spiritual progeny around the world reserved the right to halakic autonomy.

E. Premises of the Halakah

The provenance of halakah, whether in Palestine or in Babylonia, did not affect the underlying philosophy or premises of halakah, which were already in place before the first century and were responsible for the direction proto-rabbinic and rabbinic halakah took from the beginning.

Halakah—religious practice, whether cultic, ritualistic, or ethical—was a major preoccupation of the ancient rabbis. They emerged from the ashes of the war of 66-73 C.E. as heirs to the leadership of a widely diversified community, in which a plethora of pietistic and ascetic groups had vied for hegemony with the priestly establishment and its Sadducean supporters. Most of these groups evaporated in the smoke that rose from the rubble of Jerusalem. An inchoate and battered population remained leaderless, the surviving priests having been long discredited. The priests were in no position to reassert authority with their base—the Temple—in ruins, and with their rationale for being—the sacrificial cult—swept away. The natural leaders to fill this vacuum and to reconstitute a living theological Israel as a renewed religious community were the individuals long known as *hakamim,* whom I style proto-rabbis, and who of late had been largely concentrated in Yabneh.

Their leading figure, Yohanan ben Zakkai, as previously noted, introduced ordination and created the institution we know as the rabbinate (B. San. 14a). These new rabbis and their predecessors had already been functioning as proto-rabbis for over two centuries, and during this period a pattern of hermeneutics and a set of principles had developed that were now further applied at Yabneh. These principles allowed them to affirm the divine revelation of Scripture, and simultaneously to legislate new halakah, interpret and transform old halakah, abrogate obsolete practices, and innovate new ones. They had a set of criteria upon which they based their activity.

The rabbinic halakah was informed by a variety of criteria, which included humanitarianism, historic continuity, aesthetics in ritual, and adaptation to social custom and the surrounding milieu.[5] With these concepts, the rabbis shaped the halakah, both in their exegesis of the Torah and in their various abrogations of the old halakah and innovations of the new. Along with consideration of scientific data available to them at the time, a variety of principles infused these criteria. Among them the leading philosophical formulations were: (a) *dina demalkutah dina* (sovereign law of the state is binding), freeing the Jew from the necessity of resistance to government; (b) *miphney tikkun haolam* (the general social welfare); (c) *miphney darkey shalom* (domestic and civic tranquility); (d) the principle that one should not introduce a decree which the majority of a community cannot be expected to accept; and (e) *liphnim meshurat hadin* (adoption of a higher standard

---

5. These criteria are more fully discussed in my *New Dimensions in Judaism.*

than that of the letter of the law). All of these were underpinned by the concept of *middat hasidut,* the quality of love, or basing one's decision making upon the love command. All of these principles had the result of working toward leniency in the halakah, although this by no means implies that halakah became monolithic or that there were no longer powerful and numerous forces operating in favor of stringency and restrictiveness in the halakah. These later rabbis carried forward the old standards of *Perushim,* many of whose pietistic stringencies in the halakah were adapted and integrated into the rabbinic halakah.

The tension between leniency and stringency, which is often delineated as liberalism versus conservatism in the modern world, was present in the development of halakah from the earliest times. On the one hand, Ezraic-Nehemian conservatism was reflected in the book of Jubilees and the Zadokite Fragments and served well for those who vigorously opposed Hellenism. On the other hand, as Hellenism progressed, the rise of the definable group I refer to as proto-rabbis, originating with Simon the Just, Ben Sira, and their younger contemporary Yosi ben Yoezer, represented a powerful swing toward leniency and moderation in halakic decision making. Yosi acquired the epithet "the permitter," and from his time on leniency appears to have been the preferred approach. This is clearly evident in the controversies reflected in the halakic midrashim and talmudic literature. Nevertheless, the option of *humrah,* the stringent or restrictive interpretation, was always open to the devout when leniency, or *kulah,* received majority support. And similarly, when conditions were reversed, the believer was free to adopt leniency. This right to options in the halakah was sometimes abridged by secular power, whether by a gentile government recognizing only one rabbinic authority in a given area, or by secular Judaic community power where a civil government gave the corporate community such power over resident Jews. But the periodic denial of freedom in the practice of halakic options was contrary to historic halakic philosophy. Options in halakah were historically indigenous to Judaism and were of the warp and woof of the theological presuppositions of the faith.

Chapter Four

The Medieval Era I:
From Diaspora Goes Forth Torah

I. AUTHORITARIANISM AND DISSENT

A. The *Geonim*

1. Their Influence

The title *Gaon,* "excellency," was accorded the rabbis of Babylonia from approximately the sixth to the twelfth centuries—somewhat before or during the Islamic period. The *geonim* expanded a genre already known from the Talmud—the epistle. Letters were written by rabbis either to respond to religious questions from the diaspora or to offer unsolicited direction. These questions took the form both of (a) theology, matters of doctrine and faith; and (b) halakah, problems of ritual practice, domestic relations, and even civil and criminal law. The letters written by the various *geonim* over a period of some five centuries formed a massive new body of Judaic religious literature known as *sheelot uteshubot* (literally, "Questions and Answers"), or the "responsa literature."

The Babylonian *geonim* were in direct rivalry for religious authority with Palestinian rabbinic leaders, who presided over a dwindling community, especially after the Byzantine and Persian wars of the fifth and sixth centuries. Nevertheless, the community was still sufficiently vital from the seventh to the eleventh century to have created a considerable body of midrashic literature, the Masoretic text of Scripture, and liturgical poetry. But the Babylonians gained hegemony by their near-monopoly on the responsa that influenced all of North Africa and Europe. With this hegemony, the Babylonian Talmud became the repository of Judaic halakah most frequently researched and followed. The Babylonian Talmud continues to be the more prominent of the two Talmuds, although in recent generations more attention has been given to the Palestinian Talmud, and in some cases Palestinian traditions are revived in the contemporary Western world.

Despite the *geonic* influence, however, Judaism did not become monolithic. For one thing, not all *geonim* had the same approach to doctrine and practice. But even more important was the geographic factor, the vast stretches over which Jewish communities settled, from India to the Atlantic and from Africa and the Persian Gulf to the North, Baltic, Black, and Caspian Seas. They lived among widely variegated pagan, Christian, and Moslem populations. Indigenous cultures operating in their respective ambiences had the inevitable impact upon Judaic custom and lifestyle. These, in turn, influenced halakah. Thus, for example, to anticipate what became a major modern controversy, the covering of the head at worship was influenced by oriental custom and spread throughout the Islamic world, but was of less significance in the Christian European lands until the seventeenth century. And as the eighteenth century drew to a close and central Europe witnessed the belated Jewish Reformation, whether covering the head at worship was required became a major issue and became one of the basic distinctions between the new Reform movement and those styled Orthodox and Conservative.

Geography was significant in many ways. The heat of the Near East and the cold of northern Europe, the varying occupations Jews engaged in as a function of their geographic distribution, the attitudes of the gentile governments and the Church, the distances between Jewish communities, all played a role in shaping local traditions. These in turn influenced ever-widening concentric circles. Historically, *minhag* (custom) often evolved into halakah, or was considered as valid as halakah, if not more so, by virtue of which it came to possess the power of halakah. As a result, local custom in time became the mode of practice in the proliferating digests of halakah that appeared all around the Jewish diaspora.

Judaism was unified throughout this vast diaspora by the incessant labors of the *geonim,* who brought forth a basic approach to liturgy, food practices, Sabbath and holy days, and the observance of life-cycle events. But this developing homogeneity never became uniformity. And as great new centers arose, with significant schools presided over by emerging or migrating scholars, a tendency toward

111

widespread independence developed. As Babylonians had asserted their autonomy from Palestinians, so did Italians, North Africans, Spaniards, Provencal and northern Frenchmen, Germans, and ultimately east Europeans, all in turn assert their independence from the Babylonian *geonim*. They all built upon the Babylonian foundations, however, and this background explains why amidst great diversity there remained a permanent semblance of similarity.

Much of our knowledge concerning the *geonic* era is relatively recent. It became available to us with the retrieval of a massive *genizah* trove—a vast yield of medieval literary documents including liturgy, collections of halakah, responsa, commentaries, and even enlightening commercial documents. This find provided great new raw material, hitherto unknown, which could help scholars ascertain the medieval development of Judaism. Much of this vast find still remains to be read.[1]

Sura in Babylonia (modern Iraq) was the center of the largest literary output during the four centuries from the close of the Talmud (perhaps best dated at 600 to ca. 1000), after which rabbinic hegemony shifted to North Africa and Europe. Two classics stand out as paradigms of all future Judaic religious literary effort: the *Halakot Gedolot* and the *Seder Rabbi Amram*. The first is a comprehensive collection of religious practice. The second is an annotated description of the order of religious worship. Both have influenced every area of Jewish religious life to this day, but I will here discuss only the first.

2. Halakot Gedolot

Some scholars attribute this work to Rabbi Yehudai, *Gaon* of Sura 757-761 (or 760-764), while others attribute it to Simon Kayyara, a ninth-century scholar. The most likely view is the compromise that attributes an original collection of halakot to Yehudai and a later expanded form to Simon. The technical details of this literary problem are not our concern. What is of moment here is that *Halakot Gedolot,* by serving as a new Mishnah, a new comprehensive digest of relevant halakah, asserted the Babylonian claim to hegemony and helped institutionalize it. The massive talmudic literature was inaccessible to many. The purpose of a digest such as *Halakot Gedolot,* which, like the Mishnah, was not a "code of law," was to extract suggested and recommended

---

1. For an original discussion of the genizah see Solomon Schechter, *Studies in Judaism,* Second Series (Philadelphia: Jewish Publication Society, 1908-1924).

halakic views for quick decisions and easy reference. Undoubtedly, the disorientation of communities by recurring Byzantine-Persian and Persian-Arab wars with consequent sociopolitical and economic hardships in part prompted this work of halakic extraction.

But more significant might have been the role played by the emerging dissenting force called *Karaism*. Once before, the rise of Christianity had influenced the gathering of holy Scripture into a definable corpus, and its successful spread led to the editing of the Mishnah to serve as an authoritative guide to Jewish religious life. In this way now *Halakot Gedolot* was a response to the challenge of Karaism.[2] The Karaites, dissenting from the halakah of Rabbinism, arose in part from the shadowy remains of Sadduceeism, Qumran pietism, Christian Judaism, and the eastern Iranian remnants of the so-called lost tribes of Israel. In his *Halakot Gedolot,* Yehudai sought to clarify the differences between Rabbinic Judaism and Karaism, and to establish the former as authoritative.

If such response to challenge was Yehudai's purpose, he succeeded in a way he hardly intended, for while he did not stem the rise of Karaism, he set an interesting precedent with far-reaching consequences for Jewish religious development. His style and format, patterned after the Mishnah, became the halakic model for future rabbis. An aspect of that style was the omission of aggadic material. This omission further deepened the tendency in Judaism to give less credence to aggadah, especially when it taxes credulity and demands commitment to the miraculous and mysterious. The central question Yehudai implicitly propounded was not "What do I believe," but "How do I express my faith in practice?" Furthermore, Yehudai omitted halakah he regarded as no longer applicable, which sharpened the notion that halakic relevance has validity, and that halakah can become obsolete. Moreover, he omitted talmudic discussion that led up to a decision, which allowed his halakic successors the freedom similarly to extract material that expressed new views on old subjects, or to select precedents other than those in vogue. The process of extraction is selectivity, and selectivity became the hallmark of halakic evolution. Yehudai was emphasizing relevance by selectivity, disregarding the tension between divine revelation and human authority by virtue of the same selectivity, and furthering the historical propriety of the primacy of contemporary authority over the halakah of the past.

---

2. Karaism will be more fully discussed later in this chapter.

Although all of these notions are already prefigured and embodied in the Mishnah, a religious corpus tends to develop a mystique over many centuries, and the Mishnah, like the Torah, stood alone and apart as a unique religious document, thus obscuring these verities of halakic philosophy. By 750, a new Mishnah was greatly desired to share some of the authority of the earlier one and to reassert the religious philosophy implicit in the earlier one. *Gaon* Yehudai supplied it, thus bringing about a cultural revolution which evoked much opposition from other *geonim*. He was attacked for his omissions, for providing a halakah without the rationale, for opening new avenues of religious independence, and for challenging the supremacy of the Talmud. Nevertheless, the book played a major role and set a precedent for many to follow from the eighth to the twentieth century. Above all, Yehudai's ambiguous use of the talmudic source material as both authoritative and revisable institutionalized the primacy of contemporary authority.

3. Ambiguity and Authority

The ambiguity of *geonic* authority was inevitable, if only because there were two great Babylonian centers, at Sura and Pumbedita, which had shared influence and differed in outlook since early talmudic times. This differentiation was underscored by the Islamic state recognizing both *geonim* equally. The *geonim* sought to institutionalize their authority by promoting their viewpoint in digests of halakah which, while supporting diversity, acted as well to curb multiplicity. But the backing of Islamic state power prompted the *geonim* to attempt to enforce an uncharacteristic authoritarian approach to Jewish life modeled after Christian and Islamic centralized orthodoxy. It had some of the features of the defunct Patriarchate of Roman Palestine, and was sustained by an Exilarchate in Babylonia, in which a "ruler of the Exile" officially held authority over an organized Jewish community.

Such efforts to centralize authority, buttressed by frequent use of excommunication of recalcitrants, did not succeed. Thus, when Palestinian and Babylonian emigrants settled in Fustat, a suburb of Cairo, Egypt, each group established its own synagogue and followed its own inherited tradition, despite the *geonic* efforts to hold authority over Egypt and other areas of North Africa. In the eighth century, a long period of conflict ensued between the *geonim* and the Karaites, which produced a reactionary trend among *geonim* in their search for authority. They even used secret police to spy upon the people, and engaged in corporal punishment of those who violated ritual practices. One historian has termed these *geonic* efforts as a pan-Babylonian program to establish Babylonian tradition as the monolithic uniform pattern of Jewish religious observance.[3] The *geonim* succeeded in making the Babylonian Talmud the primary source of reference, research, and study in Judaism. But this success was largely because Babylonia was the center of Arabic culture, and therefore became the center of Jewish religious culture, with students coming to Babylonia from Spain, Provence, Italy, and other European and African lands, acquiring Babylonian hermeneutics and tradition. But they never succeeded in imposing uniformity of practice or belief. Local autonomy and scholarly independence always reasserted itself, and soon Kairouan and then Cordoba in Spain claimed equal authority with Sura.

Despite his conservatism, Yehudai was one of those who perhaps unwittingly, but nevertheless realistically, contributed to innovation and became an indirect source for modern revisionism. For in truth, Yehudai was not as conservative as some peers in the ninth century attested. He prohibited fasting on Rosh Hashanah and abolished absolution of vows and the study of the tractate Nedarim (Vows), all radical changes of the halakah then current.

We see in the activity of the *geonim* the tension between the tradition of relative halakic freedom and the *geonic* drive for centralized authority. It was the latter which resulted in excesses that led to much dissension in Judaism. Some Jews migrated far northward and eastward to the Iranian frontier to escape the power of the *geonim*. These immigrant colonists left the urban centers of Jewish life and followed the Arabian armies for adventure and economic reasons, at times seeking independence from the heavy *geonic* authority. At this juncture a number of factors coalesced to bring about the rise of Karaism.

B. Karaism

1. Origins

The name *Karaism* (or Qaraism) is derived from *qara,* "Scripture," and signifies "Scripturalists." At the beginning, its adherents professed a reliance upon a more literalistic approach to Scripture and an abandonment of the interpretation and the amplified ritualism of Rab-

---

3. See Salo Baron, *A Social and Religious History of the Jews,* V (Philadelphia: Jewish Publication Society, 1952), 181.

binism. Three major factors contributed to its rise: (1) the migrations mentioned earlier; (2) the relatively recent imposition of the Talmud, which had undergone its final editing in the late sixth or early seventh century and had left memories of historic factions that had conflicted with proto-rabbinic and rabbinic groups; and (3) the Moslem example which was then witnessing the rise of the Shiites, a major dissenting sect.

Although it took some time for Karaism to crystallize, and like Rabbinism it eventually was characterized by more than one movement, the basic outlines of its philosophy may be seen in the following: (1) it rejected the Talmud as authoritative; (2) it rejected the authority of the *geonim;* (3) it espoused a vigorous messianic zeal; (4) it espoused a more ascetic program than Rabbinism; and (5) as a movement arising from a rural populace, it eschewed the class structure of the urban metropolitan middle- and upper-class stratification.

The messianic zeal of the Karaites was fueled by the cataclysmic events of the time in which massive armies were frequently deadlocked in great combat. The mighty Byzantine empires in the East and the Visigothic kingdom in the West crumbled. The host of Arabs penetrated eastward deep into Asia, and westward out to the Atlantic, overthrowing historic and powerful empires, transforming the culture of half the known world, and even arranging its battering rams to point at the heart of Christian Europe. Vast populations were uprooted and replanted, diffused into distant new frontiers, and vigorous missionary activity was let loose by Islam, Christianity, and Zoroastrianism. Gnosticism penetrated all the groups. All this turmoil left some Jews ripe for conversion, others for syncretism, and others for dissent. Considerable segments of Jews were living isolated lives in the vastness of the Arabian peninsula and northeast Iran, where remnants of ancient Israel were still settled, all of these distant from the systematic Judaism of orderly, traditional *geonic* scholarship and influence. Many of these Jews encountered long-forgotten residues of Qumran, Christian Judaism, and other dissenting sects of long ago, as well as Samaritans and survivors of anti-rabbinic Sadduceeism.

It was out of the complex admixture of many such groups with dissenting members of *geonic* society that Karaism arose. According to one twelfth-century historian, Abu'l Fath Muhammad ash-Shahrastani, during the *geonic* period 600-1300, seventy-one sects arose, all of them characteristically Judaic in their adherence to monotheism, the Torah, the Sabbath, and the doctrine of messiah, and differentiated from Christianity and Islam by rejection of the Christian Testament and the Koran, respectively, and by the affirmation of the seventh-day Sabbath. Karaism was the one movement that flourished and survived, and at times became a menacing rival to Rabbinism.

Anan ben David was the founder of Karaism, and he provided a manual of nonrabbinic theology and halakạh for the movement in his *Book of Precepts* ca. 770. During the ninth century Saadia *Gaon* of Sura took up the challenge, and a protracted age of Rabbanite-Karaite polemics was opened. As Karaite scholarship gained and Karaism became first stabilized and later expansionary, the movement spread into the Balkans and out to Spain, and even far north as Lithuania. Karaism was affected by an almost contradictory tendency to insist upon individuality in interpretation, and at the same time to preserve a rigid conservatism that eschewed reinterpretation. Karaism argued that Rabbinism makes religion too convenient, and within its own purview Karaism preserved its independent traditions so rigidly that radical changes in its halakah were not in evidence until the fifteenth century.

2. Karaite Religious Thought

The rejection of Talmudism and a return to a literalist approach to Scripture initially had ramifications for Karaism, such as the abandonment of all dietary practices related to the mixture of meat and dairy. Anan took Exodus 23:19—that one is not to boil a kid in its mother's milk—literally, as a cultic command unrelated to the institution of kashrut (dietary practice). Karaites did not observe Hanukkah or Purim, since they were not pentateuchal, and rejected such liturgical ritual symbols as the tefillin (phylacteries) and mezuzah (capsule with Torah passages nailed to the doorpost).

In time, Karaites found that one cannot live by Scripture alone and developed a new Karaite halakah, which makes its first appearance in the *Sepher Dinim* (Book of Rules) during the ninth century. The author, Benjamin Al-Nahawandi, conceded to a degree of rabbinic halakah and included some as optional for Karaites. Some Karaite scholars saw Karaites as the true "Israel," however, and regarded the belief in the revelation of rabbinic interpretative torah as heresy.

Karaism rejected anthropomorphism and all mystical ideas related to heavenly hosts and demons. Its adherents regarded belief in the potency of evil spirits and magical remedies as witchcraft and contrary to Torah, thereby placing rabbinic literature into a posture of heresy. These rationalist elements in Karaism were as important as the

117

rise of Islamic philosophical and theological rationalism in bringing about the development of rationalist philosophy among Jews from the ninth century onward, both in Babylonia and in Spain.

Despite the wide discrepancy between them on halakic matters, Karaites and Rabbanites intermarried. This intermarriage continued until Rabbi David ibn Zimra of Egypt prohibited it during the sixteenth century, after which Karaism declined and was regarded as prohibited. Karaites used a *ketubah* (marriage certificate), and the bride and groom each protected his or her religious prerogatives by writing them explicitly into the *ketubah*. Karaites observed the same religious days as Rabbanites, but rejected the diaspora second day of the festivals as having no basis in the Torah. They did not observe festivals on the same day as other Jews, because they did not accept the standardized computed rabbinic calendar, but reverted to reliance upon eyewitness testimony to the appearance of the new moon. The Karaites observed the "first day of the seventh month" (Num. 29:1; Neh. 8:9), but rejected the Rabbanite view of Rosh Hashanah, and with it all of the ideas related to this holy day as a time of creation, repentance, judgment, and the ramifications thereof—in sum the entire theology of Rosh Hashanah. Similarly, Karaites rejected rabbinic halakah related to ritual slaughter and the making of wine, and eschewed the meat and wine of a Rabbanite Jew, a condition which was reciprocated by Rabbanites.

Doctrinally the Karaites differed little from Rabbanites as far as articles of theological belief were concerned. Elijah Basyatchi summarized Karaite theology in ten principles which are strikingly similar to the thirteen of Maimonides. These ten principles included: (1) creation; (2) the eternity of God; (3) the oneness of God; (4) the supremacy of Moses; (5) the revelation as given to Moses; (6) the truth of prophecy; (7) resurrection; (8) reward and punishment; (9) the messianic idea; and (10) the requirement that believers know Scripture. Of these ten Maimonides did not include the last principle. For his part, Basyatchi rejected Maimonides's principle that the two Torahs—written and interpretative—are a complete whole. Furthermore, Basyatchi did not include (although Karaism did not reject) Maimonides's doctrines that God knows human actions and that God alone is worthy of worship. Basyatchi regarded these as self-evident in his doctrine of God.

The liturgy of the Karaites was generally confined to Psalms and other biblical passages, eliminating rabbinic accretion. Later Karaites allowed nonbiblical compositions to be used in their liturgy, and even hymns composed by non-Karaites. They instituted the traditional prayer quorum of ten and used the fringed prayer shawl. As happened in Rabbinism, diverse prayerbooks arose among Karaites. They rejected the *maarib* (evening worship) because they considered it to be of rabbinic origin, and maintained the biblical twice-daily worship represented by the morning and afternoon *oleh tamid* sacrifice (the perpetual whole burnt offering). Many elements of the liturgy which Karaites shared with Rabbanites were nevertheless regularly differentiated. Thus the *berakah* (blessing) form was retained in Karaism on an extensive basis, but the wording was varied to hew more closely to biblical phrases. Interestingly, despite their intense affinity with Scripture, because the Torah included no festival for the purpose, the Karaites observed no festival in honor either of revelation or of rejoicing in the Torah akin to the rabbinic approach to Shabuot and to Simhat Torah, respectively. They simply celebrated the Torah on the Sabbath, when the reading of Genesis was begun each year in the renewal of the cycle of pentateuchal readings.

There were times when Karaites might have constituted the majority of the Jewish community. Certainly they were very numerous in the Ottoman empire, and when they predominated, their writers referred to the Rabbanites as "dissenters." Otherwise the Karaites were the great dissenters of Jewish history, setting an interesting precedent for the modern Reform and Conservative movements. They did not become more numerous and spread everywhere, and failed to gain permanent mass adherence, but rather declined, because of several factors. First, the raw political power of Rabbinism suppressed and isolated them. Second, the ascetic strain upheld by Karaism was unattractive to the masses. Third, despite the fact that it was a dissenting movement, it represented a status-quo approach compared to the dynamism of Rabbinism. Religions which show adaptability and successful acculturation to new societies, yet preserve their basic tenets as a perennial stream of tradition, have greater promise of survival and growth. Leniency in the halakah is a hallmark of Rabbinism which Karaism never emulated. Joyous festivals became days of self-denial; liturgy was deprived of the warmth and extensive variety of that of the rabbinic synagogue. Finally, Rabbinic Judaism's capacity to adapt to changing circumstances enabled it to flourish and enter the modern world in its wide variety of religious expression. The less adaptable conservatism inherent in Karaism resulted in its decreasing vitality as a major expression of Judaism.

II. GLORY AND TRAGEDY

A. England

Although Jewish settlement and the practice of Judaism in England during Roman times and its perseverance into Norman times are attested, little is known of it until the records of the twelfth century evince expansion, prosperity, and security for Jews in England. Thus, the effort to build an Anglo-Judaic center had an auspicious beginning but was early aborted.

It appears that the so-called blood libel against Jews, which arose in Europe from time to time, originated in England ca. 1144, when the Jews of Norwich were accused of torturing a Christian child before Easter and hanging him crucifixion-style on Good Friday. The "blood accusation," in its various forms and locales, basically alleged that Jews killed Christian children at Easter time either in order to reenact the crucifixion or to use the child's blood in their Passover observance, or both. Despite the patent absurdity of the charge and the fact that it was never proven and was repeatedly denounced by a sequence of popes, the libel was often resurrected in England and elsewhere. In England, it was said to have played a role in the expulsion of Jews by Edward I in 1290. That expulsion ended the Anglo-Judaic center for four centuries. Although sporadic settlement and religious life did continue mysteriously and quietly from 1290 to 1700, Judaism did not begin to flourish again in England until the eighteenth century. By then, the heart of Judaism was in eastern Europe, and the center of modernistic trends was in Germany and a few select areas in central Europe. The development of a significant English-speaking Judaic center had to await the growth of Jewish immigration to the New World.

In medieval English society, as in all of medieval Europe, Jews were not citizens of the countries in which they resided, but lived by their own halakah, governed by special charters granted by kings. The English Jewish community had rabbis, known in documents of thirteenth-century England as *Rav* in Hebrew and *magister* in Latin. Another functionary of Jews in England was the Jewish consultant to a government agency called the Exchequer of the Jews, which dealt with monetary tallages and tithes of Jews. The office of this consultant, known as *Presbyter Judaeorum* (literally, "the Jewish elder") has too frequently been misinterpreted as an early form of "Chief Rabbi." Careless English scribes often called him *sacerdos* or *pontifex,* thus connoting a sacred, clerical function. In reality, however, the Presbyter was not a religious functionary, this role having been filled by the *Magister-Rav*. It is possible that even the *Magister* was not always a rabbi, and that some rabbis were called *Dayan Umoreh Tzedek* (literally, "judge and teacher of righteousness"), another documented title used in the thirteenth century. This particular title, being so intimately related to the chief figure of the Dead Sea Scrolls, might have been attractive to some Karaites, and its presence in England might attest to the presence of Karaites there, an otherwise obscure matter. The only other singularly interesting item pointing to a Karaite presence in England is the evidence of serious scholarly activity to preserve the biblical text, which was a specialization of Karaites.

The Jews of England at that time spoke French, which, along with their stone houses—a symbol of affluence—did not endear them to the English, and only exacerbated their already basic isolation as a result of religious separation. But since the time of Henry II they were slowly acculturating to English life. They had highly organized synagogues with at least two paid officials: the *shohet,* who prepared meat according to ritually appropriate norms; and a *chanteur,* or cantor, who conducted the worship. As on the continent, the office of salaried rabbis was not yet in evidence.

From the sparse number of English Jewish scholars who became historical figures, it is generally thought that English Jews drew their religious inspiration, leadership, and learning from the continent. But this continental influence must not be overemphasized at the expense of undervaluing English autonomy and the quality of Jewish spiritual life. A number of scholars there were cited in continental commentaries and were regarded as significant authorities. Continental bibliophiles attest to the proliferation of books among England's Jews where Judaica libraries abounded. Jewish grammarians, exegetes, and talmudists flourished in England. Original works were written there, among them halakic digests and works of liturgy, including original compositions for synagogue use, as well as commentaries and a lexicon. Roger Bacon learned Hebrew during the thirteenth century from Jewish grammarian Masoretes.

Continental halakists might have preferred not to share authority with the English, but that the English scholars were not to be slighted as insignificant is evident from the stream of visiting continental scholars who found it worthwhile to go to England and who are listed in English books. Apparently, Rabbi Moses ben Isaac, who composed a lexicon, was styled "son of a countess" (in Hebrew: *hanassiah*). It appears that Jewish life and learning had sufficiently progressed in England so as to produce a typical halakic variegation and disputation. The presence of the thirteenth-century German variety of *hasid* (devout one) in England is attested, and from a dispute over observance of the Sabbath, it is clear that other sectarians were there. These sectarians argued that the Sabbath commenced at dawn on Saturday morning and ended at dawn on Sunday morning. Both the Rabbanites and Karaites, who believed the Sabbath begins and ends at sundown, regarded this view of the Sabbath, held by a sect on Cyprus, as heterodox.

By the time of the expulsion in 1290, Judaic learning had made much progress, and the historic tendency of recognizing local authority was at work in England. English Jews had their own prayerbook, a liturgy ostracized by the well-known Judah the Hasid, who objected to both its additions and omissions. That English Jews were capable of producing their own talmudic-halakic scholars is evident from a careful description of their educational system available to us. The young men were trained in the Targum, the Aramaic translation of Scripture, in order to facilitate their ability to study rabbinic halakah. They had a segment of young men called "the separated ones" *(perushim),* composed of one son of each family dedicated to intensive study for seven years.

The English liturgy perhaps best pointed up English autonomy and therefore called forth the anathema of German Hasidim. However, the expression of heterodox ideas or the omission of traditional theological concepts in the English liturgy was not the cause of tension between the English and German Jews. The hostility between them developed because the English exercised the Jewish inclination to assert local and contemporary authority.

B. Spain

1. The Golden Age (950-1150)

The "Golden Age of Spain" was a period of Jewish participation in the field that might broadly be termed the liberal arts and humanities—especially in poetry, the sciences, finance, and government—in both Islamic and Christian Spain. During this era, Spain also became a major center of Judaic biblical and rabbinic learning, and ultimately of philosophy and the rudimentary stirrings of a resurgence of earlier medieval mysticism. The considerable accomplishments of Jews in Spain in astronomy, mathematics, mapmaking, the navigational arts, trade, guilds, government administration, and diplomacy are of little consequence to the evolution of Judaism and will not detain us here, anymore than such sociopolitical and economic matters will occupy our attention in nineteenth- and twentieth-century Europe and North America.[4]

It is important, in focusing on the evolution and great flourishing of Judaic religious and philosophical writing, to redefine the "Golden Age" of Judaism in Spain as really occurring from 1200 to 1490. Interestingly, the extensive participation of Jews in the sociopolitical and cultural life of Spain did not adversely affect their preservation and expansion of Judaic religious learning and their deepening of spiritual perceptions, especially in the field of religious philosophy. The Judaic experience in Spain reflects vividly how challenge and response relate. The Islamic environmental challenge in the south, especially, brought about what historians have termed a "symbiosis" between Judaism and Islam. On the one hand, the Spanish experience of Judaic acculturation and religious accommodation, accompanied by a deepening of spiritual perspective, followed the Hellenistic paradigm, and in turn has served as a paradigm for succeeding centuries. On the other hand, this acculturation led some rabbis to retrench—to promote separatism and to reject the scientific, philosophical, and literary developments among Jews during the thirteenth-fifteenth centuries.

We know little about Jewish life in Spain from the first century, when Paul yearned to go there and preach the gospel to his fellow Jews, until the ninth century. Spanish Judaism was a variant of Babylonian Judaism. But again, historic diversification manifested itself, and religious practice, if not doctrine, differed from province to province, and even from city to city within a province. Spain received the first published worship order in Judaism from Babylonian *geonim* and sought Babylonian guidance in the early centuries. Ultimately, however, Spanish rabbis asserted their halakic independence and promoted local custom.

Spain began to succeed to leadership in rabbinic learning when Isaac of Fez moved there in the eleventh century and signaled the transfer of the major center of learning from North Africa to southern Europe, not long after Italian scholars moved to the Franco-German Rhineland area and signaled the transfer of major Judaic development to northern Europe. Both centers, however, soon eclipsed both Baby-

---

4. Philosophy and mysticism will be dealt with separately in Chapter Five.

lonia and North Africa. Significant centers arose in Seville, Granada, Cordoba, Barcelona, Toledo, and Malaga. In a way not experienced by the Babylonian *geonim,* however, Spanish Jews were acculturating to all aspects of the flourishing Arabic culture, which posed new challenges of accommodation.

In Jewish adaptation to Arabic culture, poetry played a major role. The composition of liturgical poems and hymns proliferated in Spain, and such major poets as Solomon ibn Gabirol, Abraham ibn Ezra, and Yehuda Halevi are inordinately represented in the prayerbook of the French Rabbi Simhah of Vitry. The poets were also rabbinic scholars and philosophers. The earliest important figure of whom we have knowledge, who gave strong impetus to the religio-intellectual evolution of Spanish Judaism, was Hasdai ibn Shaprut (915-970). As a wealthy patron of learning, he was a forerunner of the modern concept of offering grants, stipends, and fellowships. After him, Samuel ibn Nagrela, or haNagid (993-1063), maintained a "factory" in which he funded scribes to copy manuscripts of prayerbooks, Bibles, and Talmuds, and financed an academy and library at Granada. Ibn Nagrela was himself a philosopher, poet, and rabbinic scholar and wrote a Hebrew dictionary, an introduction to the Talmud, and an important halakic work, *Hilkata Gavrata.* The last work has not survived, but it is described in one of Samuel's poems, where he indicates that an important motivation for him was responding to the challenge of Karaism. Here we have verification of the thesis that Karaism influenced rabbinic learning in that it challenged rabbis to systematize the halakah and to sum up extensive, complex material for easier access in the debate with Karaism.

Samuel played an important role in establishing Spanish Jewish independence from Babylonia by his patronage of Spanish scholars and of literary production and by his personal scholarship and theory of authority. He overstated Spain's role in Judaism as extending to the days of the first exile from Jerusalem (597-587 B.C.E.), but in this way he asserted his independence from Babylonia, just as the Babylonian *geonim* had used the same argument to assert their independence from Palestinian rabbis. At the same time, two other significant scholars compiled considerable halakic collections devoted mainly to the ritual observances of festivals and to liturgy. These efforts were also aimed at establishing an orthodoxy against Karaites. For the average Jew the lines between Karaism and Rabbinism could easily be blurred, for the former adhered to the major theological doctrines (except as they related to the authority and inspiration of rabbis) and were pietistic and messianic. One could easily wonder whether Karaites were not as correct as rabbis in their halakic views, as once the differing options of the schools of Hillel and Shammai were equally accepted. To overcome this blurring of distinction the Spanish rabbis inaugurated a strenuous anti-Karaite program and engaged in severe purges of Karaites.

As was the case with Babylonian *geonim,* Spanish rabbis were prolific in writing responsa. There is historical coincidence between the drying up of the stream of responsa from Babylonia and the beginning of a great flow from Spain, France, and Germany. During the thirteenth and fourteenth centuries, Rabbi Solomon ben Abraham ibn Aderet of Barcelona (1235-1310) and Rabbi Asher ben Yehiel of Toledo (1250-1328) were alone responsible for over four thousand responsa. Through the many disciples he acquired, Rabbi Asher became, in a very real sense, the "father" of contemporary Judaism.

2. The Marranos

Since earliest times, Jews were compelled to undergo conversion to Christianity. These involuntary converts were called *anusim* ("the compelled ones") in the traditional religious literature, and were looked upon more sympathetically than voluntary apostates. This phenomenon was not confined to Spain, but in Spain a very distinct development took place that was historically unprecedented and was not present in France or Germany. This was the development of "marranism," a condition of Jewish life which virtually became a hereditary culture. While some *anusim* frequently returned to Judaism, others remained permanently Christian, raising progeny that remained Christian into the future generations. But some of the Spanish and Portuguese *anusim* underwent a totally different experience. They were baptized into Christianity and lived their outward lives as Christians, attending church and taking the sacraments, but in their private, secret lives, they lived as Jews. As time passed, succeeding generations raised in this manner might have become far less cognizant of their Judaism; yet, out of a sense of preserving a sacred tradition which carried a solemn mystique, they continued to observe certain rudimentary rituals, even if often incorrectly.

The massive problem, which acquired historical notoriety, was the product of an unprecedented summer of violence in 1391, when the Jewish community of Barcelona was decimated and hundreds of thousands of Jews were either massacred or forced into baptism in Aragon and Castille. From then on into the fifteenth century, Jews continued to be forcefully baptized. These Jews were called *Nuevos Cristianos* (New Christians) or *conversos* (converts). In popular terms they were pejoratively referred to as *marranos,* either an old Spanish term meaning "swine," or a word derived from a term meaning "sheep." Although the Church frowned upon this type of mass compulsory conversion, once the person was converted, any deviation from the true faith on the part of the convert constituted "heresy." Marranism, therefore, resulted in the diffusion of a mass of people throughout Christian society that was in contempt of Christian doctrine while pretending to follow it, and that, at the same time, gained prominence in high Church and State positions as "Christians."

The Church understood this condition to open the perpetrators to investigation for heresy. The suspicion was that these so-called Christians took their children to baptism and then washed off the baptism at home; that they received the sacrament of marriage from the priest and then another Judaic marriage rite at home; and that they observed the Sabbath, ate *kasher* meat, practiced circumcision, and secretly sent donations to synagogues. They dissimulated so far that they formed societies under the patronage of a Roman Catholic saint as a front for a religious fellowship in which to observe Judaism.

The "Edict of Faith," issued by the Inquisition when it began its work on the suspects in 1480, lists the Judaic religious practices of the Marranos and exposes the evidence for their culpability of heresy. The sentence of heresy, which required burning at the stake unless the heretic recanted, was known as the *auto de fe* (*auto-da-fé* in Portugal). Although not all scholars agree that the work of the Inquisition was designed to root out heresy among the New Christians, and some argue that it was really aimed at rooting Marranos out of Spain, the evidence more clearly sustains the former. For one thing, the Church defined Jews in terms of religion, so that if Jews became Christians they were perpetually born-again Christians, and deviation on their part opened them to charges of heresy. Second, if there were also racial and political aspects to the anti-Jewish drive in late fifteenth-century Spain, it was due to the yearning of Queen Isabella and King Ferdinand to confiscate Jewish wealth. This motive was the state's parallel to the Church's motive to clear the Jews out of Spain and thereby leave the Marranos rudderless and consequently more likely to settle peacefully into their Christianity. In sum, the goal of the 1480 Inquisition was to purify Marranos by a baptism of fire; the Inquisition, however, was not aimed at Jews. The post-1490 Edict of Expulsion of Jews sought to seize their wealth, and itself stated explicitly that it was aimed at preventing them from further damaging Christianity by their role as paradigm and support for Marranos. That it was not directed at those Jews who were loyal New Christians or Jews willing to convert is evident in the protection it offered these people, and by virtue of its not applying at all to Marranos.

For some decades prior to the expulsion, Judaism in Spain was going through crises. Followers of Averroeist[5] philosophy argued against immortality, creation, and providence. Furthermore, they maintained that Aristotelian natural ethics was superior to the Torah and that all the ritual mitzvot were allegories, and they urged the young to study philosophy rather than the Talmud. Between the Averroeists and *conversos* Judaism was considerably weakened. Reaction to them led to a more inward-oriented and stringent approach to thought and observance, and to mystical speculation. After Islam was driven from the Spanish peninsula and a purely Christian Spain was possible, the Jews were expelled in 1492. Whether Judaism would ever have been regenerated to its "golden age" levels is a moot point, for the expulsion of 1492 settled the destiny of Spanish Judaism.

C. France

The Jewish communities of France were developing as major Judaic centers at the same time as Judaism flourished in Islamic lands from Iran to Portugal. French Jewish centers, like their German counterparts, did not produce the same abundance of poets and philosophers as the communities in Islamic lands. They specialized in breeding talmudists, halakists, and commentators. It can with reason be affirmed that Judaism underwent internal symbiosis. The halakah of the Franco-German rabbis traveled to Spain, and the theology of the philosophers of the Islamic countries from Iran to Spain streamed northward into northern and central Europe. As we will see, the resultant mix of halakah and piety in Germany ultimately gained ascendancy in eastern Europe, and out of that vast reservoir came North American Judaism.

From French scholars came some of the classical commentaries

---

5. Averroeists were followers of the thirteenth-century Arab philosopher ibn Rushd.

on both Bible and Talmud, the former frequently having a profound influence upon Christian scholars. Jews had lived in Gaul since Roman times, and Church councils paid untoward attention to their presence, finding enough of them in the environs to necessitate a ban on Christians marrying them and on Jews converting their slaves to Judaism. It was not until the ninth century, however, that meaningful development of Judaism in France began. Even then little is known of the spiritual life of Jews until the eleventh century. Religious scholarship first became rooted in France at Narbonne in 802, and by the twelfth century a great school existed at Lunel. This school welcomed students from all over, provided free education, room and board, and clothing. It was a school that had precedents in the East and in Spain, but historically might in itself be seen as a paradigm of the east European yeshiva, frequently still emulated in North America. By the twelfth century, the famous traveler Benjamin of Tudela wrote that in France there are scholars "unequalled in the whole world, who study Torah day and night." This was French Judaism at its apex, and it served as the forerunner of the prolific yeshiva culture of eastern Europe some centuries later.

In France, as in Babylonia and Spain, responsa became a major genre of literature, embodying the abundant religious learning and life that transpired there. We know of this activity in the ninth century from a responsum written by an Italian scholar who moved to Germany and wrote to a rabbi in Provence. In fact, northern European scholarship was deeply influenced by antecedents in both Provence, France, and Mayence, Germany. The father of this abundant tradition, who sent forth many disciples, and whose disciples in turn brought French and German halakah to Spain, Poland, Turkey, and back to the East to Palestine, was Rabbi Gershom of Mayence.

Within the confines of this survey it is not possible to discuss even a small number of the dozens of significant rabbinic scholars who flourished throughout the French realms, both in the North and in Provence. It will have to suffice to mention briefly the scholar who wrote what became the classic commentary on Bible and Talmud: Rashi, or Rabbi Solomon ben Isaac of Troyes (1040-1105). Prior to the decimation of the Rhineland communities in the first crusade of 1096, Jewish communities in France took their leadership from Mayence and Worms in Germany. But after that crusade Rashi rose to prominence. His forte was his ability to present lucid and simple explanations of texts. He briefly interpreted terminology, copied out midrashim, and provided philological explanations. He did not write extended excursuses, did not reflect upon great principles, and did not conceptualize. He was not a creative thinker, but he recorded massive explanatory glosses which opened the Bible and Talmud to the novice.

A contemporary of Rashi's, Alfasi, or Rabbi Isaac of Fez, who flourished in Lucena, Spain, was a major halakist upon whose work all later halakah was in some way based. A second contemporary, Nathan ben Yehiel of Rome, composed the *Aruk,* a talmudic lexicon which became an indispensable tool. These three scholars—Alfasi, Rashi, and Rabbi Nathan—became the tripod upon which was erected medieval Judaic studies.

Although Rashi's role in history is not primarily as halakist, he wrote responsa which reflect a relatively conservative position, due to his reluctance to accept innovation, yet sympathy for those who accepted baptism under compulsion. He did not leave a philosophical legacy or a major halakic compilation, but his biblical and talmudic commentaries eventually spread out of northeast France to Provence, and from there across the mountains to Spain and to Italy and on to Africa. They moved through Germany into southern and eastern Europe, and on to Asia. Rabbi Solomon fertilized many a scholar's writing and thinking and indirectly affected philosophy and halakah, thus influencing the future direction of Judaism. His commentaries were so popular that right into the twentieth century they became the first text for children to study after becoming familiar with the Pentateuch and with the Targum. This type of curriculum for youngsters continues to be standard in Orthodox schools today. But even more interesting is how his influence spread through Christian scholarly circles. His commentaries were used by Nicholas de Lyra, and through him and others they passed into the researches and thinking of many Christians, including Martin Luther and John Calvin. It was through Rashi that Christian scholars frequently made their entry into rabbinic literature.[6]

Rashi also influenced liturgy, for there was great dependence upon him by Rabbi Simhah of Vitry. The *Mahzon Vitry (The Cycle of Worship,* composed in the city of Vitry, France) was a comprehensive compilation of the liturgy and of the halakah relating to it. Furthermore, Rashi had a powerful influence upon his sons-in-law and grandsons, who were the pillars of a group of scholars over several generations called Tosafists, those who compiled the Tosafot (Supplements),

---

6. More will be said of this in Chapter Five.

a commentary on the Talmud, largely the work of German scholars. Through these Tosafists the influence of Rashi passed through to Rabbi Meir of Rothenburg, who became a conduit of learning and thought to eastern Europe, and to Rabbi Asher ben Yehiel, who moved from Germany to Toledo, Spain. Rashi's work also became a conduit to Rabbi Joseph Karo, whose compilation of halakah, the *Shulhan Aruk,* became the backbone of eastern European Orthodoxy.

As German scholarship had fertilized France through the disciples of Rabbi Gershom, the French scholars bequeathed their influence to the Germans through Rabbi Meir of Rothenburg and Mordecai ben Hillel. The latter's commentary-halakic abridgment on the Talmud became a leading resource and was ultimately almost canonized by Rabbi Moses Isserles, whose notes on the *Shulhan Aruk* made that work palatable to eastern European Jews and made possible its increasing hegemony in the sixteenth and seventeenth centuries. In this way, a great chain stretched from tenth-century Rabbi Gershom of Mayence to seventeenth-century Poland and Russia. And when the scholars of eastern and central Europe began to migrate to North America during the nineteenth century, they brought with them a religious perspective and a religious culture that had been influenced in concentric circles from small centers of northern France and the Rhineland since the tenth century. Through these tenth-, eleventh-, and twelfth-century scholars of France and Germany, the talmudic centers of these countries gained ascendancy from Spain to India. They eclipsed Babylon, North Africa, and Spain, until they were in turn eclipsed by those of Poland, Lithuania, and Russia.

D. Germany

Unverified legend attributes the effective founding of Jewish learning in Germany to Charlemagne (742-814), when he invited the Italian Rabbi Kalonymus from Lucca to settle in Mayence. There might, however, have been a historical conflation with an ancestor of this Rabbi Kalonymus, for Rabbi Kalonymus (author of the earliest surviving European rabbinic literature) lived from 880 to 960. From the earliest times German rabbis, like their French and Spanish counterparts, asserted their halakic independence. Thus Rabbi Gershom said that his teacher Rabbi Leontin had opinions "more acceptable to [him]" than those of the Babylonian *geonim.*

Rabbi Gershom (960-1028) is partially an enigma, little being known of his life. But his learning was so widely cited and his disciples so numerous that he was called "Light of the Diaspora." His responsa are the primary remains of his work. These exhibit his intellectual mastery and independence of judgment. His views on apostasy, polygamy, and divorce revolutionized Judaism. He rejected the notion that Christianity was to be subsumed under the rubric *abodah zarah* (idolatry). His teaching was subsequently followed by Rashi and became the consensus among Jewish sages since. Rabbi Gershom put an end to polygamy among Jews, still technically permitted by both the Bible and the Talmud, but we do not have the original text and cannot be certain of his reasoning. A third major halakic position he advanced was prohibiting the divorce of a wife without her consent.

In one area Rabbi Gershom was stymied. He preferred mandatory communal decision and brought about his changes by decisions of synods or councils. Traditionally, however, Jewish religious life and halakic decision making were not governed by synods, but by the scholarly conclusion of a specialist whose authority was accepted within a given area. It rested upon individualism and rabbinic independence. While there were advantages to Rabbi Gershom's view, which would mandate that a majority decision be followed by all, this would have the potential of stultifying ritual life and circumventing the classical concept of halakic options being available to followers of diverse schools of thought. The French scholars, especially in later generations, led by the arguments of Rabbi Tam, grandson of the famed Rashi, prevented the hegemony of community council decisions or the expanded control of federations of communities and preserved the classical concept of the supremacy of individual authority and rabbinic independence. Although the German scholars later agreed with their German predecessors and Rabbi Meir ben Baruk of Rothenburg favored the synodal system, and although such efforts were attempted from time to time in eastern Europe, they ultimately failed. Individualistic authority and a form of congregationalism retained their hegemony and have remained essentially the Judaic religious pattern among all denominations.

Rabbi Gershom stands out, in a sense, as a founder of both German and French talmudism. After the remarkable growth of the two communities through equally remarkable vicissitudes, including riots, massacres, compulsory baptism, and expulsions which decimated Jewish communities, the level of learning and religious life remained high. Eventually, however, socioeconomic and political hardships took their toll. The closing chapter of medieval German Jewry was largely dominated by Rabbi Meir ben Baruk of Rothenburg (1215-1293). In the unprecedented mass slaughter of Jews in 1336-37, and after the Black Death of 1348-49, the medieval German experience approached its end.

Rabbi Meir attracted the most brilliant disciples, and through them he placed his stamp upon Judaism for over five centuries. Only within the rising modern movements after 1750 did rabbis and scholars turn to a Rabbi Meir or a Rashi as research resources rather than definitive authorities.[7]

One aspect of Hasidism was its emphasis that every prayer, every ritual formula, and every halakic pattern had to be precise and consistent. Religious behaviorism became immensely significant. Rabbi Meir aided this process, or responded to it, as is evident from his writings—especially his responsa—and by his devotion to the minutiae of ritual observance. Rabbi Meir also dampened the traditional ardor for contemporary authority by stressing the authority of past scholars, particularly such intellectual giants as the *geonim,* Rabbi Alfasi, Maimonides, and his own teachers and peers among the Tosafists. Yet, with all his pietism and devotion to the past, he retained the open-door policy to innovation by stressing that the talmudic rabbis always considered the public interest, and that priority must be given to intergroup relations when Jews live in a predominantly Christian society. Nevertheless, it was his pietistic and authority-oriented side that became the legacy of future generations of eastern European Judaism. German Judaism itself might have been dealt a mortal blow by a synod in Frankfort in 1603, which was loyal to that form of piety. The synod was designed to regenerate German Judaism, but what was really attempted there was to restore the impositions of the thirteenth century. There were no new or imaginative ideas on how to confront the new world arising out of humanism, the Renaissance and Reformation, and scientific discoveries and explorations.

After a long series of repeated attacks and expulsions during the fourteenth century, the fifteenth century witnessed a consistently deteriorating Judaic community life, and with the banishment of the Jews of Rothenburg in 1520, Jewish learning and spiritual life in Germany effectively ended. Much of the problem was the result of political chaos in Germany itself, which was a medley of nationalities and

---

7. During the thirteenth century both Christianity and Judaism experienced a pietistic revival, and this brought forth the thirteenth-century Hasidic movement in Germany, to be discussed in Chapter Five.

tribes, and made Jews unexpectedly vulnerable throughout Germanic lands. Spreading peasant and worker social revolution during the fourteenth century indicated how exposed the Jews were as convenient scapegoats. Their status under state law and their status in the eyes of Christian theology both militated against recovery at that time. Out of the vicissitudes of German realities was born mysticism, the kabalist movement, and the detailed ritualism which were passed on to Poland, Lithuania, Galicia, Hungary, and Russia. The element of Christian-Jewish relations, however, is not to be underestimated. While Christian theology had much to do with Jewish suffering, no straight line should be drawn from medieval Church documents to Auschwitz, nor should the coincidence of one form of German persecution during the Middle Ages and another form from 1933 to 1945 be used as support for a racial judgment on the nature of Germans.

III. CHRISTIAN-JEWISH RELATIONS

The medieval relationship between Christians and Jews existed on two levels. One was the secular level, including the everyday commercial relationship of customers and tradespeople, or the social contacts among neighbors, which were often quite friendly. The other level was the theological, the formal position taken by Christian theology that pronounced Judaism to be subordinate to Christianity and regarded all Jews as potential converts and subjects of evangelization. Frequently the two levels were blurred. Theological subordination led to secular animosity and governmental suppression of Jews and Judaism. This suppression often took the form of special oppressive taxation, confiscation of property, and expulsion of Jews from cities or regions, or, as in the case of England in 1290, from the entire country. These processes are known from the earliest western European Church councils.

The basic papal policy, formulated by Gregory the Great (590-604), declared that Jews were to receive the protection of law, but were not to exceed the privileges the law gives them to live in Christian countries and to practice their religion freely. Letters reformulating this basic attitude to protect Jews from unjust attacks and riots as well as compulsory baptism were issued by a great number of popes. In time this view was titled in canon law as *Constitutiones pro Iudaeis*. Even those people who preferred that the conversion of Jews take place sooner rather than later saw this conversion as happening in God's own time. Thus the policy of conversion was really theological expectation rather than program. There were exceptions to this policy, such as Nicholas III, who in 1278 instructed Franciscans and Dominicans to preach to Jews. In contrast to this, in 1422 Pope Martin V wrote to monks of the same order that their type of activity in rousing the people against Jews caused Jews to persist in their refusal to convert. But he had no intention of programming such conversion. Conversionary sermons directed by the papacy did not actually begin before 1548, when Pope Gregory XIII suggested they be delivered each Sabbath, and preferably in Hebrew.

This brief reference to a few popes over many centuries reveals what error can arise from speaking of Christian-Jewish relations as if we are confronted by a monolithic process. The relations, the laws, the suffering, and the privileges differed from country to country and from century to century. Thus violent suppression of Judaism was attempted early in Spain by the Visigothic king Sisebut in 613, and by the Frankish king Dagobert in France as early as 633. Yet Spanish Judaism flourished. In 1182, Philip II Augustus of France expelled all Jews from his realms for several reasons. One reason was the belief that Jews killed a Christian each Easter as a surrogate for the re-crucifixion of Jesus, in contempt of Christianity. Probably the more authentic reason was that Jews seized church vessels as surety for loans and possessed huge real estate holdings in Paris. Although Jews were recalled in 1198, French Judaism was never again the same.

Historians have documented a high degree of social interaction among Jews and Christians in France. Jews used the French language and took French names, indulged in local fashion in dress, and had neighborly relations with each other. The *Sepher Hasidim,* a major pietistic work written in Germany, disapproved of Jewish acculturation in France as it had of independent English liturgy. Yehudah ben Samuel writes, "As are the customs of the gentiles so are the customs of the Jews in the majority of places."

The view of some historians that the Crusades, and therefore 1096, was a watershed for Jewish life in medieval Europe is overstated. At Rouen, for instance, the crusaders applied rigorous logic when they argued, "After traversing great distances, we desire to attack the enemies of God in the East, although the Jews, of all races the worst foe of God, are before our eyes. That is doing our work backward."[8] The

---

8. Robert Chazan, *Medieval Jewry in Northern France* (Baltimore: Johns Hopkins University Press, 1972), p. 26.

subsequent massacre spared all Jews who accepted Christianity. Nevertheless, Rouen was an exception in France. The Rhineland suffered more severely in the first and in subsequent crusades. Yet it remains a fact of history that these lands were populated by large masses of immigrating Jews all through the twelfth and subsequent centuries, and the great centers of learning continued to thrive. Indeed, King William II of England and Normandy allowed the Jews who were baptized under compulsion in the attack on Rouen to return to Judaism without penalty, and Emperor Henry IV of Germany offered the same indulgence to Jews there.

These forced conversions, exacerbated at different times by massive anti-Jewish riots, by the successive crusades, or by the masses gone mad at such junctures as the Black Death of 1348, produced many apostates in the Jewish community. That there were also many Jews who voluntarily became Christian—for socioeconomic advancement, or out of a genuine religious experience—is reflected in the responsa throughout the period. Usually the question of apostasy involved the status of a person who wished to reintegrate himself or herself into Judaism, or a descendant of an apostate who wished to do so. Rashi expresses the tone of most halakic decisions by adopting the position of the earlier Rabbi Gershom, who was lenient in matters of apostasy. Rashi writes, "the general rule is: an apostate has the status of a Jew suspected of heresy."[9] But since it carried with it the obverse, that the apostate was still really a Jew and therefore subject to the halakah, it could also cause much undue hardship in exceptional situations. For example, some scholars insisted on this basis that an apostate must still serve as a *levir*[10] to free his widowed sister-in-law, through the rite of *halitzah,* a ritual which symbolically sets the widow free. This view ran counter to the older halakah of the *geonim* who said the levirate ceremony was not necessary and could result in such a widow never being eligible for remarriage. For an apostate went off frequently to distant places to start a new life, or might be indifferent and unwilling to participate in what he regarded as a bizarre rite of his erstwhile Jewish coreligionists. This condition gave rise to the famous problem

9. Cited by Irving Agus, *Urban Civilization in Pre-Crusade Europe* (New York: Yeshiva University Press, 1968), pp. 707-708.

10. A *levir* is the brother of a deceased man who is obligated to marry his childless widow. If the *levir* refuses to fulfill this responsibility, he must undergo the ceremony of *halitzah,* whereby the widow removes his sandal and spits in his face (Deut. 25:5-9).

of the *agunah* ("the chained one"), a woman bound to her first husband who had abandoned her. In modern times this condition exists when the *levir* refuses to perform *halitzah,* regarding it to be offensive to his religious perceptions, or when a husband refuses to execute a ritual divorce after he and his wife have been divorced civilly. In all of the foregoing instances the woman is unable to remarry. This hardship has persisted for the Orthodox to the present time, although it is no longer related to the problem of apostasy. The Reform movement abandoned both *halitzah* and ritual divorce in the nineteenth century, and both Reform men and women may remarry after a civil divorce. Although the Conservative movement has preserved both *halitzah* and ritual divorce, it has circumvented the *agunah* difficulty by vastly modifying the requirement of *halitzah* and even waiving it, and by instituting annulment proceedings conducted by an ecclesiastical tribunal.

Theologically, Jews were entitled to save their lives by accepting baptism under compulsion. Judaism required martyrdom only under very limited circumstances (B. San. 74a). Martyrdom was common during medieval times, and there was prolific memorialization of those who died *al kiddush hashem* ("for the sanctification of the Name [of God]"), as martyrdom was called. Mass suicides frequently took the place of mass conversions; especially in the Rhineland, during the First Crusade, whole communities participated in killing one another. Such instances were inspired by extremely devout townspeople or rabbis. But the individual who submitted to baptism was entitled to bear no stigma. Public baptism, attendance at church, even genuflections to church dignitaries were not considered idolatrous; and when such Jews reverted to Judaism they were not to be reminded of their prior lapse.

The Second and Third Crusades also took their toll in Germany, but they did not affect French Judaism. The celebrated Bernard of Clairvaux preached against harming Jews during the Second Crusade, arguing, "They are living symbols for us, reminding us always of the Lord's Passion. . . . When the time is ripe all Israel shall be saved."[11] In this way, the ecclesiastical leaders often prevented the unruly mobs from venting their frustration and fury upon the Jews in the path of the crusading hordes. The paradox in this situation is that, on the one hand, the theological power which declared the subordination of Judaism, and therefore left Jews vulnerable to attack, humiliation, and disability, frequently protected and saved them. On the other hand, the secu-

---

11. See Baron, *Social and Religious History of the Jews,* IV, 121-22.

lar power, through whose agency everyday social and economic life of the community exhibited quite good relationships with Jews on a one-to-one basis, was found wanting in times of crisis. They frequently unleashed the restive peasant mobs and allowed them a diversion from rebellion and insurrection by scapegoating the Jew. They worked their will upon the Jews, to whom they were in debt or of whom they were envious because they were not frozen in the lowest step of a rigid feudal hierarchy.

The envy of the peasant was undoubtedly natural. Mention has been made earlier of the stone houses built by English Jews. Similarly, French Jews were described as wealthy from gain by usury and exploitation. And frequently the parish priest could arouse his people by reminding them that the Jewish moneylender holds the Church's ritual objects and sacred relics as surety for loans. But this situation could not have sufficed for the decline, for instance, of the French center. Rather, these historical collapses must be viewed from the perspective of the historic coalescence of three personalities complementing one another. France can serve as a paradigm.

The first was Pope Innocent III, one of the greatest occupants of the papacy, the first to call himself "Vicar of Christ." The second was King Louis IX of France, a devout son of the Church. The third was Nicholas Donin, an exceptional Jewish convert. Louis IX, "the Saint," reigned from 1226 to 1270, and was as devoted to reminding the Jew of his destiny to suffer as he was to overwhelming the Islamic "infidel." His campaign against Jewish usury as oppression of Christians destroyed the economic base of French Jews. Donin's campaign against the Talmud, as a perversion of faith and as morally offensive as well as blasphemous of Jesus and Christianity, undermined the Jew's spiritual resources.

The papacy was now, as generally, seeking to protect the physical well-being of the Jew, and a papal critique of thirteenth-century anti-Jewish suppression was issued, which said, "Such kindliness must be shown to Jews by Christians as we hope might be shown to Christians who live in pagan lands." But while the Church was correct that Jews could live without usury, it was blind to think they could live without their religious books upon which a massive assault was being made in western Europe in the thirteenth century, highlighted by the famous burning of the Talmud at Paris in 1242.

The condemnation of the Talmud led to emigration by students and rabbis, an end to immigration of foreign students, and the decline of great academies at Rameru, Dampierre, and Paris. Simultaneously, conversions of learned Jews to Christianity increased. It was through some of these converts—Nicholas Donin, Theobold of Sens, and Pablo Christiani among them—that wider avenues were formed along which Judaic rabbinic learning passed to Christian scholars and ultimately influenced the Reformation.

The inspiration of this turn in Jewish-Christian relations during the thirteenth century was Pope Innocent III. His theological presuppositions were canonized at the Fourth Lateran Council in 1215 and governed Jewish-Catholic relations, more or less, until Vatican II. The Reformation and rise of nationalism and democracy, however, made for massive mitigations of Innocent's theology in the actual life of the Jew in Protestant countries. Later, emancipation was secured in secular democracies during the period from the seventeenth to the nineteenth centuries. Meanwhile, the theological underpinnings stressed by Innocent III made for very serious tension during the thirteenth century and beyond.

Innocent III initiated no new theological concepts. He merely emphasized that the need to subordinate Judaism to Christianity validated laws suppressing Jews in their socioeconomic and political status. In this way Jews would more intensely be subjected to impoverishment, segregation, and degradation. Laws that assured this humiliating condition were hundreds of years old, and few new ones were needed. However, the renewal of old laws long neglected went on apace. Behind all this persecution was the ancient theological doctrine that Jews were condemned to eternal servitude, as Augustine had proclaimed in exegesis of Genesis 25:23, where Esau the elder is doomed to serve Jacob the younger. Augustinian exegesis had placed the Jew into the position of Esau and the Church into the position of Jacob. The Jews, by their degradation, were to expiate their sin of the crucifixion. Innocent III referred repeatedly to this theological premise and strengthened it, while its theological credibility was underscored by St. Thomas Aquinas (1225-1274).

There were times when Jews were compelled to hear Christian sermons. Bishop Robert Grosseteste of Leicester helped Jews avert expulsion for over twenty years in the hope that he would convert them. That neither the Church nor the State was able to find a solution to the problem of living with Jews goes deeper than Jewish usury, coin clipping, or wealth. Christians practiced usury, amassed great wealth, and were guilty of many crimes against the state. The basis of the Christian-Jewish tension was theological, and was in some deep and inexplicable manner an atavistic fear and anxiety deeply embedded in the Christian psyche. The crucifixion hovered over all, and medieval theorists were persuaded that one must either abandon the theology of Jewish culpability for the crucifixion or act on its reality. They apparently failed to grasp the fact that Jewish culpability in the year 30 or so had nothing to do with living Jews in their own day. They were as yet incapable of discovering a format of dialogue with Jews that transcended the concept of debate. In debate after debate in medieval Europe, the object was not to reach mutual understanding but to prove the truth of Christianity to the Jews and to convert them to that truth.

Although the Church had taught, since the beginning, that the Jews remain the covenant people, it was incapable of liberating itself from a theological dilemma: it taught, on the one hand, that Judaism must be subordinated, and, on the other hand, that Christians must desist from harming Jews. A study of Pope Innocent III reveals a microcosm of this ambivalence. His emphasis upon the perpetual servitude of the Jew, taken from the exegesis of Genesis 25:23, led Frederick II in 1236, "faithful to the duties of a Catholic prince," to exclude all Jews from any public office in his Germanic lands. This exclusion was a disability never suffered in Spain and not a formal factor in France or England. The *Berliner Stadtbuch* of 1397 finally reached a crescendo in this medieval tension. While it was secular state law, its provisions for Jews were wholly founded upon theological conceptions. Jews were allowed to live in a Christian country, it stated, only because of the gratitude Christians owed to Jews. Furthermore, Christians were obligated to Jews because the Torah was the testimony for Jesus, and Jesus' humanity was taken from their forefathers. Moreover, the law maintained, there was hope of converting them and they were a remembrance of Christ.

Church policy inspired State policy, and Church policy was an inevitable product of Church doctrine. Furthermore, the Roman Catholic Church was a universal forum and an ecumenical institution, its law and influence stretching across Europe and thereby creating an international problem for Jews. To this extent, canon law is to be faulted for Jewish suffering during the Middle Ages. While Innocent III was a leading proponent in subjecting the Jew to degradation, he was merely reviving the oldest Christian policies and doctrines. Laws that subjected Jews to a variety of socioeconomic and political disabilities go back to the fourth century, even before Christianity fell heir to Roman imperial power. The Council of Elvira, in 306, had already begun the parade of prohibitions against Jews. Myriads of laws were repeatedly renewed in medieval Spain, France, Germany, and elsewhere, because Christians were not obeying and enforcing them. Laws were passed between 300 and 800 by Roman emperors, by Visigothic and Frankish kings, and by Church councils. These laws ran the gamut from serious economic restrictions to silly rules, such as prohibiting a Christian from eating unleavened bread with a Jew. These laws were still basically the same ones enforced between 800 and 1700 in varying degrees in different places.

Christian theological antagonism affected the development of European Judaism in a wide variety of ways. But above all, it enforced a separation upon the Jew which in some ways crippled the Jew's self-identification. The ghetto succeeded in making Jews different, and into modern times many a Jew's psyche is still strongly dominated by a tendency to separatism, a condition which leads to much ambiguity over self-identification as ethnic unit or religious group. When Franks first conquered Gaul, they found Jews in a typical state of acculturation, speaking Latin and having Roman names. That eastern European Jews in the nineteenth century were rooted in a Yiddish culture, were largely inward oriented, and lived by a multiplication of ritualistic minutiae is a product of Innocent III's fidelity to an ancient theological exegesis which stood the Bible on its head. That exegesis made the Jew into Esau and the Christian into Jacob, and eventually gave rise to the ghetto.

This cursory review of Christian-Jewish relations would not be complete without emphasizing that papal policy varied, and frequently popes, bishops, and priests defended Jews. Reference was made earlier, for instance, to Pope Martin V, who opposed Franciscan preachers that aroused people against Jews in 1422 and again in 1429. Yet, as Innocent III furthered a process which was often neglected—the subordination of Judaism by having its visible symbol, the Jew, degraded—Pope Paul IV, in 1555, sealed the process by instituting the ghetto. The ghetto was not a formal arrangement during earlier centuries, although at times in different places local laws restricted Jews to special residential quarters, as in Castile, Spain, under what are termed the laws of Valladolid. Generally, however, when Jews lived in self-contained neighborhoods they did so voluntarily for religious convenience (walking distance to a synagogue, *kasher* food, and life-cycle celebrations with family and friends). These neighborhoods were not legally set aside for Jewish occupation, however, and Jews were not confined to them. Paul IV changed that situation with his Papal Bull *Cum nimis absurdum*, July 17, 1555. In this bull he also labored at changing the ancient policy of not pressing conversion upon the Jews, by linking toleration of Jews to their recognizing the need to shed their error and see the light of Catholic faith. From the time of Paul IV to the nineteenth century, the papacy conducted an active evangelical program to win Jews to the Church. Paul IV drastically reversed a course which had taken some liberal turns during the sixteenth century. Pope Leo X had employed Jewish physicians and allowed Jews to teach at some universities. Undoubtedly, the Renaissance and Reformation and the consequent upheavals in the Roman Catholic domain inspired Paul IV to his drastic changes. What Paul IV basically did was to enforce all restrictions and remove all leniencies in Christian relationships with Jews. He carried laws ten centuries old, aimed at subordinating the Jew, to their logical conclusion. In order to be sure there would be no relationship which might contaminate the Christian, and in order to offer no opportunity for a Jew to lord it over Christians, the Jew was to be wholly segregated from any contact with Christians.

There is also another side to the coin of Christian-Jewish relations—the attitude of Jews toward Christianity. The Jewish attitude had its practical results, and undoubtedly served both to buttress Jewish anxiety and to frustrate Christians. Jews did not eschew their belief in the doctrine of the election until modern times, and even then it remains articulated among most religious groups and in the standard liturgy. The traditional view was that all gentiles fall into the category of "sons of Noah," and as such are obligated to the rabbinic "seven mitzvot of the sons of Noah," or as often termed, the Noahide Commandments. The righteous gentile achieves salvation, but for Judaism that implied that the righteous gentile will abide by those standards set by Judaism. The Jewish attitude toward the salvation of any gentile, Christian or otherwise, would revolve around that requirement. No amount of Jewish physical and mental suffering and social degradation caused Jews to doubt their election and their possession of the revealed truth. When much suffering and degradation did cause such doubt, Jews were more susceptible to converting to Christianity or to Islam.

Jews regarded Christianity as monotheistic, but they did not regard Christians as being in covenant with God. They sometimes included them in the general designation of *umot haolam* (the nations of the world) of rabbinic literature, offering them a higher status than the other nations for their monotheism, but not a covenantal status. Where rabbinic halakah appeared most discriminatory against pagans, medieval rabbis excluded Christians. But if Christian exegesis identified the Jew as Esau, synagogue liturgical poetry (the *piyyutim*) and midrashim clearly taught that Esau, formerly a symbol of the Roman empire, now referred to the Church. It must be underscored that, although Jews suffered much physical, mental, and emotional misery at the hands of Christians, this suffering did not weaken their vigorous apologia for the faith. When Christian theologians argued that the threefold reference to God in the Shema (Deut. 6:4), "Hear, O Israel, the *Lord* our *God,* the *Lord* is one," prefigures the Trinity, Jewish scholars countered that the verse explicitly rejects this concept by stressing the oneness of God. Rabbi Moses of Coucy, a thirteenth-century scholar, seems to have undertaken a speaking itinerary through France and Spain in 1236. It can be assumed that he urged the people to persistence in their faith with the same words he wrote in his *Sepher Mitzvot Gadol,* a halakic compendium. There he wrote that God told Moses He would directly reveal His Word at Sinai to all Israel (Exod. 19:9), in order that in later times, when Christians and Moslems claimed they had miracles and signs that showed the Torah was superseded, the Jew could respond that even a multiplicity of signs means nothing, that they must hear the very voice of God declaring it. So too Rabbi Moses of Coucy preached that the meaning of the end of the book of Malachi, "I will send you Elijah the prophet" (4:5; 3:23 in Hebrew), is that there will be no more prophets until God sends Elijah to herald the messiah, and that until Elijah comes nobody should be accepted as a prophet.

Christians had the eschatological (end-time) expectation of Jewish conversion. The reverse was no less true. Medieval Jewish scholars saw ancient rabbinic statements of gentile affiliation with Judaism preceding the actual day of redemption. Whereas popes often argued that kindness would do more to bring Jews into the Church, rabbis argued conversely that by being upright and moral and setting the highest example of how the people of God are to live, Jews would attract the gentile to Judaism. In times of severe trial and crisis, such as the thirteenth century, some rabbis were so incensed at Christians that they uncharacteristically referred to them as idolaters, which was undoubtedly one way they hoped to deter Jewish conversions. But when these occurred, as mentioned earlier, many halakic leniencies were applied to the apostate. Even the pietistic *Sepher Hasidim* takes a positive attitude to allowing apostates to contribute Torah scrolls to synagogues and to accepting charity from them. The reasoning was always quite logical: that at heart apostates remain Jews, and therefore all positive gestures on their part should be graciously received. There were, after all, recorded cases of Jews who became Christians by conviction, became priests, and then recanted and reentered the Jewish faith.

While Jewish conversion to the majority faith is an understandable process, Christian conversion to Judaism in an age when Jews lived on the edge of a precipice is an enigma. Moreover, one could never know when the authorities would invoke the law requiring capital punishment and the confiscation of the property of the Jew who converted a Christian to Judaism. That the Jew risked life and property to teach and to receive proselytes attests to the strong countervailing Jewish attitude to that of the Christian that ultimate truth is found in Judaism. The gentile who became a Jew was referred to as *ger tzedeq,* "a righteous proselyte."

Yet to be explored, on a theological and psychological level, is the readiness a Christian had to become a Jew or of a Jew to become a Christian by conviction in a society so heavy with the power, symbolism, and mystique of each faith within its respective parameters. Deep in the psyche of each there must have been an attraction to the other, precisely because each was forbidden fruit to the other. The very incidence of Jewish martyrdom so widespread in the Middle Ages attested to Jewish contempt for Christianity. But it also affirmed the conviction that it was the Jewish role unto death to bear witness as God's people to the Word of God, and that this Word was embodied in Judaism and in no other faith. The two communities have come a distance toward mutual accommodation and mutual recognition during recent decades that would have been unthinkable during the Middle Ages.

Chapter Five

The Medieval Era II:
Philosophy and Mysticism

I. PHILOSOPHY

A. Introduction

The following discussion of medieval Jewish philosophy can only survey highlights. It should also be noted that within the constraints of this essay the terms *philosophy* and *theology* are interchangeable, since my premise is that philosophy which centers around a God-idea is by its very nature a form of theology.

The major impulse for the cultivation of philosophy arose from the need of thinkers to accommodate faith based upon revelation with knowledge acquired through the processes of reason. The Jewish philosophers legitimated going beyond the Bible and rabbinic literature for their understanding of religion by arguing that although revelation is primary, the senses and reason, which include judgment and logic, are also sources of knowledge. Furthermore, they desired to harmonize the inchoate, unsystematic thought of the Bible and rabbinic literature with the thought of Aristotle, which held sway over medieval minds. Later, when Averroes supplanted Aristotle, this Arabic philosopher became the primary source of philosophical reflection. In some cases, where Plato or Neoplatonism was supreme, Jewish philosophers attempted to reconcile Judaism with that point of view.

Basically, the medieval Jewish philosophers, from ca. 900 to 1500, were situated in Islamic countries and wrote in Arabic or Hebrew, but toward the end of that period philosophy emerged in Christian Spain and southern France. The flowering of Judaic philosophy in Islamic lands took place under the inspiration of the Arabic cultural renaissance.

The spread of Hellenism firmly implanted Greek science and philosophy in the Near East. As Christianity spread, Greek learning also advanced in Africa and Asia. Greek writings were translated into Syriac, and after the rise and spread of Islam, they were translated from Syriac into Arabic. It was from the growing Arabic schools that Jews learned Greek thought, and in time, as the Middle Eastern Christians had mediated Greek thought to the Arabs, so Jews played a large role in mediating the Islamic mode of Greek thought in Arabic to Christians in Europe during the thirteenth century. In this way, Jewish thinkers had a hand in stimulating the Renaissance and Reformation, which, in turn, led to their own stirrings of acculturation in Italy and Holland and to the formation of modern Judaism.

B. Philosophical Themes

1. General Themes

A number of great issues agitated the thinkers of the Middle Ages. Jews were especially interested in those themes that already had venerable acceptance as theological doctrine by their inclusion and daily reiteration in the liturgy. These themes were creation, election, revelation, redemption, and ideas associated with eschatology, such as the messianic theme, reward and punishment, last judgment, resurrection, hell and heaven, and immortality. A continual problem was whether human accountability to God is fair, whether the human being enjoys free will or labors under a deterministic system. Upon this crux turned all questions related to the very essence of faith. This problem penetrated to the very heart of religion. A whole school of thought would argue that without freedom of choice there can be no responsibility for sin, and no sense to the doctrines of repentance and atonement. In sum, all the themes can be subsumed under three rubrics: creation, revelation, and redemption. Revelation includes all themes related to God's manifestation to Israel, and therefore incorporates all those ideas related to covenant and election; redemption includes all eschatological themes, therefore incorporating all ideas related to sin, punishment, and atonement.

2. The Influence of Kalam

An important influence upon Judaic philosophers was the school of Arabic philosophy known as Kalam, which had two factions. One taught that human beings enjoyed free will; the other argued for determinism. Since the concept of determinism brought into focus skepticism toward God's justice, the Islamic school of Mutazila, or Mutakallimun, took up the cudgels for free will. This school also opposed Aristotle on the doctrine of creation, denying the eternity of matter. Furthermore, they argued for a metaphorical understanding of all the anthropomorphic statements in the Koran concerning God.

It would take us too far afield here to explore the matter, but modern scholarship has frequently argued that all of these views, and others held by Mutakallimun, were in reality developed from pre-Islamic targumic and rabbinic sources, and possibly in part from early Christian patristic literature. Thus, influences ran both ways: from Judaism and Christianity to Islam and back again to medieval Jewish and Christian philosophy.

3. The Influence of Sufism

Another influential school of thought in the Middle Ages was Sufism, a sect of Islamic mysticism. The Sufis were influenced by eastern asceticism and Christian monastic movements. In their effort to reconcile how a spiritual deity can be connected with a material universe, they followed the Neoplatonic view. Neoplatonism tried to explain this enigma by a theory of divine emanations; this theory later penetrated medieval Jewish mysticism.

4. God's Attributes

Other subjects dealt with at length in Jewish philosophy were the attributes of God, most notably God's existence, unity, and incorporeality. While Christian thinkers saw the three attributes of deity— life, power, and reason—as reinforcing the idea of trinity, Jewish thinkers maintained that one can find many more attributes (the rabbis had selected thirteen based on Exod. 34:6-7). The chief problem for Jewish philosophers was how to reconcile God's possession of multiple attributes with God's unity.

5. Virtue

In analyzing virtue, Jewish philosophers distinguished between practical and intellectual virtues, and adopted the Aristotelian idea of moderation. Furthermore, the consideration of the primacy of ethics led them to reconcile ritual practices with the ethical objectives of Judaism. Although this problem had already been treated by Philo and others in the Hellenistic world, medieval Jewish philosophers attacked it anew.

C. Philosophers

1. Introduction

It is possible that many more Jewish philosophers will come to light in future literary discoveries, or when more of the Genizah fragments found in Cairo are explored.[1] In all, there might have been over forty major medieval Jewish philosophers, some of whom were Karaites. Only half that number gained prominence, and only the few who played a large role in Judaic thought will be surveyed here.

2. Saadia ben Joseph (882-942)

The earliest Jewish philosopher of significance since Philo was Saadia (or Saadiah) ben Joseph, who became *Gaon* of Sura in Babylonia. He was in the vanguard of new medieval studies in philology, philosophy, Bible, commentaries, liturgy, and rabbinic literature. In 933 he wrote his major philosophical treatise (in Arabic), entitled *Kitat al-Amanat wal Itiqadat*. This work was later translated into Hebrew as *Sepher Haemunot Wehadeot* (The Book of Beliefs and Opinions). Saadia was also the first to translate the Bible into Arabic, and he founded the disciplines of Hebrew grammar and lexicography. Moreover, he was a leading scholar of rabbinics, having written an introduction to the Talmud and having compiled a prayerbook and annotated it with liturgical halakah. He became the leading apologist for Rabbanism against Karaism and was a major influence in stemming the growth of Karaism for a while. In his variegated literary efforts, he influenced both Spanish Jewish poets and northern European pietists, the former with his work in language and liturgy, the latter with his rigorous halakic positions, often taken in the face of Karaite challenge.

3. Solomon ibn Gabirol (1021-1058 or 1070)

Jewish philosophy makes its appearance in Western circles with Solomon ibn Gabirol. When the Umayyad dynasty befriended and elevated to power the patron of Jewish learning, Hasdai ibn Shaprut, mentioned

---

1. The Cairo Genizah was a storehouse of medieval documents, found at the end of the 19th century, which has shed much light on medieval Jewry in the Islamic world.

earlier, it allowed Judaic development in Islamic Spain. Out of this ambience came Solomon, not only the first Jewish philosopher in Spain, but the first person to write philosophy there. His major work was *Fons Vitae*, a Latin translation of his *Mekor Hayyim* (Fountain of Life), which was preserved in Christian circles under the name Avicebron rather than Solomon. It was, in fact, not until 1845 that Avicebron was discovered to have been the Jewish Spanish poet Solomon ibn Gabirol, when a Hebrew epitome of *Fons Vitae*, prepared in the thirteenth century, was discovered in Paris. Solomon was sometimes thought of as a Moslem and sometimes as a Christian, but not as a Jew. This ambiguity attests to the universality of his thought, despite his having been a significant composer of synagogue liturgy. He was indeed denounced by the twelfth-century philosopher Abraham ibn David as having ideas dangerous to Judaism.

4. Abraham ibn David (1110-1180)

Another major Spanish Jewish philosopher was Abraham ibn David, who best articulated the idea that Judaism is based upon philosophical principles. He argued that moral precepts are attainable by reason, and that one need not profess Judaism to practice them. Moreover, ibn David believed that gentiles would be impressed by the wisdom of Judaism (as indicated at Deut. 4:6) when they understood that revelation provided Israel with the philosophical principles it took gentiles thousands of years to develop. He did not seem to realize, however, that it could be proposed that since gentiles had evolved the same principles by reason and logic, there might be no further need for revealed religion. This mode of argumentation often led to the kind of cul-de-sac philosophers ended up in when seeking to prove that revelation was superior to, but inherently harmonious with, reason.

5. Yehudah Halevi (ca. 1075-1141)

It was undoubtedly against the effort to reconcile faith with reason, among other things, that the great medieval poet Yehudah Halevi rebelled and insisted, in his role as philosopher, that revelation alone must be the measure of truth. Born in Toledo, Spain, during an age when the cross and the crescent began to engage in an incipient struggle for control of Spain, Halevi perceived that Judaism, Christianity, and Islam made three equally fervent claims to possessing the truth. Watching the danger that confronted Judaism from both Christian and Islamic Spain, Halevi became concerned with the religious destiny of Jews.

Using his rich imagination and felicity with words, in his book *The Kuzari* he placed his philosophy into fictional conversations among representatives of Judaism, Christianity, and Islam who seek to convert the king of the Khazars to their respective faiths. The Khazars were a people who inhabited an area that is part of the contemporary Soviet Union north and east of the Black Sea, extending as far as the Caspian Sea. The Jew is Halevi's protagonist, and, as in all Platonic dialogues, upon which the book is modeled, the protagonist wins and converts the king in the story to Judaism. *The Kuzari* is an enigma based upon a historical episode in which a Turkish people, living in the Black Sea area in Russia, followed their king into Judaism.

Halevi began with the premise that God's will is unknowable by human reason and therefore can only be discovered through revelation. In a very real sense, Halevi took what twentieth-century existentialists came to call a "leap of faith." While he stressed the superiority of Judaism in *The Kuzari,* the very plot of the dialogues—the effort to convert a gentile kingdom to Judaism—points the way to a nonracial, nonethnic conception of Jewish identity. Halevi implied that those who adopt the faith of Judaism are Jews, and all human beings are welcome. This was a bold position on the part of Halevi in an age when Judaism, as he himself indicated in the title of one of his manuscripts, was a "despised faith."

6. Hasdai Crescas (1340-1410)

Hasdai Crescas was one of the latest medieval Jewish philosophers. He worked in Christian Spain and wrote *Or Adonai* (Light of the Lord). Crescas elevated the nonrational to religious truth, emphasizing faith as superior to reason. He comes close to the Christian idea of original sin in his teaching that "the entire race of mankind became predisposed to degeneration and oblivion." For Crescas, therefore, circumcision is a continuous sacrifice of the flesh and blood to atone for Adam's sin. Furthermore, Crescas implies his knowledge of the old tradition that Abraham actually sacrificed Isaac, contrary to the denouement in Genesis 22, and that God accepted this sacrifice as atonement for Adam's sin on behalf of all the future progeny of Abraham and anyone who entered the covenant.

7. Moses ben Maimon (Maimonides) (1135-1204)

Overshadowing all these figures in philosophy, as he overshadowed all halakic scholars, was Moses Maimonides. He has aptly been called "by far the most comprehensive mind of medieval Jewry."[2] His genius did not assure him of universal acceptance in his own time, however, and for many years he was the center of venomous controversy. Born in Spain, he settled in Fostat, Egypt, a suburb of Cairo, where he supported himself as a physician to Sultan Saladin.

Maimonides articulated his philosophy most comprehensively in his Arabic book *Dalalat al-Hairin (The Guide for the Perplexed)*. This work was translated into Latin and influenced both Albertus Magnus and Thomas Aquinas. Within Judaism, however, it was attacked for its rejection of all anthropomorphism (the tendency to speak of God in human terms) as heretical and for what some believed was its lukewarm attitude toward resurrection, among other matters.

With regard to his objection to anthropomorphism, Maimonides argued that all expressions in the Bible referring to God's organs, such as God's ear, arm, or mouth, or to God's emotions, such as love or anger, were to be understood metaphorically. Many of Maimonides's antagonists feared that a metaphorical interpretation of any part of the Bible might lead to metaphorical explanations of other parts of Scripture. An example of their concern is the biblical verse whose literal reading is the basis for the ritual of tefillin: "You shall fasten them [the words of God] on your hand as a sign and on your forehead as a circlet" (Deut. 6:9). This verse, referring to Moses' assertion that *Yahweh* is one and that Israel should love *Yahweh,* was read literally by the rabbis. Accordingly, they linked this verse to the custom of wearing tefillin, leather boxes containing this verse and others fastened on the arm and forehead. If Jews read this verse metaphorically, the rabbis feared, they would not observe the ceremony of donning tefillin.

An even graver issue than anthropomorphism between the Maimunists (supporters of Maimonides) and the anti-Maimunists was stimulated by the complex of doctrines related to eschatology. The anti-Maimunists suspected that Maimonides did not believe in the doctrine of literal resurrection, and continued to doubt his belief in it even after he wrote a defensive tract on the subject to clear the air. His opponents believed that his treatise, which was not meant for the philosopher, but for "women and ignorant people," would lead the uninitiated to anxiety and the sophisticated to disbelief.

---

2. Gershom G. Scholem, *On the Kabbalah and Its Symbolism,* trans. Ralph Manheim (New York: Schocken, 1965), p. 344.

Maimonides is famous for his thirteen principles of faith, which summarize his basic theological creed. This core of beliefs, found in his commentary on the Mishnah, is as follows: (1) God is the Creator; (2) God is one; (3) God is incorporeal; (4) God is eternal; (5) God alone must be worshiped; (6) the prophets are true; (7) Moses was the greatest of all prophets; (8) the entire Torah was divinely given to Moses; (9) the Torah is immutable; (10) God knows all the acts and thoughts of human beings; (11) God rewards and punishes; (12) the Messiah will come; and (13) there will be resurrection.

Maimonides affirmed belief in human free will, even arguing that human freedom to choose is unlimited and that any degree of determinism could make a mockery of prophetic exhortation to a high quality of morality and would render divine justice impossible. For God to exercise the power of reward and punishment, Maimonides argued, it is necessary to acknowledge the human right to choose. Only then can there be accountability for one's actions. But Maimonides also affirmed a doctrine of providence, limiting freedom of choice to the moral sphere. He attributed human destiny, events in nature, life and death, and similar phenomena to providence, to a power beyond human control, influence, or choice.

While Maimonides averred a doctrine of reward and punishment, he was not always firm on traditional views. He implied there was no lurid place of punishment which has been termed "hell," and that the ultimate post-resurrection punishment was the absence of bliss, a total annihilation of life, rather than actual extended torment.

These views of Maimonides on free will and reward and punishment raised many a conundrum among scholars, as did his messianic idea. They feared that the Maimonidean way of articulating traditional theology held implicit dangers for faith. For example, his messianic idea contained the basic traditional notion that a Davidic king would rule over a regenerated nation in this world. He saw the world continuing just as it was, except for the redemption of Israel, and affirmed the idea of a world to come which would be eternal and would be inaugurated at some unknown time after the advent of the this-worldly messianic kingdom. Maimonides, however, did not ascribe importance to the apocalyptic ideas held by a consensus of medieval scholars. He expected no miracles of the messiah, and denied that any changes would take place in nature, thus causing many to doubt that he was authentically biblical in his messianic doctrine. In sum, he saw the messianic era as designed to render Israel "free to devote itself to the Torah and its wisdom, with no one to oppress or disturb it, and thus be worthy of life in the world to come" (M.T. Mel. 12:1, 4).

D. Conclusion

From the time of Moses to the rise of the modern State of Israel, no significant philosopher of Judaism per se arose in the Holy Land— each one was a product of the diaspora. The Torah and rabbinic literature were primarily halakic in character, delineating conduct rather than creed. Where biblical books, whether Pentateuch, Prophets, or Writings, and rabbinic midrashim did exhort to faith and articulate doctrines, these were never presented in any cohesive, systematic form. When thinkers arose who tried to present Judaism in some form of systematic philosophy worthy of ancient Greek or medieval Islamic philosophy, it was done as a reaction to the challenge of the environment or as a form of acculturation.

Historically, philosophy consisted of abstract thought subject to logical analysis and rational criticism, while biblical and rabbinic religion were subject to faith and proclamation. In essence, the philosophy of Judaism, as expressed in the Hellenistic and medieval writers, and later in modern Europe, was a synthesis of foreign ideas with Judaic faith. Thus, for example, Philo is to be understood essentially in the light of Plato; Maimonides largely in the light of Aristotle; and, in modern times, Hermann Cohen in relation to Immanuel Kant, and Mordecai Kaplan as a disciple of a whole constellation of modern thinkers from Auguste Comte through Matthew Arnold to John Dewey.

As early as the second century B.C.E., the realization that Judaism needed the reinforcement of foreign philosophical thought to survive led the Alexandrian Jew Aristobulus to write a remarkable apologetic. Aristobulus maintained that Greek philosophy and all Hellenistic learning owed their origin and development to Judaism. This ingenious idea was embraced by other Hellenistic writers down to Josephus and was also adopted by Christian writers. As late as the Middle Ages, Maimonides continued to affirm that idea in his *Guide for the Perplexed*.

The foregoing Jewish thinkers attempted to preserve Jewish fidelity to Judaism in a world of other conflicting monotheisms, each claiming to be the truth, and of philosophies opposing all religion. The thirteenth and fourteenth centuries brought repeated calamity to Jews in Germany and Spain. By the fifteenth century, rationalism was losing its hold as persecution increased. As a consequence, the conversion of Jewish intellectuals to Christianity, mysticism, pietism, and even obscurantism began to grow. Reaction to rationalism was accompanied by socioeconomic and political deterioration in the Jewish community. These events led, first, to the emergence of the German pietistic and mystical movement of the Hasidim, and later, stimulated by the anti-intellectualism of Hasdai Crescas, to the full flowering of the kabalistic movement.

II. PIETISM, MYSTICISM, AND KABALISM

A. Hasidism

German Jews did not engage in the rational philosophical thought that evolved in Islamic Spain and the Islamic East. They brought forth another religious form which spawned a different theological approach. *Geonic* halakic influences, harsh physical and political conditions of the thirteenth century, and contemporary pietistic movements among Christians (such as Franciscan revivalism) all contributed to the rise of the medieval Hasidic movement. This movement is not to be confused with eighteenth-century Hasidism, which was a variety of popular kabalism. The earlier Hasidism was the kernel out of which kabalism emerged. While there are points of contact between them, as there would be among all pietistic movements, the earlier movement did not give rise to a rabbinic system which resembled a personality cult, as did the later one. Furthermore, it was predominantly rigorous in ritualism, asceticism, and scholasticism, and did not emphasize the celebrations in music, dance, and fellowship meals in the manner of the eighteenth-century Hasidim.

The earlier Hasidim and kabalists were esoteric sects, while the later Hasidim were among the common people. The earlier Hasidic ideas, however, had a lasting impact upon Judaic folk-religion. It is possible that the nineteenth-century rabbinic dynasties which emerged in later Hasidism were modeled after the accident of the hereditary leadership that fell to three outstanding personalities who were the apparent founders of thirteenth-century Hasidism: Samuel the Hasid, his son Yehudah the Hasid, and grandson Eliezer. Aside from these three men, however, there were no rabbinic dynasties around whom separate sects rallied in medieval Hasidism.

Comparable to his Christian contemporary, St. Francis of Assisi, Yehudah became "the Hasid" par excellence, and his work *Sepher Hasidim* became the major literary expression of the pietism, ethics, and morality of the movement. The old *merkabah* (chariot) mysticism, going back to the *geonic* period and tracing itself to Ezekiel's throne-chariot, was reinvigorated by the Hasidim and influenced the emergent kabalistic trends.

The adherents of *merkabah* mysticism called themselves *yordey merkabah,* "chariot-riders," and believed that only those who meticulously observe all the halakic minutiae were capable of penetrating the divine realms. These Eastern notions reached the Germans through the synagogue *piyyutim* (prayer-poems and hymns) superimposed upon the regular rabbinic liturgy. The disguised mysticism embedded in these poems undoubtedly motivated some opposition to them among medieval rabbinic halakists. They nevertheless remained in the liturgy, because Rabbi Gershom accepted their legitimacy on the basis of decisions made by Rabbi Meshullam ben Kalonymus, who was actually a scion of the family which transmitted esoteric lore from generation to generation from a certain Abu Aron of Baghdad.

Sepher Hasidim basically agreed with the theology and halakah of other elements of Judaism, with perhaps a stronger emphasis upon eschatology. But here and there concepts were stressed which later became embedded in Judaic folk-religion. The concept called *hibbut haqeber,* "the terrors of the grave," which afflict a person soon after burial, for example, remained part of Jewish folk-religion into modern times. Here we have an example of an idea which is neither biblical nor rabbinic. Saadia mentioned this concept earlier as a three-day period, and might have derived it from Islam, which in turn might have adopted it from Zoroastrianism.

The Hasidic philosophy of history was based upon the notion of "profane history" originating in the sin of Adam that alienates the human being from God. The only way this human alienation could be overcome was by religious perfection, achieved through asceticism and altruism. While rabbinic thought affirmed that *derek eretz* (the ordinary worldly life) should be brought into harmony with the study of torah (M. Ab. 2:2; 3:21), *Sepher Hasidim* avowed that the road to perfection is via *atzibat derek eretz,* "the abandonment of the worldly way" (§ 861). In direct antithesis to the rabbinic halakic philosophy, the Hasidim argued that even what is permitted halakically may be sinful and punishable, in the same way as it is possible that what has been declared legal by secular law is immoral by what one believes to be a higher divine standard. Despite Hasidic asceticism, however, no Hasidim emulated the monk's vow of celibacy.

The masses saw the avowed Hasid as one who has mastered esoteric forces. It was out of their own literature, which also asserted the possibility of utilizing the power inherent in God's name for the creation and control of a *golem* (a Frankenstein, robot-type of demonic power), that Christians accused Jews of magic and sorcery, which made it easier for them to associate Jews with the diabolical power of Satan.

Prayer was influenced by Hasidic emphasis upon the number of words, the numerical value of words, or of phrases and parts of sentences. All were linked with the names and attributes of God and angels. Prayer was seen to be a ladder upon which the devout ascended to heaven. Formulas were created for magical purposes and to create *kavanah*—the intensive mental concentration that characterized mystics. The Hasid also engaged in fits of ecstasy and penitence; the former derived from mental concentration, the latter was exercised in such activities as sitting in snow and ice during the winter. Hasidism speculated in theosophy, which in its doctrine of the immanence of God took anthropomorphism to its outer limits. Thus, in one of the Hasidim's most significant liturgical hymns, the *Shir Hakabod* (The Hymn of Glory), God is seen as an old man with a hoary head, as a youth with raven hair, and as a warrior armed for battle.

Sepher Hasidim reflected the tendency to intolerance found in pietistic revival movements. In such circles, both adherence to one's own religious "truth" and aversion to other religions became more intense. Jewish suffering of the thirteenth century, aggravated by Innocent III, caused Hasidism to express its disdain for Christianity and Christians in no uncertain terms. The anti-gentilism and aversion to the precincts of a church that one may at times detect in Judaic religious writing since medieval times and in the folk-religion of eastern Europe into modern times owes much to *Sepher Hasidim*. The book prohibits the Jew from relating to Christian ceremonies or objects, from entering the courtyard or the vicinity of a church, and from even having windows in his house from which he can see a church (*S.H.* 1353-59). It also bans teaching Hebrew to a priest (*S.H.* 348). Such precepts can be multiplied many times over, but for the most part the bigotry and religious revulsion to all things Christian evident in *Sepher Hasidim* generally cannot be paralleled in the Talmud. Where it can be remotely paralleled, *Sepher Hasidim* adopts the stringent minority view from multiple opinions expressed (*S.H.* 726). Furthermore, occasionally it applies a pejorative talmudic view aimed at pagans to the Christians of its own period.

Modern philosophers of religion would explain the Hasidic re-vulsion against Christians in the following way. Hasidism understood an object used by a person of another religion as possessing per-manently the essence transmitted by that person. This meant that Jews could not degrade their own objects by allowing gentiles to use them, and would be on the edge of idolatry if they used the gentiles' objects.

In these anti-Christian precepts, as well as in other restrictions and stringencies, Hasidism expected more than the masses could per-form. There is no information on how widespread adherence to these Hasidic teachings was, and some scholars even deny there was ever such a movement as Hasidism in the Middle Ages, or anything more than scattered individuals who practiced these esoteric ideas and rigorous precepts. Furthermore, there is even a degree of ambivalence toward these anti-Christian attitudes within *Sepher Hasidim*. For ex-ample, it is clear from *Sepher Hasidim* itself that Jews and Christians continued to have economic and social dealings with each other, and that Hasidim even continued to employ gentile servants. Only the rare Hasid refused to accept food prepared by a gentile servant, and *Sepher Hasidim* itself permitted bread baked by a gentile for the public at large (*S.H.* 1940). Hasidim were also encouraged to dispute religious mat-ters with Christians if they had confidence that they could prevail. Al-though a Jew was not to save a Christian's life if it meant desecrating the Sabbath, all Jews were honor-bound to save a gentile when they knew a Jew plotted to kill him (*S.H.* 1849). At times it is difficult to know whether the Hasid was moral or only pragmatic. Thus, because a Jewish cheater of a gentile might generate danger to all Jews who stood to lose their residence privileges in a town as a result of collec-tive punishment, the Hasid declared it to be a greater sin for a Jew to cheat a gentile than to rob a Jew (*S.H.* 632).

In contrast to the basic Hasidic intolerance toward Christianity, there was a countervailing view predominantly expressed by Rabbi Menahem haMeiri of Provence in the late thirteenth and early four-teenth century. He looked upon Christianity and Islam as monotheis-tic and therefore entirely excluded from any halakic disabilities that applied to pagans. Although earlier halakists had already taken this position, Rabbi Menahem refashioned their view into a more compel-ling philosophy, and stressed that nobody obeyed the anti-pagan tal-mudic regulations any longer. Nevertheless, haMeiri, no less than *Sepher Hasidim,* was somewhat ambivalent about Christians, for he would not permit Jews and Christians to eat together, even when the food was *kasher,* because it might lead to their undue mingling (*Bet Habehirah* A.Z. 132).

B. Kabalism

The word *kabalah* (or cabalah) means "tradition," and originally had reference to nonscriptural tradition. Later it took on the more exclusive sense of mysticism. Jewish mysticism, not unlike other forms of mysticism, strives for an immediate and intimate contact between the person and God. One cannot dichotomize religion into two separate types, the rational and the mystical. All religion consists of both elements, and in Judaism there was always a two-track development. Rabbinic intellectualism evinced in the Talmud also includes mystifying aggadic passages dealing with eschatology, apocalyptic, and other themes that arise in both Jewish Scripture and intertestamental literature, which are the seminal core of later kabalism. This commingling of rationalism and mysticism remained the hallmark of later thinkers. The truly religious personality was partly mystical, and when the mystic sought to delineate the halakah by which to live, he approached it through rational processes.

The major significance of kabalism is its emphasis upon the sense of *mystery* in Judaism, transforming a mitzvah into a sacrament, a term that has been avoided by Jewish thinkers. The major weakness of kabalism, however, is its emphasis upon the demonic as an active cosmic force, and its stimulus to ideas and practices that border on magic and superstition. The mystics taught that demons and evil spirits populate the world and that various ritualistic forms are needed to frustrate them. This teaching led to a number of life-cycle events being circumscribed by prohibitory practices and celebrated by newly designed rituals that emerged from medieval superstition. Belief in spirit-possession stimulated a far-reaching confidence in and practice of exorcism that remained part of the nineteenth-century eastern European Hasidic movement.

The antecedents to kabalah are already present in Scripture and rabbinic literature. A source of much mystical discussion, for example, is biblical anthropomorphism, in which God speaks, hears, intrudes, becomes angry, loves, and hates like a human being. Maimonidean thought vigorously opposed this attitude, but kabalistic opposition to Maimonidean rationalism restored the anthropomorphic deity with its biblical validation. Furthermore, talmudic literature is replete with angelology and demonology, and these were therefore regarded as fully validated. The *merkabah* (chariot) rider, referred to above, explored the *hekalot,* or halls and palaces of the heavens, on the way to the divine throne, thus producing out of Ezekiel 1 and Isaiah 6 an extensive *merkabah* and *hekalot* mysticism. Another major aspect of mystical thought was *maaseh bereshit,* the creation, with all of its cosmological ramifications, involving the mystery of how an infinite, incorporeal deity can produce finite matter doomed to decomposition.

The road of Jewish mysticism ran from Genesis and Ezekiel through Enoch and Philonic Hellenistic mysticism until the *Sepher Yetzirah* (Book of Creation) emerged. This tract takes up the doctrine of emanations, or *hamshakah,* asserting that there are ten *sephirot,* or intermediary stages, by which the *sapir,* divine radiance (Exod. 24:9-11), produces the material world. It thus teaches that all existing things are divine radiations. *Sepher Yetzirah* further teaches that God created the letters of the alphabet, and that the letters are the prime cause of the material world. All real entities in the world—in time and within the human body—emerged out of the relationship of the twenty-two letters of the alphabet, which produced an infinite variety of material products. This book unquestionably influenced the element of magic within kabalism that stressed creative and potent powers in letters and words. In this aspect of kabalah we have one of its more damaging influences upon later Judaism, especially eastern European Hasidism.

Better known than *Sepher Yetzirah,* however, is *Sepher haZohar* (The Book of Splendor). This book was written in Castile, Spain, during the thirteenth century by Moses ben Shem Tov de Leon. Designed as a running commentary on the Pentateuch, Song of Songs, Ruth, and a few miscellaneous writings, it is actually similar to a rabbinic midrash, and is generally homiletical in character. The book is theosophical, searching for an understanding of the mysteries of how God functions in the world. It engages in cosmogony, psychology, and anthropology, searching for the answer to the riddle of how the world came into being, the nature and destiny of human beings, their alienation from God through sin, and the avenues that might lead to redemption. The *Zohar* represents God as *ein-soph* (the infinite) and as King, and sees the shekinah (the Divine Indwelling Presence) as His queenly consort. The shekinah—the feminine principle in God—has its roots in Scripture in the conception of *hokmah* (Wisdom) and is seen in the Apocrypha as God's consort. It was elevated and intensified by kabalism under the influence of both Gnosticism and the role of Mary in Roman Catholicism. According to the *Zohar,* Adam's sin shattered the male-female unity in deity, a unity not destined to be restored until eschatological redemption took place. Thus, careful observance of religious acts was important, for they would bring about divine unity in microcosm, leading ultimately to permanent cosmic unity in redemption.

The *Zohar* teaches that God's left hand—the *sephirah* of judgment and punishment—is moderated by the *sephirah* of love. At times, however, the *sephirah* of evil is torn free and becomes a satanic force in the world, partaking of the *sitra ahra,* "the other side," or the demonic. This element of Jewish mysticism found its way into Christian mysticism through the writings of Jacob Boehme. He, too, saw evil as the negative principle in God, and this concept influenced Christian mystics in Germany, Holland, and England. This theory allowed for the independent existence of evil, which is either let loose by God or activated by human beings. Moreover, it has its roots in the Bible: "I am Yahweh. . . . I make good fortune and create calamity" (Isa. 45:7). The *Zohar* also teaches that this demonic area is the one from which gentile souls derive. This teaching thus served as a bridge, in its aversion to all things non-Jewish, between German Hasidism and the eighteenth-century Hasidic movement.

In its *Zoharic* form kabalism espoused the concept of *gilgul,* a Pythagorean theory of reincarnation which also signifies the transmigration of souls, or as otherwise known, "metempsychosis." Reincarnation generally signifies that the same soul inhabits various bodies sequentially, but metempsychosis affirms that the soul that once inhabited human bodies might sometimes inhabit bodies of animals and even plants and inorganic matter. While the philosophers held that the injustice of undeserved suffering in this world will be balanced by eternal bliss in the world to come, the kabalists saw the balance in different *gilgulim* (cycles of reincarnation). Alternatively, some kabalists asserted that new *gilgulim* are opportunities for sinners to overcome the errors of their previous life, while others espoused the notion that infant mortality is to be explained by the punishment of one who sinned in a previous *gilgul* by causing that person to die immediately in the new one.

Refugees from the cataclysmic events in Spain and Portugal from 1350 to 1500 swelled Jewish settlement in Palestine, and mystics especially settled at Safed. There they were inspired, among others, by Rabbi Moses Cordovero (1522-1570) and Rabbi Isaac Luria (1534-1572). Luria's life was surrounded with metaphysical and miraculous anecdotes. Thus it was believed that his father had a vision in which Elijah revealed to him that he would have a son who would be named Isaac and who would, like the atoning Isaac of the *aqedah,* redeem Israel from the forces of evil. Divine messages are said to have continued to direct Luria's life, and under these auspices he spent six days a week in solitude, fasting, prayer, ablutions, and mortifications, until he attained communion with Elijah and the gift of the Holy Spirit. In his nocturnal ecstasy, Luria was believed to ascend to heaven and there, in the celestial realms, to receive the teaching of past masters.

Lurianic ideas were largely transmitted by Hayyim Vital (1543-1620). Vital describes Luria's notion of how one receives the Holy Spirit and asserts that a *maggid* (speaker) is created through the sounds of the human voice expressed in study, prayer, and pious conduct carried forth in mystical concentration. Since, in kabalistic thinking, everything below acts upon everything above, every minute religious act and word has a magical potency and can even create celestial beings. Lurianic kabalists learned from the *Zohar* that celestial beings created by the voices of human beings return to teach them. The source for this is the Mishnah (Ab. 4:13), which states that every mitzvah performed brings forth a paraclete—a heavenly advocate—and each sin brings forth a prosecutor. For the kabalists this teaching signifies that the purity of one's sounds and pious deeds will result in the creation of a *maggid,* which will convey the Holy Spirit or revelation to the perfect mystic. The term *maggid* is pre-Lurianic and is used by Rabbi Joseph Karo (1488-1575).[3] Karo emphasized that his *maggid* appeared to him as the Mishnah personified, and revealed the works of God in response to his recitation of passages of the Mishnah and practice of mortifications. He kept a diary of the *maggid's* variegated teachings, admonitions, and exhortations, which he entitled *Sepher haMaggid.* Cordovero believed that an angel enters people's souls and speaks to them in their own voice, and termed this angel a *maggid.* This teaching or revelation is what speaks forth after the angel has left.

The theory of *maggidism* entered into Sabbatianism and later eighteenth-century Hasidism as one of the many significant influences of Lurianic kabalah upon both movements. But Luria's influence, like that of kabalism in general, was perhaps greatest upon the folk-religion which predominated in eastern Europe after 1650. The following are

---

3. R. J. Zwi Werblowsky, *Joseph Karo, Lawyer and Mystic* (Oxford: Oxford University Press, 1962).

ceremonies that were influenced by him: prayer formulas invoking the union of God and Shekinah through the performance of a given mitz-vah; special liturgies for midnight and all-night vigils; a variety of *tik-kunim* (rites of restoration); the elevation of Shabuot from a festival commemorating the Sinai event to the celebration of the mystical marriage of God and Shekinah; a variety of fasts and forms of penance; ritualistic embellishments permeated by music and ecstasy; the Friday night liturgy known as *Kabalat Shabbat* (welcoming the Sabbath), and religious table songs. Naturally, in some cases Luria and kabalism only reworked older forms, and sometimes kabalist views were rejected by halakists. But generally the two views prevailed among different segments of Jews. Kabalism became highly popularized in eighteenth-century Hasidism, and therefore many of its rites were integrated into eastern European Orthodoxy.

Kabalism was a major factor in the rise of Sabbatianism, a messianic movement sparked by Shabbatai Zvi (or Tzevi) (1626-1676) in Turkey that swept European Jewry. A variety of factors had escalated mystical messianic fervor among the Jews of Europe when Shabbatai came upon the scene: the repetitious local expulsions of Jews from many regions of France and Germany and their total expulsion from Spain; the trauma of forced baptisms in Aragon and Castile in 1391; the devastating attacks against Polish Jews by Bogden Chmielnicki (or Khmelnytsky) in 1648; and the disorientation of massive resettlement in Poland and the Ottoman empire. There were always sporadic messianic movements, such as the mission of David Reubeni in 1524. Appearing as the long awaited messiah, Reubeni set the stage for an even more zealous movement led by Shabbatai Zvi during the seventeenth century.

Devotees of the *Zohar* saw the Jewish lunar year 5408 as the year of resurrection of the dead and messianic redemption. Apologists, however, who were astonished by its being a year of convulsion and catastrophe in which the Cossack rebellion of Chmielnicki wreaked unprecedented havoc among the Jews of Poland, had to seek a rationale, which they found in numerology. The letters of *heblay mashiah,* "pangs of the messiah," add up to 408, and 1648 was equivalent to the year (5)408 in the Jewish calendar. They reasoned that it was not the Messiah who was to come in 5408/1648, but pre-messianic suffering, and that this suffering portended the messianic advent. It was in this kabalistic-intellectual environment, and in a climate of socioeconomic and political despair, that Shabbatai Zvi arose. A manic-depressive ordained scholar who practiced kabalistic ablutions and mortifications, he experienced a visionary moment of self-revelation as the Messiah in 1648.

One cannot always precisely determine the direction of the flow of influences. But it is of interest in the history of religion that chiliastic and millenarian Christian groups saw 1666 as the year of the advent of Christ. For that reason, during the 1650s English millenarians were interested in the return of Jews to England to assure the Second Coming. Under kabalistic influences, taking advantage of yearnings similar to those of the millenarians, Menasseh ben Israel worked for this return. Simultaneous with the activity of Menasseh ben Israel, Shabbatai Zvi proclaimed his mission in 1665-1666, thus launching massive messianic ardor in Jewish communities all across Europe and the Near East. Books published in Amsterdam in 1667 had title pages on which were attested, "Published in the year the Messiah son of David arrived," and hundreds of thousands of Jews hailed Shabbatai Zvi as Messiah and began to plan a trek to the Holy Land. Zvi, however, responding to Turkish demands that he accept Islam or prove his messiahship by a direct significant miracle, accepted Islam. His followers suffered no trauma over his apostasy. Instead they saw in it the counterpart of Jesus' passion and vicarious atonement—the need of the Messiah to suffer degradation in the world of darkness until he vanquishes it and reappears. The ultimate Christianization of Sabbatianism is present in the legend that his brother Elijah found Shabbatai Zvi's grave empty on the third day and declared, "Neither our Lord nor anything else was in the cave, but it was full of light." Sabbatians that persisted into the twentieth century in the Donmeh sect of Greece and Turkey believed that Shabbatai Zvi was a returned Moses, and they celebrated the important dates of his life as religious festivals.

Sabbatianism discredited kabalistic enthusiasm in many circles, and the countervailing influences of the Dutch and Italian Renaissances helped the ultimate spread of a new rationalism and yearnings for acculturation and European integration. These yearnings were escalated by the stirrings first of the French revolutionary climate during the 1700s, and ultimately by the Napoleonic supremacy. Nevertheless, the kabalistic elements that continued in Hasidism influenced eighteenth-century romantic Zionism to some extent and continue to stir deep impulses in contemporary Jews.

C. Conclusion

Hasidism and kabalism were in large measure the product of the Crusades, which led to a climate in Christian Europe that encouraged Jews to retreat within a shell of ritualism and pietism. Although more rational talmudics and halakah remained the staple of Jewish scholarship, on a higher than popular level, the pietistic impulse expressed itself in ecstaticism and technical mysticism. For Hasidism this impulse meant shifting the emphasis from talmudics to esoteric interests, from speculation on meaning in religious study to preoccupation with fixed formulas and exactitude in ritual. Magic was interwoven with faith as the followers of Hasidism moved from quiet confidence in God's response to an effort to compel God's response with the usage of the right choice of words, the right number of words, and the correct incantation of these words.

These magical elements of Hasidism, combined with the detailed punctiliousness of Rabbi Meier of Rothenburg's regimen of ritualistic fastidiousness discussed earlier, accompanied the Jew to eastern Europe. Out of this matrix emerged eastern European Judaism and its by-product—the latter-day Hasidic movement inaugurated during the eighteenth century. It was this combination of esoteric pietism and meticulous ritualism which became characteristic of that group which called itself "Orthodox" during the nineteenth century, and remains the canon by which "Orthodoxy" continues to measure itself as we approach the twenty-first century.

Kabalism enriched Judaism on many levels, especially in spirituality and liturgical composition. But its countervailing tendencies presented a potent dilemma. Kabalism is the most particularistic form of Judaism ever developed, not only for teaching that Jews are the center of the cosmic drama, or that only by the mitzvot of Judaism practiced by Jews alone can the shattered divine unity be restored and redemption become a reality, but because of the ethnic self-exaltation it engenders, and even worse because of its abnegation of all things gentile.

III. PIETISM AND THE RISE OF "PROTO-ORTHODOXY" IN EASTERN EUROPE

The geographic area under discussion includes what in the twentieth century constitutes the Baltic States, Poland, and the Soviet Union; but between 1400 and 1900 the major areas of Jewish learning and religious growth were in the smaller segments better identified as Lithuania (the Baltic States), Poland, Galicia (alternately held by Poland or Austria), Ukraine, and White Russia. A secondary area was Hungary, Bohemia, and Romania. The inner life of the Jew reached its zenith in this geographic area during the seventeenth century, persisted on a plateau from 1650 to 1850, and then began a slow decline. Its extinction, however, did not result from inner disorientation, but rather from the twentieth-century Hitlerian program of physical extermination and the Stalinist program of spiritual annihilation.

Many streams and tributaries out of western Europe converged on Poland as the disciples of Rabbi Mordecai ben Hillel and Rabbi Meir of Rothenburg issued forth in such new luminaries as Rabbi Solomon Luria (not to be confused with the mystic) and Rabbi Moses Isserles. It is the teaching of Rabbis Mordecai and Meir and their subsequent "canonization" among their disciples after 1650 that must be referred to as "proto-Orthodoxy," for the distinctive designation "Orthodox" did not appear until the opponents of the reformation after 1800 adopted this term for self-identity and differentiation from all reforming and dissenting tendencies emerging since 1750.

An example of this long chain of tradition with its diversified points of origin is Rabbi Jacob ben Moses Segal of Mulln, known as Maharil (1360-1427), born in Austria. Maharil was undoubtedly influenced by Austrian disciples of Rabbi Meir of Rothenburg and became, in turn, the major source for the Polish Rabbi Moses Isserles (1520-1572). Maharil innovated many rituals that became embedded in the halakah surrounding marriage, burial, and synagogue ritual. Similarly, as the waves of Spanish Jews joined the Polish Jewish community, there was a need to accommodate both the Sephardic customs of the former and Ashkenazic customs of the latter. Furthermore, the kabalistic influences that spread to Europe generated the use of kabalah-inspired prayerbooks, which were identified as "Sephardic" and were later adopted by the Ashkenazic Hasidim. In the early stages of these crosscurrents, Moses Isserles and the mystic-halakist Joseph Karo of Safed corresponded. Isserles felt strongly about upholding local and contemporary halakic authority, against the array of Sephardic halakic literature embodied in the massive tomes of Moses Maimonides, Jacob ben Asher, and Joseph Karo. Thus, when Joseph Karo compiled his *Shulhan Aruk* (The Prepared Table), a digest of halakah to serve as a convenient reference for his students, Isserles appended to it his glosses, called *Mapah* (Tablecloth), which supplied the Ashkenazic customs that Karo had neglected. The two works appeared together in 1571, and this dual collection remains to this day the basic authority for what is termed "Orthodoxy," although several other collections of halakah compiled since 1600 are frequently referred to in preference to the work of Karo and Isserles.

Neither Karo nor Isserles ever envisaged their compilations as compulsory definitive "codes," and they state this idea lucidly in their introductions. The juxtaposition of the two works symbolizes in the profoundest way the historic principle of diversity and flexibility in halakah, and the concomitant concept that halakah is *not "law."*[4] Independent halakic judgment was preserved after 1571 as an increasing flow of halakic commentaries and digests contained either implied or explicit critiques of the *Shulhan Aruk* and *Mapah*.

Nevertheless, after 1650 the situation was altered. An increasing flow of literature, written under the shadow of disorientation caused by Sabbatianism, the Chmielnicki attacks, and internal political upheavals in Poland, sought to entrench piety and create a definitive all-embracing authority and to dissociate dissenters. The *Shulhan Aruk* was thus elevated to near "canonical" status.

When the "Orthodox" school of thought arose during the nineteenth-century polemic with the emergent reforming groups, its basic platform and its regimen of observance was the *Shulhan Aruk*. As was always true historically, some scholars differed with others about how to observe some details of the given rituals. But the differences in observance between a devout follower of the Karo-Isserles digest of 1571 and an observer of one of the manuals of halakah such as the twentieth-century *Mishnah Berurah* would not be noticeable to the unpracticed eye or the halakic novice. Included in the latter digest, written by Rabbi Meir of Radin (Poland), were discussions of how to deal with new questions that arose from modern business techniques, means of travel, new food technology, and marketing systems. On the whole, however, Rabbi Meir neither recommended the abolition of old ritual to thin out the heavy ritualism of eastern European Orthodoxy, nor did he innovate new liturgical or life-cycle practices that would speak to a modern, Western-educated person.

---

4. See my "Halakah Is Not Law," *The Jewish Spectator* (February 1971), 15-18.

Chapter Six
Proto-Modernity:
Renaissance and Reformation

I. INTRODUCTION

The profound currents that swept Europe after 1650, making for a Western cultural revolution, included the industrial revolution, advances in science and technology, and the rise of the national democratic state. The by-products of these phenomenal events included: (1) the application of scientific study and the concept of evolution in the form of historicism to the humanities, liberal arts, social sciences, and the study of religions, including Judaism; and (2) the extension of the democratic idea to Jews. Furthermore, these developments led to significant phenomena in Judaism: a secular view of Jewish history, and a developmental perception of Judaic belief and practice from the standpoint of historicism. Historicism led to the idea that Jewish survival was not the gift of a miraculous, divine salvation-history, but must be understood by normative historical analysis. Furthermore, the conclusion was reached that the theological and ethical precepts and the ritual practices of Judaism were not revealed at one time, but arose and changed within a historical context and are neither mandatory nor eternal.

Historicism frequently led to abandonment of faith and practice, and secularism led to ethnicity in Judaic communal self-perception. The European Enlightenment was paralleled by its Jewish counterpart—the *Haskalah*—which, in its negative elements, intensified the secularization and ethnicization of Judaism. The *Haskalah* combined with messianic nationalism to create modern political Zionism, in time bringing Israel back full circle to the theory denounced by the ancient preacher Samuel, "Let us be like all the nations."

The great social philosophers like John Locke and his successors brought feudal thought to a close. Feudalism was characterized by the idea that human beings are structured in groups. Whether one enjoyed political freedom, economic or educational opportunity, and social mobility depended upon the group into which one was locked. The individual was not judged or dealt with on the basis of individual merit. It was this static hierarchical society that came to an end with the rise to supremacy of the thought of the social philosophers who inaugurated the modern era. As the basis for social relationship shifted to individual merit, individual people gained the dignity of no longer being locked-in to the group into which they were born. This shift made it possible to transform Jews from ghetto denizens into acculturated western Europeans.

Nevertheless, we must acknowledge that John Locke and his confreres stood on the shoulders of earlier humanists, and in some cases, of Reformation thinkers. Similarly, Jewish scholars who brought changes during the eighteenth and nineteenth centuries were already indebted to a few pioneers of the Italian and Dutch Renaissance and to developments that arose out of the Protestant Reformation. It is to these antecedents that we must give some attention.

II THE INFLUENCE OF THE RENAISSANCE ON JUDAISM

A. General Remarks

It is not possible here to examine the full influence of the Italian Renaissance upon Judaism, a task carried forward more extensively in the third volume of my *Emergence of Contemporary Judaism.*[1] In this chapter, we will see, at least through a brief survey of several major figures, how this cultural effulgence influenced some Italian Jews. We will also note how the Italian Renaissance, humanism, and Protestantism in Holland, which opened the way there for Jewish acculturation, had their impact upon the Jewish reformation that occurred in Germany after 1780. The several men to be discussed by no means

---

1. See especially chapter 4.

represented the majority of their coreligionists, from whom they differed radically in lifestyle and in religious thought and sometimes practice. They serve, however, as paradigms for later emulation. Prior to the nineteenth century, when eastern European Orthodoxy in its massive numbers held hegemony in Judaism, men considered in this chapter, such as Azariah dei Rossi, Yoseph Delmedigo, Leone da Modena, and Menasseh ben Israel, were of little importance in Judaic study. While some lived after the Renaissance, the forces that shaped them and made them precursors of modern Judaism are of that period. And while scholars might deny they could have played a significant role in the reforming tendencies of the nineteenth century, it is important to see these men, first, as paradigms and precursors, and second, as sowers of seeds from which grew prolific sprouts.

The eighteenth century saw much tension in Judaic thought, which was generated by these humanist Renaissance scholars and which clashed with the residue of the Sabbatian messianic movement. This tension is highlighted in a paradigmatic struggle between Rabbi Jacob Emden (1697-1776) and Rabbi Yonathan Eibeschutz (d. 1764) in Germany. On the one hand, Emden, as conservative as he was, represented a new breed of scholar who engaged in the study of non-Jewish sources, the sciences, languages, and philosophy, as did the Italian and Dutch humanists. On the other hand, Eibeschutz is the embodiment of the kabalistic and esoteric residue of the post-Sabbatian era. Both Emden and Eibeschutz, however, contributed in strange and contradictory ways to the Reformation, and behind them stood such figures as Azariah dei Rossi and Menasseh ben Israel.

B. Azariah dei Rossi (1513-1578)

Modern Jewish historiography goes back to Azariah dei Rossi, the Italian physician-scholar of Mantua. He produced a collection of essays in *Meor Einayim* under the influence of Renaissance culture. Dei Rossi exhibited the humanist spirit and engaged in what we today call historical criticism. He subjected talmudic passages to comparative criticism and rejected the rabbinic computation of the age of the world. He used Roman historians to document the date and manner in which Titus, the conqueror of Jerusalem, died, and rejected the talmudic aggadah in which Titus is punished by God with a mosquito that enters his nostril and works its way up into his head, ultimately driving him mad and to his death. From Prague in central Europe to Safed in Palestine, dei Rossi was denounced and his book banned.

II. THE INFLUENCE OF THE RENAISSANCE ON JUDAISM

Dei Rossi had no significant successors until the nineteenth century historian Isaac Marcus Jost (1793-1860). Similarly, Baruch (or Benedict) Spinoza (1634-1677), who argued in his *Tractatus Theologico-Politicus* that the perseverance of the Jewish diaspora is not a marvel but dependent upon historical events, had no successors until the secularization of Jewish history in the nineteenth century. But both dei Rossi and Spinoza were read by scholars, as they had read earlier thinkers, and their teachings and the teachings of other Renaissance and pre-modern scholars penetrated the minds of modern Judaic scholars.

Dei Rossi used Roman, Greek, and Christian sources, including the church fathers, and was the first to study Philo and to rehabilitate him as a Jewish philosopher. But while he displayed many features of the modernist, he was in the tradition of the Protestant Reformation and Catholic Counter-Reformation in stressing revelation over reason. There are ambiguities in his work. He accepted the role of demons and miracles in human affairs and such doctrines as immortality and resurrection, despite their nonscientific and nonrational nature. However, he rejected talmudic views of events and phenomena where these were contradicted by science. While the medieval tendency was to harmonize all past religious thought with currently accepted science and philosophy, Azariah dei Rossi evinced the modern tendency to prefer science and reason even at the cost of implying talmudic errancy. Similarly, with intellectual certainty he picked up on the ancient Hellenistic argument that all wisdom and civilization came from the Jews. Nevertheless, he conceded that Jews took their knowledge of astronomy from Hipparchus and Ptolemy and used them in the development of their calendar, thus conceding gentile influence on the occurrence of the holy days. Most interesting of all was dei Rossi's advocacy of international peace. He argued that because Jews are scattered internationally the Jeremiac injunction that they pray for the peace of the land in which they live must be a prayer for universal peace, for the nationalist and feudal wars frustrated the Jewish prayer in the various lands in which it was recited.

Antedating modern scholars by two centuries, dei Rossi anticipated modern intellectual tolerance with his objective and laudatory opinions of Christian scholars such as Augustine, Eusebius, Jerome, and Aquinas. This "softness" on Christians incurred much antagonism, as it did for another Renaissance scholar, Yoseph Shelomo Delmedigo, and dei Rossi was accused of heresy. Yet, dei Rossi rejected all halakic change, even denying the right to change *minhag* (custom). In many ways dei Rossi is the proto-modern scholar-rabbi who reminds us of his first heirs, such as Moses Mendelssohn. Mendelssohn maintained that Judaism is essentially a system of halakic observance, and while he now and then reluctantly favored some modifications, he persisted in defending the inherited regimen.

C. Yoseph Delmedigo (1591-1655)

Delmedigo, also known as Yashar, was born in Candia, Crete, lived later in Padua and ultimately at Frankfurt am Main. He experienced the period when the influence of kabalah was great and when anti-rational, esoteric elements of Judaism were in ascendancy. At the same time, he was also aware of the advance of scientific and naturalistic ideas among Western intellectuals. He embraced the new scientific rationalism, as did others in Italy and Holland, such as Yehudah Aryeh (Leone) da Modena in Venice, and Uriel da Costa and Baruch Spinoza in Amsterdam.

Literary sources give evidence that personal religious observance and synagogue attendance were very weak in Crete. It was an acculturated community, and its savants engaged in humanist studies. Delmedigo studied traditional rabbinical literature, but he also studied Greek and translated parts of Philo. At Padua, Delmedigo experienced a typical secular-humanist education of the seventeenth century, including astronomy with Galileo. He traveled distantly, but everywhere he criticized the cultural narrowness and intellectual confinement of Jewish communities, lamenting the lack of secular studies and the uselessness of the intricate talmudic dialectic in which they engaged, especially in Poland. Wherever he traveled Delmedigo maintained close relationships with Karaites. For a while he lived in Hamburg, where the Reform movement had its origins in the nineteenth century. He taught in a yeshiva (academy of higher rabbinic learning) in Amsterdam, where Menasseh ben Israel befriended him.

It is clear from this brief survey that Delmedigo had many opportunities to sow seeds of Italian humanist modernity in Germany, and to reinforce the same tendency in Holland. His wide reading in a lifelong pursuit of knowledge with a mind open to a great variety of influences and viewpoints resulted in his being eclectic. Thus, his writing sometimes reflects ambivalences in his thinking. At times he is an Aristotelian rationalist, at other times a Platonic mystic. At times he tends toward the European rationalist Enlightenment; at other times he is caught up in the Judaic-centered kabalistic resurgence of the seventeenth century. He would come by his antirationalist moments quite honestly under the influence of his Renaissance predecessors such as Yehudah Moscato (1532-1590), Azariah Figo (1579-1647), and Azariah dei Rossi. It was quite common during the sixteenth century for seminal rationalists to preserve a modicum of belief in magic, astrology, alchemy, and other spheres of occult knowledge. Both a leading Frenchman and an Englishman—Jean Bodin (1530-1596) and Francis Bacon (1561-1626), respectively—share this characteristic.

Delmedigo anticipated Spinoza in pre-modern higher biblical criticism. He attributed errors to copyists, argued that there are insertions by Masoretes, and discussed the influences of foreign languages on the text. He downgraded the importance of Talmud and ridiculed much of the aggadic literature. On the one hand, he attacked the Polish rabbinate for its opposition to secular studies and the general religious lifestyle there; on the other hand, he found much to be positive about in Karaite Jews. Karaism would naturally appeal to Delmedigo as a paradigm of dissent. He attacked the kabalist view that gentiles are impure and do not share in the immortal celestial destiny of the Jew.

In his critique of Jewish parochialism, Delmedigo is a forerunner of the eighteenth- and nineteenth-century scholars, as he is with his emphasis upon secular education. Influenced by these views, Moses Mendelssohn and Herz Wessely introduced secular education into Jewish curricula. Furthermore, Delmedigo is a precursor of the modern scholar in critical study of the Bible, rabbinic literature, and halakah; in the general utilization of modern methodology; and in an ecumenical approach to relationships with all branches of Judaism and with Christianity.

D. Leone da Modena (1571-1648)

Leone da Modena not only perpetuated the Jewish synthesis of the Italian Renaissance with Judaism and was a rabbinic forerunner of the Reforming rabbi of the nineteenth century, but was also a precursor of those who conducted intensive ecumenical interchange with Christian scholars. He was the first Jewish scholar to vindicate Jesus as a Jew. He accepted the Christian Scriptures as a historical source. He anticipated a wide segment of modern scholarship by surmising that Jesus was a Pharisee, and in a vigorous apologetic he denied the role of Jews in the crucifixion. Scholars may now take positions that can be substantiated somewhat more, but da Modena's views nevertheless remain part of Judaic apologetic. The amazing aspect of his views does not concern the correctness of his positions, but that in his time he stepped so far forward in his Christian studies and interests, and in interchange with Christian scholars. Perhaps the most interesting result of this interest was his authorship of *Riti Ebraica* (Rites and Ceremonies of the Jews), translated into English by Edmund Chilmead in 1650. This was a presentation of Jewish religious practice and belief written for James I of England as an indirect reply to Buxtorf's *Synagoga Hebraica*. This aspect of da Modena is of special interest, for unlike Delmedigo, he was not an itinerant scholar but a stable communal rabbi. In this capacity he was not as independent as Delmedigo in his choice of interests and pursuits, which is evident in his sermons to be discussed below. *Riti Ebraica,* however, played a very special role as a source of many English writers on Judaism, such as John Selden (1584-1654).

The century in which da Modena flourished saw a concerted turning away from revelation as a source of knowledge to reliance upon nature and reason. Such luminaries as Descartes, Galileo, Bacon, Spinoza, Newton, Locke, Leibniz, and numerous others influenced Jewish minds. Rabbinic halakah appeared unnecessary and irrational, and its minutiae too restrictive. Such men as Uriel da Costa in Amsterdam ridiculed the aggadah and kabalah. They believed they were as competent as Rashi to set forth biblical exegesis, and empowered to be selective in their halakah. Some, like da Costa, attacked ritual observances such as tefillin as unscriptural, thus appealing to Karaism, and denied doctrines such as immortality as not explicit in Scripture. This type of religious critique was constantly recurring, but usually its advocates were alienated from Judaism and were like branches lopped off a tree.

Leone da Modena joined other Italian rabbis, like Immanuel Aboab, to defend Rabbinic Judaism. Yet these defenders were also frequently acculturated and critical, studied secular literature, did not cover their heads, played tennis on the Sabbath, ate gentile foods and drank gentile wine, and in many other particulars were radically different from those who promoted the *Shulhan Aruk.* Da Modena favored adjusting halakah to time and place, and wrote an early responsum to defend bareheadedness and choral singing in the synagogue. It is of interest, in examining da Modena's liberal halakic postures, that he was born in the year 1571, when the joint Karo-Isserles digest came to public view, and died in the ominous year of 1648, by which time that digest had gained hegemony in eastern Europe and among Sephardic and Ashkenazic Jews elsewhere as well. Nevertheless, Da Modena stands out as a forerunner of the lenient modernist rabbis. These rabbis attempted to restore the ancient halakic moderation of the proto-rabbinic and rabbinic teachers of the talmudic period, when leniency was the rule of thumb in the halakic decision-making process.

The roles of scholar and preacher were often diametrically opposed. Thus da Modena, the scholar, differed from da Modena, the celebrated preacher, who was much in demand in Venice, Ferrara, Florence, and elsewhere. For example, in his sermons he betrayed none of his interest in Christian studies and ecumenism, in which he engaged. Unlike his celebrated predecessor, Moscata, who championed classical studies and drew on these sources for his preaching, da Modena's sermons were designed to edify and elevate his listeners by using Jewish literature alone. To this extent, Moscata, rather than da Modena, is the forerunner of the modern preachers who draw upon world literature, science, philosophy, and history to illustrate their sermons. Furthermore, in his sermons da Modena allowed his listeners to hear what they probably yearned to hear: that Judaism and Jews are superior to Christianity and Christians. Da Modena preached after the papacy had introduced the ghetto and thereby had aborted the opportunities for acculturation on the part of the masses. As a result, he expressed his frustration with this papal enactment in the conservative orientation of his sermons. Another reason for the narrowness of da Modena's sermons was due to the influence, at the end of the sixteenth century, of a group of leading rabbis of a wide variety of cities in Italy, Greece, and Turkey. These rabbis invoked an old fourteenth-century ban by Rabbi Solomon ibn Aderet against a preacher in Mantua that prohibited pagan and secular allusions in synagogue teaching and preaching. We see here a rather significant coalition of rabbis that was turning the Renaissance clock back. Following the papal lead, which ghettoized the Jewish body, this group escalated the ghettoization of the Jewish mind, thus aborting modernity between 1600 and 1800.

III. HOLLAND

A. Pre-Modern Dissent

The phenomenon witnessed in Italy was also present in Holland. Proto-modern spirits and reactionary traditionalists encountered a new age.

The traditionalists, like their counterparts in Italy, sought to suppress dissent to preserve Judaism. Dutch society was relatively open-minded for its time, and many Jews, especially Marranos who came back to full Judaism, were often acculturated and inspired by this environment to critical examination of Judaism and opposition to traditionalist rabbinic authoritarianism. Rabbi Saul Morteira (1596-1660) was one who labored to suppress liberal thought and was instrumental in the excommunication of the two well-known dissenters—Uriel da Costa (1585-1640) and Baruch Spinoza. By twentieth-century standards, da Costa was simply of a reforming tendency, opposed to excessive ritualism and skeptical of some theological doctrines, and finally espousing a naturalistic religion which has affinities with the present-day Reconstructionist movement. He was no different from large masses of twentieth-century Jews who are loyal adherents of synagogues. But da Costa, ahead of his time and far in advance of men like Menasseh ben Israel, ended a tragic suicide.

Whether Spinoza was indirectly influenced by da Costa is uncertain. But Spinoza was a more profoundly educated person, who was deeply influenced by René Descartes, the harbinger of a radically new philosophical age. He was also a friend of Gottfried Leibniz and other major figures of intellectual stature. Spinoza was a dedicated rationalist and abandoned faith in all metaphysical ideas of Judaism that in his view ran contrary to reason, such as angelology and immortality. He rejected an offer by Morteira of a lifelong grant to remain silent about his beliefs, and found spiritual and intellectual satisfaction among the Mennonite Collegiants, working as a lens grinder and writing philosophy prolifically.

Spinoza's great work, *Tractatus Theologico-Politicus,* was a significant critique of revealed religion; it anticipated higher biblical criticism and rejected all miracles as contrary to the laws of nature. He regarded the cultic practices of Judaism and the whole range of ritual as nondivine, historically evolved, and wholly superfluous. In his ethics, Spinoza developed a pantheistic theory in which he saw all material things and individual human souls as part of the infinite divine substance. He also posited a philosophy of determinism, according to which human beings are subject to the inexorable laws of nature. For him, human salvation was in people's rising to the blessed state in which they understand all these things and are no longer burdened by illusory hopes or vain fears in the present or the hereafter, but endeavor to fulfill their natural powers.

B. Menasseh ben Israel (1605-1657)

Spinoza's fate would have been different in 1956 than it was in 1656. It might even have been different in 1656 had his teacher, Rabbi Menasseh ben Israel, been in Amsterdam instead of in England seeking the readmission of Jews to that country. In Menasseh's absence, Morteira expedited Spinoza's excommunication. But Rabbi Menasseh was of a different stripe. Between the extremes of Uriel da Costa and Baruch Spinoza on the one hand, and Rabbi Saul Morteira on the other, there strode this unusual figure, the prototype of Judaic modernity.

Menasseh ben Israel was born a Marrano in Madeira, but was brought back into full Judaism in Amsterdam. His familiar memories apparently did not obscure his vision, and he maintained an affinity and empathy for the Christian world. He probably transmitted some of his proto-modernism to his pupil Baruch Spinoza. But while Menasseh anticipated the eighteenth century, Spinoza was a model for the twentieth and was as yet too radical for acceptance. In founding Amsterdam's first Hebrew publishing company, Menasseh made an important contribution to the spread of Judaica. Versed in Latin and in Christian theology and philosophy, he did much of his writing for Christian audiences. Friend of Hugo Grotius and Rembrandt, and correspondent of Queen Christina of Sweden, he exemplified a new type of rabbi. By far his most interesting Christian friend and admirer, however, was Anna Maria von Schurman of Utrecht, a woman savant even more versatile than Menasseh in languages, erudite in kabalistic and rabbinic learning and in modern literature. She composed poetry and music and conducted a Hebrew correspondence with other women Hebraists. She was apparently friendly enough with Menasseh to have received as a gift from him an autographed copy of David Kimhi's Hebrew grammar.

Menasseh was also a mystic, deeply attached to Lurianic kabalism, and one of those who helped prepare Amsterdam for its disastrous attachment to the messianic pretender Shabbatai Zvi, whose advent and wretched aftermath Menasseh mercifully did not live to witness. It is reasonably certain that Menasseh would have taken the view of his colleague Rabbi Jacob Sasportas (1610-1698), who had accompanied him to England, that there was no warrant in Judaic messianism to accept the claims of Shabbatai Zvi.

Rabbi Menasseh had long been interested in the readmission of Jews to England, and took a vigorously active role to bring this about during the Puritan Revolution and the tenure of Oliver Cromwell. He wrote a pamphlet in 1655 which was translated into English with the title page addressed to the Lord Protector of the Commonwealth, Oliver Cromwell. In two parts, these "Humble Addresses," as they were termed, expounded upon the advantages of readmitting the Jews, and upon how faithful Jews were to the lands of their residence.

Menasseh's wide-ranging reading, from the most ancient of sources right up to an English author like Sir Thomas Browne (1605-1682), is seen in all his writings, but especially in *Vindiciae Judaeorum*. In this critique of the blood libel against Jews, the charge that Jews annually kill a Christian in order to use his blood in the Passover wine and to reenact the crucifixion, Menasseh displays knowledge of Josephus's work *Contra Apion,* in which Josephus accuses Apion of inventing this libel in the Hellenistic era. But Menasseh was not only a new breed of Jewish scholar who read Josephus and Philo—he also demonstrates his familiarity with church fathers such as Justin and Tertullian when he discusses their denunciation of the same blood libel used by pagans against early Christians.

The significant aspect of Menasseh's scholarly work is his proto-modern apologia. Even when he was wrong, for example, in denying that the ancient *amidah* prayer contained a curse upon Christians, he was correct in signifying that Jews did not recite it. It is quite possible that Menasseh never saw a version of the prayer that included the word *notzrim* (followers of the man of Nazareth) in the curse and relied upon the authority of Maimonides that the prayer as worded in his time referred only to a variety of deviant Jews.

Unlike the more traditional rabbis of eastern Europe and Italy, the kabalists, and rabbis of other regions, Menasseh read the current literature on Judaism by gentile scholars such as Johannes Buxtorf, John Selden, and Alexander Ross. Menasseh also read the medieval Christian writers—especially those who expounded upon the anti-Christian details in the so-called six-hundred and thirteen commandments—and sought to make an enormous leap over what he regarded as obsolete medieval and ancient views expressing only one strand within a widely variegated Judaism. Thus, while Maimonides argued that one may exact usury from a gentile "in order to harm him," Rabbi Menasseh could appeal to a contrary view in the Talmud (B. B. Mes. 70b). Though unabashedly apologetic, in effect Menasseh, by appealing to the more universalist strains within Judaism, was bringing Judaism into a posture of ecumenical relationship that has still not been fully consummated three hundred years later. Thus, in his pattern of study, intellectual interests, and outreach to the gentile community, Menasseh anticipated nineteenth- and twentieth-century rabbis. Whereas medieval Jewish scholars were involved in disputations with Christians, Menasseh opened an era of apologetics which could more fruitfully lead to genuine dialogue. Rabbi Menasseh in effect adopted the position that anti-gentile halakah found in early rabbinic literature applied to idolaters and not to monotheists, and argued that since Christians are monotheists neither this halakah nor other pejorative comments apply to them.

These interreligious apologetic labors of Menasseh ben Israel were necessitated by a widely developing coterie of Christian scholars who emerged from the humanistic phenomenon of the Renaissance and from the biblicist orientation of the Reformation. Both tendencies, the interest in Greek classics and the interest in Hebraic biblical studies, inspired people like Menasseh and his Italian colleagues, and brought them into closer intellectual proximity with non-Jews with whom they met and corresponded. Thus, they anticipated twentieth-century interreligious dialogue by three hundred years.

IV. THE PROTESTANT REFORMATION

A. Introduction

There is no truly comprehensive study of the impact of the Protestant Reformation upon Judaism, or of Judaism's influence upon the Reformation. Nevertheless, on the basis of research already done and studies published we can surmise that the Protestant Reformation and Judaism were directly interrelated in some important ways.[2] One of the significant consequences of the Reformation was its contribution to the disintegration of the concept of corporate society and its role in promoting individual conscience. This development in itself ultimately had a strong influence upon the destiny of Judaism, especially in the northern and western European spheres and in North America. Similarly, intellectual tracings can be made from humanist and Renaissance studies to the Reformation that suggest powerful influences of

---

2. See Salo Baron, *A Social and Religious History of the Jews*, XII (Philadelphia: Jewish Publication Society, 1952), 206-96; H. H. Ben-Sasson, "The Reformation in Contemporary Jewish Eyes," *Proceedings of the Israel Academy of the Sciences and Humanities* 4 (1970), 239-326 [English]; 62-116 [Hebrew].

Judaism upon biblical studies, and consequently upon the direction taken by early Reformers and their successors.

During the fifteenth and sixteenth centuries the entire spectrum of European history began to undergo wondrous transformation. Global exploration, the growth of primitive nationalism, and the rise of proto-capitalism all disturbed the traditional institutions of culture, money, and government. The emergence of Protestantism, influenced by all the other forces of change and influencing them in turn, further shook the foundations of medieval Europe. Protestantism arose primarily because intellectually astute and spiritually zealous persons dissented from the corruption and hypocrisy they charged were part of the Roman Catholic Church and the papacy itself. In time the Reformation had important influence in the secularization of governments and religious diversity, both of which affected Judaism in a positive manner.

In essence, the Reformers were searching for pristine Christianity. But just as Thomas Aquinas developed his great synthesis of classical and Christian thought by imbibing Islamic and Jewish philosophy, so too the Reformers were deeply influenced by both humanism and Judaic exegesis of Scripture. The Protestant Reformation influenced study of Judaica, but study of Judaica also influenced the repeated secessions from Rome. Humanism played a great role in Protestantism, especially through the medium of philosophical criticism which influenced biblical translations. Humanist criticism led devout Catholic scholars to skepticism about many Vulgate (the Latin translation of the Bible) renditions, and then inevitably about traditional interpretations of scriptural passages. The discrediting of the Vulgate in turn led to a greater emphasis upon a return to the original Hebrew of the Jewish Bible and to the Greek of the Christian Scriptures, and this emphasis became a hallmark of Protestant dissent. Furthermore, while capitalism imbued people with a fervor for individual enterprise, and humanism for independence in the arts and sciences, the Protestant emphasis upon individual conscience contributed to religious diversity and self-reliance as opposed to submission to papal authoritarianism. In time this emphasis had a beneficial effect upon the equality enjoyed by Judaism in Western societies.

B. The Christian Study of Judaism

The progressive phenomena we have briefly scanned would not have been possible without the invention of the printing press. This invention made accessible for study both biblical and rabbinic writings in

Hebrew and Aramaic all across Europe. Initially this study was given impetus by the Bomberg family's publication of *Mikraot Gedolot,* an edition of Scripture which contained within it all the major Targums and commentaries. The Italian rabbi Elijah Levita, who made important contributions to Masoretic and targumic studies, influenced Sebastian Münster (1489-1552), who became the leading Protestant Hebraist. Münster had been preceded by other translators, like Martin Luther, but his translation was a more scholarly product. He refers in his writings to many Judaic commentaries, and evinces the likelihood that his Latin translation of the Bible is a significant intermediary between medieval Jewish exegetes, Talmud and midrash, and the ultimate English translation of Scripture. Along with many specialized studies and other works, Münster translated the Gospel of Matthew, the Epistle to the Hebrews, and the Apostolic Creed into Hebrew. In his Hebrew and Latin dedication of the biblical translations to Henry VIII of England he discussed Judaism and Christianity, and also published pamphlets examining the two religions in the form of dialogue. Münster's objective was a new type of missionary approach to win Jews to Christianity, and he avoided the invective and polemic of Martin Luther or John Calvin.

Renaissance emphasis upon classical studies influenced the study of Hebrew in Germany, England, France, and elsewhere. Frequently the interest in Hebrew was only in the hope of converting Jews by indicating how the Jewish Scriptures foreshadow the Christian Scriptures. But whatever the motive, rabbinic lore came to Christian scholars either through medieval biblical exegesis or the actual study of talmudic and midrashic sources. Phillipus Ferdinandus Polonus, born a Jew in Poland in 1555, first turned Roman Catholic and later Protestant. He lived in England and later in Leyden (Leiden), and served as an important conduit of Judaic learning to Christians. Although Münster had already discussed systematically the so-called six hundred and thirteen commandments, basing himself on Moses of Coucy's work, Polonus did so as well. This theme attracted many Christian scholars. Polonus also expounded on Maimonides's Thirteen Articles of Faith and on the hermeneutical rules attributed to Rabbi Ishmael of the first century. Polonus also reflects the period's interest in mysticism and discusses *gematriot* (numerology) and other esoteric elements of kabalah. Furthermore, Polonus is known to have influenced Puritan scholars, among them John Selden.

During the peak period of Lorenzo's Florentine Renaissance, Pico della Mirandola (1463-1494) had been among the first known Christian students of the kabalah. His work emphasized the notion that kabalah can be used to prove the divinity of Christ. He understood the kabalah as the application of Neoplatonism to the Bible, and through his writings, especially his *Apology,* he introduced kabalah to such Christian scholars as Johann Reuchlin (1455-1522). For Reuchlin, kabalah was a means of applying the Renaissance to the burgeoning Reformation. In kabalah, Reuchlin, like Pico, found every major doctrine of Christology: the Trinity, incarnation, original sin, and atonement through Christ. Their interest in kabalah in turn led them to extend their Hebraic studies and to influence others to undertake such studies.

Reuchlin believed that the truth of Christianity stems from the primary revelation which God made to Jews, and which contains all religious, scientific, and moral truth. Therefore, he argued for the necessity of studying Hebrew in order to gain direct access to the primary biblical and rabbinic materials. His *De Rudimentis Hebraicis,* published in 1506, virtually opened the world of Hebrew study to Christians. He promoted the study of Hebrew in European universities, which, although slow in coming, ultimately came.

In the earlier period, Christian scholars were compelled to study Judaic materials in order to engage in disputations with Jews to convert them by pointing to alleged Christian evidence in Jewish religious texts. Frequently, Jewish converts to Christianity were active in these activities, for example, Abner of Burgos (d. 1345). The Dominicans engaged in much study of Hebrew and Aramaic texts, and it was from them that one of the most illustrious medieval students of Judaism, Raimundus Martini, gained his learning and became capable of writing one of the greatest of medieval works, *Pugio Fidei.* A Franciscan, Petrus Galatinus, plagiarized Martini's work ca. 1520 in his *De Arcanis Catholicae Ventatis.* Nevertheless, Galatinus's work and others he wrote were important sources for sixteenth-century students.

The *Pugio* was republished during the seventeenth century with much supplementary material by its new editor, Joseph Voisin, including many rabbinic parallels to the Christian Bible. The Reformation spurred efforts among Protestant scholars to extend this type of work from a Protestant viewpoint. Out of this effort there emerged a major work by Surenhusius—a Latin translation of the text of the Mishnah, along with its leading commentaries, accompanied by Christian notes. Similar works emerged on the Talmud and midrashim, and it became stylish to include rabbinic materials in commentaries on Christian

Scriptures. Most of the seventeenth- and eighteenth-century scholars who pursued this effort owed a significant debt to Johannes Buxtorf the Elder's *Lexicon Chaldaicum Talmudicum et Rabbinicum,* published in 1640. Of great importance as well was John Lightfoot's *Horae Hebraicae et Talmudicae,* published between 1658 and 1678.

During the seventeenth century, the study of Jewish antiquities and rabbinic literature went on in such major universities as Leyden and Utrecht. The *Biblia Rabbinica (Mikraot Gedolot)* published by Johannes Buxtorf in 1619 reflected the high level of Judaic studies in Protestant universities. Reference has already been made to the English translation of Leone da Modena's *Rites and Ceremonies of the Jews,* published in English in 1650. Even the backlash to Menasseh ben Israel's efforts to engineer the readmission of the Jews to England was indebted to the rise of Judaic scholarship. These studies made possible and provided a market for such works as William Prynne's *A Short Demurrer to the Jews* and Alexander Ross's *View of the Jewish Religion.* Joseph Meade wrote *The Key to the Revelation,* which contained an appendix on rabbinic views of the eschatological hope with which the author endeavored to show that his view was ancient and was authentically Jewish. Judaic influence upon the millenarian movement in Puritan England was quite extensive. This movement brought forth a spate of books, such as Thomas Brightman's *Revelation of Revelation.*

The millenarian movement had a strong role to play in the readmission of Jews to England, and thus had a historical role in the expansion of Judaism in the English-speaking and Calvinist societies in the eighteenth and nineteenth centuries. The seventeenth and eighteenth centuries were the years of greatest intensity in Judaic learning by Christian scholars, but this learning came to a pause ca. 1750. It resumed in the later part of the nineteenth century, when it relied upon the new Jewish learning that was characterized by the researches of the scholars who formed the *Wissenschaft des Judentum,* and especially the writings of Leopold Zunz. August Friedrich Gfrorer (1803-1861) became the first known Christian scholar to study first-century Judaism as the matrix of Christianity.

C. The Protestant Reformation and
Its Relationship to Judaism

Christian study of Judaism opened new perspectives for Christians, and in some cases offered them more resources for their traditional hope of converting Jews and bringing closer the hour of the Second

Coming. But this was only one of the many ramifications of the humanist Renaissance. The humanists, of whom the most significant was Erasmus, remained Roman Catholic for the most part, but in time they undermined the Roman church and its authority. The emphasis upon classics resulted in a new interest in biblical translations from Greek and Hebrew into Latin and other languages. Soon the return to Scripture in the original was urged as the only valid source of religious truth, with personal conscience rather than traditional interpretations as guide. This emergent independent attitude to religion was only one more aspect of the general turn to individualism that accompanied the great cultural revolution sweeping Europe.

Corporate religious authority was to be secondary to that of the individual confronting the text of Scripture with the aid of the Holy Spirit, which became one more means of penetrating medieval corporate structure and contributed to opening the sluices for Jews to gain identity as individuals. However, neither the Protestant Reformation nor its impact upon Judaism should be simplified in these terms. The early Protestant founders such as Martin Luther (1483-1546), John Calvin (1509-1564), John Knox (1513-1572), and others had ambivalent attitudes toward, but were nevertheless in some measure influenced by, biblical Judaism in their quest for the pristine church, and were strong influences upon the direction of modern Judaism in Protestant countries.

Some scholars date the Reformation to John Wycliffe in England (1330-1384). Wycliffe was master of Balliol College, which possessed the old synagogue of Oxford and a considerable Judaica library left behind at the time of the expulsion of 1290. What influences these had upon him is unclear, but what is certain is that Wycliffe initiated the first English translation of the Bible. In effect, he argued that the apostles used the vernacular, for which the tradition of ancient targum and the Greek translations were supportive evidence. He used the example of the priesthood in Jewish Scripture to argue against the clergy holding private property. Nevertheless, one cannot go too far in assessing the relationship of Wycliffe to Judaism, because, as yet, there is no comprehensive study of his writings to ascertain this relationship.

For whatever historical reasons, Wycliffe had a strong influence upon Jan Hus (John Huss) in Bohemia (1373-1415). Hus was accused of having "counseled with the Jews" before he was burned at the stake. Moreover, Jews were blamed for the Hussite opposition to indulgences, to the church's reverence for saints and relics, and to the hierarchy. But the extent of the influence of Jewish teaching upon Hus is unclear. What is clear is his anger over Jewish rejection of the Trinity and his repetition in his writings of many negative traditions concerning Jews and Judaism. But he did not identify Jews with the antichrist, a frequent medieval sophistry. And some sectarian offshoots of the Hussite movement became so-called Judaizers by demanding a return to biblical dietary practices, including the rabbinic mode of ritual slaughter. More important, however, than the Hussite reformation and its rebellious aftermath, which led to a ten-year violent struggle in which Jews suffered from both Catholics and Hussites, was the indirect outgrowth of the Hussite movement—the Lutheran Reformation.

Martin Luther (1483-1546) expressed great compassion for Jews in 1519 when he charged that Catholic preachers "exaggerate the Jews' misdeeds against Christ," and in his celebrated "Ninety-five Theses" he called for a Judaic-type repentance rather than the traditional Roman Catholic indulgences. He was deeply influenced by his study of the Latin biblical commentaries of Nicholas de Lyra. De Lyra had gained much rabbinic tradition from the medieval Jewish commentator Rashi, and his work is evidenced in both Luther's German translation of the Bible and in his exegetical writings. Luther's awareness of the Judaic heritage in his studies led him to his early outreach to Jews. Luther had anticipated that Jews would be more pleased to adhere to what he considered a purified Christian faith than to the obscurantist Roman Catholic Church. But when this adherence did not occur, he went from a warm attitude in his 1523 tract, *That Jesus Christ Was Born a Jew,* to serious hostility in his *Table Talks* during the 1530s and 1540s.

Luther's theology became distinctly inimical to Judaism because of his misinterpretation of Paul's doctrine concerning faith and works. His vigorous emphasis upon faith led to the vehement rejection of Judaism's ritual content. He compared those he called "the papists" (the Roman Catholics) to the Jews in their demand for observance of traditional ritual, and promised that for this reason "the papists" would perish like Jews. Nevertheless, he sought to win Jews by more moderate means than heretofore extended. He urged that Jews first be taught about Jesus the man, and only after the convert loved him as a person should he be introduced to the subject of Jesus' divinity and be led on to the dogma of the Trinity.

On the whole, however, Jews rejected Luther's blandishments. Furthermore, when some Lutherans saw in Martin Luther the Elijah of pre-messianic days, some Jews (e.g., Rabbi Joseph of Arli) countered with the ironic notion that Luther's contribution to the disintegration of Christian unity and the rise of many sects may rather be a harbinger of the Jewish messiah. Ultimately, therefore, when Luther became entangled in rising German nationalism against international papalism, he became a force for mistreatment of Jews as aliens and as loyal to the Holy Roman Emperor. His opposition to Jews, he surmised, might also reduce the Catholic charge that reformers were "Judaizers," a term that had implied strong abhorrence since early Christian times. To his theological and literary attacks were soon added disjointed fulminations against Jews in the most vile and vituperous language. Whether this attitude was truly what in modern times is called "anti-Semitism" may be questioned, since inquiry into the texts indicates that Luther spoke with the same venomous tongue of princes and bishops, calling even the pope a "son of depravity," and the noted Jew-hater Elector Joachim I of Brandenburg a "mad bloodhound . . . dirty pig." Nevertheless, he also urged that Jews be given over to forced labor and, in his last sermon in 1546, to conversion or banishment. He was no more successful in exhortations, however, than he was in his advocacy of "expelling" the Epistle of James from the Christian Bible for its being too Jewish.

Martin Luther's attacks on Jews are important because his crudities remained enmeshed in German Lutheranism and could be appealed to in the later, more racist nationalism that allowed for the Hitlerian aberration. Whether Luther, who could watch the ravishing of the peasant, could have been silent during the Hitlerian era must remain a matter of speculation. The scope of this chapter does not permit more extensive treatment of Luther's followers, like Philipp Melanchthon (1497-1560) or Andreas Osiander (1498-1552).[3] These and others were milder than Luther but did not undo some of his harshest influence.

Ulrich Zwingli (1484-1531) influenced new directions in the burgeoning Protestant movement, but ultimately his version of reformation was displaced by that of John Calvin. They and other Reformation figures, like Martin Bucer (Butzer, 1491-1551) and Wolfgang Capito (Kopfel, 1478-1541), studied the works referred to earlier that conveyed Judaica and especially rabbinica, which certainly colored their thinking—sometimes positively, sometimes negatively. They also con-

---

3. See my *Emergence of Contemporary Judaism*, III, 51-52.

sulted living Jews, such as the celebrated Josel of Rosheim, on both Judaism and Jewish life. Men like Josel were themselves versed in Christian matters and even attended Christian sermons and lectures (Josel attended Capito's). Although they defended toleration and pluralism for themselves vis-à-vis Rome, none of these Christian Reformation figures was yet able to rise to a theory of equality for Judaism. A person like John Knox might have been vindictive and authoritarian in his day, but his stand for the right to dissent and to resist tyranny went far beyond the confines of the Presbyterian movement.

It is not possible to discuss every initiator of Protestant tendencies, but on the whole the major ones like Luther, Calvin, Knox, and John Wesley (1703-1791), sometimes despite themselves, had a longterm, beneficial influence upon Western democracy. Thus, in 1517, when Luther took the momentous step of posting his famous ninetyfive theses on the door of the church in Wittenberg, and in 1520, when he burned the papal bull that threatened him with excommunication, he sowed the seeds of freedom represented by the Protestant Reformation. Furthermore, although Luther had little use for defectors from his own movement, or for Jews who remained aloof contrary to his expectations, the concept of religious self-determination that he initiated was all-important and had its historic impact. The new attitude, breaking through the dense underbrush of medieval Roman Catholic conformity and authoritarian suppression, led to the hospitable spirit that was amenable to Jewish settlement and development in Holland.

The Reformation aided this hospitable spirit in a variety of countries, though there were exceptions among some Anabaptist radicals. Still, some Anabaptists engaged in true ecumenicity for a short time in Münster. The Reformation, like Judaism, was not monolithic, and developed differently in Germany, Switzerland, the Scandinavian countries, France, Holland, England, and Scotland. On the whole, this complex succession of events and transformations, which we call the Reformation, had a significant impact upon social and intellectual history. In a certain sense it ushered in what is called the "modern era" in history, and it is therefore no surprise that Judaic modernity took root earliest in Protestant countries, while in Counter-Reformation Italy, where it had shown great promise during the Renaissance, it was aborted.

Martin Luther's influence, however, exacerbated anti-Jewish elements in German nationalism. His influence upon followers and disciples led to the perpetuation of anti-Judaic attitudes that were only eliminated in secular constitutional democracies. Protestant intellectuals were no different from theologians. For example, a Heidelberg historian, Heinrich Alting, felt inclined to attack the papacy with the charge that it absorbed too much Judaism. Possibly the smaller proliferating sects contributed to religious liberty and therefore Jewish religious equality more than mainline Reformation groups. But space does not permit a discussion of sects such as the Sabbatarians in Transylvania, or the complex called "Anabaptists," who incorporated many widely differing groups having in common only opposition to infant baptism.[4] The interrelationship of all these groups with Jews and Judaism, and their attitudes, which might have influenced the future of Judaism, have yet to be comprehensively set forth.

Such a study is still required for John Calvin (1509-1564) as well. Calvin contributed significantly to Protestant Bible study and interest in Judaica by his emphasis upon study and its broad application to Hebrew at his academy in Geneva, where students absorbed eight weekly lectures in Hebrew. Calvin's furtherance of the Christian study of Judaica cannot be underestimated in evaluating the direction of English Puritan intellectualism. It helps explain the great spate of books on Judaism during the remainder of the sixteenth and through the seventeenth century.

Calvinists made little headway in Germanic lands, and, as Huguenots, were driven out of France in 1685. But Calvinism became predominant in Holland, and was the leading dissenting group in the British Isles. Although it was relegated to a dissenter status by the established Church of England, Calvinism in England, in France, and in other English-speaking lands had an enduring influence. The emergence of Calvinism inevitably affected Jews and Judaism strongly, despite the fact that Calvin had little to do with Jews before his residence in Strassburg (1539-41). Some question whether, with his weak knowledge of German, he read Luther's virulent attacks on Jews contained in certain of his pamphlets. But, as was the case with other reformers and Christian theologians in general, Judaism was inevitably on Calvin's mind and Judaic exegesis, even by the disdained rabbis, was imbibed in his studies. Ultimately, Calvin, like other clergy, was prone to inject Judaic notions into his christological commentaries and sermons. Sensitive to this reality, he projected upon others what he

---

4. See my *Emergence of Contemporary Judaism*, III, 56-59.

feared was his own flaw. Thus, when Calvin met Philipp Melanchthon, who insisted upon using Hebrew in the church, he accused the Lutheran liturgy of being too Jewish.

Scholars believe that Calvin did not make extensive use of Nicholas de Lyra's *Postillae,* a major medieval source of rabbinic commentary drawn upon by many Christian scholars. It is apparent, however, that Calvin read Rabbi Isaac Abarbanel, or sources that cited him. Calvin's commentaries have remarks about the strength in grammar evident in rabbinical biblical commentaries, a fact which itself points to his having imbibed this type of influence. But the influences that worked upon Calvin have not been exhaustively extrapolated from his writings. For instance, he studied Judaic sources in the writings of Michael Servetus (Miguel Serveto) (1511-1553), but he attacked Servetus for his "Judaizing." Servetus was antitrinitarian and a forerunner of modern Unitarianism, but was nevertheless insistent that the Christian Scriptures fully displaced the Jewish, and that Jews ought to accept the inevitable. Servetus became the first victim of Calvinist heresy-hunting, being burned at the stake in 1553.

Ultimately, however, the Protestant Reformation led to toleration and advocacy of pluralism in religion in Western democratic societies. Calvin's dictatorial theocracy in Geneva did not survive. Out of the admixture of humanist principles and Protestant dissent came a climate of opinion that led to the equality of Judaism. The return to the Jewish Bible, interest in rabbinic exegesis, and Calvinist rabbinic-like emphasis upon "law" all built unprecedented bridges to facilitate Protestant-Jewish relationships. Although the Catholic Counter-Reformation set back Catholic-Jewish interchange for centuries, the Church Council Vatican II in the 1960s instituted a new age which has yet to be brought to fruition.

Chapter Seven

The Modern and Contemporary Periods

I. SOCIAL, POLITICAL, ECONOMIC, AND CULTURAL INFLUENCES

A. Introduction

The fifteenth to the nineteenth centuries witnessed the growth of humanism, the Italian Renaissance, and the Protestant Reformation, all of which contributed positively to the evolution of Judaism. New global exploration and colonization introduced new physical and intellectual horizons to all people, but especially to Jews in pursuit of new frontiers offering greater personal freedom. Science, global travel, technology, and the transformation of the medieval feudal mind-set all contributed to new directions in Judaic thought and practice. Moreover, the Industrial and French Revolutions brought many of the changes in Judaism to fruition.

The jurist Sir Henry Maine characterized medieval Europe as a "status society," with a status pyramid extending from king to serf. This societal structure excluded Jews, who were unable to take the Christian oath which bound it all together. Jews were wards of the king living in any given area by sufferance of the king alone, subject to specific contractual arrangements. Individual Jews derived their status only from membership in a corporate entity—the Jewish community. The corporate Jewish community, the *Kahal* (or *Qahal*), had virtual religious autonomy, and its oligarchic leadership enjoyed a great measure of authority over all of its members, leaving little room for dissent, denominationalism, and religious innovation. Furthermore, this authority helps explain why so little substantive change occurred in either halakah or theology between the eleventh and eighteenth centuries. During that period there was constant accretion of practices related to the life-cycle, and a proliferation of liturgy. Uniformity was enforced within communities, though Judaic ritual practice and liturgy varied among Jews in different locales, among ethnic groups, and between mystics and rationalists.

All these conditions underwent radical change when the medieval "contract society" gave way to the modern emphasis upon the individual. The Jew was no longer to be dealt with as a "Jew" but as a "person." The French Revolution brought this social and intellectual development to a head. The process of Jewish transformation took a long time. Its lines, however, were clearly patterned by 1880, first in western England and northern and western continental Europe; later, albeit less comprehensively, in Poland, Russia, and the Baltic and Balkan states. Jews of Galicia, a sometime province of Russia or Poland, became part of the Austro-Hungarian empire during the eighteenth century and therefore emerged among leaders of a new Western-oriented *haskalah* (enlightenment) earlier than those of others in the East.

This process of Jewish entry into the society around them and their consequent acculturation during the eighteenth and nineteenth centuries is called "Emancipation." The process was checkered throughout Europe, with Jews of the West and those in Protestant countries more influenced earlier by humanism, the Renaissance, and the Reformation than those of the East. *Musar* (moralistic) literature of the seventeenth century already deplored Jewish interest in the theater, an activity which required a degree of acculturation and a measure of social mingling between Jews and Christians. It cannot be determined how early these acculturated Jews began to think of themselves as "Europeans," but sources verify that such views, with a consequent lack of desire to return to Palestine, were already current in Holland at the turn of the seventeenth century.

Jewish acculturation to secular society was facilitated by the travels of such Renaissance figures as Delmedigo, who sowed its seeds all across Europe. Furthermore, the growing interest of Jews in their surrounding culture is evident in Poland, where Solomon Maimon (1753-1800) discovered liberating secular books in his father's library. The process was influenced by the change in Christian outlook deeply inspired by John Locke's *Letter Concerning Toleration* written in 1688, in which Locke defended offering civil rights to pagans, Moslems, and Jews. The first concrete expression of this toleration was

Emperor Joseph II's Edict of Toleration in 1781-82 in Austria. French Jews, however, were the first to receive actual citizenship, in 1790-91, and Jewish emancipation spread across Europe with Napoleon's French armies.

Social relationships between Jews and Christians always took place, either openly or surreptitiously. But such relationships became more intensified during the eighteenth century, especially in Berlin. Aaron Solomon Gumperz, Moses Mendelssohn, and Solomon Maimon all belonged to and frequented intellectual societies and coffeehouses with Christians. Nevertheless, the Christian mentality was not yet capable of understanding how Jews could be acculturated and preserve their Judaism. Thus, even an enlightened monarch like Frederick IV refused to ratify the election of Moses Mendelssohn to the Academy of Science. Indeed, the Christian thinker Johann Kaspar Lavater challenged Mendelssohn to take what Lavater regarded as the natural step from acculturation to Christianity. But Mendelssohn's position was that Judaism is in full conformity with a rational philosophical outlook and is therefore the proper place for a philosopher.

The process of Jewish-Christian intellectual integration was a long one. Here and there efforts were made to hasten it by orienting one to the other through intellectual communion and mutual familiarity with their religious symbols. One such formal society was the Order of the Asiatic Brethren founded in 1781 in Vienna, with branches in many cities. But it lasted only until 1792. More productive were the celebrated salons conducted by acculturated Jewish women in Berlin and Vienna where Jews were able to meet and dialogue with Christian statesmen, literary figures, and intellectuals.

Christian Wilhelm Dohm (1751-1820), economist and historian, published *Über die burgliche Verbesserung der Juden* in 1781, a work symptomatic of the growing philosophical attitude which helped change the intellectual climate of Europe and bring about the full emancipation of Jews and their subsequent comprehensive cultural integration. Dohm came to the significant insight that the mutual antipathy of the two religious groups which have a common origin has persisted longer than the philosophical mind would guess and desire after such a long time. This statement of basic recognition that Judaism and Christianity have a common origin, and that the mutual antipathy over what happened almost two millennia earlier is no longer rational, epitomizes the intellectual progress which made possible the consummation of modern Judaism.

I. SOCIAL, POLITICAL, ECONOMIC, CULTURAL INFLUENCES

The calls of such men as Locke and Dohm to grant Jews full naturalization into European societies received a strong impetus from the French Revolution. Nevertheless, opposition continued, and Napoleon therefore decided in 1806 to call for an Assembly of Jewish notables to convene in Paris, in order to indicate by their answers to crucial questions whether indeed Jews were capable of being loyal citizens, fully willing to conform to the laws of the land and the requirements of patriotic duty.

The Assembly debated twelve questions submitted by Napoleon, and a "Sanhedrin" convoked by him in 1807 ratified the conclusions reached. In essence, the "Sanhedrin" reinforced the principle of *dina demalkutah dina* (sovereign law is binding), and selected lenient options and innovative interpretations of the halakah whenever possible without any radical break with older tradition. The most interesting formulation was probably the response to whether a Jew may marry a Christian, in which the rabbis indicated that the Torah's ban extends only to Canaanites, and that even the Ezraic-Nehemian extension of the ban is applicable only to idolaters and consequently does not apply to Christians. They said that although the marriage sacrament, the kiddushin, is not possible between a believer and a nonbeliever, civil marriage between a Jew and a Christian would be a valid marriage. This and other replies paved the way for the spread of emancipation as well as for new approaches to the halakah in the soon-to-emerge Reform and Conservative movements.

B. Moses Mendelssohn (1729-1786)

Mendelssohn has become the figure around whom the mystique of the rise of modern Judaism has been woven. But one must be aware that he stood upon the shoulders of the Italian and Dutch figures discussed earlier and based his studies and his pattern of Judaic development upon other precedents among rabbinic figures who indulged their intellectual curiosity. Furthermore, he was part of a coterie of contemporaries breaking through the old mold and not only contributing to new directions in Judaism but also to the general culture. For example, Solomon Maimon was considered the greatest Jewish thinker since Spinoza and a major force in post-Kantian philosophy.

Mendelssohn was born on September 6, 1729, in Dessau, Germany. Dessau was a vital intellectual center in a century when the humanist-Renaissance influences were expressed in a new German *Aufklärung* which emphasized the universality of human nature, natural law, and reason, and which proclaimed all human beings equal. Mendelssohn was attracted to Locke and to his disciple John Toland, who considered anti-Jewish behavior a form of inhumanity and called for civil equality for Jews in the British Isles. While Mendelssohn received a traditional talmudic-oriented education, he early digressed into the study of the Hebrew language, Bible, philosophy, and secular subjects. From Moses Maimonides's *Guide for the Perplexed,* which he found among many other literary products in science and philosophy in the bookstores of the publishing center of Dessau, he branched out into several other areas and soon developed into a kind of proto-*haskalah* scholar. Coming under the influence of a Galician Jew, Israel ben Moses halevi Samosz (1700-1772), a great synthesizer of rabbinics and philosophy, Mendelssohn went on to study Latin, French, and English and was further influenced by an Italian Renaissance type, Aaron Solomon Gumperz (1723-1769). Mendelssohn was attracted to Rabbi Menasseh ben Israel and Baruch Spinoza, thus adding Dutch Jewish humanism to the variegated influences that shaped his thought. In 1782 he wrote a preface to a German translation of Menasseh's *Vindiciae Judaeorum.* Mendelssohn's co-worker, the educational pioneer Naphtali Herz Wessely, also appealed to Menasseh for support in bringing the sciences, arts, and crafts into Jewish education.

In his *Jerusalem,* Mendelssohn called for greater freedom of conscience within the Jewish community, possibly having in mind the hostility of such traditionalists as Rabbi Raphael Cohen of Hamburg-Altona to Jewish enlightenment and specifically to his own recent German translation of the Pentateuch. Mendelssohn's call for a modicum of freedom from excessive ecclesiastical authority provoked some thinkers to challenge him to surmount old rabbinic authority and to allow for greater conformity to Christianity. But Mendelssohn's apologetic veered from that course. Although he rejected punitive ecclesiastical authority as not in keeping with the spirit of religion and urged religious pluralism within Judaism, he nonetheless upheld the basic regimen of ritual as the essence of God's revelation. For Mendelssohn Judaism was "revealed legislation" designed for Jews alone, although he claimed that Judaism also possesses the natural religion of humankind.

The winds of change in European Judaism were evident from Mendelssohn's ability to have a close relationship with a traditionalist like Rabbi Jacob Emden, who cherished secular erudition, who studied the Christian Bible, and who avowed respect for the historical Jesus.

I. SOCIAL, POLITICAL, ECONOMIC, CULTURAL INFLUENCES

It is not possible in this chapter to examine Mendelssohn's religious philosophy in depth. Suffice it to say that Mendelssohn believed that reason was capable of arriving at the truths of Judaism, but that Judaism had no dogmas. Moreover, he maintained that action (fulfillment of the "revealed legislation"), not belief, is the criterion of salvation. He argued further that if Christianity would eschew the irrational, with which he identified Christology, Judaism could accept Jesus as a prophetic teacher to the gentiles. Thus he did not go so far as to say Jesus could be readmitted to the Jewish pantheon of prophets and sages, but he was radically advancing the grounds of ecumenical interchange. For with this view of how Christianity could be accommodated to Judaism, Mendelssohn was anticipating certain aspects of twentieth-century dual covenant theology. Dual covenant theology maintains that the mysterious will of God might have intended two paths—Judaism and Christianity—to salvation. But Mendelssohn was not yet prepared to concede that the two figures, Moses and Jesus, might serve on both tracks, that just as Moses is a teacher to Christians, Jesus could be a teacher to Jews.

Mendelssohn, however, failed to persuade his generation. Above all, he seemed to paint himself into a corner with his emphasis upon the validity of traditional ritual as "revealed legislation." It was precisely this regimen of minutiae that obstructed the enlightened Jew from freely joining in the society around him. For the need to observe dietary practices and to abstain from work when the Sabbath and holy days occurred on regular work days prevented Jews from mixing with gentiles and entering new occupations. Perhaps because Mendelssohn had a personal emotional bond in his maternal lineage that led back to Moses Isserles, the sixteenth-century Polish halakic authority who put his stamp upon eastern European traditionalism, he was incapable of transmitting a viable form of Judaism to his own children and many of his followers. The one great desideratum—halakic reform—was an idea foreign to Mendelssohn and was the chief cause of his basic failure. The description of eighteenth-century Jewish life in Berlin as a place where Jews already "buy and sell on Saturdays, eat all forbidden foods, keep no fast days" pointed to the great challenge halakic scholars faced, a challenge Mendelssohn avoided. He died believing in freedom of conscience but conformity in practice. Modern Jews needed the same freedom in practice as in conscience. They could not live by a theology conforming to universalist naturalist humanism while still bound by thirteenth-century halakah embodied in the sixteenth-century Karo-Issereles compilation. A spiritual breakdown took place in Mendelssohn's own generation, followed by a great wave of conversion to Christianity in the nineteenth century, until it was stemmed by the success of the vigorous drive for the reformation of Judaism.

C. Educational Reform

It is an axiom that at the heart of all social change must be change in the education of the young. The *Maskilim* (enlighteners) who followed Mendelssohn labored at bringing about change in the curricula of Jewish schools and in a variety of publishing endeavors. Naphtali Herz Wessely (1725-1805), a foremost Hebraist who had collaborated on Mendelssohn's Pentateuch, was a leading influence. He was involved in both the Hebrew-language journal *Hameaseph* (The Gatherer) and in the transformation of curricula from exclusive talmudic emphasis to secular and vocational education in order to facilitate the integration of the rising generation into the surrounding culture. The task was to train the youth in the sciences, languages, mathematics, history, and geography.

Traditionalists bitterly opposed the changes. Some decades earlier the same traditionalist elements had at first prevented Solomon Maimon from settling in Berlin, which Maimon attributed to their suspicions that his desire to study medicine there was only a cloak for devoting himself to science. Traditionalists regarded the pursuit of science with no greater approbation in 1778, still believing that it was inimical to the religious life. They also assailed both the absence of rabbinics and the effort to reorient the thought-pattern of the young to the intellectual interests of the larger society in *Hameaseph*. They were even more antagonistic when the *Maskilim* established the German-language periodical *Sulamith* in 1806 "to promote culture and humanism" among Jews.

Despite the opposition of the traditionalists, more schools of the Wessely pattern followed in many cities, spreading to Austria and Czechoslovakia. These schools broke the hold of traditional talmudism upon the curriculum and consequently upon individual conduct. They emphasized the vernacular over the Yiddish language and moral principles over ritual.

Many educators were true to their master, Mendelssohn, by remaining relatively traditional in their observance and by teaching traditional ceremonials to their students. Others, however, believing that

much of the ritual had lost its meaning, worked toward radical reformation of religious patterns. In effect, the more liberal educators reversed Mendelssohn's dictum that Judaism's special feature beyond natural religion was its ritual, declaring that it was rather its doctrines that were unique to the faith.

D. Stirrings of Religious Reform

1. Introduction

Many Jews were dissatisfied with services where worshipers prayed aloud—each at his or her own pace—creating an atmosphere of anarchy and bustle rather than devotion and meditation. This discontent with what was considered a nonaesthetic environment in the synagogue promoted a quest for major religious reform. As early as the 1790s, Rabbi Saul Berlin of Frankfort-an-der-Oder favored such reforms as allowing gentile wine, shortening the daily prayers, and not requiring early burial—all matters of considerable dispute. In Westphalia, Israel Jacobson innovated changes in liturgy, including choral and instrumental music, and repealed the medieval prohibition on the use of rice and legumes on Passover.

2. Saul Ascher (1767-1822)

In 1794, Saul Ascher wrote *Leviathan,* in which he argued for an underlying historical right to change ritual while preserving its essence. In this book Ascher planted the seeds of the coming reformation, a term which he himself used. Unlike Spinoza, who believed that ancient and medieval usages were no longer vital, and who abandoned Judaism, Ascher determined to revitalize and preserve his faith. Consequently, he emphasized the theological tenets of Judaism, and even used the term *dogma* to denote them. Ascher posited the centrality of belief in the existence of God, revelation, the covenant, resurrection, and redemption—the last, however, without national restoration. Moreover, he declared that rituals could be changed, except for the indispensable practices of circumcision, the Sabbath, holy days, and atonement.

3. David Friedländer (1750-1834)

David Friedländer, regarded as Mendelssohn's successor in Berlin, translated the Jewish prayerbook into German under Mendelssohn's supervision. It appeared in 1786, but contained no innovation, abridgment, or omission, and reaffirmed the prayers for the restoration of

Jerusalem and the sacrificial cult. Although he considered the boisterous form of Purim observance disgraceful, Friedländer nevertheless defended it. After Mendelssohn's death, however, Friedländer became more radical. From his correspondence with a certain Meir Eger of Glogan, we learn of his intention to introduce drastic reforms. He castigated the rabbis as medieval, clinging to outworn and irrelevant traditions. In 1793, Lazarus BenDavid called for a natural biblical religion devoid of the ritual, a position with which Friedländer agreed. Like Solomon Maimon and others, Friedländer even toyed with the idea of entering Christianity. He now argued that the ritual practices were introduced by Moses, not revealed by God, and were designed to free a new people from old idolatrous practices, a purpose no longer significant. In a Christianity devoid of Christology and a ritual-less Judaism he could see common ground.

Friedländer expounded his position in a letter to the enlightened theologian William Abraham Teller, but it encountered negative critique from both Christians and Jews. Meanwhile, Friedländer's hope for reform improved in 1806, when he was elected as elder by the Berlin Jewish Community, and when the edict declaring Jews equal citizens in Prussia was promulgated on March 11, 1812. He now proposed extensive liturgical changes, including the use of the vernacular, removal of prayers for national restoration, and elimination of large segments of liturgy which he regarded as irrelevant. A storm of opposition arose. Reform was aborted in Berlin, but Friedländer and others worked at it in other newly established congregations. Traditionalists vigorously opposed these efforts and were able to convince the Prussian government, which was opposed to all forms of divisiveness, that reform leads to sectarianism. The government abolished the reform congregations in 1823. Discouraged by this turn of events, Friedländer again began to urge a fusion of enlightened Judaism and Christianity, but once again, no substantial move was made in this direction. For the rest of his life Friedländer persevered in the Society for the Scientific Study of Judaism and was a close friend of Leopold Zunz.

II. THE JUDAIC REFORMATION

A. The Science of Judaism

The Society for the Scientific Study of Judaism, which promulgated the modern critical and historical methods for the study of "The Science

of Judaism," was an important factor in transforming modern Jewish scholarship and contributed to the establishment of both the Reform and Conservative movements in Judaism. At its inception, the most notable motivating figure in this endeavor was Leopold Zunz (1794-1886). Zunz was born into a traditionalist environment and was subjected to the traditionalist talmudic curriculum. Early in life, however, he discovered the abridged work of Josephus, *Josippon.* In 1807 his school turned to *haskalah* and introduced secular subjects and the rite of confirmation. Zunz later lived in Berlin, where he prayed in a Reform congregation, and, like David Friedländer, when he was discouraged by the lack of progress in Reform, he toyed with the notion of converting to Christianity. After 1815, his studies at the University of Berlin brought him to a recognition of the importance of applying *Wissenschaft,* scientific method and historicism, to Judaism. In 1816 he joined a *Wissenschaftszirkel,* a cultural discussion group. This group only lasted a year, but ultimately some of its members regrouped in 1819 as a *Verein* (a society or club) and later organized as *Der Verein für Cultur und Wissenschaft der Juden,* which published a periodical, *Zeitschrift für die Wissenschaft des Judentums.* The *Verein* lasted only until 1824 but had an enduring impact upon modern Judaic scholarship.

Zunz published seminal articles in the *Zeitschrift,* but his most notable contribution was his celebrated *Die Gottesdienstlichen Vorträge der Juden,* which investigated the evolution of Judaism through the development of its liturgy and the synagogue. This investigation was the paradigm for how a modern scholar was to apply the critical method to ancient sources and sift the massive literature to discriminate between the pertinent and the irrelevant. By 1840, he abandoned his earlier interest in reform, being more circumspect in his role as director of the Berlin Teachers Seminary. In 1843, he defended the use of tefillin, a ritual eschewed by reformers, and in a letter to Abraham Geiger in 1845 he attacked the abandonment of the dietary practices. Nevertheless, his work significantly motivated men like Isaac Marcus Jost and Heinrich Graetz, the earliest modern Jewish historians, and even more importantly such religious leaders as Abraham Geiger (1810-1874) and Zechariah Frankel (1801-1875), two prominent mid-century advocates of Reform Judaism and of what was to become the Conservative movement in Judaism.

The *Verein* precipitated scientific research similar to the work of Zunz in France and Italy, and ultimately the Jewish Theological Seminary in Breslau was committed to the critical study of Judaica.

Moreover, the same pattern of scientific study of Judaism was extended to England and North America.

B. The Founding of the Reform Movement

1. Israel Jacobson (1768-1828)

Israel Jacobson founded a modern nonsectarian school in Seesen in 1801, where Christians taught secular subjects and Jews taught Judaic subjects. He also formed a small chapel, which he called a temple, in order to inaugurate reforms that could not be effected in the community synagogue. He abbreviated the liturgy and introduced hymnal singing and a regular sermon. In 1808, he installed an organ and a mixed male and female choir. He repeated these activities in Cassel, where in 1810 he introduced the rite of confirmation. It was confirmation, carried out in the form of a Protestant rite, even including a catechetical public examination of the confirmand, that evoked the strongest protest from traditionalists. With these basic changes one might say Reform Judaism was formally inaugurated. In 1813, Jacobson moved to Berlin, where he and others attempted to establish a Reform synagogue, but the opposition elicited a declaration by the government, in 1823, that Jewish worship must be conducted without any modifications from tradition. This aborted reform in Berlin for twenty years. As one scholar has noted, the traditionalists had achieved a Pyrrhic victory, for a wave of conversions swept Prussia.

2. Eduard Kley (1789-1867)

Other characteristics of Reform Judaism began to take root. In 1818, Eduard Kley established a Reform temple in Hamburg where prayers for redemption were reformulated to include not only Jews but all humanity, and messianic prayers were changed to prayers for a new age of peace and justice for all humankind. Confirmation was introduced at Hamburg for girls as well as boys, and soon thereafter, wherever a Reform temple opened, this ceremony was observed for both sexes, generally at Shabuot. Despite his liberal attitude toward secular learning, Rabbi Isaac Bernays (1792-1849) vigorously denounced these reforms and banned the Hamburg temple's prayerbook.

3. Polemics with Traditionalists

Israel Jacobson enlisted the halakic participation of international scholars in assessing the legitimacy of Reform innovation. Two rabbis

from Italy and two from Hungary wrote responsa in which they supported the use of instrumental music and vernacular prayer. Jacobson's agent in this matter, Eliezer Liebermann, published the responsa in a book called *Nogah Hatzedeq* (Light of Righteousness). Hamburg traditionalist rabbis followed this book with the publication of twenty-two responsa in a collection called *Elleh Dibrey Haberit* (These Are the Words of the Covenant), which condemned the Hamburg innovations. This collection also resorted to a stern polemic, which accused the Reformers of being infidels and rascals, "neither Jews nor Christians." The Reformers answered with satire, and the traditionalists began to speak of expulsion. Both sides appealed for government support, and while the traditionalists managed to close the Berlin temple, the Reformers were able, after 1833, to secure a government order in Saxe Weimar to conduct worship in German and to eliminate specific prayers. These Reform beginnings spread from Vienna to other places in Bohemia and Hungary, and to Denmark, America, and England. Ironically, they spread to Prague in 1837, from which only eighteen years earlier all innovations were strongly condemned.

4. Abraham Geiger (1810-1874)

Abraham Geiger was a leading scholar of Zunz's *Wissenschaft* group. Like Zunz he was born into typical German traditionalism. Geiger became a rabbinic scholar, but later went on to study philology and history at Heidelberg and Bonn. As a young rabbi he was an early Reformer, and became involved in a bitter conflict which went on for years with his senior rabbi, Solomon Tiktin in Breslau. This conflict was a microcosm of the great tension and controversy in nineteenth-century Judaism. Geiger began calling for a conference of progressive rabbis as early as 1837 to discuss the essentials of Judaism and how to resolve the great conflicts between modern life and inherited tradition. The first such conference was called at Brunswick in 1844, and gathered modernist rabbis from a wide geographical sweep.

Geiger was a broad, original scholar and prolific writer. He argued that Judaism, like all religion, and religion, like all human institutions, underwent continuous development, and that every generation has a right to modify the practices and rethink and recast the ideas of the past. Geiger saw Judaism as having passed through three stages: the creative age of revelation, the dynamic talmudic age, and the stultified medieval period, which he believed had come to a close. He argued that Judaism was now in its fourth period, in which the narrower scope of ritualism and particularism was to be broadened into a universalist ethical system.

Geiger held that, as an evolving faith, Judaism must discard obsolete ritual, for ritual is but a manner of expressing an idea, and while the idea may be eternally valid, the mode in which it is concretized in rite can vary. He understood correctly that circumcision is a sacrificial act, and therefore he advocated its abrogation, holding that it no longer had significance in a more spiritualized faith. Similarly, he regarded dietary practices as relics of ancient taboos and rejected them. He espoused the idea that Jews were elected servants of God with a religious mission; consequently, he rejected ethnicity and nationalism and called for full acculturation. Furthermore, he excised all liturgical references to the Messiah and the restoration of Jerusalem in his Breslau prayerbook of 1854. He reserved only a minimal role for Hebrew in worship and favored German hymns over the older Hebrew ones.

5. Samuel Holdheim (1806-1860)

Geiger was supported by people like Samuel Holdheim, who went even beyond his views. Holdheim argued that the destruction of Jerusalem and the end of the Jewish state in the year 70 forever brought an end to the nationalist element of Judaism. He went so far as to argue that while a seventh-day Sabbath was in keeping with sovereignty in its own land, Judaism may observe a Sabbath that is in keeping with diaspora reality. He therefore urged moving the Sabbath to Sunday and discarding all its restrictions. He advocated the replacement of all halakah of marriage and divorce with civil law and permitting mixed marriage, especially with Christians who did not come under the biblical interdiction. Since it is birth that gives status to a Jewish child, rather than circumcision, Holdheim argued that circumcision was neither mandatory nor desirable under modern conditions. He introduced a female choir into the synagogue, desegregated the sexes at worship, abandoned the tallit, and inaugurated bareheaded worship. Furthermore, he abolished the shofar on Rosh Hashanah, and gave the rabbi the duty of pronouncing the priestly benediction (formerly reserved for Jews presumably descended from the ancient priests). A good proportion of Holdheim's changes in Berlin became the pattern for Reform Judaism in America but never prevailed in Germany.

C. Dissent from Reform: The Positive-Historical School

1. Zechariah Frankel (1801-1875)

It was largely Geiger's views on liturgy which led to Zechariah Frankel's dissent from the reforming rabbis. Frankel was also a *Wissenschaft* leader. He was born in Prague and received both a traditional talmudic and a secular education. In 1831 he received both a doctorate and rabbinic ordination, and in his synagogues at Teplitz and Dresden he introduced a number of reforms. By later standards these appear mild: a male choir, the sermon in German, and the omission of certain medieval *piyyutim* (hymns). Frankel was a halakist and a scholar of rabbinics, writing an introduction to the Mishnah which was a rudimentary history of halakah, and an introduction to the Palestinian Talmud. In his halakic history he followed Nachman Krochmal's theory that rabbinic halakah was not of Sinaitic origin, a view that elicited severe reprimand from the emerging orthodox segment.

Frankel also took his cue from a contemporary German Romantic school of thought which stressed the concept of *Volksgeist* (folk-spirit). Frankel's counterpart to the German school became known as the Positive-Historical School. He saw Judaism as the spirit of the Jewish people. This view meant that central to Judaic reality is its existence as an ethnic entity with an historically evolved religious expression. He taught that the Jews received a revelation which they amplified from the written Torah in the oral interpretative torah. This historical view did not meet with traditionalist approval; but while it was closer to Geiger's perceptions, it did not coincide with all of the practical conclusions drawn by Geiger.

For example, Frankel believed that an important criterion for omitting a segment of liturgy was whether the omission violated the emotional power it had upon the people, and whether it damaged the unity of the people. Thus Frankel opposed the new Reform prayerbook in Hamburg, in 1842, as vehemently as the traditionalist Isaac Bernays, but not on halakic grounds, and not with an interdiction, as the latter did. For the same reason Frankel opposed the deletion of messianic prayers and prayers for the restoration of Jerusalem and the Temple. Prefiguring twentieth-century debate, the Reformers were concerned that prayers for a return to Zion implied dual loyalties and a lack of patriotism to one's country, but Frankel argued that there is no contradiction between absolute loyalty to one's country and the dream of national regeneration. Nevertheless, fully conscious of the modern trend for Jews to receive full citizenship in Western countries, and of the need for Jews to prove themselves true citizens, Frankel contradicted himself by advocating the divestiture of Jewish nationalism from prayer wherever the Jew has full equality. In one place he even expressed the idea that Jewish nationalism was imposed upon Jews by their oppressors, who made them aliens, and was not inherent in Judaism. In reality, Frankel had nothing that could be identified as a Zionist theory, despite the fact that such theories had already begun to germinate since the early part of the nineteenth century.

2. Solomon Judah Rapaport (1790-1868)

Another vigorous advocate of the Historical School, Solomon Judah Rapaport, was also opposed by all branches of traditionalism, Hasidic and non-Hasidic. However, he feared that Geiger and his followers had gone too far and would bring about a serious schism in Judaism. Rapaport believed that time and nature would take their course, as they had in the past, to sweep away fossilized relics of Jewish custom. He therefore opposed the Reformers' abolition of the diaspora's second day of festivals and the dietary practices, and changes in the halakah of *kiddushin* (marriage) and *gittin* (divorce). He saw the Reformers repeating the history of the Samaritans and Karaites by becoming an impotent and disappearing sect in Judaism.

D. Reform Conferences

At first, despite the obvious differences between Frankel and Geiger, when Ludwig Philipson convened the Brunswick conference of 1844, Frankel was not among those present, although he was certainly a "reforming" rabbi in Germany. Frankel was a strong critic of the conference's lenient position toward all ritual. But his criticism was mild compared to that of seventy-seven traditionalist rabbis of Germany, France, and Hungary. They accused the Reformers of erecting "the idol of convenience and sensuality," and declared the conference's resolutions "false and condemnable." Despite the virulent opposition of traditionalists, the progressive forces met again in 1845 at Frankfurt am Main, and this time Zechariah Frankel attended. But it was there that the question of the use of Hebrew in worship became the central symbol of the disagreement among the Reformers. On the one hand, Geiger and others argued that Hebrew is a nationalist ingredient in Judaism, has a segregating influence, is not understood by the people, and was never regarded in the halakah as the mandatory language of worship. Furthermore, they submitted that language does not sanctify prayer, but rather is itself hallowed by prayer. On the other hand, Frankel argued that Hebrew is the holy language in which the pristine faith was expressed, adds mystery to worship, cannot be adequately translated, will be abandoned in study as well if given up in worship, and serves to unify the international Jewish community. The majority upheld Geiger, but only mildly, stating that it was "advisable" to retain Hebrew in worship. Frankel withdrew from the conference, arguing that the resolution opened the way for the gradual abolition of Hebrew, and that it should therefore have read that Hebrew was "essential." With this withdrawal was born what eventually came to be called the Conservative movement.

There were many more differences among the Jewish Reformers. Those who now constituted the Reform movement as over against the Historical School argued for the abandonment of most minutiae in the massive regimen of ritual in Judaism. By contrast, Frankel's group argued that ritual is inseparable from doctrine. Nevertheless, Frankel was not at home with traditionalists who rejected acculturation, and showed in his historical researches how Judaism in the past had indeed undergone many halakic adjustments, how rabbis had introduced halakic innovations and had even effected abrogations.

Unlike the Reform rabbis, Frankel rejected the idea that a group of rabbis can exercise authority to change religious practice. He conceded that groups of rabbis and individuals had altered religious practice throughout history, but argued that the Reform movement was weakening loyalty to the rites, whereas in the past changes were effected to strengthen such loyalty to mitzvot. The Reformers were quite possibly being more consistent with historical reality, and more authentically understanding that Judaism can be a pluralistic faith, with some Jews going one way, others going another way, each following its own rabbinical representatives. Although Frankel never organized a new movement, he and his seminary in Breslau were opposed by the same right-wing traditionalists who had opposed Reform since 1800.

The third Reform rabbinical conference took place in Breslau in 1846. Although other questions were debated, here the matter of chief interest was Sabbath observance. The conference resolved to work toward more devoted consecration of the Sabbath in the home and a more edifying service in the synagogue. But it declared as no longer binding the manifold restrictions on personal activities. Although the resolutions on the equality of women were not debated, their basic recommendations became the practice of Reform congregations. These included the equality of women with men in matters of ritual, including being counted in the prayer quorum (minyan), the abolition of the morning blessing in which God is thanked for "not making me a woman," and the recognition of women at age thirteen in a manner similar to men.

Such reforms were introduced in congregations all over Germany and elsewhere, but unevenly and decreasingly. The Breslau seminary, headed by Zechariah Frankel, helped a conservative reaction against the Reformers to slow the pace of their changes. Perhaps of even greater significance was the development of a new type of orthodoxy. Geiger began to agitate for new conferences, and one was held in Cassel in 1868 that called for a synod in Leipzig in 1869, which was to be "catholic" in format—neither Reform nor traditional. Rabbis from many countries gathered, but none of the traditionalist wing, and none from Russia and Poland. It was therefore basically a Western Reform synod, as was that of Augsburg in 1870. Subsequently, one hundred and thirty-three rabbis of various European countries declared in effect that all Reform rabbis were ineligible to preside over marriages. The lines had been drawn. There were now several movements in Judaism: an "Orthodoxy," a separatist Hasidic movement, Frankel's Positive-Historical School, and Reform Judaism.

III. VARIETIES OF TRADITIONALIST OPPOSITION TO REFORM

A. Introduction

Political emancipation and religious reform were two sides of a coin that gave rise to increasing articulation of the traditionalist status quo. After the Brunswick Conference of 1844, the traditionalist rabbis proclaimed, "Neither we nor any person ha[s] the power to abrogate even the least of the religious laws." In this sentence is contained the basic philosophy of that segment of Judaism which styles itself "Orthodox." It is precisely this position which has inspired two centuries of modern religious reform since the French Revolution. In total disregard of historical fact, the Orthodox school of thought believed that radical transmogrification of Judaism can only take place in the Holy Land in the days of the messiah. However, the eighteenth and nineteenth centuries saw the increasing yearning of Jews to be permanent, integrated citizens in the countries of their residence rather than to return to the Holy Land, and liberal scholars and congregations undertook radical changes without benefit of the messianic advent and the return to Zion. The traditionalists would not change their theory, and no amount of invective or excommunication on their part was able to stem the tide of Reform.

Reference has already been made to the many modern influences that operated in the emergence of contemporary Judaism. Although there were dormant historic seeds of Reform in Amsterdam, in 1772 an Amsterdam rabbi saw a threatening reality that no longer lay dormant. In a poem entitled "A New World," he bemoaned the Jewish pursuit of new fashions in hair and dress, shaving with razors, attendance at theater and opera, indulgence in cardplaying, laxity in synagogue attendance and Sabbath observance, neglect of the fast of the ninth of Ab, and pursuit of university education by the sons of the wealthy. As can be seen from the sermons of the time, this laxity in Jewish observance and changing lifestyle, including even a freer sexual life, was endemic throughout Europe.

The new educational programs and ritual changes referred to above were catalysts for a powerful reaction. Among the earliest castigators of Reform was Eleazar Fleckeles, a rabbi in Prague who attacked laxity in dietary practices and the increasing turn to secular learning. When the dispute broke out over burial customs, the modernists attacked the traditionalists for their insistence on early burial of the dead. The reforming generation, however, was not monolithic. Some who favored educational reform remained conservative in halakah. Nevertheless, traditionalists began to sense the danger to their perspective of tradition and increasingly attacked and ridiculed the innovators.

B. Non-Hasidic Ultra-Orthodoxy:
Rabbi Moses Sofer (1763-1839)

One of the great nineteenth-century halakic authorities, Rabbi Moses Sofer (or Schreiber) of Pressburg, became a leading zealot against Reform. He offered his contemporaries no option, demanding that they accept the entire corpus of tradition in its culturally isolated form, or not at all. Sofer's position was that even the idiom of tradition had to be preserved unchanged, and that to translate the texts into any European vernacular was unacceptable. For Sofer, social and cultural isolation was a worthy price to pay for preservation of the tradition as then inherited. He founded a yeshiva that banned any form or subject of study related to Western enlightenment. In a very real sense, he became the first of a new genre of *roshey yeshiva* (heads of academies), charismatic counterparts of the Hasidic zaddik (or tzaddik) (see section D below), to whom the student was fully devoted and who completely controlled the student's spiritual and everyday life, a type still prevalent even in North America and in modern Israel. In 1811, he preached a sermon in which he condemned a modern school in Pressburg and declared that the founders and all associated with it were severed from Judaism. Some historians have seen this sermon as the first salvo in the growing traditionalist tendency to exclude Reformers from Judaism. The Reformers, however, following the authority of their own rabbis, were not intimidated by Sofer's effort to ostracize them.

This traditionalist segment was called the "Ultra-Orthodox" or the *Altglaubigen* (Old Believers) by the Reformers. They had a fundamentalist approach to the Talmud and to later halakic computations, centering a nearly absolute authority in the *Shulhan Aruk* and in their own interpretation of its dicta. They were augmented by Hasidism, and were especially vocal and powerful in eastern Europe.

C. Neo-Orthodoxy

1. Introduction

In Germany, however, there arose a milder form of opposition to the Reformers, in which the protagonists, like Rabbis Isaac Bernays and Samson Raphael Hirsch, received university educations. This group, known as "Neo-Orthodox," was willing to attempt to adjust in some minimum way to the new world in which Jews enjoyed political rights and the potential for acculturation. Neo-Orthodoxy upheld the concept of revelation as binding upon both written Torah and its continuation in the Talmud, and in this respect parted with the Frankel school.

2. Samson Raphael Hirsch (1808-1888)

Samson Raphael Hirsch, a major leader of Neo-Orthodoxy, was born in Hamburg, a seedbed of Reform. He had a strict traditionalist upbringing and was a disciple of Bernays. He attended the University of Bonn as a colleague of Abraham Geiger and became a rabbi in 1830. Hirsch engaged in some reforming activities, but in 1851 he became the rabbi of the partially secessionist orthodox group in Frankfort, where he gave full expression to a new type of orthodoxy. By 1876 he won governmental right for a total split from the central Jewish community, a wholly new development in Jewish life since the Middle Ages. In this split was born modern Jewish denominationalism, characterized by orthodox separatism, and a movement known as *Trennungs Orthodoxie.* This movement became the model for the refusal of orthodox groups since that time to enter into religious ecumenism with other Jewish denominations.

Hirsch believed that all of Judaism was a single revelation. He saw no need to reconcile Judaism with modern rationalist thought, and he emphasized the continued observance of all the ritualistic minutiae. Where these seemed to be out of harmony with the modern lifestyle he tried to impress their symbolic value upon his congregation. Furthermore, he advocated secular learning, and recognized the need to replace the old dialectical method of talmudic study, known as *pilpul,* by a more modern approach to the text. But he denied the historicism of *Wissenschaft,* and although he granted the right to pray in a language one understood, he rejected any other tampering with the liturgy. Finally, Hirsch differed with religious supporters of proto-Zionism who arose in his day, and argued that one must not hasten the end-time. He rejected the idea of restoring a Jewish state without divine intervention, and argued that the Jewish people are, in any case, not a nation like other nations. He went so far as to advocate Hegel's idea that citizens owe their loyalty even to an evil government. But he nevertheless opposed all liturgical reforms that removed Zion, national restoration, and mourning for the Temple.

3. Samuel David Luzzato (1800-1865)

Italy also produced a leading exponent of Neo-Orthodoxy—Samuel David Luzzato of Trieste. But Luzzato had a higher regard for *Wissenschaft* and often employed the critical method in his commentary to the Pentateuch. Luzzato was a scion of an old Italian family and imbibed the residue of the Italian Renaissance and the thought of Rousseau and John Locke. Luzzato wavered between rationalism and romanticism, and thus, although he engaged in *Wissenschaft* and acknowledged its historical perspective, he upheld the contrary view that every Jew must believe in divine revelation. He argued that any other position than this fundamental one would lead to the abrogation of all Judaic practices as invalid. He opposed Reform vigorously, but, unlike Hirsch, he had a strong romantic nationalist bent.

The foregoing brief survey points to a strong traditionalist complex in nineteenth-century Judaism. There were at least three visible types of so-called orthodoxy. But there was also a fourth, a pietistic revivalist group which outnumbered the others and dominated the east European Jewish masses for over half a century.

D. Hasidism

1. Introduction

The Hasidic movement of the eighteenth century should not be confused with the ascetic, kabalistic individuals known as Hasidim in thirteenth-century Germany. The new Hasidim, unlike the earlier pietists, did not believe in mortification of the body, which was then still practiced by pietistic penitents. On the contrary, they believed that the whole person should serve God, and that it was appropriate to satisfy the senses in the service of God.

2. Rabbi Israel Baal Shem Tov (the "Besht") (1700-1760)

The movement which came to be called Hasidism regarded its founder to be Israel ben Eliezer of Okopy and Medzibozh. His birth was associated in Hasidic legend with divine involvement through a visit from Elijah on the Sabbath in the form of a traveling beggar. It was believed that because Israel's father, Eliezer, took him in and did not disparage Elijah's violation of the Sabbath, Elijah promised him a son who would be a light to the Jews. Israel was popularly called Baal Shem Tov (The Master of the Good Name), and this epithet was contracted to "Besht."

His followers believed that the Besht's fervor was so intense that he could reach celestial realms. In time, the faithful saw him as embodying divinity in a way superior to all other creatures who enjoyed the immanence of deity. His life had been marked by special circumstances, and these were elevated in legend to produce an extraordinary aura around him. Little is known of his life, and that sparse information largely consists of miracle tales in part compiled by Jacob Joseph hakohen of Polonea (d. 1782) in a collection of sermons, and later, in 1815, amplified in a book entitled *Shibhey Habesht* (Praises of the Besht).

As an adult, he first made a poor living as a lime-digger in the Carpathian mountains, curiously distant from any Jewish settlement. It is there that he learned herbal medicine and became an effective healer. As he grew aware of his religious consciousness and the powers he attained from the mystical solitude in which he indulged, he began to go about as a *baal shem*—a type then quite prolific—and offer his healing and his teaching to both Christians and Jews. In the language of mystics, Israel "revealed himself" at age thirty-six. He conveyed his teachings in fables and aphorisms grasped by the illiterate.

The leading teachings which legend and tradition attributed to the Besht were all, in one form or another, from classical Jewish sources: the midrashim, talmudic aggadah, and kabalist works. But the Besht escalated the importance of certain nuances in these texts. Thus, he taught so intense a theory of God's pervasive presence in all things that some have adjudged him to having been a pantheist. This judgment is inaccurate, however, because the Besht and later Hasidim continued to teach a complementary notion of God's transcendence. Some more recent scholars attribute *panentheism*—a theory that maintains a rather opposite view to that of pantheism—to the Besht. Panentheism holds that all things are in God, but that God is more than all things. The Besht taught that all existence, whether organic or inorganic, at any given moment derives from God's will, and that this principle holds true for evil as well as for good.

For the Besht, the chief vehicle by which one could reach celestial radiance was prayer. Furthermore, his central message was that human beings must always live with hope and gladness (Ps. 100:2). He therefore rejected Lurianic asceticism and stressed the need for exuberant singing and dancing and losing oneself in prayer. As a result, his followers developed a style of worship that included swaying, bending, hopping, crying out loud, and walking up and down the synagogue. The Besht's teachings won allegiance for a variety of reasons: the poetry and drama in Jewish ritual had been washed out by supercilious attention to halakic minutiae; the love of learning had been soured by emphasis upon subtle dialectic called *pilpul;* and prayer had become fossilized by concentration upon liturgical formalism. Whereas the elitist rabbinate engaged in abstruse intellectual exercises, the Hasidim stressed religious fervor over theoretical knowledge to elevate the soul.

3. The Zaddik (or Rebbe)

The Hasidim placed great reliance upon their spiritual leaders, whom they called the *zaddik* (righteous one), or *rebbe*. These disciples of the

Besht became virtual objects of a charismatic personality cult with a system of dynastic succession.

Great differences obtained and continue to exist among various *rebbes* in scholarship, mode of prayer, emphasis upon miracles, faith healing, the use of amulets, etc. Nevertheless, a unique lifestyle is common to all Hasidic sects. A Hasid who visits a *rebbe* often presents a *kvittel* (note), which relates the petitioner's request for health, a child, a mate, or any other simple or complex need. Such notes are often placed at the graves of *rebbes*. The *rebbe* conducts fellowship meals and says words of Torah. At the close of the meal the Hasidim sing and share his leftover food, called *shirayim*, which they believe has been sanctified by the *rebbe*. The Sabbath meal is a special holy time to spend with the *rebbe*, and the Hasid precedes this meal with a visit to the *miqvah* (ritual bath). Twelve loaves are used at this Sabbath feast, on the basis of Leviticus 24:4, thus indicating the conception that the fellowship meal partakes of the holiness of the ancient cult. Hasidim sing and sway at these meals, for cultic, not social or entertainment, purposes. One of the most solemn Sabbath meals is the third one of the day, at which the Hasidim linger long after dark and conclude with a great celebration known as *melaveh malkah* (escorting the queen), dedicated to Queen Sabbath.

Down to the present, the *rebbe* and many of his followers still wear their traditional costume: a kaftan (or caftan; a long black coat), a *gartel* (a sash worn around the waist to separate the genitals from heart and mind), sometimes breeches and white socks in place of regular trousers, and a tallit undergarment with fringes displayed on the outside. Hasidim usually eschew the tie and reject trimming their beards or earlocks.

4. Foremost Hasidic Leaders

a. Introduction. The Baal Shem's disciple, Dov Baer of Meseritz (1710-1773), became the real founder and leading apostle of Hasidism. He was the Paul of Hasidism, having raised up all the great Hasidic masters of the nineteenth century: Levi Isaac of Berdichev, Menhem Mendel of Vitebsk, Aaron of Karlin, and Shneur Zalman of Ladi, among others. Space does not allow for a full discussion of the masters of Hasidism whose names are legendary in the history of Judaism. Below we will consider but two of them: Shneur Zalman of Ladi and Nahman of Bratslav.

b. Shneur Zalman of Ladi (1746-1812). Shneur Zalman founded a sect within the Hasidic movement called Lubavitch, the name of the city where it began. This sect combined the emotionalism of the Besht with renewed emphasis upon intellectualism, and consequently spurred further sectarianism within Hasidism. In his philosophical-ethical work *Tanya* (It Has Been Taught), Shneur Zalman revived kabalistic dualism. He saw human beings as struggling between their divine and animal souls—a microcosm of the great cosmic war between good and evil. The *Tanya* teaches that the evil person succumbs to sin, but the zaddik is fully motivated by the divine soul, a gift obtained by few. With this view, Shneur Zalman underlined the dependence of his followers upon the zaddik. Lubavitch Hasidism also came to be known as *HaBaD,* an acronym for the three segments of the intellect: *hokmah* (wisdom), *binah* (understanding), and *daat* (knowledge).

c. Nahman of Bratslav (1772-1810). Rabbi Nahman of Bratslav was renowned for his profound mysticism and knowledge of kabalah. He became a virtual mediator between his disciples and God, with a hint of messianic pretensions. He believed he could make atonement for his disciples, and they regularly confessed their sins to him. Like Jesus of Nazareth, under other circumstances, when he was about to die, Rabbi Nahman assured his disciples, "I will be with you always." His Hasidim were ostracized by other Hasidim, and henceforth frequent internecine conflict raged among various Hasidic sects.

5. The Mitnagdim and Elijah of Vilna (1720-1797)

This growth of Hasidism was opposed by many traditionalist rabbis and their congregations. These opponents were named by the Hebrew word for opposition, *mitnagdim.* Among the *mitnagdim* was the greatest and most learned of the rabbis of the eighteenth century, Elijah (ben Solomon) of Vilna (1720-1797), who holds an almost unparalleled position in the history of Jewish scholarship. Elijah was known as the *Gaon* (genius) of Vilna, an honorific title attached to him as it had not been to any scholar in almost seven centuries. He taught his students to examine primary texts meticulously and not to rely upon supposed authoritative interpretations. He argued for simple exegesis of texts and opposed the dialectics of Polish scholars. In this remarkable way, and probably unconsciously, Elijah became a forerunner of modern Jewish scientific research of Scripture and talmudic texts, even showing how some interpretations were based on texts corrupted in transmission.

Elijah opposed Hasidism because of what appeared to him to be its denigration of Jewish learning and overemphasis upon strange emotionalism in worship. He also feared that the popularization of kabalah by Hasidism could lead to the rise of another false messiah. Such a debacle had just occurred in the disaster of the messianic claim of Jacob Frank (1726-1791), who believed he was the incarnation of Shabbatai Zvi. For his part, Elijah seemed to incarnate the zeal of biblical Elijah in his fastidious adherence to every minute detail of halakah and in his war on Hasidism. The relative freedom and spontaneity prevalent in early Hasidism, the charismatic tendencies, the zaddik cult, and other patterns that appeared strange antagonized Elijah, and he determined virtually to destroy the movement. He took part in excommunicating the entire movement in 1772, and in 1781 he asked communities to enforce a *herem* (ban) that would achieve the following: make Hasidic worship impossible, ban their literature and meat, and reject any Hasid as rabbi, cantor, ritual slaughterer, or religious school-teacher. In 1794 Hasidic writings were burned in public in Vilna. Yet, by the time he died in 1797, the Vilna *Gaon* had utterly failed. Internecine struggle continued until 1804, when the Czarist regime gave Jewish groups the right to build separate synagogues and elect preferred rabbis other than those of the officially recognized community. As a result, Jewish denominationalism became institutionalized for the first time, almost a decade before the actual rise of the Reform movement, and over half a century before such formal pluralism was recognized in Germany. Thus Hasidism, in a very real sense, was the first of the modern Jewish denominations to emerge as a separate religious movement.

6. Hasidic Schools

During the twentieth century, Hasidim in eastern Europe identified with the Agudat Yisrael, a proliferating Ultra-Orthodox movement that maintained a network of religious and parochial schools, newspapers, a publishing house, and youth and women's organizations—all doing battle against modernity and religious change. The great Lithuanian *mitnagdic* centers of Jewish learning—Mir and Slabodka—were soon rivaled by Hasidic study halls and the great school at Lublin. In Galicia, the Belz dynasty was equaled by that of Bobov (Bobowa), which also set up a network of schools. The same process went on in Hungary. The second rabbi of Husiatyn, Israel Friedman (1858-1933), moved to Vienna during World War I and espoused vocational yeshivot where students could become proficient in both learning and an occupation. During the twentieth century, many Hasidic rabbis established themselves and their schools in North America.

7. Conclusion

Hasidism spread from the southern areas of Podolia, Ukraine, White Russia, and Galicia northward and eastward to engulf Poland, constantly dividing into new dynasties of *rebbes* until it became a hydra-headed complex. It was Orthodox but fully distinguishable from all other varieties of Orthodox experience. *Rebbes* differed from one another and from other traditionalists, just as Sofer, Hirsch, Luzzato, Geiger, and Frankel differed from one another. This variegation of rabbis among Hasidim, traditionalists, and nontraditionalists points up how inaccurate it is to stereotype Judaism, or even one segment of it.

During the nineteenth century, as the *Haskalah* movement and reforming tendencies proliferated, Hasidism became increasingly antagonistic to modernity and change. Mutual antagonism between *Maskilim* and Hasidim arose in Galicia and in Russia when the *Haskalah* emerged there. Hasidic leaders, opposing every slight adjustment in Jewish style and tradition by the *Maskilim*, stressed their own east European lifestyle, including their distinct costume and speech.

The Hasidic movement was persecuted and took vengeance. Its rabbis and adherents were excommunicated, and they in turn ostracized those whom they believed to be heretics. *Mitnagdim, Maskilim,* and Reformers excoriated them, and they repaid in kind.

In time, Hasidism gained power, influence, and respectability, but it also became subject to inner decay. The leadership of rabbinic dynasties lost the charismatic spontaneity of the first zaddikim, and the reliance of the masses upon the *rebbe's* miracles resulted in a degree of charlatanism and fraudulent disbursement of amulets for money. Further, the fervor and obedience of the Hasidim to their *rebbes* led to their enthronement in a "court" with all the trappings of royalty. Hasidism taught the Hasid to relate to God with *kavanah* (inner concentration), *debekut* (clinging to the divine), and *hitlahabut* (enthusiasm)—stages which allowed the believer to withdraw from his physical environment to commune with God. Its early experience of religious fervor, however, was later deadened by mechanical forms that were passed on as accepted method and doctrine. While at first their rabbis argued for halakic freedom, in time their own pattern of observance became for them a new orthodoxy. Each Hasidic sect became locked into its own discipline of obedience. Shneur Zalman of Ladi even wrote his own *Shulhan Aruk de Rab* (The Rabbi's Shulhan Aruk) to provide his followers with a replacement for the Karo-Isserles work.

The foregoing has described a varied Hasidic movement of dissent and protest that became at once pietistic, disciplined, rigorous, and demanding, as well as spontaneous, joyful, and hopeful. It soared on music and exhausted itself in dance. It consoled the ignorant and elevated the learned. It sought to heal the sick of heart and mind and exalt the poor. It espoused equality and the fraternity of poverty, and yet tolerated and advanced the regal splendor and great wealth of its *rebbes*. Hasidism was accompanied by irrationality, superstition, and often self-delusion. The primeval powers of myth and mysticism operative in Hasidism captivated large segments of depressed masses along with middle- and upper-class people seeking a spiritual haven from an increasingly menacing industrial and scientific society.

IV. JUDAISM IN NORTH AMERICA

A. Introduction

Most Judaic responses to the challenge of the modern world originated in Europe and were transported to America by immigrants. In the United States there originated only two indigenous movements, Reconstructionism and Humanistic Judaism. These two movements are interrelated in that both deny the traditional idea of a personal God and reject beliefs in the traditional doctrines of divine revelation and election. Both reinterpret other doctrines, such as creation and redemption, in modernistic, naturalistic, and humanistic terms.

The earliest Jews to settle in North America were traditionalist Sephardim, descended from Spanish and Portuguese Jews, and more recently from those who lived in the Ottoman empire, including pre-World War I Balkan countries. They differed from the Ashkenazim, who were descended from Jews hailing from those parts of Europe which were predominantly Christian during the Middle Ages. However, the differences between Sephardim and Ashkenazim were not major. Ashkenaz and Sephard traditionalists shared the same basic theology, and, aside from their respective allegiance to Isserles or to Karo, they regarded the *Shulhan Aruk* as their basic source of halakic authority. The larger differences between them might be in synagogue liturgy. In the early period, the small numbers of Ashkenaz Jews who came from Germany, Holland, and England before 1730 integrated themselves into the Sephardic communities. This changed, however, during the eighteenth century.

B. Reform Judaism

It was in a Sephardic congregation in Charleston, South Carolina, in 1824, that the first stirrings of Reform were heard in North America. A group seceded from the congregation to organize its own synagogue on the pattern of the Hamburg congregation. It introduced instrumental music, worshiped with bare heads, and made a variety of liturgical adjustments. The first Reform rabbi in America, Gustav Poznanski, soon arrived and added another characteristic Reform feature in his preaching: the anti-nationalist position that America is Palestine, Charleston is Jerusalem, and the synagogue the ancient Temple. In this way, Poznanski emphasized that the prayers for a national restoration in Palestine had no further relevance, and he set the tone for American Reform for over a century.

Further development of Reform took place in Baltimore, New York City, Albany, Philadelphia, Cincinnati, and other cities. By 1880 most synagogues were Reform. This development was inspired by Isaac Mayer Wise (1819-1900), who came to the United States in 1846. Wise introduced the typical pattern of Reform in Albany and then continued his ministry in Cincinnati. Generally, in those early years, the Reform pattern in the United States consisted of the introduction of a new prayerbook, an organ, and confirmation; the abolition of the second day of festivals observed in the diaspora; worship with bared heads; a mixed choir; family pews; and a wide variety of liturgical modifications, including the elimination of prayers thought no longer compatible with modern religious sentiment.

Although Wise did not believe that in Judaism salvation depended upon faith in any dogma or mystery, he did teach the doctrine of revelation, but limited it to the Decalogue. He therefore argued that the Ten Commandments stand as a universal religious core of Judaism, and that the particularistic elements developed in the process of national life in Palestine could be abandoned. Furthermore, Wise saw the universalist ethic of Judaism already incorporated into the moral and political system of the United States.

Judaism had had a long history of congregational autonomy, interrupted or aborted only when secular power was accorded a central community council in order to demand and impose uniformity. Since

America was a land of free association, and "congregationalism" was the natural tendency, the Reform movement was able to prosper. As early as 1739, a certain Abigail Franks wrote, "I cannot help condemning the many superstitions we are clogged with. . . . I don't think religion consists in idle ceremonies." This complaint about minutiae long antedates the rise of Reform, and because it was even more difficult to live the traditional halakah in America's frontier society, Reform Judaism was natural for the United States. Therefore, in a way American Reform may be said to have arisen from indigenous need, but when it arose it functioned with European scholarship and rabbis.

Wise was by no means the only significant Reform leader, but he was a founder, a mentor, and a moving spirit of the Reform movement. He spearheaded the founding of Hebrew Union College, of the lay and rabbinic institutions of the Reform movement, and of its synods. In a series of conferences, American Reform established itself and articulated its positions. The first was at Philadelphia in 1869, where many theological views were reinterpreted and many religious practices revised. At the 1869 conference the Messiah was no longer defined as a person, but as a time of universal human unity—as a messianic era—which would not include a restoration of the Jewish nation or of the sacrificial cult. Furthermore, the "chosen people" idea, or the doctrine of election, was interpreted as a mission; bodily resurrection was rejected; and prayer in the vernacular was emphasized. Additionally, a variety of modifications were made in the practices of marriage and divorce. In the case of marriage, for example, contrary to the tradition where the groom consecrated the bride to himself, mutual consecration was introduced.

The most significant conference of the nineteenth century took place in Pittsburgh in 1885, when the "Pittsburgh Platform" was issued as a formal theological statement of Reform Judaism, which prevailed until about 1940. In the Pittsburgh statement, the most important affirmations were that monotheism is the highest concept of God; Jews must pursue interfaith efforts with Christianity and Islam; the soul is immortal; moral principles of the Torah are binding; and social concern is the Torah's highest command. Among the notable observances that were rejected were prescriptions for diet, purity, the priestly cult, dress, and the like. The nation concept was declared obsolete, and Jews were perceived as constituting a religious community. Although in theory Wise and his colleagues and their successors rejected the binding character of halakah and its process, in practice the pursuit of halakah continued to characterize the Reform movement as it did the Conservative movement, and does so until this day.

Reform introduced late Friday evening worship as an alternative for Jews no longer able to reach a synagogue for sunset Sabbath worship. It made an effort, which ultimately failed, to shift the major worship service from Saturday to Sunday, in order to accommodate the realities of North American life where Jews invariably labored on Saturday and had leisure on Sunday. Equality was accorded to women in synagogue ritual; conversion of gentiles was eased because of growing mixed marriage; and circumcision and immersion were no longer required of proselytes, a statement affirming the faith being regarded as adequate. In general, the home rituals, such as Sabbath candles, the kiddush before meals, large elements of the Passover seder, the kindling of Hanukkah lights, and others were relaxed or abandoned on the basis of their being nonbiblical.

By 1937, however, new "Guiding Principles" were issued which began to reverse the anti-Zionist tendency of the movement and to encourage the reintroduction of a variety of the long-abandoned private and family rituals. Now "the *preservation* of the Sabbath, festivals and holy days, the *retention* and development of such customs and symbols and ceremonies as possess inspirational value" was resolved. While in 1937 only the "upbuilding" of Palestine was given support, in 1943 Zionism and Reform Judaism were declared compatible, thus reversing a century and a half of Reform ideology. Since that time, the nuances of the "Guiding Principles" of 1937 and the interest in the State of Israel have both been extended, and a new prayerbook has been issued that enlarges the use of traditional liturgy and the quantity of Hebrew used in the service. In some Reform temples the skullcap and prayer shawl are worn as an option, and other liturgical symbols, such as the *lulab* and *etrog,* have been reintroduced on Sukkot. Furthermore, a wide variety of private and family home rituals have been encouraged with the same sociological and quasi-theological rationales as in the Conservative movement.

One historian has called Reform's "return" to tradition a reflection of a "failure of nerve," as the term is used by the philosopher Sidney Hook. This "return" signifies a reorientation to ritual and mysticism as a reaction to science and rationalism, similar to the retreat of Hellenistic populations into salvational cults to surmount the cultural voids created by the internationalism, rationalism, and technology of that time. Reform's reversion to tradition is what I consider to be "inner orientation" as compared to outward acculturation. The tendency to turn inward is evidenced in such eras of Jewish crisis as the Nehemian period after the Babylonian exile; the period of the separatist *Perushim*-Pharisees; post-70 rabbinism; and various post-talmudic developments such as German Hasidism, Palestinian kabalism, and seventeenth-century east European pietism and halakic stringency. An orientation toward traditionalism was the route taken by Hirsch's Neo-Orthodoxy and marks the tendency of Neo-Reform. But American Reform, on the whole, continues to espouse a distinct freedom of ritual and acculturation, and its future direction is still uncertain.

C. Conservative Judaism

The Conservative movement arose in reaction to the elements of the Reform movement's Pittsburgh Platform that were incompatible with Frankel's Positive-Historical School, and in response to the massive influx of traditionalist east European Jews into North America between 1880 and 1914. Reform's renunciation of the binding authority of halakah, Jewish nationhood, and certain aspects of the afterlife all made a withdrawal from the Reform movement, like Frankel's from Frankfort in 1845, inevitable in America after 1885. Furthermore, the natural haven for the mass of immigrants was a religious movement that facilitated acculturation while it accommodated the emotion and nostalgia entwined with their traditionalist customs and ritual.

In 1887, Sabato Morais, a Sephardic rabbi, along with several others, organized the Jewish Theological Seminary, and a number of synagogues identified themselves with this institution. Some of these synagogues had organs, and all had mixed pews and used English in their worship. However, they were unwilling to discard other traditions eschewed by Reform: the head covering, the reading of the book of Esther on Purim, the second day of festivals, and a large number of other private family and synagogue rituals. Like Frankel, if they still did not support the rising Zionist movement as such, they did affirm at least eschatological nationhood for the Jewish people in Palestine. Furthermore, the dietary practices—both those observed on a daily basis and those performed during Passover—constituted a significant divide which could not be bridged between the Reform and the Conservative movements.

The rabbis and theologians who supported Morais, however, were keenly aware that they were not orthodox. They advocated "historicism" in their studies of Judaism, maintained at least a limited right to change historic halakah and to innovate new custom, and encouraged adaptation of Jews to the American cultural milieu. Here again, as in the case of Reform, certain individuals inspired the ideas and engineered the development and expansion of institutions that reflected the new tendency in Judaism. Solomon Schechter, the Romanian disciple of Frankel's Positive-Historical School, came to America in 1902 to preside over the reorganization of the Seminary, which had fallen into difficult times. Schechter was later followed by one of his disciples, Louis Finkelstein, who presided over an expansion of the Jewish Theological Seminary through the middle third of the twentieth century, a development which went in tandem with the vast expansion of Conservative synagogues and a Conservative rabbinate.

The Conservative movement, however, must not be seen as different in kind from the Reform movement. As in Europe, so in America, it was different in degree. Frankel's romantic philosophy of the *Volksgeist* (the spirit of the people) was translated by Schechter into the concept of "Catholic Israel." Schechter's idea of "Catholic Israel" held that the practices which grew out of the communal experience of observing Jews was legitimate. The converse of this concept was that those observances which fell into disuse might be abandoned without sacrificing the doctrine of revelation. Furthermore, whatever old customs still provided spiritual meaningfulness might be retained and enhanced. Schechter held that Jewish religious authority does not reside in a book, a person or a period, but that "the norm . . . is the practice actually in vogue. . . . The Torah is not in heaven. Its interpretation is left to the conscience of Catholic Israel." But an identifiable consensus which conformed to Schechter's idea of "Catholic Israel" never arose.

Schechter's thinking opened the door to change, innovation, and abrogation of Jewish religious practice. Flexibility and variety, therefore, predominated in the Conservative movement as in Reform. Conservatism early adopted modifications very similar to those of Reform: mixed choirs and pews; a modicum of liturgical reform, which was radical when measured by traditionalist standards and rather mild when measured by Reform innovation; the use of an organ;[1] and the relaxation of the severe restrictive regimen of the *Shulhan Aruk*. Through its Committee on Jewish Law and Standards,[2] the Conserva-

---

1. See my "The Organ and Jewish Worship," *Conservative Judaism* (Spring-Summer 1963), 93-105.

2. I have served on this committee for more than a quarter century.

tive Rabbinical Assembly has in recent decades made even more radical modifications. Sabbath restrictions have been modified by permission to use electricity and drive an automobile to synagogue, activities still prohibited by Orthodoxy. Furthermore, the observance of the diaspora second day of festivals was declared optional.[3] In the area of women's rights, successive stages of ritual participation of women on an equal basis with men have developed from a responsum affirming the eligibility of women to serve in a prayer quorum (minyan).[4] More major breakthroughs enabling fuller involvement of women in the religious life of the Conservative movement occurred when the Jewish Theological Seminary of America ordained its first woman rabbi in 1985 and graduated its first women cantors in 1986.

The remaining differences between Conservatism and Reform are largely in orientation to the Sabbath halakah. The Conservative movement retains more traditionalism in liturgy and synagogue ritual and in the custom of worshipers wearing *kiphot* (skullcaps). Further, Conservatism emphasizes and encourages the practice of dietary tradition at home and in the synagogue. There are other areas where Conservative Jews preserve more tradition, as, for instance, in the custom of *shivah*—a seven-day mourning period—and in their effort to maintain daily morning public worship.

D. Orthodoxy and Modern or Neo-Orthodoxy

The east European traditionalists understood correctly that Conservative Judaism differs from Reform Judaism essentially only in degree. They therefore rejected it and organized their own institutions. At first, as in Europe, Orthodoxy opposed secular education and every manner of change in halakah or lifestyle, and its earliest yeshivot were established on this principle. But soon the impress of the Samson Raphael Hirsch form of German Neo-Orthodoxy made itself felt in America. Again, it was an individual who inspired its ideas and institutions: Bernard Revel, who came to America in 1906. Like Wise and Schechter, he was a Western-type scholar, and curiously specialized in Karaism. In 1915, he became head of the Rabbi Isaac Elhanan Yeshiva in New York and set the groundwork for the emergence of a movement that

---

3. See my "A Responsum on Yom Tov Sheni Shel Galuyot," *Conservative Judaism* (Winter 1970), 22-33.

4. See my "Women in a Prayer Quorum" in *Conservative Judaism and Jewish Law,* ed. Seymour Siegel (New York: Ktav, 1977), pp. 281-92.

was the logical conclusion of Neo-Orthodoxy's emphasis upon secular education. Revel founded the first Jewish College of Liberal Arts, Yeshiva College, which became a full university in 1945. He handed over to his successor, Samuel Belkin, the basic building blocks of Modern Orthodoxy. Like Finkelstein in the Conservative movement, Belkin, a Hellenistic scholar, presided over the vast expansion of Yeshiva University and Modern Orthodoxy during the middle third of the twentieth century.

This acceptance of and emphasis upon full Western secular learning in all the sciences and arts marks the great divide between the organized Modern or Neo-Orthodox Yeshiva University tendency and all other branches of American traditionalism. The traditionalist element of Orthodoxy, inspired by the European brand of Moses Sofer and Hasidism, rejected Modern Orthodoxy, which resulted in a variety of separatist Orthodox groups.

Modern Orthodoxy theoretically rejected all changes in the halakah of Sabbath, liturgy, domestic relations, and the status of women, but in reality has allowed a wide variety of innovations quietly to intrude into the sanctuary and the home, and above all in the acculturated lifestyle of the individual Jew. Relationships between the sexes, for example, are not nearly as puritanical as among Hasidim or other so-called Ultra-Orthodox types. A minimum of English and modern Western decorum have been introduced into the synagogue, and riding to the synagogue on the Sabbath is no longer futilely excoriated, as it was a generation ago.

The significant boundary marker, however, between all Orthodoxies on the one hand and all non-Orthodoxies on the other, is the doctrine of revelation. Despite over a century of Neo-Orthodox dedication to secular learning, the thinkers of the movement have never made peace with historicism. They still adhere theoretically to a doctrine of revelation of both written Torah and rabbinic halakah. Other basic theological propositions, which are accepted in their more literal traditionalist form than they are by Conservative and Reform ideologists, are those of resurrection and a personal Davidic messiah. While Conservative and Reform theologians, rabbis, and adherents will question variegated aspects of Maimonides's thirteen principles of faith, the Neo-Orthodox, like the older Orthodox groups, will theoretically subscribe to all thirteen.

Studies of Jewish Americans and Judaism in America have revealed what is termed a "non-observant Orthodox" Jew, a description which readily fits myriads of members of the Reform and Conservative movements as well. Such studies have indicated that the more recent self-designation of "Torah-true Jew" by observant Orthodox Jews might apply to no more than about five percent of the Jewish population, who are separated into a multiplicity of sects, both Hasidic and non-Hasidic, with the Hasidic in turn proliferating into a great variety of separatist tendencies.

E. Reconstructionism

Reconstructionism was founded in 1920 by Rabbi Mordecai M. Kaplan (1881-1983), a member of the faculty of the Jewish Theological Seminary of America. It arose out of the Conservative movement, and was inspired by the sociological, philosophical, religious, and educational ideas of men like Emile Durkheim, Matthew Arnold, and John Dewey. In 1922, Kaplan founded a synagogue called the Society for the Advancement of Judaism, and set out to implement his basic concept of "Judaism as a civilization." He argued that the Reform movement abandoned too much tradition and erred in rejecting the "peoplehood" of Israel, the term Kaplan substituted for "nation." He saw Orthodoxy as incompatible with the modern world in its supernaturalism and its general lifestyle, but rejected secularism in favor of an approach to Judaism that could satisfy the Jew's religious needs. Kaplan found Conservatism to be too vague as a meaningful option in American Judaism. He sought to impress his more precise philosophy upon the Conservative movement and transform it into the Reconstructionist movement, but failed. After his retirement, a separate denomination was organized, with all of its institutional organs: a seminary, a synagogue association, and a rabbinic fellowship.

Kaplan believed that Judaism is a *religious civilization* and that the elements of nationhood, language, folk customs, art, and the like are all essential to its preservation. He therefore saw the people, Israel, as the hub of a wheel with the diaspora as its spokes; and in the diaspora he saw the organic community and "community centers" as surrogate hubs. In later years, however, Kaplan began to emphasize the concept of "*synagogue* center." In rejecting supernaturalism, he denied the doctrine of a personal God, although he retained the term God, seeing deity rather as a "cosmic power that makes for salvation." Along with this theological concept, he rejected the traditional doctrines of creation, election, revelation, and the afterlife, although he reinterpreted and recast all of them except election. To further these ideas and to achieve intellectual integrity he issued a new Prayerbook in 1945, which, however, cannot be said to be consistent with Kaplan's theology. He transformed the idea of halakah from mitzvah (a sense of obligation or command) to folk custom or "folkways," but urged their general observance for their role as the poetry, song, and drama of life, and for their significant symbolism. Kaplan believed that salvation was no longer that which God's grace supplies, but rather the this-worldly striving for fulfillment of human destiny. God, he argued, does not hear prayer: prayer serves the person as an opportunity to verbalize hopes and fears, give strength for crises, and aid in releasing tension and sorrows.

The Reconstructionist movement remained small because most Conservative and Reform Jews were unable to subscribe to many of its tenets. By a freer approach to "folkways" as over against halakah, however, Reconstructionism became the more liberal wing of the Conservative movement, and contributed to many of the changes noted earlier. Reform and Conservative, and in many cases even Orthodox, rabbis adopted Kaplan's terminology of "peoplehood," "community," and "civilization" to define the nature of Judaism in terms of its poetry, art, drama, and music. As the end of the twentieth century approaches, Kaplanist terminology has pervaded every denomination, even if his naturalistic theology has not. Nevertheless, many who empathized with Kaplanism found his concept of an "organic Jewish community" as retrogressive to the medieval concept of the kabal, and his emphasis upon Zionism and Israel as contributive to secularist nationalism. In retirement he moved to Jerusalem, and, recognizing the flaws of expansionist nationalism, in his later years Kaplan began to call for a "New Zionism" in which the State of Israel would remain true to the ethical and moral values of Judaism and eschew expansionism and militarism.

F. Conclusion

The foregoing survey of Jewish American denominationalism does not exhaust all options for the contemporary Jew. Some individuals affiliate with organizations that have no specific religious teaching, and some have no institutional affiliation whatsoever. Nonaffiliated Jews may "purchase" whatever religious needs they have: synagogue seats for high holy day worship, cemetery plots, circumcision ceremonies, weddings, and the like. The "unsynagogued" Jews in North America are considerable in number, but their lack of affiliation does not signify that they are not religious and do not espouse Judaic spiritual and moral values.

America is a land of prolific experimentation, and so, in addition to the formal denominations, a variety of other religious experiences are available to Jews: humanism; Jewish science, akin to Christian Science; and a variety of Black Judaisms.

V. ZIONISM, THE HOLOCAUST, AND THE STATE OF ISRAEL

A. Introduction

The history of the Zionist movement, the rise of the State of Israel in 1948, the relationship of Israel to the Palestinians and to its Arab neighbors, and the wars since 1948 are not subjects for a survey of religion, and therefore are omitted from consideration here. Similarly, this is not the place for tracing the event known as the Holocaust in terms of its historical background in Germany between 1918 and 1933 that led to the persecution of the Jews from 1933 to 1939, the conquest of Europe, and the ultimate policy of extermination from 1942 to 1945 known as the "Final Solution."

The following sections, therefore, deal essentially with the spiritual tensions within Zionism and with theological reflections upon the Holocaust and the State of Israel.

B. Zionism

The age of the subordination of Judaism, which began in 312 when Emperor Constantine became a Christian, theoretically ended everywhere by 1850, except in Czarist Russia. The Russian term for "devastation," *pogrom,* became the term that characterized the condition of Jews who endured unprovoked intermittent attacks upon civilians in their homes between 1881 and 1907. These assaults upon Jewish communities led to massive migration and played a major role in the development of Zionism.

The "return" or "ingathering" of Israel to its land was a theological doctrine. This doctrine was reiterated in the liturgy, in the rituals of festivals, and in the wedding rite. The spiritual connection between the Jew and the Holy Land was never disrupted, and now and then it erupted into a temporary flowering, such as the rise of the community of kabalists, inspired by messianic enthusiasm, in the Palestinian city of Safed in the sixteenth century. During the nineteenth century, under the impact of a mix of Greek nationalism and Jewish kabalism, the Serbian rabbi Yehudai (Judah) Alkalai (1798-1878) advocated the colonization of the Holy land. One of Alkalai's admirers was Simon Herzl, grandfather of Theodore Herzl (1860-1904), who ultimately founded a secular political movement called Zionism. Similarly, influenced by Polish nationalism, Rabbi Zvi Hirsch Kalischer (1795-1874) was instrumental in founding a religious counterpart to Herzl's Zionist movement.

Thus, there entered into the Zionist enterprise from the beginning a tension between religion and secularism. At first, the religious expression of Zionism was an anti-reform orthodoxy. Since the prevailing nationalist views were a modern transmutation of classical messianism, however, Zionism did not seize the imagination of the ultra-traditionalists who believed that the messiah could be brought only by divine providence, not by human effort. At first, nationalism attracted neither the modern religious movements nor certain secularists who placed their hope for the survival of Jews in emancipation, integration, and religious reform within the countries in which they resided. Furthermore, Neo-Orthodoxy opposed Zionism because it encouraged the resurgence of Hebrew as a secular language and because it was identified with the secularism of the *Haskalah*.

Theodore Herzl, a charismatic figure who strode across the stage of Jewish history in a flash, left the legacy of political Zionism which evolved into the modern State of Israel. After the devastating Russian pogroms of 1881 and the French Dreyfus affair[5] in the 1890s, Herzl despaired that anti-Semitism would ever cease, and in the depths of this despair he abandoned the ideal of Western acculturation. In his play *The New Ghetto,* he argued that an acculturated Western Jew continues to endure an invisible ghetto into which he is cast by anti-Semitism. Religious movements accepted the tension inherent in this reality, finding consolation in the expected messianic advent. While some religious movements sought to ease the tension between tradition and acculturation, Zionism denied that the tension could be relieved anywhere other than in a Jewish state.

---

5. Alfred Dreyfus was a Jewish captain in the French army who was falsely accused of spying for Germany. Following his conviction for treason, a wave of anti-Semitism swept France. Although Dreyfus was eventually acquitted of the charges against him, many Jews lost confidence in their emancipation in Europe because of the Dreyfus affair.

Zionism was not monolithic. In addition to the religious expression of Zionism there arose the cultural Zionism of Asher Zvi Ginzberg (also known as Ahad Haam; 1856-1927). He rejected the despair and the raw political methods and interests of political Zionism. In his essay "This is Not the Way," he stressed the spiritual and ethical aspects of a Jewish revival in Palestine, a vision that remains unconsummated. In 1904 he continued his arguments, in his essay "Flesh and Spirit," to advocate a moral society rather than a political state, believing with Nietzsche that the "superman" is best suited by nature to hold power, while the Jew, whose moral hero is the zaddik or scholar, is least suited. In 1897, he wrote "The Jewish State and the Jewish Problem," an essay with remarkable prescience in which he outlined all the basic humanitarian and moral dilemmas that continue to this day to confront the State of Israel.

C. The Holocaust and Jewish Theology

The term *Holocaust* refers to the genocidal extermination of some six million Jews by Adolf Hitler's Nazi regime in Germany between 1942 and 1945. Hitler's program was conceived early in his career and was first implemented by the degradation of Jewish Germans from 1933 to 1939. It constituted a unique genocidal event, unprecedented in motive and magnitude, made possible by Hitler's conquest of Europe and modern technology.

The Holocaust victims are often spoken of pejoratively as having gone to their slaughter "like sheep." This image is an offense to their memory. Judaism teaches that we must judge others only when we stand in their place, endure their trials, and experience their condition. Resistance to Nazi guards by their Jewish prisoners meant certain death, whereas submission to orders appeared to hold out hope for their survival. Nevertheless, when all hope was lost, collective resistance was organized in various ghettos, of which the Warsaw ghetto uprising is the most famous, but not the only one. German Jews and European Jews in general are tragically maligned when they are accused of naivete, or worse, for not leaving Germany or other countries. In fact, at least half the Jews in Germany departed between 1933 and 1940, when the war made emigration impossible. As for other European Jews, none of them could have known that Hitler would conquer Europe in nine months and trap so many millions of Jews, or, even given that eventuality, that he would divert his human, natural, and technological resources from a life-and-death struggle with the Soviet

Union and the Western allies between 1942 and 1945 to exterminate harmless Jews in concentration camps. Adolf Hitler must be adjudged what he was—a truly bizarre, unique, and demonic creature. He is in no way to be seen as characteristic of Germany, nor his program as the natural outcome of Christianity's medieval doctrine of the subordination of Judaism. His racism is not to be interpreted as a permanent biological stigma to be borne by Germans. To use Hitler as a criterion by which to evaluate Germans as a whole is to submit to Hitlerist stereotyping of whole peoples and to concede his triumph over the Judaic theology of compassion and forgiveness.

When Jesus, in his self-perception as Isaac enduring the *aqedah*, died in the consciousness of being Israel, Servant of the Lord, he concluded his living ministry with the words, "Father, forgive them; they know not what they do" (Luke 23:34). In accord with Judaic perceptions that the Servant of the Lord is collective Israel, it is appropriate for Israel, entwined in its own Isaac-line *aqedah* (binding), undergoing its crucifixion on behalf of humankind, to proclaim the grace of atonement to those who were blind to the human spirit. This theological perspective might envision the smoke that rose from the crematoria to be the smoke of the *olah* of atonement, the whole burnt offering, called in Greek *holokaustos*.

The most challenging problem arising from the Holocaust is the unanswerable question of *why?* The questioner grinds out again and again the same perplexing enigma: where was God throughout the trauma of millions of people, including innocent children, when they were undergoing incredible suffering without having committed a crime? The very essence of faith in a loving and compassionate God requires that the challenge be made even if a response is not possible. Every committed believer must wrestle with inherited theological imperatives. But to start with Judaic premises is to assume that God wants justice and that God is available to save innocent human beings. Abraham demanded justice of God before the Sodom-Gomorrah holocaust, and Job on the dung heap insisted that the God who allowed his undeserved suffering "will surely be [his] salvation" (13:16). Nevertheless, Sodom and Gomorrah were destroyed, and Job's suffering continued. The European experience from 1942 to 1945 was an incomprehensible orgy of undeserved suffering prefigured in the debilitated person of Job. There can be seen in it no purpose, no reason, no justification—only mystery. To declare this mystery is not to do violence to faith in God. On the contrary, it is because one affirms the loving, forgiving God that one can raise the question at all. Job's friends strove to defend and justify God. Job questioned God's justice while he reaffirmed his faith. Israel at Auschwitz need not justify God; despite their repeated undeserved suffering, however, the response of Jews to it, whether on the individual level or on the collective level, is Job's "my redeemer lives" (19:25).

A very real element of Judaic theology that theologians grappled with insufficiently down through the centuries is the tragedy of the "divine eclipse," *hester panim* ("the concealment of the Presence"). In the drama of the Holocaust God seemed to have turned away, as God warned in the Bible, "I shall hide my face" (Deut. 31:18). It appears from that verse and from the whole tenor of moral retribution warned about in the Bible that suffering is the product of sin. A large number of biblical references to *hester panim,* taken along with their targumic and midrashic interpretations, imply that sin causes the Shekinah to depart from Israel, resulting in the *hester panim.* This interpretation awards approval to the friends of Job, who were certain Job had sinned, for they held the traditional views that suffering is punishment or discipline, but never "undeserved."

Like Job, the pre-Holocaust Jew of every previous century in almost every land of Europe would have had reason to cry out with the psalmist, "How long will you hide your face from me?" (Ps. 13:1). The psalmist was not admitting to sin, however, and promised no penitence. He was cut of the same cloth as Job, and both are perhaps of a school of thought more fully expressed by Deutero-Isaiah. That preacher saw that sin and suffering are not precisely related. Deutero-Isaiah understood Israel's suffering as vicarious atonement, in the doctrine of the Servant of the Lord. The author of Job worked from the premise that there is no nexus between sin and suffering. While Deutero-Isaiah spoke of national suffering, the author of Job explored the undeserved suffering of an individual, and concluded that it is wrapped in mystery. One can extrapolate from the individual back again to collective suffering that all suffering is a mystery and that it is futile to seek either an explanation of it or a theodicy in God's defense.

The modern Jew will respond to the suffering of the Jews who experienced the Holocaust either by declaring "there is neither justice nor judge," or by submitting to the mystery of life and death, suffering and joy, and reaffirming the belief that there is both a righteous judge and justice. When the ancient rabbis attributed the fall of Jerusalem to the sins of countless generations, they did not mean to attribute all human suffering to sin. To do so would have been to make a mockery of God and God's love. It would also be a denial of the equally compelling Judaic theological notion of freedom of choice in moral behavior. A Hitler may exterminate, and God, even if present, is concealed by the flood of demonic evil over the world. Deutero-Isaiah, who several times speaks of *hester panim,* might have glimpsed a very sophisticated truth when he discovered that it is the God who is the savior who also hides Himself (Isa. 45:15). The mystery of deity is in the enigma that the same God who is absent in *hester panim* is the savior. The *hester panim* is absolutely essential if the human being is to be free. Part of the mystery of evil, therefore, is in the nature of the human being whose humanity is expressed in freedom—even the freedom to spread affliction.

Eliezer Berkovitz, an Israeli thinker, has speculated that the Holocaust was the product of irrational metaphysical fear, the fear demonic forces have of the power of God. This thinker ruminated that for the Nazis the destruction of the Jews would signal the death of God to whom the mysterious survival of the Jews in history is testimony. When you remove the testimony, you remove the object testified about. Berkovitz sees this as the meaning of Isaiah 43:12, "You are my witness, I am God," to which the rabbis added, "*when* you are my witnesses, I am God." Thus the Final Solution Nazi leaders planned for the extirpation of all Jews becomes the great Anti-Christ, the final victory of Satan over God's people. And yet, in the apocalyptic mysteries with which Judaism and Christianity function, it is God who must triumph over Satan. Nazi Germany was, therefore, foredoomed. The presence of God is then perceived in the powerlessness of God's people. The very Holocaust in which there was *hester panim,* reaching its denouement in the survival of God's people, becomes the symbol of God's presence. This witness to God's presence in His absence appears to be a theological conundrum and in no way justifies the event as Job's friends sought to justify God's ways. While it does not justify God, it does affirm the mystery. Faith, whether Jewish or Christian, functions within the mystery, as Paul had finally concluded, "How rich are the depths of God—how deep his wisdom and knowledge—and how impossible to penetrate his motives or understand his methods!" (Rom. 11:33).

The *aqedah* opens Jewish (and Christian) salvation history. It is with this proleptic event that the history of Israel as Servant of the Lord and cosmic vicarious atonement begins. Christianity individualized the Israel-*aqedah*-servant figure into Jesus of Nazareth, who took on the role of corporate Israel. In this servant theology Auschwitz might be considered the end of salvation history, if indeed the world were now perceived to be living in messianic times. The rise and consistent triumph of Israel, especially since 1967, became the messianic signal for many Orthodox Jews and for fundamentalist Christians alike. But the paradox in this triumph is that Israel became the same as all other world powers, no longer the powerless servant-*aqedah,* but capable of vast power, conquest, and oppression. This is a new post-Auschwitz posture and raises the question whether in this form Israel can still testify to God.

Theologically, it is impossible to regard a state that lives in concrete history by the dictates of powers as the cosmic witness. Witness to God was presented by the experience of survival despite powerlessness, which marked the history and testimony of Israel. The miracle and mystery of Israel was precisely in Israel's Job-like endurance despite the *hester panim* of God. *Hester panim* made possible suffering, but no degree of periodic suffering, not even Auschwitz, became a Final Solution. Can the current triumphalism of Israel be explained as the ultimate cosmic eschaton? Karl Barth saw it as an eschatological sign in 1967. But it might be perceived as a temporary Hasmonean resurgence with all the worldly temptations of power to deflect Israel, the "light to the nations," from its true elected spiritual course. In that event, it remains up to "theological" Israel, the affirmers of Judaism regardless of national identity, to remain the witnesses, the elect, and the light.

One of the enduring truths of Israel's history was its ability, without physical power and without national sovereignty, to surmount all degradation and decimation and to survive. This truth offers an interesting challenge in the post-Hiroshima nuclear age. If Israel is perceived as the Servant, its suffering may be paradigmatic of the potential suffering of all humanity in a nuclear holocaust. The symmetry of creation and eschaton is always to be borne in mind. In this connection it should be recalled that at the very time when Hitler's Final Solution against the Jews was in progress between 1942 and 1945, there was also in progress in Chicago and New Mexico the development of the first atom bomb, and concrete realization of a consequent possible Final Solution for the entire human race. In such an age, Israel's historic testimony speaks out clearly to all humanity. The crucified Israel of the Holocaust, a function of sophisticated technology, emerges either as proleptic of a crucified humanity by its sophisticated use of nuclear-weapon technology, or as a caution against the possession of the power of national sovereignty.

That Jews should have served in this role is neither a justification of God's ways nor an explanation of the Holocaust. It only highlights the profound mystery and suggests to both Jewish and Christian theologians the need to begin to plumb the depths of the mystery of *hester panim*, its relationship to the *aqedah*-servant theology, and the implications for two groups who each claim to be the covenanted people of God.

Chapter Eight
Judaism Distilled

I. INTRODUCTION

Judaism encountered many religions over its long odyssey. Predominant among them in the earliest period were primitive Egyptian, Canaanite, and Mesopotamian religions. To these were added the Greco-Roman and Hellenistic religions, Zoroastrianism, Christianity, and Islam. Eastern religions, such as Buddhism and Hinduism, undoubtedly penetrated the outer rim of Judaism during late biblical and rabbinic times. Moreover, Jewish scholars and theologians have been influenced by those of other faiths as well as by nonreligious thinkers, from Pythagoras to Whitehead and the modern phenomenologists, existentialists, and process theologians. Influences from all of these spiritual quests were absorbed into Judaic thought. When one wishes to distill the essence of Judaism, however, one must mine the extensive biblical and rabbinic literature and penetrate to the heart of its liturgy. The foregoing chapters have presented the development of Judaism in all its diversity embodied in three areas: theology, ethics, and ritual. This chapter will bring together these three aspects of the faith in a cohesive summary.

II. THEOLOGY

A. An Overview of Basic Doctrines

Judaism has never had a mechanism by which to formulate an authoritative creed which called for mandatory adherence as a condition for remaining an affiliate of the community of faith and being eligible for

232

salvation. Efforts were made to do so at certain times (M. San. 10:1), but these failed. At best, the variegated strata of the literature—the Bible, the rabbinic midrashim, the Talmuds, and the medieval and modern philosophical writings—have *reflected* efforts to articulate a complex of beliefs. But no instrument of "canonization" of a formal creed to be recited at stated occasions has ever been employed.

Nevertheless, if one reviews the prayer-psalm of Nehemiah 9, one discovers a legitimate source for the basic theology current ca. 400 B.C.E. This core theology remains the background of Judaic theology, and in it are accentuated the predominant doctrines of creation, revelation, and redemption. Furthermore, the doctrines of Nehemiah 9 continued the earlier preexilic religion of Israel and Judah. Briefly stated, the doctrines both explicit and implicit at Nehemiah 9 are: (1) God is creator; (2) God selected Abraham; (3) God entered into a covenant with Abraham; (4) God redeemed Israel from Egypt; (5) God's will was revealed at Sinai; (6) God renewed the Abrahamic covenant with all Israel at Sinai; (7) Moses was the mediator of God's word; (8) other preachers were sent by God to speak God's word; (9) history is governed by God; (10) God intrudes into history to punish sin; (11) God is forgiving; and (12) God's essence is one of compassion, love, grace, and patience. The unspoken belief hovering over all the above doctrines and requiring no articulation is the concept of monotheism.

The foregoing outline may be supplemented by Maimonides's thirteen principles of faith (see Chapter Five above), which are the basis for the hymn *Yigdal* ("May [God] be magnified"), which opens traditional daily morning worship, and *"Ani Maamin"* ("I believe"), which closes the morning liturgy.

B. Redemption and the Messianic Idea

1. Redemption

The roles of God as Creator and Redeemer are frequently interwoven in Scripture, creation and redemption being the two poles of the mystery which is God's purpose for Israel. The two events represent birth and rebirth. Redemption in such events as the Exodus from Egypt prefigures the eschaton, the end-time when a new creation and a new covenant will issue forth from God. At the eschaton, God will inaugurate that which frequently has been called *yemot hamashiah* (the messianic era) or *malkut shamayim* (the kingdom of heaven). The advent of divine sovereignty represents the return to that condition which obtained before the defiance by the human beings in primeval paradise, or before the imposition of a human monarchy over Israel by an act of rebellion against God (1 Sam. 8:7).

Before the final redemption, many generations will pass, and believers must be assured that the intrusion of death will not rob them of salvation. Doctrines concerning the afterlife provide this assurance. The concepts of the immortality of the soul and of resurrection—whether physical or spiritual—promise survival in *olam haba* (the world to come). At that time, all the immortal souls will be resurrected for judgment—either for damnation or eternal bliss (Dan. 12:2).

The experience of the Exodus from Egypt became for Judaic theology the paradigm for all redemption. Israel sang of God's *pele* ("the marvellous"), the incomprehensible miracle of God's splitting of the Sea of Reeds (Exod. 15:11). The same God of *pele,* however, is the God who was mute while Israel was in bondage. The mute God was in a condition of *hester panim* ("concealment of the presence"). This concealment becomes the supreme mystery of the covenant relationship between God and Israel. Thus, for Israel, God never cancels the covenant, but suspends this relationship by a mute turning away. This doctrine is reiterated on all levels of Scripture—the Pentateuch, Prophets, and Writings. The sequence of *hester panim* and *pele* are significant. First comes the *hester,* then follows the *pele.* Suffering precedes salvation. One point of view in Judaism even insists that suffering is a sine qua non of the human condition, or there can be no redemption. Thus, Jacob must go down into Egypt in order that God may bring forth Israel from Egypt (Gen. 46:4). *Olam hazeh* (the world of history) is the arena of suffering. *Olam haba* (the world to come)—the metahistorical world in which God's sovereignty will be manifest—is the world of salvation.

2. The Messianic Idea

It is difficult to determine how early the rudiments of a messianic idea developed and became universalized in Israel. As early as Amos (9:11) it appears as a concept of the restoration of the Davidic dynasty to the Northern Kingdom. Thus the earliest messianic idea, although not referred to in those terms, can be seen before the fall of the Northern Kingdom in 721 B.C.E., and therefore part of the fabric of the ancient religion of Israel.

The redeemer figure, though never called "messiah" in Scripture, has come to be called by that term. There are significant differences in both Scripture and postscriptural sources as to whether the messiah-redeemer figure will be a political liberator who is a scion of the dynasty of David or even God (as in Isa. 63:1-6). The sources are also ambivalent as to whether the redeemer will be a victorious sovereign or the servant of *Yhwh* who will suffer, and even die, in order that the people attain atonement.

3. Conclusion

In modern times, the classical doctrines of Judaism outlined above have been modified, reinterpreted, and in some cases even abandoned by nontraditionalists. For example, the concept of God's election of Israel was rejected by Mordecai Kaplan as smacking of chauvinism; moreover, Kaplan dismissed all beliefs rooted in supernatural phenomena such as revelation and the afterlife. In the nineteenth century, the Reform movement transformed the idea of a messiah into the notion of a messianic era, a time when the world will be characterized by human and natural harmony. Furthermore, most liberal Jews today eschew the doctrines regarding heaven and hell, and many reinterpret immortality symbolically as the survival of personality and achievements in this world.

The evolving theology of Judaism reflects the quest of all religions for answers to the ultimate questions of human existence and destiny. Even a rationalist and genial skeptic like Ecclesiastes turned in radical amazement to the profoundest of his discoveries: "That which is far off, exceedingly deep; who can discover it?" (Eccl. 7:23ff.). Judaism partakes of this mystery both as subject of it and as its source of teaching, and therefore the Jew stands at the precipice of ignorance as the cosmic mysteries of the twentieth century unfold. The more we penetrate the profundities of nature and the human mind, the more are we baffled by the atrocities of a Holocaust or a Vietnam and by the ultimate Holocaust of nuclear war that threatens to wipe out all of God's creation.

Modern Jewish theologians drew upon modern non-Jewish philosophers, such as Kant, Schelling, and Hegel, just as medieval ones drew upon Plato, Aristotle, and Islamic thinkers. No longer feeling compelled to harmonize Judaism with Greek philosophy, they had as their major purpose to establish Judaism's superior rationality over Christianity and its ethical monotheism. This tendency was part of the trend to emphasize the ethics of Judaism as its essence rather than its theological doctrines and mystical elements. For example, Hermann Cohen (1842-1918) stressed the role of the moral life as an end in itself, and argued that it was Jewish monotheism that discovered the idea of loving one's fellow human beings. In addition, he emphasized the idea of God as the archetype of universal compassion and the patron of the exploited and disfranchised.

Finally, the twentieth century has seen the emergence of Jewish existentialists, such as Martin Buber (1878-1965), Franz Rosenzweig (1886-1929), and Emil Fackenheim (b. 1916). Furthermore, this century has witnessed a mixture of existentialist and Kantian in J. B. Soloveitchik (b. 1903), primary leader and halakist of Modern Orthodoxy. A major contemporary theologian, Abraham Joshua Heschel (1907-1972), has been regarded as a Jewish counterpart of Neo-Orthodox Protestant thinkers like Karl Barth and Reinhold Niebuhr. In this way Judaic theological speculation and affirmation continues to be filtered through variegated tendencies of thought.

III. ETHICS

A. Fundamental Concepts

The ethics of Judaism are predicated upon the commandments of God. The Jews are commanded to be holy (Lev. 19:2), to love the stranger (19:34), to love their fellow human beings, not to bear a grudge or take vengeance (19:18), and to observe a host of other ethical precepts. God asserts that the reason for these moral imperatives is that *ani Yhwh* ("I am *Yhwh*") and "I *Yhwh* your God am holy" (19:2). It is my view that the refrain *"ani Yhwh"* throughout the chapter from which these ethical injunctions are drawn is merely a truncated repetition of "for I *Yhwh* your God am holy." This basic statement grounds Jewish ethics in the divine. It is highly instructive that some of the most humanitarian precepts of the religion of Israel/Judaism appear in the midst of the cultic procedures discussed in Leviticus. Chapters 1–18 in Leviticus are devoted to the sacrificial system and to the complex purity-impurity taboos and rites. All of these cultic arrangements seem only to be leading to chapter 19 as their purpose and climax. This chapter ordains the attainment of holiness largely by the performance of humanitarian deeds, and by the concrete expression of love through beneficent acts on behalf of the unfortunate, unprotected, and disadvantaged people. The rest of Leviticus amplifies the first nineteen chapters, adds a programmatic holy day roster (Lev. 23), and warns Israel of the consequences of rebellion against God.

Rooted in these precepts, found so abundantly in Leviticus and amply reinforced by similar and additional ones in Exodus and Deuteronomy, Judaism is to be viewed as a religion which emphasizes the worth of the individual. Moral imperatives are the commands of God, but the human potential to fulfill these commands and each person's right to be treated in accordance with them are more solidly rooted in the doctrine of human creation. Judaism affirms that each human being is created in the image of God (Gen. 1:27; 9:6), and for this reason no person of whatever race, nationality, ethnic segment, or religion is in any way superior to another (Amos 9:7). It is true that in the vicissitudes of raw history Jews employed naked power discriminately against "gentiles," and often Israel-Judah was guilty of persecution of the downtrodden. But it is to the teachings of the faith that one must turn, as contrasted with the realities of humanly polluted history. Thus one does not judge Judaic ethics by the hypocrisy, corruption, oppression, and persecution practiced by the rulers and the wealthy who are denounced by the classical prophets. Rather, one takes one's perspective on Judaic ethics from that which the prophets taught. This principle holds true for all humanistic religious systems, whether informed by theism or not, as it also holds true for political systems, such as democracy. The human facilitators of the historical currents do not always fulfill the divine intent. Thus, the worth of the individual, preservation of life, social justice, and charity toward the poor, the homeless, the disfranchised, and disadvantaged always loomed high in teachings of Judaism. Along with the study of Torah and the worship of God, the ancient rabbis gave equality of sacred significance to *gemilut hasadim,* the doing of loving deeds (M. Ab. 1:2). Rabbinic halakah in general, even that affecting ritual practices, was therefore deeply infused by concern for the poor, leniency, compassion for the suffering, and very careful investigation of witnesses lest innocent people be condemned. The rights of labor, restriction of profit, and concern for the consumer were among the issues that the rabbis weighed.

As is well known, Judaic ethics were fundamentally established upon that group of precepts known as the Ten Commandments (Exod. 20:1-17), and especially upon commandments five through ten (vv. 12-17). This segment of the Torah is at the heart of the entire ethical system in terms of family relationships; respect for the human person;

the sanctity of life and of one's own body and one's own property; and the central importance of truthfulness in social and juridical proceedings. In his extensive study *The Special Laws,* Philo of Alexandria based the heart of his work on the Ten Commandments, and in all its phases, rabbinic halakah was rooted in these fundamental principles. It is no accident that the segment of the Torah known in modern biblical scholarship as the "Covenant Code" follows immediately upon the Ten Commandments. This section (Exod. 21:1–24:8), along with its revisions and amplifications in Deuteronomy, is in turn the basis of most rabbinic halakah, embodied in the orders of the Mishnah, Tosefta, and Talmud, which pertain to domestic relations, juridical procedures, and civil and criminal law.

B. Modern Challenges

A serious challenge to Judaic ethics arises from modern technology, mainly from nuclear technology, which provides the power to destroy God's creation and the human race made in God's image. Furthermore, modern technology has confronted Judaism, as well as religious ethicists in general, with dilemmas in biomedical ethics. While some segments of Judaism justify birth control, limited abortion, a restrained form of euthanasia, and other progressive approaches, many adamantly oppose all of these in any degree.

Modern Judaic thought has not yet produced a comprehensive approach to these problems. Indeed, the last systematic ethical treatise written in Judaism was that of Moritz Lazarus, *Die Ethik des Judenthums,* published in 1898. For this reason it is appropriate here to suggest aspects of an ethical response for the future. The traditional Judaic interest in the preservation of life and conservation of resources implies a current interest in ecology, a call for reduction of pollution of water, air, and land, opposition to undue exploitation of national resources, and a reversal of the trend to release increasing amounts of toxic wastes into our environment, endangering human health on many levels as well as the genetic future of the human race. The nuclear threat that hovers over humanity calls for a new exploration of the meaning of a "just war," or, as it was called in Judaic terms, the *milhemet mitzvah,* the war which is considered a mitzvah or a holy action. The danger inherent in any concept of a *milhemet mitzvah* is apparent in the modern Middle East, where each war of Israel against its neighbors has been adjudged by its proponents to be a mitzvah since it is fought for holy soil. Using the *milhemet mitzvah* as a rationale, extremists were able to include the Sinai Peninsula and Lebanon in the same category as preemptive defenses of the holy soil. But beyond that rationale, the devastating potential of nuclear power suggests that the entire concept of *milhemet mitzvah* is obsolete, and that what is called for is a new theologically rooted Judeo-Christian ethic of nonviolence. The basis for this ethic in Judaic thought is that one of the names of God is given as *shalom* (peace), and this name is regarded as God's seal—the very expression of God's fundamental identity.

In an age of escalating ethnicity and nationalism, the universality of the pre-Tower of Babel human family depicted in Genesis is often thought to be doomed. But some segments of Judaism continue to cherish that universalist vision. It is true that since ancient times some authorities of the halakah were what today would be considered racist, treating pagans as inferior, discriminating against them, and later against Christians and Moslems. Many unfriendly Jews remember and cite repeatedly the dictum of Rabbi Simon ben Yohai, "the best of the gentiles is for killing," a dictum said in the heat of resentment over persecution during Roman times. But it is also true that the Talmud yields advocates of the idea that concern for the welfare of gentiles be on a par with concern for Jews. It is frequently important, in regard to the massive rabbinic literature, to ignore sayings of individuals and examine what became institutionalized in Jewish life. Thus one will find that the great, humane, charitable arrangements in every town were open to gentiles as well as to Jews.

Regarding the contemporary issue of feminism, the ancient rabbis and their medieval successors were not in favor of granting equality to women. However, they were generally concerned for the welfare of women. This concern serves as a distinct and invaluable precedent for contemporary reversal of all forms of discrimination. In modern times, as in other eras, Jews do not agree, and scholars reach diametrically opposed conclusions. Some rabbis argue for full equality for women in all things—secular and religious; others oppose equalizing women's religious status with men's; and yet a third group would be prepared for a variety of compromises.

The modern era has presented a challenge to Judaic ethics in the area of civil disobedience. The Jewish ethic historically asserted the principle of *dina demalkutah dina,* which enjoined Jews to obey the sovereign law of the state. Should Jews have participated in civil rights demonstrations in the United States during the 1960s, or in the various anti-nuclear and peace demonstrations in Europe? In discussing certain exorbitant taxes, medieval Jewish scholars often took the view that when a king's law is unjust it is not protected by the principle of *dina demalkutah dina*. Modern Jewish ethical perspectives can build upon a precedent of that nature. The problem becomes highly subjective, however, when confronted with the need to determine what is a just law. Many would regard as unjust, and therefore subject to disobedience, laws offending human personal dignity on the basis of race, religion, sex, or national origin; laws requiring punishment that seems too severe; and laws depriving people of basic human liberties, civil rights, and equal access to the political and judicial systems.

IV. RITUAL

A. Liturgy

The Jewish liturgy is arranged in three daily worship orders: *shahrit* (morning worship), *minhah* (afternoon worship), and *maarib* (evening worship). Sabbaths and other holy days, as well as certain select days of the year, have an additional *musaph* (supplementary) worship order. Yom Kippur alone has yet an additional one, the last worship order known as *neilah*. This term signified the closing of the Temple gates in Jerusalem, and later was taken metaphorically to refer to the closing of the heavens, the last opportunity for prayer to reach God.

Although private devotion is acceptable in Judaism, public worship is theologically regarded as superior, and more likely to influence God's compassion. The theory is that while an individual might be inadequate to reach God, the strength of the praying community in worship transcends the weaknesses of each individual. A public worship service requires the participation of a minimum of ten persons. These are to be males, according to the Orthodox, while females are eligible to serve in the quorum in the Conservative, Reconstructionist, and Reform synagogues.

The traditional worship order is relatively standard. For example, each *shahrit, minhah,* and *maarib* is the same in the daily services. There are variations in some prayers and in the wording of some individual passages to conform with varying occasions. For example, the *amidah*—recited silently in standing devotion—contains variations for weekdays, Sabbaths, and each different holy day. Thus, there is much fixity and little spontaneity in synagogue worship. This was not so at the beginning of Rabbinic Judaism, when the rabbis encouraged spontaneity. Free expression in prayer ceased with the passage of time and the printing of standard prayerbooks. Nevertheless, in spite of a high degree of similarity in all the worship orders, there is a wide variety of prayerbooks among the various denominations. Another feature of modern worship, which seeks to alleviate the burden of reciting all the prayers accumulated over centuries, is the tendency to engage in selection. Different prayers are selected or omitted almost on an ad hoc basis.

The prayerbook is a major witness to what Jews have believed. The content of worship is an accurate index of ancient and medieval Jewish theology. In modern times, however, this is no longer necessarily the case. The wording of prayers is frequently retained and recited with nostalgia, even when faith in the meaning of the words has evaporated. Often the communal singing rouses an emotional response, regardless of the inherent incompatibility of the worshiper's beliefs and the prayer's words.

A very important aspect of Judaic liturgy, and almost omnipresent in all worship orders, is the *berakah* (plural: *berakot*). That term is best left untranslated. To call it a "blessing," as is frequently done, is inappropriate, for the worshiper does not bless God. One thanks and offers praise to God for God's abundant love. A *berakah*, therefore, is a verbal thank-you note sent to God for blessings. The *berakah* formulation not only occurs throughout the worship order, but it also predominates in grace after meals and is recited before the devout Jew partakes of any benefit at all. The standard formula is *Baruk attah adonay* ("We thank you, Lord"). This formula is usually followed by *elohenu melek haolam* ("our God, eternal sovereign") and the reason for thanks. Sometimes, especially when a ritual is to be performed, this formula is followed by "who sanctifies us with His commandments and commands us to. . . ," and the ritual is then named. In this way the *berakah* is the humble acknowledgment that all that the person possesses and enjoys and the ritual one enacts are the will of God. The *berakah* has been termed "the basic structural element" of Judaic liturgy.

Shahrit and *maarib* are structured around the Shema. These prayers, which express faith in God as creator, revealer, and redeemer, along with the creedal profession of monotheism, all lead to the *amidah*, a complex of *berakot* and petitions that is recited at every service every day of the year.

In addition to these regular features of the daily and holy day liturgical cycle, prayers are inserted on the High Holy Days, on certain other festivals, and on the festival of the New Moon. Kiddush, the proclamation of the holiness of the Sabbath and holy days, is recited at the opening dinner of a sacred day. And habdalah—the prayer separating the holy day from the profane ones that follow it—closes the Sabbath and holy days.

B. Holy Days

1. Introduction

The fullest roster of the holy days of Judaism is given at Leviticus 23 and Numbers 28–29.[1] The reader will notice that of the familiar names of holy days on the modern Jewish calendar the Bible did not name the following four days: Rosh Hashanah, Simhat Torah, Hanukkah, and Purim. Rosh Hashanah, however, was known in the Pentateuch as the "first day of the seventh month" (Num. 29:1). The other three were introduced after the period of the Pentateuch. Purim was derived from the story of the biblical book of Esther; Hanukkah was introduced by the Hasmoneans; and Simhat Torah was innovated in the Middle Ages.

The holy days must be understood as having a very profound theological function. The rituals related to them are deeply symbolic and often have mystical nuances. The fundamental principle underlying every holy day is its function in bringing the observer of the day into direct relationship with God's saving and redeeming power, or with God's role as revealer of the Word.

2. Rosh Hashanah

Although Rosh Hashanah is the first day of the seventh month, it is considered the "New Year Day." This is actually a theological consideration rather than a chronological one, for it celebrates the creation of the universe and hence the beginning of all things. It is referred to as "the trumpeting of remembrance" (Lev. 23:23), but it is not possible to know what this phrase signified in biblical times. In later times, certainly apparent in rabbinic literature, along with being called *yom hazikkaron* (day of remembrance), it was called *yom hadin* (day of judgment)—the day when God remembers and judges all human beings. As a day of judgment, it became a day for reflection and introspection, for "return" or what is commonly called "repentance." It

---

1. For a discussion of the sacred days in the Pentateuch see Chapter One above.

ushered in ten days of penitence, when believers were to undergo a spiritual transformation climaxed by their atonement on Yom Kippur. The celebration of creation was thus transformed into the celebration of all spiritual renewal.

The theological complex of Rosh Hashanah thus encompasses the doctrines of creation and redemption, in this case, personal redemption issuing from the atonement by grace. It also embodies the doctrines connected with reward and punishment, God's knowledge of human deeds, God's love and forgiveness, and the human being's freedom to choose the good way. Unlike other holy days which in some way celebrate a historical occasion, Rosh Hashanah and Yom Kippur focus entirely on the intimate relationship between the human being and God. In early traditions, Moses is said to have ascended Mt. Sinai on the first day of the lunar month Elul (which precedes Rosh Hashanah) and remained there for forty days. This forty-day period ends with Yom Kippur, when he is said to have descended. In this light, the Christian Lent is a reminiscence of this forty-day penitential period of Judaism.

The most characteristic feature of Rosh Hashanah is the sounding of the shofar, the ram's horn. This event recalls the binding of Isaac (for vicarious atonement) which, although one tradition had it take place at Passover, according to another, occurred on Rosh Hashanah. For, as targumic tradition emphasizes, God looked upon Abraham's sacrifice of Isaac as Isaac's vicarious expiation for Israel's sins throughout history. Accordingly, the sacrifice of Isaac virtually prefigured the sacrificial *olah* (the holocaust offered on the Temple's altar), which is conjured up and affirmed in the solemn liturgical rite of the shofar. The sounding of the shofar is also related to the messianic theme, and, in one tradition, Rosh Hashanah is said to be the time of the ultimate redemption. Thus, in addition to the normal daily orientation of the liturgy to the themes of creation, revelation, redemption, and the profession of monotheism, the New Year liturgy takes on cosmic dimensions. The prayers in many different ways allude to God's enthronement, for the kingship (kingdom) of heaven materializes with the advent of the Messiah, who presides over the last judgment.

Rosh Hashanah calls Jews to repentance and penitence, to a full turnaround *(shubah)*, and reminds them with the shofar that the kingship of heaven is near. The theme of Rosh Hashanah is the theme of John the Baptist and Jesus in their early teaching, and it is quite likely that they began their respective ministries at Rosh Hashanah. Since Jesus was the *aqedah*-Isaac—hence the Servant-Lamb—it was appropriate that he open his teaching with the Isaac Rosh Hashanah tradition and close it with the Isaac Passover tradition. While non-Christian Judaism did not follow the cross, its rabbinic leaders, beginning in the first century, centered the Rosh Hashanah liturgy around the shofar in the triune theme of *malkiyot, shopherot,* and *zikronot,* which signified God's sovereignty, enthronement, and judgment—all messianic themes. The celebration of creation is no less eschatological, for the eschaton is to be characterized by a new creation.

3. Yom Kippur

Yom Kippur, the tenth day of the lunar month, Tishri, is a twenty-four-hour cycle of prayer and fasting—the outward symbols of inward transformation. One element of the Yom Kippur observance is the ascetic strain of ancient pietism adverting to the Torah's injunction that one is to practice self-abasement (or afflict oneself) on this day (Lev. 16:29; 23:27). The penitent believer withdraws from eating, drinking, bathing, anointing, wearing shoes, and having sexual relations. Yom Kippur is thus designed to be a day of spiritual regeneration leading to the promised atonement (Lev. 23:28). The basic premise of this *shabbat shabbaton* (Lev. 23:32), "sabbath of sabbaths," is that the grace of God is bestowed upon the contrite heart. It sums up Judaism's teaching of salvation by grace, a necessary gift of God to help human beings bypass their inability to fulfill all God's expectations that they be holy "as Yhwh [is] holy." Human salvation by merit alone is impossible. God's grace is an absolute need, and Yom Kippur teaches that it is an absolute and free gift of God.

Philosophical tradition, beginning at least with Philo of Alexandria, saw Yom Kippur's requirement of self-restraint as teaching the human being a modicum of detachment from the perpetual quest for materialistic objectives. It is of some significance that Yom Kippur repeats the basic liturgical themes of Rosh Hashanah and also daily theological themes alluded to earlier. But Yom Kippur adds a characteristic emphasis upon confession, with confessional prayers recurring many times throughout the cycle of worship. The heart of this confessional is found in the famous *al het* ("for the sin") prayer. It is significant that this entire lengthy confessional, as well as other shorter confessional passages, consists solely of moral and ethical transgressions that occur between one individual and others, or between one person and collective society. None is a sin of ritual. The importance of moral deeds in Judaism was profoundly misunderstood by theologians like Martin Luther, who believed that Jews could achieve salvation by ceremonial observance alone. Violation of the so-called ceremonial law, if indeed nonobservance can even be called "violation," need not be confessed in Judaism. Ceremonials or rituals are expressions of human piety—a quest for drama, color, poetry, and music that enrich mundane existence. At its spiritual best, a ritual is part of the search for sacramental relationship with God. Rituals, however, are not of the essence of righteousness. They constitute methodology and form, not substantive essence.

Just as the sounding of the shofar at the first of Elul began the forty-day period which Yom Kippur climaxes, the sounding of the shofar at the end of Yom Kippur closes the penitential season. Thus the eschatological enthronement of God is again the theme, recalling once more the messianic advent and judgment, but now more firmly, the redemption that comes from atonement.

4. Sukkot, Shemini Atzeret, and Simhat Torah

Nine days of festival observance are ushered in from the fifteenth day of the lunar month, Tishri. The seven days of Sukkot (tabernacles) are followed by "the assembly of the eighth day," Shemini Atzeret. The eighth-day festival is concluded with a ninth-day festival, Simhat Torah, which was instituted in the tenth century. When Judaism was de-paganized, Sukkot was reinterpreted from its original purpose as an agricultural harvest celebration into a historical commemoration of the Exodus from Egypt. Though the original purpose of the booths was to provide shelter for the Israelite farmers during the harvest, they were now declared a remembrance of the dwellings of the wilderness during the wanderings of ancient Israel after the Exodus. Cognizant of the fact that no such booths are described in the entire account of Israel's sojourn in the wilderness, however, some Jewish scholars interpreted the booths as symbolic of God's overarching protection and shielding of Israel when they were redeemed from Egypt. In this way, even the historical reinterpretation was more fully theologized. For the post-Rabbinic era, Sukkot became fully expressive of the redemption. That Sukkot is a possible alternative to Passover as the time of future redemption can already be noticed at Zechariah 14:16-21.

At Sukkot time the liturgy again has one of its periodic variations with the carrying of a *lulab* and *etrog* in processions around the synagogue. The *lulab* consists of a central palm branch flanked by willow and myrtle twigs, accompanied by the *etrog,* or citron, which is a lemonlike fruit. One procession is made around the synagogue each day. In order to accentuate the redemptive nature of the Sukkot celebration, *hoshanah* prayers evolved that express past miraculous acts of divine salvation which prefigure the end-time salvation. The *lulab* and *etrog* go back to the agricultural state of the festival, but have been reinterpreted symbolically to signify organs of the body joined in worship of the Creator, or types in the community united in worship. The *geshem* liturgy, prayers for rain, survived all the vicissitudes of history with the change of the Jewish faith community from an agricultural society to an urban one, and the transformation of the liturgy from an orientation to the pagan fertility cults to a theological emphasis upon redemption. Prayers for rain take place on Shemini Atzeret, as does the *yizkor,* or memorial prayers for the deceased.

The precise origin of Simhat Torah (rejoicing with the Torah) is obscure, but the name surfaced in the early Middle Ages. The Torah was then concluded in its Babylonian annual reading cycle with the reading of the last part of Deuteronomy, and was immediately begun again with the reading of Genesis. Processions were introduced in which Torah scrolls were carried around the synagogue in a series of processions.

5. Hanukkah and Purim

The name *Hanukkah* is derived from the Hebrew word for "dedication," and refers to the time when Judah the Maccabee rededicated the Jerusalem Temple to monotheistic worship in 164 B.C.E. The major symbol of the festival is again a liturgical one: the kindling of lights to recall the kindling of the ancient menorah in the sanctuary. Hanukkah is essentially a mini-commemoration of an event which celebrated the miracle of redemption.

Even if less spiritually uplifting, Purim is also a celebration of redemption. The story of Purim is related in the book of Esther and tells of the salvation of the Jews from a destructive plot of a certain Haman in the Persian empire. The main liturgical characteristic of Purim is the reading of the *megillat Esther,* the scroll of Esther, which consists of the biblical book of Esther. The customary noisemaking, still practiced in modern synagogues, was originally opposed by leading halakists. But the carnival atmosphere of the season penetrated the synagogue until it came to be regarded as legitimate.

Originally it was not at Hanukkah but at Purim that Jews exchanged gifts. In modern times, in lands where Christmas gift giving prevails, Jews have moved their gift giving to the Hanukkah season.

6. Pesach

The Passover occurs on the eve of the fifteenth day of the lunar month of Nisan. The name *Pesach* (or Pesah) is derived from the verb *pasah,* "to stand astride" or "defend," signifying the time God protected the Israelite homes in Egypt from the "destroyer" who killed the Egyptian firstborn (Exod. 12:1-20). This festival is also called *Hag Hamatzot,* "the festival of the unleavened bread," pointing to the ancient merger of the two separate pre-Israelite festivals into one. And finally, it is also called *zeman herutenu,* "the season of our freedom." In all its forms, the festival commemorates the Exodus of ancient Israel from Egypt where its males served as slave-laborers. This historic event became a theological paradigm that pointed to future redemption and took on cosmic proportions. Its miracles, recorded in the book of Exodus, pointed to the great upheavals that will take place at the end-time, involving the forces of nature and a totally new creation of heaven and earth.

The seder, the ritual meal of the first night, is the celebration of the historical event in the form of a communion dinner. A special liturgical manual, the Haggadah, is used to guide participants in the rituals of the seder, and in the prayers, psalms, and midrashim (interpretative material) that are recited. The symbols used and the rituals enacted are meant to dramatize the bondage and the redemption, and the participants are bidden to see themselves as if they had departed from Egypt. Parsley, termed *karpas,* is taken and dipped into salt water to recall the season of spring and the miracle of the crossing of the Sea of Reeds. Matzah, the unleavened bread, is the reminder of the hasty departure from affliction. *Maror,* the pungent vegetable, is reminiscent of the bitterness of the slave-labor condition. A mortar-like mixture of wine, apples, nuts, and cinnamon, called *haroset,* serves as a condiment for the *maror,* and recalls that the bitterness came as a result of the building projects to which Israel's adult males had been conscripted. There are four junctures at which wine is sipped, each sip recalling one of the four redemptive expressions used by God in the promise to Moses that He will liberate Israel (Exod. 6:6-7). Since the destruction of Jerusalem in 70 C.E., the Paschal lamb has not been eaten, and a bone rests upon a central demonstration plate at each seder to recall the lamb. An egg also reposes on the seder plate as a double symbol. First, it symbolizes mourning for the atonement rites of the ancient Temple. Second, it serves as a sign of regeneration—the promised resurrection to come with the advent of the Messiah, which in one rabbinic view will occur at Passover.

Reference has been made previously to the "second diaspora day" of festivals. For those who still observe this day, the second night of Passover is celebrated with a seder identical to that of the first night. Furthermore, the second day of the festival is considered sacred, and a sacred eighth day is added after the seven days ordained by the Bible. For those who observe the prohibition against leaven in a strict fashion, all dishes, utensils, tableware, pots, and pans are set aside, and special Passover duplicates are used. However, a process of *kashering*—scouring vessels and utensils in boiling water—can be practiced upon glassware and metalware in order to transform the regular ones for purified Passover use.

Passover, as noted, is inextricably bound up with the doctrine of redemption. The goal of the redemption was to stand at Sinai to receive the revelation (Exod. 3:12 and 6:7 taken in the light of 19:5-6). Originally, the entire Paschal lamb was consumed by the participants, who became one with it in psychic or figurative communion, the lamb thus serving a vicarious expiatory purpose. This idea survives in the Christian eucharist, which is the transformed Paschal rite, and in the seder, when each participant is declared to have gone forth with the generation of the Exodus. When each of the four sips of wine is taken, for example, the participants identify themselves with the gift of salvation offered in Egypt and experience personal redemption, and, indirectly, the expiation that the redeemed generation underwent through the rites of the Paschal lamb. An integral segment of the seder is the formula of Gamaliel I, in which the expiatory-communion aspect of the rite is preserved, and which became the model for Paul's eucharistic formula (1 Cor. 11:23-25). Paul's formula ("This is my body . . . do this as a memorial of me. . . . This cup is the new covenant in my blood . . . do this as a memorial of me") echoes Gamaliel's exhortation to the participants in the seder ritual to observe the three Passover symbols (*pesah,* matza, and *maror*) in remembrance of various themes related to the Exodus.

7. Shabuot

Following the institution of the Passover in the roster in Leviticus, the Torah ordains that a sheaf of the first grain be offered on "the morrow of the Sabbath" (Lev. 23:9-14). Ultimately, in Rabbinic Judaism, "the morrow of the Sabbath" was taken to be the second day of Passover. The *sephira* period—the counting of forty-nine days—then (vv. 15-22), commenced with that day, and the fiftieth day from the second day of Passover was designated as a holy day. By Greek-speaking Jews, this was called the Festival of the Fiftieth Day, or Pentecost. This Fiftieth Day Festival is generally identified with Shabuot (Exod. 34:22; Deut. 16:9-10), the "Festival of Weeks" culminating the seven-week period. It is also called *Yom Habikkurim,* "the day of firstfruits" (Num. 28:26), and *Hag Haqatzir,* the harvest festival (Exod. 23:16).

As noted earlier, ancient agricultural festivals were historicized in the Torah itself. For example, the association of Sukkot with the Exodus (Lev. 23:39-43) was the product of an ongoing alienation of evolving Judaism from the pagan agricultural, fertility-oriented religions. Judaism sought to celebrate the mighty and miraculous acts of God centered in the three great cosmic concepts of creation, revelation, and redemption. Shabuot thus became the sacred day of commemorating the revelation at Sinai. The process by which Shabuot was linked to the giving of the Decalogue at Sinai cannot be accurately reconstructed, but we find Pentecost already related to the Sinai covenant in early Hellenistic times (Jub. 6:21).

In any event, Rabbinic Judaism celebrated this day as the day of revelation, and instituted the reading of the Ten Commandments as the synagogue lection of the day to embody liturgically the concept of revelation. In reference to a tradition that King David was born on Shabuot, the book of Ruth was read on this festival in order to recapitulate David's genealogy and to link Shabuot to the Davidic redemption. Others believed the book of Ruth was appropriate to read because it described Ruth's consecration and commitment to Judaism, a personal act of faith reminiscent of Israel's acceptance of the revelation and covenantal commitment at Sinai. For the same reason, in modern times, the confirmation of adolescents in certain synagogues is conducted on Shabuot.

8. The Minor Festivals and Fasts

There are many other days on the Judaic religious calendar. Some are termed "festivals," but are not *holy* days; and some are fasts, which are also not considered holy, except for Yom Kippur. The concept "holy day" is reserved for those days referred to specifically in Scripture as *miqra qodesh,* "holy convocations."

The minor festivals include Rosh Hodesh, the new moon; Lag b'Omer, the thirty-third day of the forty-nine-day *Sephirah* period between Passover and Shabuot; and *Tu beShebat,* the fifteenth day of the lunar month of Shebat, the Palestinian arbor day.

The fast days consist of many public and private fasts; but basically five major public fasts, other than Yom Kippur, have retained a strong hold in Orthodox circles, while in Conservative and Reform circles only Yom Kippur plays its historic role. The five fasts other than Yom Kippur are: (1) the fast of Esther, preceding Purim (Esth. 4:16); (2) *asarah betebet,* commemorating the beginning of the siege of Jerusalem in 587 B.C.E. on the tenth day of the month of Tebet (2 Kgs. 25:1); (3) *shivah asar betammuz,* for the breaching of the walls on the seventeenth of Tammuz (2 Kgs. 25:3); (4) *tisha beab,* for the destruction of the Temple on the ninth of Ab (2 Kgs. 25:9); and (5) the mourning of the assassination of Gedaliah, governor of Jerusalem, on the third of Tishri (2 Kgs. 25:22-26), which escalated the consequences of the debacle of 587 B.C.E. The last four fasts, related to the destruction of Jerusalem, seem to have already been in vogue during postexilic times (Zech. 8:19), although the dates of the third and the fourth, as given in the Bible, are not the same as the dates standardized by Rabbinic Judaism.

The minor festivals are observed by minor adjustments in synagogue liturgy, although Lag b'Omer still plays a major role for the Orthodox in relieving them of the stringencies they practice in a Lent-like penitential observance between Passover and Shabuot, when they countenance no music or enjoyment, do not shave or trim the hair, and do not solemnize marriages.

Similarly, fast days are marked with certain liturgical adjustments and scriptural readings, even in Conservative synagogues when fasting is not practiced. Fasting is basically a form of abstinence from worldly and sensual pursuits as a means of elevating spiritual consciousness in order to expiate sin. Even where fasting is no longer in vogue, the metaphor of the paradigmatic story of the sin of the Golden Calf and the prophetic lection of Isaiah 55:6–56:8, which reassures the community of God's love, remain with the standard scriptural reading.

9. The Sabbath

The Sabbath was of central covenantal significance. The paradigmatic passage is Exodus 31:13-17, where the Sabbath is designated both as *ot,* a sign, and *berit olam,* a perpetual covenant. The Sabbath was perceived to celebrate both creation (Exod. 20:11) and redemption (Deut. 5:15). As symbol of the covenant, the Sabbath reaffirms the election, and in this way observance of the Sabbath is of the nature of a creedal statement. While the comprehensive theological understanding of the Sabbath is already present in preexilic pentateuchal literature, it is clear from Jeremiah and Nehemiah and from other allusions to it that its observance was not as strict and its restrictions not as fulsome as they became in the postexilic era. The dismantling of the cult after 587 B.C.E. made the Sabbath, along with other distinctive rituals, more significant in the worship system of Judaism. The importance of differentiating ritualism became especially marked in the Hellenistic era, and thus Jubilees and the Dead Sea Scrolls evince a restrictive, pietistic, and quietistic Sabbath. Rabbinic Judaism eventually absorbed much of this approach, although in its earlier phases, the proto-rabbis were at odds with this stringent approach to the Sabbath, and like Jesus in the Gospels, they based a more lenient Sabbath observance upon principles that were both humanitarian and reasonable.

The Sabbath had another important aspect to it. From the same verse that they inferred scrupulous restraint from activity (Isa. 58:13), the rabbis also noted the suggestion for *oneg,* namely, to see in the Sabbath a time of enjoyment and delight. For this reason, good food, drink, clothing, music, and aesthetics in general were all stressed for elevating the atmosphere and the human spirit on the Sabbath. Thus, the more elegant Friday night Sabbath dinner evolved as the high point of the Jewish family celebration and, indeed, of the week. The Talmud relates how certain rabbis regarded it as proper, if necessary, to fast a goodly part of the week in order to conserve available funds for the family Sabbath dinner. But lest this become merely a secular meal in which the appetite is indulged, it was transformed into a sacramental meal by the ritual of lighting Sabbath candles and reciting the kiddush—the proclamation of the sanctity of the occasion. The kiddush contains within it the entire complex of Sabbath theology: election, the Sabbath as remembrance of both creation and redemption, and its divinely bestowed sanctity. In order to facilitate the understanding of the kiddush as a sacramental rite, it was recited with wine, which had been the normal accompaniment as a libation at altar sacrifices. Like the seder, by virtue of the kiddush and its liturgy the Sabbath meal and that of each holy day were thus all considered sacred meals, with the table as altar and the family as priests (Exod. 19:6).

Similarly, the Sabbath is closed with the habdalah ritual, which declares the moment of "separation," the separation of the holy from the profane—the right to reenter the mundane world and engage in worldly tasks once more. At this ritual, wine is taken again, making of it a cultic act with its remembrance of libation. Spices are sniffed to symbolize the prayer for a fragrant week, and a *berakah* is recited, thanking God for the creation of light. Light was the first creation by the word of God (Gen. 1:3), and is therefore celebrated in the habdalah ritual, which ushers in the first day of creation in the ever-recurring weekly cycle of six creation-days and Sabbath.

C. The Life Cycle

Judaism possesses multifarious rituals connected with every aspect of life and its rites of passage. Birth, marriage, and death are all surrounded with theology and practice. But it must also be borne in mind that a prolific number of customs, which are not integral to the basic life-cycle rituals, arose over the centuries in different communities. Some were adapted from the medieval environment, and some are rooted in superstition. A reader must be very discerning when consulting books on Judaic life-cycle "customs and ceremonies" not to mistake medieval superstitious customs for authentic rituals.

1. Circumcision and Naming

The halakah governing the naming of children is sparse, but it is abundant on circumcision. As the sacramental rite bringing the child into the covenant relationship with God, naming was always the birth ritual that was greatly emphasized. Boys were named at circumcision, while girls were at first named at home, and later in the synagogue. In modern times, many rabbis are having both girls and boys brought to the synagogue, thus equalizing the naming ceremony for both genders. Circumcision must be done on the eighth day (Gen. 17:12; Lev. 12:3), while naming can be at any time. Circumcision is delayed beyond the eighth day, however, when medical reasons require it. (In a family suffering from hemophilia, circumcision is waived.)

The basic theological presupposition of circumcision is that it consists of a sacrifice of flesh and blood on the organ that represents regeneration and perpetuity, and it thereby fulfills the traditional covenantal sacrifice rite. Although Reform Jews at one time voiced objections to this practice, it is fair to assume that it continues to be almost universally observed among Jews.

2. Pidyon Habem
(Redemption of the Firstborn; Exod. 13:1-2, 11-16)

One explanation of this rite is that it recalls the fact that Egyptian firstborn were the surrogates for Israelite firstborn in Egypt when the tenth plague struck the Egyptians. Another explanation refers to the mandate to offer all first produce or yield to the Lord by presenting it to the priests for their use. Thus, theoretically, the firstborn, who were apparently obligated to cultic service, belonged to God. This practice was later changed, and they were replaced by the Levites (Num. 3:45). While all first yield was to belong to the priestly tribe, however, the human firstborn were to be redeemed (Num. 18:15-16). As with so many other symbols and life-cycle rituals, none of the procedures of *pidyon haben* is known from the Torah. The ritual as practiced in modern times is derived from the period of the *geonim,* and is no longer widely practiced outside Orthodox circles.

3. Bar/Bat Mitzvah

Religious maturity, as an official condition in Judaism at age thirteen, is known only since mishnaic times (M. Ab. 5:21), although it undoubtedly embodies an older tradition. In any event, it signified that the young man is thenceforth personally responsible for all of his religious obligations and entitled to all rights and privileges of the faith, synagogue, or community. This rite of passage was extended to girls in the form of confirmation in the Reform movement during the nineteenth century, and as bat mitzvah in the Conservative and Reconstructionist movements during the twentieth century. Bat mitzvah, however, is not practiced in Orthodoxy. In recent decades, the Reform movement has been reintroducing bar mitzvah for boys and therefore bat mitzvah for girls as well, aside from confirmation. Confirmation at age fifteen or sixteen is also practiced in the Conservative and Reconstructionist movements.

The major feature of bar/bat mitzvah is calling the young person to the Torah, thus publicly acknowledging his or her attainment of the right to participate in public worship. The festivity accompanying bar mitzvah is known only since the fifteenth century, and the expansion of the synagogue ceremonies surrounding the bar and bat mitzvah are twentieth-century innovations.

4. Marriage

The act of betrothal in Judaism is known as *erusin*. It is also called more prominently *kiddushin,* which signifies "consecration," and gives marriage a sacramental character. Once there has been *kiddushin,* the relationship can only be dissolved by a *get* (a bill of divorce), even if the final step, *nissuin* ("elevation")—the consummation of the marriage—has not yet taken place. The *nissuin* is performed under a *huppah* or canopy, which symbolizes the home of the married couple. In earlier times there were two separate celebrations, but in early medieval times the two rites of *kiddushin* and *nissuin* were combined into one marriage ceremony.

There are no mandated customs or traditions that must be observed in the marriage ceremony, and Jews are free to adopt customs pertaining to the procession, participants, and the like that prevail in their cultural environment. Specifically, Judaic traditions include only the *huppah,* the *ketubah* (a religious marriage certificate unrelated to the civil license), and the liturgical *berakot.* Two *berakot* are recited before *kiddushin* and seven before *nissuin,* accompanied by the ubiquitous wine that is reminiscent of the altar libation and contributes to the ceremony's sacramental character. Bride and groom each drinks from both the cup of *kiddushin* and the cup of *nissuin.* Following the ceremony, a glass is broken to symbolize that even at the peak of one's joy one must be aware of the distress in the world. Earlier this ritual recalled the destruction of the Temple in 70 C.E.

The original Judaic format called only for the groom to consecrate the bride to himself. In modern times, however, outside Orthodoxy, there is an exchange of rings and mutual consecration between bride and groom. Various branches of Judaism, such as Sephardim, Yemenites, and Hasidim, among others, have distinctive customs that evolved historically but which never became universally accepted any more than modern customs became universal in all synagogues.

5. Abelut (Mourning)

It is customary for next of kin to perform *keriah* (rending a garment), or to have a symbolic black ribbon attached to their garment, before the funeral of the deceased. There are a variety of customs attached to *keriah* and differences that obtain in many communities and among the denominations. Burial was traditionally performed on the day of death, but that is no longer the case, except in Orthodox circles. The exegesis of Genesis 3:19, "to dust you shall return," has until modern times placed a literal meaning upon these words. Presently, however, the Reform movement accepts cremation and burial in a mausoleum. The Reconstructionists have no fixed position. While the Conservative movement does not formally accept a mausoleum and still prohibits cremation, rabbis will officiate at a funeral service while the body is intact, before cremation and before installation in a mausoleum.

There are three periods of *abelut* (the expression of grief following the burial): (1) *Shiba,* a seven-day period for meditation and reflection, in which next of kin remain at home, public worship is conducted at home, and the mourner abstains from various indulgences. Many moderns observe only three days strictly, but continue the worship at home in the evenings for seven days. Among the Reform Jews it is generally customary to observe only one day. (2) *Sheloshim,* a thirty-day period, which is less intense in the abstentions practiced during *Shiba.* (3) The first year, for parents only, in which frivolous events are avoided, and the kaddish, the mourner's prayer, is recited at all public worship. (The Orthodox have generally observed kaddish for only eleven months for reasons unacceptable to many modern scholars, and only men recite it.) It should be noted that the mourner's kaddish has no reference to death in it. It is wholly a doxology (a formula of praise) to God, praying for the earthly advent of the messianic era and reaffirming faith in God's assurance of resurrection even at the hour of darkest grief. Among the Conservative, Reconstructionist, and Reform groups, women say the kaddish equally with men.

Since the Middle Ages it has become customary to observe *yahreszeit,* the anniversary of death of parents and other next to kin. During that period there also arose the custom of *yizkor*—reciting certain memorial prayers for the deceased during the synagogue worship on four occasions: Yom Kippur, Shemini Atzeret, the eighth diaspora day of Passover, and on the second diaspora day of Shabuot. A memorial light is kindled on both *yahreszeit* and *yizkor* occasions.

D. Dietary Practices (Kashrut)

The dietary practices are among the most complex of Judaism's prolific ritualism. Reiterated many times is a prohibition on the private eating of blood, which was regarded as the symbol of life and was to be confined to the altar rites as a medium of atonement. The core of the other practices is found in Leviticus 11 (cf. Deut. 14:3-21), where they are given in relatively simple form: those animals, birds, insects, and fish that may be eaten and those that are prohibited. No reason is offered for the distinction between permitted and proscribed animals. Hellenistic writers ascribed humanitarian, hygienic, and symbolic explanations, but these are relative and subjective and cannot be shown to have been the original conceptualization behind the practices. The only hint of a reason for kashrut in the Torah is a call to holiness (Exod. 22:30; Lev. 11:44), and this might signify in some way a call to moral discipline.

The word *kasher* (not *kosher*) means "fit, appropriate," and refers to being ritually appropriate as food. This is not to be confused with contemporary "kosher-style" advertisements which give kashrut the nuance of a Jewish ethnic food style. There is no such thing as Jewish "ethnic" food. Jews eat all styles of cooking, the religion requiring only that foods be *kasher.* Many ancient civilizations had a variety of food taboos which are equally difficult to trace and explain. There seems, in fact, to be a confusion at times in Leviticus 11 between food prohibitions and impurity. This apparent confusion might lead an exegete to conclude that certain food taboos, for example, eating the flesh of a dead animal which was not slaughtered specifically for food (Lev. 11:39-40; Deut. 14:21), were originally part of a complex of purity-impurity taboos. It also appears that at one time the only flesh that was permitted was at a cultic meal, when the flesh was a portion of an animal offered on the altar (Lev. 17:2-9). Later, meat in general was permitted to be eaten, even in a state of impurity (Deut. 12:15, 20-22). That kashrut was not entirely standardized, and perhaps not even entirely clear to the redactors of the Pentateuch, may be seen, for example, in the contradiction between Leviticus 17:15 and Deuteronomy 14:21 on whether the *nebelah*—an animal which is dead but not slaughtered for food—is permitted to a *ger* (foreigner).

The mass of halakah pertaining to food that developed in pre-Rabbinic and Rabbinic Judaism is found largely concentrated in the talmudic tractate *Hulin.* Rabbinic Judaism ultimately attempted to standardize a massive corpus of halakic details related to preparing, cooking, and eating food, the utensils used, and the separation of meat and dairy. The restrictions and particulars were multiplied over the centuries, and the entire mass became unmanageable for the Jew of the eighteenth century and later. The Reform movement abolished the bulk of kashrut practices as no longer spiritually relevant, and as tending to separate Jews from non-Jews in a world in which mingling was deemed preferable. In modern times, kashrut observance was perceived to erect barriers in the world of commerce and finance, and made both business and recreational travel an undue hardship. The Reconstructionist and Conservative movements are in basic agreement with these modernist tendencies of thought and have adjusted certain aspects of the practices. For example, the Reconstructionists advocate the maintenance of a *kasher* home, continuing the symbolism of table as altar, but allow free indulgence outside the home. While the Conservatives continue to profess the binding authority of certain limited segments of the halakah even when eating outside the home, they have nevertheless tacitly accepted far-reaching modifications in the halakah. The Orthodox profess obedience to the most stringent practices. Thus, for example, while the Conservative movement sees the transformation of a food element into a chemical as a new product, which is no longer a food and therefore not subject to food restrictions when used as ingredients in processed food, the Orthodox continue to adjudge such chemicals to be food and subject to all food restrictions. A major example in current consideration is the eligibility of a food containing gelatin derived from animal products; the Conservatives permit it and the Orthodox prohibit it. While limiting themselves to fish or dairy foods, members of Conservative Judaism will generally eat in restaurants and in homes which do not observe kashrut, without concern for the utensils, dishes, and vessels, but the Orthodox will not.

We cannot determine precisely when the separation of meat from dairy arose as a basic element of the dietary practices. The Hellenistic writers do not indicate familiarity with these practices. There seems at some point to have arisen an exegesis of Exodus 23:19 (cf. Exod. 34:2; Deut. 14:21), "you shall not boil a kid in its mother's milk," as signifying not to cook or to eat meat and milk ingredients simultaneously. The process whereby this prohibition became universal cannot be ascertained.

An old view that boiling and eating milk and meat together was prohibited is reflected in the Palestinian Targum, but this view did not have universal authority. Philo expatiated on Exodus 23:19 as referring to a literal boiling of the calf in its own mother's milk, and saw the prohibition as humanitarian. In Galilee and in Babylonia the separation of meat and dairy was not practiced universally, and sometimes not applied to fowl. The Ugaritic tablets indicate that in ancient Canaanite fertility worship there was a rite of boiling a kid in its mother's milk; this notion—that it was part of a pagan cultic practice and should therefore be eschewed—certainly fits the context of Exodus 23 and 34. But at some later time, apparently when Deuteronomy 14:21 was authored, this Canaanite practice was either forgotten or ignored, and the prohibition was included in the dietary practices. The Targum seems to have then added the eating, and even later this passage was taken to imply all dairy and meat and all the dishes, utensils, and vessels that are used with the foods. This universal and comprehensive separation of meat from dairy continued to be normative practice in Rabbinic Judaism until the eighteenth century, when emergent reforming Jews questioned its relevance and validity.

E. Symbols

Among the paramount symbols of Judaism are the tefillin (phylacteries), tallit (prayer shawl), and mezuzah (doorpost capsule). Many regarded such ritual commands in an allegorical manner and argued that they were only to elevate one's thought and sentiment. Others believed that these objects were meant to be observed literally. This difference of view still exists.

1. Tefillin (Phylacteries)

The word *tefillin* is a plural of *tefillah*, "prayer," and signifies a prayer-accompaniment. The tefillin consist of two boxes, each containing four sections of the Torah (Exod. 13:1-10; 11:16; Deut. 6:4-9; 11:13-21), all of which contain the command, "fasten them on your hand as a sign and on your forehead as a circlet" (Deut. 6:8), while also containing affirmation of monotheism and redemption. The tefillin are called *ot*, "a sign," as is the Sabbath, and consequently are not worn on Sabbaths and Festivals (the latter generally being treated as a Sabbath in most phases of the halakah).

How the tefillin should be made or worn is not specified in the Bible, and the traditions embodied in Rabbinic Judaism were considered "halakah of Moses from Sinai," a term signifying great antiquity. The symbolism of the tefillin being placed upon the left arm facing the heart and upon the head is, in its consciousness-raising effect, bringing the worshipers into closer communion with God and reminding them of their obligation to use their faculties of mind, heart, and physical power in the correct service of God. Generally, in modern times, most Reform, Reconstructionist, and Conservative Jews no longer observe the ritual of donning tefillin.

2. Tallit (Prayer Shawl) and Zizit (Fringes)

These symbols are derived from Numbers 15:37-41 and Deuteronomy 22:12. How the zizit (or tzitzit), "fringes," become a "remembrance" of all of the Lord's commandments (Num. 15:39) is unclear (see B. Men. 43b; Sot. 17a). The earliest fringes were made with one thread of blue, probably as a symbol of Israel's priesthood and royalty. But at a certain juncture the process of extracting this blue dye from the shellfish murex on the Mediterranean was forgotten. As with the tefillin, the Torah specifies nothing about how a tallit with zizit is to be made or how it is to look, but all the traditions embodied in Rabbinic Judaism are declared to be of high antiquity. It appears clear from oldest sources that any garment should have zizit attached to the hem, but when it became socially impossible for Jews to wear the zizit all day in public, the tallit was introduced in the form of a four-cornered prayer shawl with the appropriate zizit attached, and was used only as an accoutrement for prayer. Whether one begins to don the tallit at bar mitzvah or bat mitzvah, or when one marries, varies among different segments of Judaism. Although the Reform movement abandoned the tallit in the nineteenth century, it has slowly been reintroducing it in recent years.

3. Mezuzah

The commandment to write "these words" on the doorposts is given at Deuteronomy 6:9 and 11:20. As with tefillin and zizit, many ancients, especially those in the Hellenistic milieu and those with tendencies like the modern Reformists, regarded the command to write the words on the doorposts in an allegorical manner. Others followed it literally, and in time the mezuzah as we know it—a capsule containing the first two paragraphs of the Shema (Deut. 6:4-9; 11:13-21) written on a parchment—was devised. This capsule is placed on a doorpost to the right of a person entering the house. The symbolism involved is for the people entering or leaving the home to be constantly aware of the presence of God in their lives and of their obligation to live by God's Word at home and in society.

4. Kiphah or Yarmulke (Skullcap)

The covering of the head for worship, religious study, or at any other time was not ordained by either Torah or Talmud. It arose in the Middle

Ages and was the source of a difference of opinion at least into the seventeenth century. The *Shulhan Aruk* of 1565 formulates the halakah of the skullcap, and it has remained the same for Orthodox Jews. However, it was early disputed and abandoned by the Reform movement and ultimately was generally abandoned by the Conservative and Reconstructionist movements, except for worship. The skullcap is also still worn by many Jews for religious study and for meals taken at home, especially on the Sabbath and holy days.

The headcovering which has become popular, especially for indoor wear and now almost universally in synagogues, is known as a *yarmulke* in Yiddish and as *kiphah* in Hebrew. The skullcap is undoubtedly an adaptation of the episcopal headcovering. Hasidim and some other Ultra-Orthodox still wear full hats for worship. Women are expected to cover their heads in Orthodox circles, but no longer in the Conservative, Reconstructionist, and Reform synagogues. As with other symbols, some Reform rabbis are presently reintroducing optional headcovering for worship.

F. The Synagogue

The origin of the synagogue has been discussed earlier in this work.[2] The fully developed synagogue of rabbinic times was called a *bet tefillah* (B. Git. 39b), but was originally called *moed*, the place where the *edah*, the holy congregation, gathered (Ps. 74:8), and later more frequently *bet kenesset*, "a house of assembly." From the latter term was derived the Greek *synagoge*. The synagogue often contained a *bet sepher* (an elementary school), a *bet talmud* (a high school), and a *bet midrash* (a school of advanced study). The ancient rabbis saw this institution as replacing the Temple of Jerusalem and called it a *miqdash meat*, "a small sanctuary" (B. Meg. 29a) or the "sanctuary for a while," that is, until the restoration of the eschatological sanctuary in Jerusalem.

Each synagogue and each rabbi of a synagogue is autonomous. No denominational center can dictate policies or candidates for its pulpit to any synagogue, which is governed by a Board of Directors elected by the membership at large, nor can any outside authority impose any halakah upon a rabbi. This autonomy is universal throughout Judaism and is the historic pattern since Rabbinism arose. The rabbi is an ordained person, his credentials being academic and his degree

---

2. See Chapter Three above.

called *semikah* (the "laying on of hands"). The rite was adapted from the way Moses transmitted authority to Joshua (Deut. 34:9). The rabbi's authority rests upon ancient rabbinic exegesis of Deuteronomy 17:9 and is validated by *semikah*. Ultimately, however, whether rabbis wield more or less authority in their own synagogue and among other Jews and how widespread this authority is depend upon their scholarship. The central halakic organs of the contemporary Orthodox, Conservative, and Reform movements exist for offering guidance but do not supersede individual rabbinic authority and autonomy.

In more recent centuries, the office of cantor has been professionalized, especially in larger congregations. Cantors are not ordained persons and have no halakic authority. Their role is to chant the worship order, sometimes to read the Torah, to teach religious subjects to the children, and to prepare youngsters for bar and bat mitzvah. Any layperson may serve as cantor, and in Reform, Reconstructionist, and some Conservative synagogues, women serve as cantors.

Afterword

The foregoing chapters have sought, within a very brief compass, to summarize the origin and evolution of Judaism, and to review its basic tenets and practices. Throughout it has been stressed that in all ages Judaism was not a monolithic faith and did not possess a "normative" set of practices. A number of option have been available, and different tendencies of thought and practice have been equally legitimate. Nevertheless, there have been times when some groups, such as the extreme Hasidim and Ultra-Orthodox types, have denied this legitimacy.

In its classical form, Judaism denied that non-Jews can attain salvation unless they adhered to a set of principles defined by Judaism and thereby attained the status of *hasidey umot haolam,* "the devout of the gentiles." In modern times this argument is muted by most Jews, who will assuredly make no special charge that, for example, Hinduism still does not approach the level of monotheism that would theoretically be required of a non-Jew to attain salvation. Closer to home, however, Judaism has granted, since early times, that Christianity and Islam are monotheistic faiths. In modern times a number of Jewish scholars have been prepared to discuss the essentially Judaic nature of the teachings of Jesus and of Paul. I have been engaged in researching a variety of themes that could lead reasonable Jewish and Christian theologians to a formulation of *dual covenant theology.* According to this concept, Judaism and Christianity—two authentic branches reaching upward from the same sturdy trunk—will recognize that God's will has been for the two to coexist and to work God's will in the world.

The great divide in the modern world between orthodoxy and nonorthodoxy in Judaism has its source in two fundamental questions.

The first is whether one accepts the Torah as the literal words of God and all the accumulated rituals of Judaism as equally divinely revealed and their observance as divinely required, or whether one sees the Scriptures as the human effort to describe the will of God. The second is whether one regards Rabbinism as a historically evolved interpretation of God's will, albeit with the input of the Holy Spirit. The differences between orthodoxy and nonorthodoxy hinge on historicism, which both Samuel David Luzzato in Italy and Samson Raphael Hirsch in Germany strongly attacked in the nineteenth century. In twentieth-century Germany, Franz Rosenzweig, an entirely different type of person from Luzzato and Hirsch—nonorthodox in style, existentialist in philosophy, and immersed in romanticism—also rejected historicism. These thinkers repudiated historicism and advocated a theological view, which continues to see in Judaism the absolute revealed truth and a divine gift of eternal validity, not subject to history and therefore not subject to change.

Modernists, however, see how historiography discovers and analyzes texts which sometimes challenge the stereotypical, idealized, and romanticized collective memory. Objective historical writing raises such questions as the role of provocation given by Jews to their oppressors, the viability of Zionism, the true nature of the transmission of tradition, and, most significantly, the meaning of heresy and orthodoxy in any given period. The collective memory suppresses uncomfortable facts and ideas; historiography dredges them up. Historicism suggests that religious tradition is the result of historical evolution, is undergoing constant modification, and is not the product of a one-time absolute and eternal revelation.

Thus, contemporary interest in Hasidism, arising from a search for Jewish mysticism that flows from attraction to Eastern mysticism, romanticizes the popular Hasidic development and submits to an unhistorical mystique. By contrast, historiography reveals Hasidism's undesirable aspects and unworthy tenets, its exclusion of gentiles from equality in God's sight, its dynastic rivalries, its internal corruption, and its antidemocratic absolutism.

Other contemporary issues challenge the theologian. When one considers the entire spectrum of messianism in the classical Judaic sources in tandem with modern secular nationalism or even religious nationalism of the current Moslem variety, one is bound to question whether Zionism is a natural conclusion to the messianic dream or a radical rebellion against it.

AFTERWORD

All of these matters—the plausibility of a dual covenant, the ironic possible heresy of Orthodoxy, and the apostasy of Zionism—emerge from cover in a careful summation of Judaism. It is not for me to answer all questions but to allow them to flow from an objective presentation of possibilities. What a reader must be made aware of is that the ultimate pursuit of the nature and meaning of Judaism must be effected within the primary literature of the Hebrew Testament, Hellenistic literature, the intertestamental scriptures, the Dead Sea Scrolls, the Targums, the Christian Testament, the midrashim, and the two Talmuds.

Appendix
Images of Women in Judaism
LILLIAN SIGAL

I. INTRODUCTION

In an article on the treatment of women in the classical halakah, Phillip Sigal has written, "In truth, whether we care to confess it or not, Judaism possesses distinct elements of what would currently go by the name of 'male chauvinism.'"[1] Although a general attitude of humanitarianism toward women prevailed throughout Jewish history, up until approximately the mid-1960s they have been relegated to a position inferior to men. Women's subordination in Judaism has been due to the power of patriarchy, that is, to the fact that men have written Scripture and its interpretations, have recorded the laws of Judaism, composed its liturgy, and created its institutions. Since Jewish women's lives have been circumscribed by men, the role they have played in the evolution of their faith has been marginalized and has been almost invisible.

The purpose, then, of this appendix is to make women's experience and participation in Judaism visible by focusing on the ways in which they were portrayed and treated, and by identifying certain women who did not conform to the stereotypical role assigned to their gender by their androcentric society. Furthermore, this essay will expose the presence of feminine imagery in depictions of God and Israel in the classical sources of Judaism and the persistence of goddess worship in ancient Israel.

---

1. Phillip Sigal, "Elements of Male Chauvinism in Classical Halakhah," *Judaism* 24 (1975), 226.

II. THE POSITION OF WOMEN IN ANCIENT ISRAEL

A. Introduction

Since ancient Israel was patriarchal, the status of women was low, even by ancient standards. Woman's role was that of procreator and homemaker. She called her husband *baal*, "master," or *adon*, "lord," paying him the homage that a slave or servant would pay a master. As daughter, sister, or wife, she was always subject to the authority of men. The family, not the individual, was the basic unit of society, and the family was called a "father's house," its interests being identified with those of the male head.

B. Women's Social and Economic Status

The Israelite woman was considered part of her husband's possessions. For example, the Decalogue admonishes the Israelite against coveting the possessions of his neighbor, which include his house, land, animals, slaves, and wife (Exod. 20:17; Deut. 5:21). Nevertheless, an Israelite wife was not a slave. Moreover, though foreign women were taken as booty in war (Deut. 20:14), their husbands who had taken them captive could not sell them. That Israelite women were treated as chattel is evident in the following two illustrations from the Bible. In the book of Judges (19:22-30), a Levite gives his concubine to some men who rape and abuse her until she dies, and the Bible expresses no condemnation of her husband's action. Furthermore, David's seduction of Bathsheba is presented as an offense against her husband, Uriah the Hittite, not as an outrage against her (2 Sam. 11–12).

A wife was the property not only of her husband but of his family as well. When her husband died, she became subject to the head of his family, who chose for her another member of the family as her husband. This treatment of a widow was institutionalized in the levirate marriage, in which the brother of the deceased person, or his closest kinsman, married his widow in order to perpetuate the name of the deceased by giving her a child who would be his heir.

All her life the Israelite woman remained a minor. Vows made by a daughter or wife, to be valid, needed the consent of her father or husband (Num. 30:4-17). Moreover, she could not inherit from her father or her husband, except in the absence of a male heir (Num. 27:8). If there were no kinsman to marry a widowed woman, or if the kinsman opted to undergo *halitzah*, the ritual that freed him of his obligation to marry her, she was virtually destitute if no one else would wed her. Nevertheless, biblical law did provide protection for the impoverished widow along with orphans and aliens (Exod. 22:21; Deut. 10:18), and the prophets consistently pleaded for the plight of the widow (Isa. 1:17; Jer. 7:6).

The activities of women in ancient Israel were limited to the private domain of cooking, spinning, looking after flocks, and working in the fields, and their legal rights were extremely limited. While their subordination to patriarchy reflected the general condition of women in the cultural milieu of the ancient Near East, their position was inferior to that of their counterparts in major Near Eastern countries. For example, in Egypt a wife was often head of her family, and in Babylon she could acquire property, take legal action, be a party to contracts, and inherit from her husband.

C. Domestic Relationships

1. Marriage

Parents arranged marriages for their children, although they were often initiated by the man, who would send for his designated wife. The woman was "given," "taken," "purchased," or "captured." In the story that relates Abraham's quest for a wife for Isaac, however, the text implies that a woman who was not a captive had the right to refuse an offer of marriage.

Israelite men were permitted to have many wives, as is evident in the Bible from the patriarchs (Abraham had three wives and Jacob four) through Solomon (he had seven hundred wives and three hundred concubines) and beyond. Concubinage was a very old, prebiblical arrangement which allowed for a regular sexual relationship between the man and his concubine and entitled her to support but without the legal rights of a wife. The concubine was not married ceremonially, and a divorce was not required when her husband chose to send her away. Polygamy among Jews declined when they were afforded Roman citizenship, since the practice was forbidden among the Romans. In Parthian lands, however, polygamy was a regularized institution; thus in Babylonia Jews continued practicing it. The Qumran community (associated with the Dead Sea Scrolls) and the Christian community opposed polygamy from the beginning. Ultimately, under Christian influence in Europe, Judaism ended the practice ca. 1000 C.E. Nevertheless, concubinage persisted among Jews as late as the sixteenth century, and even among Christians—Martin Luther approved it for Philip of Hesse, a Protestant prince.

Women were expected to produce progeny for their husbands, and as mothers they were honored, as is evident in the fourth commandment (Exod. 20:12; Deut. 5:16). Furthermore, a mother's advice was valued. For example, she could influence the choice of her son's spouse, as in the case of Rebekah, who determined that her son Jacob would not marry a Canaanite (Gen. 27:46). Women gained respect with the birth of their first child, especially if it was a boy. When wives were infertile they were expected to offer their maidservants to their husbands to bear their children. Thus, the matriarch Sarah gave her handmaid Hagar to Abraham so that he would not remain without an heir (Gen. 16:2). Furthermore, childlessness threatened a wife's position, since procreation was central to her wifely duties and was her raison d'être. Consequently, Rachel, despairing of her infertility, cried out to Jacob, "Give me children or I shall die" (Gen. 30:2). Rachel then gave Jacob her servant Bilhah as her surrogate to conceive his children.

2. Divorce and Sexual Infidelity

Divorce was allowed in Scripture (Deut. 24:1-4), although its procedures were not designated. It was exclusively a male prerogative, however, and remains so among traditional Jews today. Furthermore, in the Bible a divorced woman could not marry a priest.

Both men and women were liable to the death penalty if they committed adultery (Lev. 20:10; Deut. 22:22). Nevertheless, a double standard obtained regarding extramarital relations. On the one hand, if a wife were suspected of adultery, she was subjected to an ordeal (Num. 5:12-31), and if found guilty, she was punished by death. On the other hand, the fidelity of a husband under similar circumstances was not similarly tested. Additionally, law required the virginity of the bride, but not of the husband. Furthermore, if a betrayed husband were not involved, a man who violated an unmarried woman simply had to marry her and pay her father compensation. Thus, a married man who had sexual intercourse with an unmarried woman was not guilty of adultery, since adultery was considered a property crime (Deut. 22:13-21, 28-29).

Prostitutes seem to have been tolerated. For example, Judah slept with his daughter-in-law Tamar, who had disguised herself as a prostitute, with no expression of disapproval by the biblical author of the patriarch's behavior (Gen. 38:15-16). Nevertheless, prostitutes were considered social outcasts and were condemned in the Bible (Deut. 23:17-18). Moreover, harlotry was the central metaphor for religious apostasy (Hos. 1–3; Ezek. 16). In spite of the contempt in which prostitutes were held, Rahab, a harlot who sheltered two spies sent by Joshua, was rewarded for her service to Israel when they invaded Jericho (Josh. 2:1-21).

D. Women's Religious Status

Women's relationship to God was mediated through their husbands, since God's covenant with Israel was signified by male circumcision. Moreover, in most instances of biblical law God addresses the male, whose situation is regarded as the norm. For example, in the Decalogue all the commandments are directed to the masculine singular "you." This form of address is not generic and inclusive of both male and female, as evident in the last commandment of the Decalogue, which forbids the Israelite from coveting his neighbor's wife (Exod. 20:17). Typical casuistic (case) law begins with the formula, "If a man does. . . ." The Hebrew term for "man" used is not the generic *adam,* but rather the nongeneric *ish.*

Women's participation in the religious rites of ancient Israel was minimal. Only males were required to attend the three pilgrimage festivals in Jerusalem, and Israelite women were denied religious leadership as priests. The inability of women in Israel to perform the cult was due in part to the fact that they were considered impure when they had bodily emissions at their menses and after childbirth (their length of impurity being considered double if the child were a girl; Lev. 12:2, 5). In this respect they were more restricted than their Near Eastern counterparts. In the countries that surrounded Israel, female deities were venerated, and women conducted the cult as priestesses. A notable example of an ancient Sumerian priestess is Enheduanna, who flourished in the third millennium B.C.E. and wrote two cycles of hymns to the goddess Inannna. Enheduanna was distinguished as both poet and theologian and as the first nonanonymous writer in the world.[2]

Though they were exceptions to the rule, a few women in Israel performed religious roles. The Bible records the names of Miriam (Exod. 15:20), Deborah (Jgs. 4:4), Huldah (2 Kgs. 22:14), and Noadiah

---

2. William Hallo, *The Exaltation of Inanna* (New Haven: Yale University Press, 1968), pp. 1-11.

(Neh. 6:14) as prophets in Israel. Although their words were not collected in books, the Bible does include the famous Song of Deborah (Jgs. 5), which tells of her triumph, with the assistance of her general Barak, over their Canaanite enemy Sisera. Many scholars have suggested that this ancient song of victory was written by a woman.[3] In addition to being a military leader, Deborah also discharged the duties of a judge who adjudicates disputes. The aforementioned women prophets, however, are unusual in Israelite society, and male resentment toward some of them is reflected in the Bible and in the Midrash. Thus we see that Miriam is punished for her boldness in asserting her right to equal leadership with Moses. Additionally, the rabbis later deprecated Deborah and Huldah, noting that the name Deborah is derived from a word meaning "hornet," and Huldah from a word meaning "weasel."

III. FEMININE IMAGES IN THE BIBLE AND THE MIDRASH

A. Women in the Creation Accounts

1. Eve

The story of the fall of humankind in the Garden of Eden (Gen. 2:4–3:24) is generally viewed as a primary source for male hatred of women. For it is the woman in the tale, having been beguiled by the serpent into eating the forbidden fruit and having invited her companion to join her in disobeying the divine prohibition, who brings about their banishment from the bliss of Paradise. Moreover, the Midrash (rabbinic commentary on the Bible) clearly regards the woman as the villain when stating that "It required tears and lamentations on her [the woman's] part to prevail upon Adam to take the baleful step." The view that woman was the cause of human travail and suffering was of course not unique to Judaism, as is evident in the Greek myth that attributes the advent of evil in the world to the foolish curiosity of the first woman—Pandora. Although women in Greek myth, like Eve, are subject to the dictates of men, Pandora was not explicitly punished as Eve was with the curse, "Your yearning shall be for your husband, yet he will lord it over you" (Gen. 3:16).

---

3. See Paula E. Hyman, "The Jewish Woman in History," Lecture 1, Sound Recording (New York: Jewish People's University of the Air, 1980).

Phyllis Trible, a feminist bibical scholar, rejects the notion that the story of the fall confirms the right of men to dominate women.[4] She points out that the intent of this narrative of human origins is to show that in the sinless state of Paradise man and woman were equal. According to Trible, the first human being created by God from the dust of the earth is androgynous—possessing both male and female characteristics. In the Bible, the Hebrew term for this being is *adam,* which means "earth creature." Thus, when woman is created from the rib of the bisexual *adam,* his feminine part is separated from its masculine counterpart in order to complement him, to be a mate suitable and equal to him. It is only after the two primal people have sinned that their egalitarian relationship is disturbed. Furthermore, Trible argues, the view that men and women were intended from the beginning of the world to be equal is also reflected in the creation story (Gen. 1:1–2:4), which precedes that of the fall. Here we read that God created the *adam* in His own image, and that "male and female he created them" (Gen. 1:27). Man and woman, in this story, are created equal simultaneously, both having been modeled after the image of the divine.

2. Lilith

According to the rabbinic Midrash, Adam's first wife was not Eve but a woman named Lilith who, like Adam, was created from the dust of the ground.[5] Lilith did not remain with Adam, however, because he would not grant her the equality she demanded. Since she rebelled against Adam's authority, Lilith was portrayed in Jewish folklore as a demonic figure, one who murders newborn children in their cribs and who arouses the lust of men in their dreams. Adam's upstart first wife thus became the archetype of the evil femme fatale.

Since the rise of the women's liberation movement in the 1960s, however, the name Lilith has ceased being one of disrepute. Today Jewish and non-Jewish feminists alike look to Lilith as an ancient prefiguration of the modern, independent, assertive woman who insists on her personal dignity.[6] Indeed, a current Jewish women's magazine

---

4. Phyllis Trible, "Eve and Adam: Genesis 2–3 Reread," in *Womanspirit Rising,* eds. Carol Christ and Judith Plaskow (San Francisco: Harper & Row, 1979), pp. 74-83.

5. Louis Ginzberg, *The Legends of the Jews,* I (Philadelphia: Jewish Publication Society, 1954), 65-66.

6. See Rosemary R. Ruether, *Womanguides* (Boston: Beacon, 1985), passim.

called *Lilith* states that it "is named for the legendary predecessor of Eve who insisted on equality with Adam."

B. The Midwives in the Book of Exodus

The heroes, the charismatic leaders, the bearers of the divine covenant, and the shapers of the destiny of Israel in the Bible are predominantly men, not women. Biblical women are portrayed as adjuncts to men and are defined by them. Thus little attention is focused on two women who are minor characters in the story of the Exodus from Egypt, but whose boldness and courage are exemplary in the saga of the liberation of the Israelites from bondage. These women are the Hebrew midwives Shiphrah and Puah. At the beginning of the book of Exodus we read that after Joseph died, a new pharaoh arose who did not remember the beneficial deeds of the Hebrew patriarch. This new Egyptian monarch sought to reduce and weaken the Israelite population by ordering the Hebrew midwives, Puah and Shiphrah, to kill the male babies they delivered. However, the midwives "were God-fearing; they disobeyed the command of the king of Egypt and let the boys live" (Exod. 1:17). When the king asked them why they spared the boys, they answered, "The Hebrew women are not like Egyptian women, ... they are hardy, and they give birth before the midwife reaches them" (1:19). Because of their piety, God was kind to the midwives and the people of Israel kept increasing.

Though not numbered among the heroes of the faith, these two obscure women deserve to be lionized for several reasons. First, they were foreigners and members of a despised people in Egypt. Second, they were lowly women who were expected to be passive in a male-dominated society. Third, in spite of these disabilities, they had the gumption to defy the decree of their autocratic ruler and also the wit to deceive him when he questioned their nonconformity to his order. They performed a daring act of civil disobedience against a tyrannical power in the name of a higher power—the God of Israel. In this respect they are Judaic counterparts to the famous heroine of ancient Greek tragedy, Antigone, who ignored a royal edict forbidding the interment of her brother in order to fulfill a higher religious law requiring the burial of the dead. The Hebrew midwives can also be viewed as precursors of contemporary civil rights activists, such as Martin Luther King, Jr., and of advocates of third-world liberation movements.

C. Hannah

Another woman who is worthy of attention, although not counted among the major figures of the Bible, is Hannah, mother of the prophet Samuel (1 Sam. 1:1–2:11). Nehama Aschkenasy, a professor of comparative literature, provides some very illuminating insights into Hannah's experience.[7] Aschkenasy points out that, at first glance, Hannah appears to be a typical barren woman in the Bible, who, like her predecessors Sarah and Rachel, is obsessed with the desire to produce a son and is significant only as mother of her illustrious child. According to Aschkenasy, Hannah merits admiration in her own right. A character of great strength and beauty with single-minded determination, she bore herself with nobility in the face of the taunts of her husband's fertile wife, Peninnah. Moreover, her husband Elkanah seemed to be a liberated male in a sexist society in that he reassured her that his love was not contingent upon her capacity to give him a child. Indeed, when Elkanah found her weeping over her sad lot, he said to her, "Why so sad? Am I not more to you than ten sons?" (1 Sam. 1:8)

Furthermore, Hannah was a deeply spiritual woman. In search of God's help to overcome her sterility, she went to the temple at Shiloh to pray. There she petitioned God from the silent depths of her heart, vowing that if God granted her a male child she would dedicate him to God's service. The priest Eli, seeing her move her lips without uttering a sound, however, assumed that she was drunk, perhaps because he could not conceive of a woman having the ability to compose her own prayer to Yahweh. When she told the priest the reason for her pilgrimage to the sanctuary, he was impressed with her explanation and sent her forth with his blessing. After Samuel was born and weaned, Hannah took him to Shiloh to consecrate him to a religious life, in accordance with her pledge. This time when she prayed, she sang a thanksgiving hymn that was eloquent and theologically profound, comparable in beauty to many of the Psalms attributed by tradition to King David. Hannah's song of praise is also very similar to the Magnificat (Luke 1:46-55) uttered by Mary, after she visited Elizabeth (another barren wife, who became mother of John the Baptist) and shared with her the news of the annunciation of her conception of Jesus.

Hans W. Hertzberg suggests that Hannah's hymn is put into the

---

7. Nehama Aschkenasy, "A Non-Sexist Reading of the Bible," *Midstream* (June/July 1981), 51-55.

mouth of our heroine and is an editorial insertion into the story.[8] Although Hannah may not be the author of her paean to God, the narrator of the story presents her reciting a prayer which not only expresses her gratitude for the reversal of her infertility but transcends it. She expresses a significant theological idea when she acknowledges her confidence in God's power to resurrect the dead. "Yahweh gives death and life, brings down to Sheol [the netherworld] and draws up" (1 Sam. 2:6). The doctrine of resurrection of the dead is one that is generally regarded as being at the periphery of the Hebrew Bible and more clearly articulated in later rabbinic sources. Nevertheless, we see this important theological concept stated in a hymn offered by a woman in the early history of the Proto-Judaic faith.

D. The Perfect Woman

The last chapter of the book of Proverbs is a paean to the ideal wife. The poem presents a portrait of a wealthy man's wife in ancient Israel, one in whom the husband has complete confidence to run his household as well as manage his business enterprises. She is highly industrious—a virtual personification of the Jewish/Protestant work ethic. "She gets up while it is still dark" (31:10); "her lamp does not go out at night" (v. 18); and "she keeps good watch on the conduct of her household, no bread of idleness for her" (v. 27). She participates in virtually every aspect of the household chores: spinning, sewing, weaving, and cooking. Her duties are not confined to domestic chores, however, for "She sets her mind on a field, then buys it; with what her hands have earned she plants a vineyard" (v. 16). Moreover, she is charitable, for she "opens her arms to the needy" (v. 20), and she is also sensitive to the needs of all her servants, whom she keeps warmly clothed. In addition, she comports herself with dignity, speaks wisely, reveres God, and looks to the future with optimism. Here we have a woman whose activities bespeak a strong, assertive individual who has not only the skills of a housewife but also those of an executive and a commercial entrepreneur, combining these qualities with piety and a kind and cheerful personality.

The feminine paragon of virtues described in Proverbs approximates the "supermom" of today, namely, the woman who successfully shoulders the manifold burdens of marriage, motherhood, and career.

---

8. *I & II Samuel*, trans. J. S. Bowden, Old Testament Library (Philadelphia: Westminster, 1976), pp. 27-31.

There is no hint of her being a sexual object; indeed, the hymn avers that "charm is deceitful, and beauty empty; the woman who is wise is the one to be praised" (31:3). What does the husband of this exceptional woman do? He sits at the gates among the elders, presumably free to judge disputes, because he can trust that his home and business interests are in the hands of his competent spouse.

This hymn has taken on deep religious significance in Judaism. In traditional homes the Jewish husband sings it in tribute to his wife before the festive meal that celebrates the beginning of the Sabbath. It is also usually read by the rabbi who officiates at the funeral services for a woman.

E. Esther

The titular heroine of the book of Esther (also known as the Megillah) rises to the position of queen of Persia after the king chooses her, for her great beauty, to be his consort. The throne which Esther fills is vacant because the previous queen, Vashti, had the audacity to refuse to show her beauty to the king's carousing ministers. As the plot unfolds, Haman, the king's prime minister, seeks to have all of Esther's people annihilated, but Esther foils his wicked scheme and, with the aid of her cousin Mordecai, saves the Jews. The biblical story presents Esther as a courageous and clever woman, and she is traditionally accorded a position of high honor as a redeemer in Judaism. From a feminist perspective, however, she is not so favorably received. For she achieves her royal position by allowing herself to be a sex object, and later uses her sexual prowess manipulatively, thereby conforming to and fulfilling the patriarchal view of women. Throughout the story she is the pawn of her uncle Mordecai and consistently follows his directions. Furthermore, after she empowers her people to defend themselves against their enemies, she outstrips patriarchy in its use of violence by calling upon the Jews to engage in a gratuitous second day of slaughter.

Customarily, when Jewish children masquerade on the festival of Purim, which is based on the events in the Megillah, little girls are encouraged to dress up as the heroine of the story. Mary Gendler has suggested, however, that they don the costume of Vashti rather than that of Esther.[9] For by defying her husband's desire to exploit her sexuality

---

9. "The Restoration of Vashti," in *The Jewish Woman,* ed. Elizabeth Koltun (New York: Schocken, 1976), pp. 241-47.

and insisting on her dignity, it is the king's demoted queen who is a preferable model of womanhood.

IV. FEMININE IMAGES OF GOD AND ISRAEL

A. Introduction

Although Yahweh is regarded as being invisible, noncorporeal, and beyond imaging and therefore gender neutral, the God of Israel is frequently referred to in anthropomorphic terms. As the rabbis themselves indicated, the Torah speaks in the language of human beings, and therefore attributing to God humanlike qualities is unavoidable. Thus, since the society that produced the Bible was patriarchal, its references to the deity were usually masculine in nature, using such terms as king, lord, shepherd, man of war, and the masculine singular pronoun. Furthermore, the monotheistic founders of the religion of Israel sought vigorously to stamp out the worship of goddesses. Yet, despite their efforts, the worship of goddesses persisted, possibly from the time of the patriarchs until the Babylonian exile.

B. Asherah

A goddess who was venerated for a long time in Israel was Asherah, a fertility deity associated with the worship of a sacred tree or a pole (Deut. 12:2; Jgs. 6:30; 1 Kgs. 15:13). The Hebrew Bible has some forty veiled references to Asherah, who was popular in Israel until the end of the monarchy. Recent archeological evidence, based on inscriptions and pictorial evidence found at a religious center in the wilderness of northern Sinai, points to the possibility that Asherah was worshiped as a consort to Yahweh.[10] One of the inscriptions contains the following blessing: "Amaryau said to my lord . . . may you be blessed by Yahweh and His Asherah."

C. *Hokmah*

What seems to have been a need to depict God in feminine images, in spite of the patriarchal bias for masculine imagery, is evident in Proverbs 8. In this chapter we read the words of a goddess of wisdom

---

10. William G. Dever, "Asherah, Consort of Yahweh? New Evidence from Kuntillet of Ajrud," *Bulletin of the American Schools of Oriental Research* 225 (1984), 21-37.

(known by the Greeks as Sophia), or of a female personification of wisdom, who sings her own praises:

> "I, Wisdom, am mistress of discretion,
> the inventor of lucidity of thought.
>
> . . . .
> "By me monarchs rule
> and princes issue just laws.
>
> . . . .
> "Yahweh created me when his purpose first unfolded
>
> . . . .
> "when he laid down the foundations of the earth,
> I was by his side, a master craftsman"

Wisdom speaks of herself not only as a guide for human beings, including great rulers, but also as having been God's partner in creating the world.

D. Israel as God's Wife

The covenantal relationship between God and Israel is often depicted in the sermons of the classical prophets as that of a marriage between Yahweh the husband and Israel His bride, a marriage solemnized at Sinai. The marriage sours, however, when the Israelites enter the land of Canaan, where they are attracted to the fertility gods of their pagan surroundings. The prophet Hosea appropriates this marital imagery and chastises Israel for being unfaithful to her true husband, Yahweh, by whoring after a false lover, the Canaanite deity Baal. To dramatize the infidelity of Israel, Yahweh tells Hosea to marry the harlot Gomer. Hosea follows God's command and has children with Gomer who receive symbolic names such as "No-People-of-Mine" and "Unloved." Hosea then denounces his wife for her unfaithfulness and drives her away, but eventually forgives her and takes her back. Through the marriage of Hosea and Gomer, God symbolically indicts Israel's whoring after strange gods, but also recalls the time of their pristine love in the wilderness. Even as Yahweh condemns His adulterous wife, Israel, and predicts her punishment, He looks forward to her repentance and reformation. Thus we read in the midst of Yahweh's severe words of reproach to Israel his vision of her ultimate passionate reconciliation with Him.

> I will betroth you to myself for ever,
> betroth you with integrity and justice,

> with tenderness and love;
> I will betroth you to myself with faithfulness,
> And you will come to know Yahweh

(2:19-21)

The verses quoted above are recited in the Jewish ceremony of winding tefillin (phylacteries) on one's arm in preparation for worship. By invoking this passage, the Jew is metaphorically wed to God. This religious imagery is also invoked when a Roman Catholic nun is initiated into the discipline of her order and is mystically wed to Jesus.

V. WOMEN IN THE TALMUDIC PERIOD

A. Introduction

The prevalent view of women in talmudic times is summed up by the Jewish historian Josephus: "The woman, says the law, is in all things inferior to the man."[11] As was the case in the biblical period, with regard to the law, men continue to be the norm and women the exception. Thus an entire section of the Talmud is called *Nashim,* "Women," with no parallel tractate entitled *Anashim,* "Men." The absence of the latter in the Talmud is due to the fact that all the rest of the Talmud, outside of *Nashim,* deals with matters pertaining to men.

B. Women's Economic Status

Women's rights progressed most in this area and compare well with those of women in other cultures in this period. They became more than chattel and were given property rights. A woman could share in her father's estate, which would be managed by her husband. Nevertheless, the property belonged ultimately to her. The *ketubah,* the marriage contract, was introduced to assure a woman of a financial settlement should her spouse divorce her or die. This certificate represented a revolution in the economic status of women, though it also reflected her total dependence upon her husband, for she had no other source of support. On the whole, women's economic status,

---

11. See Leonard Swidler, *Women in Judaism: The Status of Women in Formative Judaism* (Metuchen, N.J.: Scarecrow, 1976).

though not made equal to men's, was consistently ameliorated. While they did not inherit property, unless there were no sons, the rabbis tried to overcome to some extent their disabilities in this area.

C. Marriage and Divorce

1. Marriage

Marriages were regarded to have been made in heaven, and the rabbis encouraged the treatment of wives with love and tenderness. The rabbis valued marriage as the means by which both men and women could achieve their greatest fulfillment. They based this view on the theology of the passage in Genesis that follows the creation of woman: "This is why a man leaves his father and mother and joins himself to his wife, and they become one body" (2:24).

In the Jewish marriage ceremony, the bride and groom stood under a canopy, signifying the bride's entry into her husband's home. The role of the wife was to make her husband happy by caring for all his personal needs, his home, and his children.

During the talmudic period monogamy became the norm in Judaism, although polygamy existed and was permitted in Islamic countries into the modern age. When the church father Justin Martyr taunted the Jew Trypho about the Jewish practice of polygamy, he was stating a reality.

According to the Mishnah, a woman is acquired in three ways: (1) by giving her a minimum coin of currency, (2) by an official document, and (3) by sexual intercourse. These modes of betrothal paralleled the ways in which a field was acquired: by money, by a document, or by taking possession. While these legal provisions suggest a less than spiritual basis for the relationship of marriage, it is significant to note that the rabbis also required the man to recite the following marriage formula: "You are hereby consecrated to me." Thus marriage was given the religious significance of a sacrament, though not in the Christian salvational sense of that theological term. The woman recited no comparable formula of her own, however, and among Orthodox Jews today the role of the woman in the marriage ceremony continues to be silent. The rabbis transformed the informal male acquisition of the female that was analogous to the purchase of a field into a religious formality. Marriage was called *kiddushin*, "sanctification," and therefore regarded as sacred, not merely a legal act. The *Zohar,* a medieval mystical work, indicated that the preferred hour for union in marriage is the Sabbath hour of midnight, for then holiness abounds.

2. Divorce

The halakah continued to permit divorce, still reserving the right to initiate the procedure to the husband. Under certain circumstances, however, the court would aid the woman in attaining a divorce. The rabbis could compel a man to divorce his wife if he were impotent, denied her conjugal rights, restricted her freedom of movement, had an unbearable disease, or worked at an obnoxious occupation.[12] Some rabbis favored the right of the husband to a divorce for trivial and arbitrary reasons, based on the biblical statement that a man could issue a writ of divorce to his wife if he found some impropriety of which to accuse her (Deut. 24:1). The followers of the sage Hillel interpreted this text to mean that he could divorce her for any reason whatsoever for which she found disfavor in his eyes. Rabbi Akiba allowed divorce if a man merely found another woman more attractive. However, the followers of the sage Shammai required that the wife be guilty of some sexual indecency before her husband could terminate their marriage.

In the context of ancient times, easy divorce put women into the position of conceding to every whim of their husbands, for it worked to their economic disadvantage in that it left them destitute. Thus, out of humanitarian concern for the plight of the woman, the rabbis introduced tactics that would delay the process by which an impulsive spouse might divorce his wife. A serious flaw in the halakah of divorce was the inability of a woman to sue for divorce if she were deserted. In such cases she was called an *agunah,* "chained" to her husband in that she could not remarry. But a man whose wife deserted him had several options, one of which was to issue her a divorce in absentia. The problem of the *agunah* continues to plague traditional Jewish women today.

D. Women's Religious Status

For religious purposes women were classed with slaves and children and therefore were exempt from certain standard rituals and barred

---

12. See Phillip Sigal, *The Emergence of Contemporary Judaism,* II (Pittsburgh: Pickwick, 1977), 381.

from public participation in them. They were obligated to all the negative commandments ("Thou shalt not . . ."), but since they were supposed to be preoccupied with their domestic duties, they were excused from the fulfillment of those positive commandments that had to be performed at a particular time. This rationale was applied inconsistently, however, for some religious obligations assigned them were related to a set time and others were not. Some of women's religious duties were the lighting of the Sabbath lamp, reading and hearing the Megillah of Esther, and observing the menstrual halakah. During the woman's menstruation she was separated from her husband for the sake of family purity. Intimacy between her and her husband was prohibited from before her flow until seven days after the last blood was seen, or for approximately a minimum of twelve days. After her flow, she was to immerse herself in a *miqvah*, a ritual pool.

Women were not counted in the minyan, the quorum of ten Jews needed for public worship, nor could they lead the liturgy. The morning prayers included the following blessing: "Praised be God, king of the universe, for not making me a woman." According to one interpretation, this liturgy expresses the gratitude of the male for the fact that he is a man so that he has the opportunity to fulfill all the commandments. In modern times, however, this prayer has been reworded or deleted from the prayerbooks of liberal Jewish denominations to avoid its sexist overtones.

While women were permitted to be included among those called to the Torah during a worship service, it was not customary to do so. To hear a woman recite the blessings at the reading of Scripture or hear her read aloud from the scroll of the Torah before the entire congregation was regarded as humiliating to the males in attendance. Other religious activities from which women were barred were wearing tefillin, reading the Megillah, sounding the shofar (the ram's horn), serving as a scribe to write sacred Hebrew documents, and serving as a rabbi.

E. Women and Education

Women were expected to care for the house and children and to enable their husbands to study the sacred texts of the faith. A notable example of a woman who sacrificed herself for the sake of her husband's scholarship was Rachel, wife of Rabbi Akiba. Since Akiba was an ignorant shepherd when Rachel married him, shortly after their wedding she urged him to leave home so that he could study at one of the great academies. Akiba left her and returned as a distinguished scholar after a separation of twelve years. Rachel represented a model for wives. The talmudic scholar Judith Hauptman characterizes women's role in in the following way: "In short, a woman's mind and energies [were] to be directed to fulfilling a man's needs, so that a man's mind and energies [could] be directed to fulfilling the broader needs of God and man."[13]

Marriage to a scholar's daughter was considered ideal for a man, and the ideal for a woman was marriage to a scholar. However, a learned woman was seen as trespassing on men's territory. Beruriah, the wife of Rabbi Meir, was an exception to the norm in the talmudic period. She was renowned for her scholarship, wisdom, piety, and emotional strength. One story indicative of her moral sensitivity tells how Rabbi Meir used to pray, in accordance with Psalm 104, that sinners should vanish from the earth. Beruriah reproved her husband for uttering this prayer and urged him to pray not for the destruction of the sinners but rather for the disappearance of evil in the world. Another story about Beruriah relates how she gently broke the news of the death of her two sons on the same day to her husband. When Rabbi Meir came home that day, she asked his advice regarding a man who had lent two jewels to her and now demanded their return. Meir's response was that they should be returned. Beruriah then led him to their sons' room and said, "These are our jewels. God has given and has taken. Blessed be his name." Beruriah's opinion in legal matters was often accepted above that of rabbis. Although the rabbis acknowledged her intellectual gifts, Beruriah is described as having a flaw regarded as typical of women, namely, sexual weakness. According to the Talmud, Rabbi Meir was coaxed into testing her virtue by asking one of his students to seduce her. Beruriah succumbed to his advances and, because of her deep shame, subsequently committed suicide.

Beruriah's tragic end suggests that the rabbis anticipated that educating a woman would lead to her ruination. Not only was a learned woman usually seen as morally suspect, but the Talmud adjured men to avoid excessive conversation with any woman lest he neglect the study of Torah out of lust for her and thus be damned to hell.

---

13. Judith Hauptman, "Images of Women in the Talmud," in *Religion and Sexism*, ed. Rosemary E. Ruether (New York: Simon & Schuster, 1974), p. 200.

VI. IMAGES OF WOMEN IN THE MIDDLE AGES

A. Women's General Status

According to the medieval rabbi Joseph Karo, "Every man is duty-bound to marry a wife in order to reproduce, and whoever does not . . . contributes to the Shekinah [the divine indwelling presence] leaving Israel."[14] Concerned that persecution and forced conversion were reducing the number of Jews, medievalists made reproduction a high priority. The same concern is evident today among Jews who advocate rejecting the concept of zero population growth in favor of large families to compensate for the massive loss of Jews in the Holocaust.

During the medieval period the status of women did not change appreciably from its condition in talmudic times; women continued to experience the same disabilities in the spheres of marriage and divorce, economics, religion, and education. Among the important halakic advancements during this period, however, was the banning of polygamy in the tenth century by Rabbi Gershom in Germany. This enactment was soon accepted by all European Jews, except those of Spain. Furthermore, Rabbi Gershom curbed the arbitrary power of husbands by issuing an edict that no divorce could be issued without a wife's consent. He also ruled that a wife beater was compelled to divorce his spouse.

During this period, misogynous statements continued to be expressed in the rabbinic texts. For example, Rashi, a French rabbinic scholar, commenting on the passage in which Rabbi Yosi ben Yoezer cautioned "Increase not conversation with a woman," stated that women were light-headed. Rashi's comment was generally interpreted as meaning that women were easily seduced. A Spanish scholar, Rabbi Yosi of Geronah, remarked, "A person should not engage in conversation with a woman lest he have sinful thoughts." Thus women continued to be perceived as lascivious, sexually alluring, and corruptive of men.

B. The Shekinah

The feminine aspect of God took on profound significance in the form of the Shekinah in the medieval texts of Jewish mysticism known as

---

14. *Shulhan Aruk,* Eben haEzer 1:1.

the Kabalah. The term *Shekinah* in the talmudic literature referred to God's omnipresence and activity in the world, especially in Israel. In the kabalistic literature, the Shekinah became a quasi-independent feminine element within God, a complement to the masculine principle in the divine. Belief in this mythical feminine principle became extremely popular among the masses, suggesting the inherent human impulse to imagine God in feminine terms. The Shekinah was seen as both woman and soul. From talmudic times, the Shekinah was regarded as having gone into exile with Israel. Whereas in the Talmud this meant that God's presence accompanied the children of Israel into exile, in the Kabalah it signified that an element of Godhead itself— its feminine part—had departed. The cleavage of the primordial divine unity, in which the masculine and feminine aspects of God had originally been fused, was attributed to the power of evil. The mystics believed that the exile of the Shekinah occurred at the fall, that it took on deep significance with the Exile, and that the Shekinah would be reunited with her masculine counterpart when the Messiah would bring about the redemption of the world.

VII. WOMEN IN THE RENAISSANCE

During the Renaissance opportunities for secular education for women began to open, as they did for men. In Italy it appears that women enjoyed a modicum of emancipation. Portraiture shows men and women playing musical instruments in mixed company. Some women, engaging in activities commonly reserved for men, were physicians, *shohtim* (ritual slaughterers of animals for food), *sopherim* (scribes of sacred texts), authors, and biblical and talmudic scholars.[15] The Jewish poet Sara Coppio Sullam conducted salons for cultured Jews and Christians, prefiguring similar activity of women in Germany one hundred years later. She was well versed in the Christian Scriptures and in the ancient historian Josephus, and carried on a considerable correspondence with a Roman Catholic priest. Nevertheless, the male chauvinist attitude toward women that had prevailed in the biblical, talmudic, and medieval eras continued apace in the Renaissance without major change until the reformation in the nineteenth century.

---

15. See Phillip Sigal, *The Emergence of Contemporary Judaism,* III, 22.

VIII. WOMEN IN THE MODERN PERIOD

A. Introduction

The emancipation of Jews from their marginalized position in Christian Europe that took place in the latter part of the eighteenth century spurred the beginnings of a comparable emancipation for women within Judaism. Access to secular learning brought about enlightenment among Jews and a questioning attitude toward many of their religious traditions that began to seem obsolete in the modern world. The reformers took to heart the rabbinic principle of *kabod habriyot*, the dignity of human beings. This principle included the extension of rights to women on the basis of one's human dignity. Many of the changes proposed by the reformers were extremely controversial and ultimately led to the formation of three movements in the nineteenth century—Reform, Conservative, and Orthodox—and the Reconstructionist movement in the twentieth century.

B. Women in the Reform Movement

1. Marriage and Divorce

The builders of the Reform movement in the nineteenth century recognized in the Mosaic legislation only its moral laws and those ceremonies that they deemed spiritually elevating; they repudiated the rabbinic halakah of the past as no longer binding. Accordingly, they eliminated the *huppah* (the canopy) and the *ketubah* from the marriage ceremony, since they considered the symbolism of the former and the protection (for the woman) of the latter no longer relevant to the social realities of their day. Moreover, they introduced the mutual consecration of the bride and groom on an equal basis in the marriage ceremony, both speaking the same formula to each other and exchanging rings. Additionally, they abolished the levirate laws relating to the obligation of a widow's brother-in-law to marry her, and they eliminated the need for a Jewish *get* (divorce), recognizing civil divorce as adequate for remarriage.

2. Religion

Reform Judaism eliminated the separation of women from men in the synagogue by a divider called a *mehitzah*. This practice had its source in the fear of women as temptresses. Whereas the American Reformers introduced mixed pews, the German Reformers never abolished separate seating of the sexes. Mixed male and female choirs, however, became a feature of Reform worship both in European and American Reform synagogues.

The ceremony of bar mitzvah, which initiated the thirteen-year-old male child into the congregation, was supplanted by the ceremony of confirmation at age fifteen or sixteen and included both girls and boys. As early as 1818, the Jews in Germany introduced confirmation for girls.

In 1885, at the time of the promulgation of the Pittsburgh Platform, which stated the principles of classical Reform Judaism, an effort was made to accord women equality with men in synagogue administration. The men were loathe to end their monopoly in this area, however, and women did not gain equality with men in the lay leadership of synagogues until approximately the 1920s.

In the late 1940s, Reform congregations began calling women up to the Torah at worship services. And in the latter half of the twentieth century, synagogues in the Reform movement began to reintroduce bar mitzvah for boys and to introduce bat mitzvah, which had been created by Reconstructionists and other liberals within the Conservative movement, for girls.

In recent times, a feminist issue that the Reformers have addressed is the presence of sexist language in the liturgy. The patriarchal references, allusions, and imagery prevent women from identifying with the liturgy. Thus, for example, to the *amidah* prayer that traditionally invokes God as the deity of Abraham, Isaac, and Jacob, they added the names of the matriarchs, Sarah, Rebekah, Rachel, and Leah.

Women in the Reform movement did not regard themselves as disadvantaged in the area of clerical leadership until the rise of feminism in the 1960s. Their impulse to render religious service to society was largely channeled into social welfare activity. A woman who was an outstanding example of ethical concern and social activism was Lillian Wald, a social worker who founded the Henry Street Settlement on New York's Lower East Side in 1895. In her efforts for social reform Wald epitomized the ideals of prophetic Judaism by being a founder of the National Child Labor Committee; by urging the establishment of parks, playgrounds, and public school nursing; and by promoting the goals of the League of Nations.

The first woman to be ordained was Regina Jones. She completed her studies at the Berlin Academy for the Science of Judaism in the late 1930s, but was denied public ordination because of her sex. She was ordained privately, however, and functioned briefly as a rabbi before she died in the the Nazi concentration camp of Theresienstadt. The first ordination of a woman rabbi in America took place in a Reform rabbinical seminary in 1972.

C. Women in the Conservative Movement

1. Introduction

As a liberal denomination in Judaism, the Conservative movement has increasingly equalized the position of women with men. Unlike the Reformers, however, the Conservatives have greatly emphasized the halakic process in instituting change, trying to build a bridge between traditionalism and modernism. As a result, the amelioration of the status of Conservative women has been more slowly achieved.

2. Marriage and Divorce

As in the case of the Reform movement, the Conservatives included mutual exchange of declarations and rings within the marriage ceremony. However, they retained the *huppah* and the *ketubah,* applying to them symbolic interpretations that made them more compatible with modern thinking. In contrast with the Reformers, they maintained the need for a religious *get* to terminate a marriage. The requirement of a *get* meant that Conservative women still had to struggle with the disability of not being able to initiate a divorce. The Conservative rabbis sought to alleviate this problem by enabling a Jewish court under certain circumstances to annul a marriage in which a civil divorce had taken place.

3. Religion

The improvement of women's rights in worship services came about in gradual stages. Pews that seated both males and females, as well as mixed choirs, became acceptable in many synagogues early in the Conservative movement.

The first bat mitzvah in Judaism was celebrated in 1922 by the daughter of Mordecai Kaplan, the founder of Reconstructionism and a professor at the seminary of the Conservative movement. The practice of bat mitzvah, however, was not widely accepted until the 1950s.

In 1955, the Conservative rabbis passed a landmark decision in the evolution of women's rights: they permitted women to have *aliyot,* the right to recite the blessings prior to and following the reading of Scripture at worship. Another milestone on the road to gender equalization was the 1973 decision to count women in the prayer quorum. The halakic reasoning for allowing this revolution in the status of women was largely based on a responsum written by Rabbi Phillip Sigal in 1972.[16]

Women's participation in the Conservative clergy was resisted for a long time. After much controversy over the issue, the Jewish Theological Seminary of America, the fountainhead of the Conservative movement, finally decided to accept women students as candidates for the rabbinate, and ordained their first woman rabbi in 1985.

The last male preserve to give way to women within the Conservative denomination was the Cantors' Institute, which trains the leaders of liturgical music in the synagogues. The first women to receive their Diploma of *Hazzan* graduated in 1987. Judith Hauptman, the first woman Ph.D. in Talmud, has argued that the normalization of women's position in Judaism can be brought about "by activating the mechanisms for change which we find on every page of the Talmud."[17] Despite the fact that the majority of Conservative rabbis have acknowledged the availability of these mechanisms to equalize the religious status of women and to welcome them to their ranks, the vehement and vocal right wing of the movement deplores their inclusion in a prayer quorum and their acceptance as rabbis and cantors. Perhaps the reason for their recalcitrance is due, as Hauptman states, to the fact that "men's validation of themselves is apparently dependent upon their subordination of women."

The need to eliminate sexist language in the liturgy, which traditionally reflected the male's experience of God in masculine terms, has been addressed somewhat by the Conservatives. Thus recent editions of Conservative prayerbooks and of the Haggadah (the Passover prayer manual) demonstrate an effort to use language inclusive of women.

D. Women in the Reconstructionist Movement

Reconstructionism was always in the vanguard of granting total equality to women. It remained an ideology within the Conservative move-

---

16. "Women in a Prayer Quorum," *Judaism* (Spring, 1974), 174-82.

17. "Women in the Rabbinate," in *Women in the Rabbinate, Priesthood, and Ministry,* ed. Lillian Sigal (Grand Rapids: Ahavas Israel Congregation, 1987), p. 9.

ment for many years, and did not break away to become an independent denomination until the 1960s. The Reconstructionist Rabbinical College ordained its first woman rabbi in 1974, more than ten years earlier than the seminary of the Conservative movement, which had been in existence since the end of the nineteenth century. Like the Conservatives, the Reconstructionists have retained the *get,* but unlike the movement from which they split, in 1980 they facilitated the first divorce initiated by a Jewish woman.

E. Women in the Orthodox Denominations

Although distinctions should be made between the practice of Modern or Neo-Orthodox Jews and that of Ultra-Orthodox Jews, in general the women in both of these right-wing camps are still subject to the inequities of their forbears in the Middle Ages and in the talmudic period. Moshe Meiselman, a spokesman for Orthodoxy, maintains that the Jewish woman today should make her primary goal in life marriage and having children. Moreover, she should cultivate the feminine virtue of *tzeniyut,* "privateness," by staying in the background like the biblical wives, and avoiding the public domain. According to Meiselman, her career is her home, family, and possibly some community activity.

Many Modern Orthodox women are nevertheless struggling with their need to come of age in the modern world, particularly in the debilitating area of divorce and in the leadership of worship, while remaining within the bounds of a male-dominated denomination. The rise of women's minyanim, prayer quorums run exclusively by women, is symptomatic of the desire of Modern Orthodox women to play a more active role in worship services. Some Modern Orthodox synagogues have introduced a celebration at puberty for girls at age twelve (rather than the customary age of thirteen for bat mitzvah) in a ceremony called bat torah. This event, however, does not take place in the sanctuary, but rather in a social room, and it is not equivalent to the bat mitzvah ceremony which initiates girls into the religious responsibilities of adulthood.

Despite the traditional exclusion of women from study of religious texts, regarded as the highest endeavor in Judaism, opportunities for Orthodox women to engage in this pursuit have opened to them. Parochial schools on the elementary and high-school level teach girls Judaism. Even college-level instruction is available to Orthodox Jewish women, for example, at Stern College for Women, a branch of Yeshivah University in New York.

F. Women in the State of Israel

In the modern State of Israel Jewish women have not made the same strides as their coreligionists in America. Many people have the mistaken impression that Jewish Israeli women are on a par with men because they are drafted into their country's armed forces (if they are not Orthodox) and because a woman—Golda Meir—has served as prime minister. Feminist consciousness raising has been late in arriving on the Israeli scene, although the 1980s have witnessed a growing awareness among Israeli women regarding their unjust treatment. A major stumbling block for these women in the achievement of religious equality with men is the monopoly of power concentrated in the hands of the Orthodox rabbinate. Orthodox Jewish law is the civil law for Jews in Israel; hence, there is strong resistance to correct the inequities to which women have been heir since ancient and medieval times. Women have no access to the modern options available to their counterparts who are affiliated with the liberal denominations in the United States and Canada, since those denominations have no authority in Israel. Israeli women are beginning to challenge the hegemony of Orthodoxy, however, as was evident in the First International Conference on Women and Judaism, held in Jerusalem in 1986.

IX. CONCLUSION

Although enactments in the talmudic and medieval periods sought to improve their condition, until the reforms of the nineteenth century and the more dramatic changes in the last half of the twentieth century, women were an oppressed group in Judaism.

The Hebrew Bible is a patriarchal text that reflects a male-dominated society. In the Bible, women were ancillary to men and important mainly in the context of male activity, a condition that was prevalent in the surrounding cultural heritage of Mesopotamia and Canaan. However, their legal position appears not to have been as high as that of their counterparts in the Near East. They suffered disabilities in inheritance, vows, and initiating divorce, having been regarded as the property of their fathers or husbands. Moreover, they were subjected to the inequities of a double standard in the area of sexual infidelity. Although the Bible recognizes a few women as heroines, these were anomalies in their society. Women did not make covenants, did not experience revelations (although a rare few served as prophets), and did not administer the cult. While they generally assumed minor roles in the drama of the Bible, women were often persuasive and influential in the lives of their husbands and sons.

The myth of women as evil as well as the legitimation of their subordination to men in Judaism has its roots in the biblical story of the fall. Thus, the Christian apostle Paul was clearly drawing upon his Jewish background when he stated, "Adam was formed first and Eve afterward, and it was not Adam who was led astray but the woman who was led astray and fell into sin" (1 Tim. 2:13-14). The religious leaders of Judaism as well as of Christianity seem to have ignored the fact that the creation accounts in Genesis suggest that at first man and woman were created equal, but that their egalitarian relationship was vitiated by the fall.

Women played a variety of roles in the Bible. Sometimes they were portrayed as courageous, pious, or wise; at other times they were depicted as manipulative, wily, and seductive. On the whole, biblical women were defined by the womb and the breast: their primary function was childbearing, and infertility was regarded as a calamity. In the Bible Yahweh was referred to in male terms. But the need among the people to worship a feminine deity or counterpart to God persisted and resisted the struggle of the prophets to extinguish goddess worship in ancient Israel.

From the postbiblical period until modern times, laws continued to be formulated from the male's point of view. They alleviated somewhat the injustices toward women but essentially perpetuated their inferiority and dependence upon men. In ceremonial and liturgical matters women were exempted or excluded. In some exceptional instances, a woman such as Beruriah was acclaimed for her intellectual gifts. But rabbinic statements about women in the Talmud and in later commentaries were frequently misogynous: women were regarded as unworthy of conversation, incapable of keeping confidences, frivolous, and seductive. If they were knowledgeable they were deemed an embarrassment to men. Nevertheless, the rabbinic literature enjoined men to treat their wives tenderly and to put them, as it were, on a pedestal, as long as they did not stray from their roles as wives, mothers, and homemakers. In sum, the rabbinic attitude toward women may be characterized as having been both chivalrous and chauvinistic.

Although later rabbis modified the oppressive marriage and divorce laws to which women were subject, women's fundamental position was not altered until the nineteenth century. The status of women, which relegated them to be enablers rather than doers, which confined them to sexually determined roles, and which treated them as an atypical category in the law, has been basically retained by Orthodoxy today. Nevertheless, Modern Orthodox women are beginning to assert themselves against male chauvinism, but strictly within the context of male religious leadership and authority.

By contrast, the liberal denominations within Judaism have currently accorded women almost complete equality with men, accepting them as lay and clerical leaders within the Jewish community at large and within the synagogue. Like their counterparts in the Protestant ministry, however, Jewish women who have been ordained still suffer from male bias when seeking pulpits, usually finding positions as assistants to senior rabbis or in small struggling synagogues.

The unique contribution that women as clergy can make to the religious life of their communities is well articulated by the Rev. Marchiene Rienstra, the first woman graduate of Calvin Seminary and the first woman to become a senior minister in the Reformed Church: "To use a Gospel metaphor given by Jesus, as women bring into the church the new wine of their unique character and experience, there will need to be new wineskins—new structures. . . . Lay people will increasingly be given power, churches will be more relationally oriented, less self-serving and like the male business model, more giving, and nurturing of those within and without the church."[18]

Rienstra's view regarding the changes that women will bring about in the church as ministers is echoed in the following statement by the Reconstructionist rabbi Sandy Eisenberg Sasso:

> Does being a woman make essentially any difference in the kind of rabbi I am and can be? I think it does. . . . Women come to the rabbinate with a different set of experiences. The findings of feminist sociologists, psychologists and moral theorists teach us that we come with different priorities, visions of reality, and relationships. Women's center of focus is on people rather than principles. Their primary concern is less with an infraction of a set of rules than with a failure of relationships. Women's vision of reality is not . . . hierarchical. . . . We have sustained hierarchies by developing talents for control over others and our environment. We sustain networks by nurturing gifts of facilitation and conservation.[19]

---

18. "Women in the Ministry," in *Women in the Rabbinate, Priesthood, and Ministry,* p. 26.

19. Susan W. Schneider, *Jewish and Female* (New York: Simon & Schuster, 1984), p. 49.

Comparative Chronological Table

Historical Period Begins (Sumer, Egypt): ca. 3000 B.C.E.

Early Dynastic period (Akkad): ca. 2800
Old Kingdom period (Egypt): ca. 2700-2400
Ebla flourishes: ca. 2500-2200
Priestess Enheduanna, first known author in the world:
ca. 2300-2200

Proto-Judaism (Israelite religion before the Babylonian exile): ca. 2000-587 B.C.E.

Middle Kingdom period (Egypt): 2100-1780
Old Babylonian period: ca. 2000-1750
Patriarchal period: ca. 2000-1700
Abraham and Sarah: ca. 1850
Old Assyrian period: ca. 1900-1400
Hammurabi: ca. 1792-1750
Hittite empire: ca. 1750-1200
Hyksos in Egypt: ca. 1700-1550
Kassite period (Babylonia): ca. 1600-1150
New Kingdom period (Egypt): ca. 1570-1085
Ugaritic texts: ca. 1500-1200
Middle Assyrian period: ca. 1400-900
Amarna period (Egypt): ca. 1400-1300
Mosaic period: ca. 1300-1200
Exodus from Egypt: ca. 1250-1230
Sea Peoples invade Egypt and Syro-Palestine: ca. 1200

COMPARATIVE CHRONOLOGICAL TABLE

Period of the Judges: ca. 1200-1000
Middle Babylonian period: ca. 1150-900
Hebrew prophets (Samuel-Malachi): ca. 1050-450
Monarchical period in Israel: ca. 1000-587
    Saul: ca. 1030-1010
    David: ca. 1010-970
    Solomon: ca. 970-931
    Secession of Northern Kingdom (Israel) from
      Southern Kingdom (Judah): ca. 931
Neo-Assyrian period: 900-612
    Northern Kingdom (Israel) destroyed: 721
    Southern Kingdom (Judah) and Temple destroyed—
      Babylonian exile: 587

Judaism after the Babylonian Exile: ca. 538 B.C.E.-70 C.E.

Persian Period: 538-333
    Edict of Cyrus (return from Exile): 538
    Temple rebuilt: 520-515
    Reformation of Ezra and Nehemiah: 450-400
    Torah (Pentateuch—first division of Jewish Scripture)
      given status as Scripture: ca. 450
Hellenistic period: 333-63
    Alexander the Great conquers Palestine: 333
    Coming of Rome to the east Mediterranean: ca. 230-146
    Prophets (second division of Jewish Scripture)
      accepted as Scripture: ca. 200
    Qumran community: ca. 200 B.C.E.-135 C.E.
    Maccabean rebellion and Hasmonean era:
      167-63 B.C.E.
Rule of Rome: ca. 146 B.C.E.-400 C.E.
    Philo Judaeus of Alexandria: ca. 13 B.C.E.-50 C.E.
    Birth of Jesus Christ: ca. 4 B.C.E.
    Death of Jesus Christ: ca. 30 C.E.
    Paul the apostle: ca. 36-67 C.E.
    Josephus: ca. 37-100
    Christian Testament written: ca. 50-90 C.E.

Talmudic Period: 70-400 C.E.

First Jewish Revolt: 66-70
Destruction of Jerusalem and the second Temple: 70

Beginning of rabbinic ordination at Yabneh: 73
Gamaliel II excludes sectarians (including Christians) from the synagogues: ca. 90-100
Bar Kokhba rebellion (Second Jewish Revolt): 132-135
Writings (third and last division of Jewish Scripture) accepted as sacred: ca. 150
Mishnah edited: ca. 200
Emperor Constantine converted: 312
Jerome: ca. 325-420
Augustine: 354-430
Talmud edited: ca. 400
Rome sacked: 410
Muhammad: ca. 570-632
Pope Gregory the Great: 590-604

Medieval Period: ca. 600-1600

Period of the *Geonim:* ca. 600-1300
Charlemagne: 742-814
Karaism founded: ca. 760
Saadia Gaon: 882-942
Golden Age in Spain: ca. 950-1150
Rashi (Rabbi Solomon ben Isaac): 1040-1105
Bernard of Clairvaux: 1090-1153
Crusades: 1095-1291
Maimonides (Rabbi Moses ben Maimon): 1135-1204
Francis of Assisi: ca. 1181-1226
Pope Innocent III: 1198-1216
The Zohar (a kabalistic book): **written ca. 13th century**
Thomas Aquinas: 1225-1274
Inquisition: ca. 1230
Expulsion of Jews from England: 1290
Italian Renaissance: 1300-1517
John Wycliffe: 1328-1384
Gutenberg Bible printed: 1456
Expulsion of Jews from Spain: 1492
Protestant Reformation: ca. 1500-1650
    Martin Luther: 1483-1546
    Thomas Cranmer: 1489-1556
    William Tyndale: ca. 1494-1536
    John Calvin: 1509-1564

Proto-Modern Period: Renaissance and Reformation: ca. 1550-1700

Pope Paul IV institutes the ghetto: 1555
Shulhan Aruk: published 1571
René Descartes: 1596-1650
Menasseh ben Israel: 1605-1657
Blaise Pascal: 1623-1662
Shabbatai Zvi: 1626-1676
Baruch Spinoza: 1632-1677
Arrival of Jews in New Amsterdam: 1654

Modern and Contemporary Periods: ca. 1700-1985

Israel Baal Shem Tov (founder of Hasidism): 1700-1760
Jonathan Edwards: 1703-1758
John and Charles Wesley: 1703-1791 and 1707-1788
Moses Mendelssohn: 1729-1786
Napoleon: 1769-1821
American Revolution: 1775-1781
French Revolution: 1789
French Jews given citizenship: 1790-1791
Founding of the Reform movement: mid-19th century
American Civil War: 1861-1865
Founding of the Conservative movement:
    end of 19th century
First Zionist congress: 1897
Founding of the Modern Orthodox movement:
    early 20th century
World War I: 1914-1918
World War II: 1939-1945
The Holocaust: 1942-1945
Declaration of independence of the State of Israel: 1948
Founding of the Reconstructionist movement (as a distinct
    denomination): 1960s
Ordination of first (Reform) woman rabbi in America: 1972
Ordination of first Reconstructionist woman rabbi: 1974
Ordination of first Conservative woman rabbi: 1985

Glossary

aggadah (adj. **aggadic**). All nonhalakic (nonlegal) matter in Talmud and midrash; folklore, legend, theosophy, biography, etc.; also spelled *haggadah,* not to be confused, however, with the Passover Manual called "The Haggadah."

am haaretz (pl. *ammey haaretz*). Lit. "people of the land"; term used in the Bible for citizens, or some particular class of citizens; in rabbinic literature, for a group that dissented from rabbinic halakah and rigorous purity and tithing norms. It sometimes signifies the unlearned. It was also used of the broad mass of the people of the 1st century C.E., who cannot be categorized into any of the sects of the time.

amidah. Lit. "standing"; the main section of prayers, recited in a standing posture; also known as *tefillah* or *shemoneh esreh.*

amora (pl. *amoraim*). Rabbinic teachers of the period of the Babylonian and Palestinian Talmuds.

amphictyony. A religious federation gathered around a sanctuary dedicated to God; an association of neighboring states or tribes in ancient Greece that banded together for common interest and protection.

anthropomorphism. The attribution of human behavior or characteristics to inanimate objects, animals, natural phenomena, or God.

apocalypse (adj. **apocalyptic**). From the Greek, meaning "revelation." A genre of literature in which the author claims he has received revelations, usually about the end-time.

Apocrypha. From the Greek, meaning "to hide." It refers to books "set apart," written in the intertestamental period. They are found in the

Septuagint and included in the Roman Catholic canon of sacred scripture, but not in the Jewish or Protestant canons.

aqedah. Lit. "binding"; biblical account of God's command to Abraham to offer his son Isaac as a sacrifice.

Ashkenazim (adj. **Ashkenazic**). The term used for Jews who resided in northern Europe and who generally followed the customs originating in medieval German Judaism. This term at first referred to the Jews of northern France and western Germany. Later it denoted all Jews whose culture originated and developed in this part of Europe and in eastern Europe, as distinct from Sephardim, whose culture originated and developed in Spain and the Mediterranean *(see Sephardim).*

berakah. Lit. "blessing"; a thank-you offering that praises God for a benefit conferred or a great event experienced.

bet midrash. Place of study, discussion, and prayer; in ancient times a school of higher learning.

Birkat Haminim. Lit. "benediction concerning heretics"; a prayer that invoked divine wrath upon Christian Jews.

canon, canonical Scripture. The books of the Bible recognized as authoritative and divinely revealed.

chiliastic. Pertaining to the Christian doctrine that Christ will reign for a thousand years; also called millenarian.

covenant. A pact between two parties. The major covenants of Judaism are God's covenant with Abraham (Gen. 15), and the Sinai covenant (Exod. 19–24) between God and Israel.

Decalogue. The Ten Commandments received by Moses on Mt. Sinai (Exod. 20:1-17; Deut. 5:1-21).

diaspora. The Jewish communities living dispersed among the gentiles outside the Holy Land.

Ebionites, Ebionism. A Judeo-Christian sect in the 2nd-4th centuries C.E.; accepted much of Mosaic Torah (circumcision, Sabbath, etc.) but rejected sacrifices; accepted Jesus as Messiah but not his divinity; opposed the doctrines of Paul.

election. A theological term indicating God's choice of Israel to receive the covenant. The choice is not based on the superiority or previous accomplishments of the people. The chosen are obligated to fulfill God's commandments.

eschatology (eschaton). A study or science dealing with the ultimate destiny or purpose of humankind and the world; ideas about the end or last period of history or existence. The eschaton is the end-time.

etrog. A citron; "the fruit of goodly trees" (Lev. 23:40) carried in procession in the synagogue with the *lulab* during the festival of Sukkot (Feast of Tabernacles).

exilarch. The head of the Jewish community in the Babylonian exile; an imperial dignitary, a member of the council of state, living in semiroyal fashion; appointed communal officers and judges; a descendant of the house of David.

Gaon (pl. ***Geonim;*** adj. ***geonic***). Lit. "excellence"; title given to the rabbis of Babylonia in the 6th to 12th centuries.

Gemara. Lit. "completion"; popularly applied to the Talmud as a whole, to discussions by rabbinic teachers on Mishnah, and to decisions reached in these discussions.

genizah. Lit. "hiding"; a hiding place or storeroom, usually connected with a synagogue, for worn-out holy books. The most famous is the Cairo Genizah, which contained books and documents that provide source material for Jewish communities living under Islamic rule from about the 9th through the 12th centuries. It was discovered at the end of the 19th century.

gittin (sing. ***get***). Jewish practice related to divorce. A *get* is a Jewish divorce.

Gnostic, Gnosticism. Derived from the Greek *gnosis,* meaning "knowledge." Various systems of belief characterized by a dualistic view of God: one God created of the material, phenomenal world, and one of pure spirit. Possession of hidden gnosis would free one from the evil material world and give access to the spiritual world. It had a great impact on the Near East in the 2nd to 4th century C.E.

habdalah. Lit. "separation"; the ceremony using wine, spices, and candles at the conclusion of the Sabbath. Smelling the spices signifies the hope for a fragrant week; the light signifies the hope for a week of brightness and joy.

Haggadah. Lit. "narration"; a liturgical manual used in the Passover seder *(see seder).*

hakam (pl. ***hakamim***). Lit. "the wise"; title given to pre-70 C.E. protorabbinic scholars and post-70 C.E. rabbinic scholars.

halakah (adj. **halakic**). Jewish religious practice (or a guide to the same) for daily life, civil and criminal law, worship, and ritual; a pattern of conduct, both ethical and ritual.

halitzah. A ceremony related to the Levirate law of marriage, which frees the widow to marry someone other than her husband's brother.

In this ceremony the widow removes a shoe from her brother-in-law's foot, which is symbolic of removing his possessive right over her. *See also levirate marriage.*

Hanukkah. Lit. "dedication"; a festival that commemorates the rededication of the Jerusalem Temple to monotheistic worship by Judah the Maccabee in 164 B.C.E.

Hasidim, Hasidism. Lit. "pious ones"; the term may refer to Jews in various periods: (1) those who flourished in the 2nd century B.C.E. in response to the persecutions of Antiochus Epiphanes; (2) pietists in the 13th century; (3) followers of the movement of Hasidism founded in the 18th century.

Haskalah. Jewish enlightenment in eighteenth- and nineteenth-century Europe.

Hasmoneans. Descendants of Hashmon, a Jewish family that included the Maccabees and the high priests and kings who ruled Judea from 142 to 63 B.C.E.

Hellenism. The civilization that spread from Greece through much of the ancient world from 333 to 63 B.C.E. As a result, many elements of Greek culture (names, language, philosophy, athletics, architecture, etc.) penetrated the Near East.

hermeneutics. Principles of interpreting Scripture.

intertestamental period. The period between the Jewish Testament and the Christian Testament (ca. late 4th century B.C.E.-1st century C.E.). The Jewish intertestamental literature includes the Apocrypha (found mainly in the Septuagint) and the Pseudepigrapha (works of a later date ascribed to ancient authors like Enoch, the patriarchs, and Moses). This literature provides important background for understanding the Christian Testament. *See Apocrypha; Pseudepigrapha.*

Kabalah (Kabalism). Lit. "receiving," "tradition"; a system of Jewish theosophy and mysticism.

kaddish. A prayer recited at the conclusion of each major section of each service; also a prayer by mourners during the first year of bereavement and on the anniversary of the death of next-of-kin.

Kahal (Qahal). Lit. "congregation, gathering"; the corporate Jewish community of medieval Europe.

Karaism, Karaites. Derived from *kara (qara),* "Scripture"; a Middle Eastern sect of Judaism which arose in opposition to Rabbinism in the Middle Ages. The Karaites had a more literalistic approach to Scripture than the followers of Rabbinism.

kasher, kashrut. *Kasher* means "ritually correct"; *kashrut* refers to ritually correct dietary practices.

kavanah. Lit. "intention"; a mystical instrument of the kabalists; a meditation which accompanies a ritual act.

ketubah. The Jewish religious marriage certificate.

kiddush. Lit. "sanctification"; derived from *kadosh (qadosh)*, "holy"; a ritual of Sabbath and other holy days, usually accompanied by a cup of wine, which proclaims the holiness of the day.

kiddushin. Lit. "consecration"; denotes betrothal for marriage, signifying the sanctity of the relationship.

kiphah. A headcovering worn for worship, religious study, meals, or at any other time; also called yarmulke.

kohen (pl. *kohanim*). A priest, generally descended from the tribe of Levi.

levirate marriage. From the Latin *levir* for the Hebrew *yabam*, brother-in-law; a biblical system of marriage in which the *levir* marries his brother's widow (Deut. 25:5-10).

logos. Lit. "the word"; divine reason; a concept found in the philosophy of Philo comparable to the Hebrew *hokmah* ("widom").

lulab. The palm branch used with other plants in the Sukkot (Feast of Tabernacles) celebration.

maggid. Lit. "a speaker"; a kabalistic notion of how the Holy Spirit is mediated to the mystic; later meant a preacher among the eighteenth-century Hasidim.

Marranos. An old Spanish term meaning "swine," used to execrate medieval Spanish Jews who converted to Christianity but secretly kept their Judaism.

Maskilim. Lit. "the enlightened ones"; eighteenth- and nineteenth-century Jews who engaged in secular studies and facilitated the acculturation of Jews to Western society; members of the *Haskalah* (*see Haskalah*).

Masoretes, Masoretic text. Derived from *masorah,* meaning "tradition"; the Masoretes were the rabbis in ninth-century Palestine who sought to preserve the traditional text of the Bible (hence called the Masoretic text), which is still used in contemporary synagogues. The Masoretes were scholars who encouraged Bible study and attempted to achieve uniformity by establishing rules for correcting the text in matters of spelling, grammar, and pronunciation.

megillah. Lit. "scroll." Usually refers to the Scroll of Esther read on the festival of Purim.

melakah. Work.

merkabah. Lit. "chariot"; the "chariot vision" was an integral element of mysticism signifying a mystical vision of divinity.

messiah. Lit "the anointed one"; ancient priests and kings of Israel were anointed with oil. The term came to mean a descendant of the dynasty of David who would restore the united kingdom of Israel and Judah and usher in an age of peace and plenty; the redeemer figure.

mezuzah (pl. mezuzot). Lit. "doorpost"; a parchment scroll with selected Torah verses (Deut. 6:4-9; 11:13-21) placed in a container and affixed to the doorposts of rooms occupied by Jews, or to the outside door of a home; the word *shaddai* (almighty) is inscribed on the back of the container.

midrash (pl. **midrashim**). From *darash,* "to inquire"; the literature which attempts to interpret Scripture to its fullest meanings; may be either aggadah, dealing with theological ideas, ethical teachings, popular philosophy, imaginative exposition, legend, allegory, animal fables, etc.; or halakah, directing the Jew to specific patterns of religious practice.

min (pl. *minim*). A heretic, sectarian, or schismatic. It was applied in earlier centuries to Christians, especially Christian Jews of the 3rd or 4th decade of the 1st century. In later times it refers to people of Gnostic tendencies *(see Gnostic).*

minyan. A quorum of ten Jews (for Orthodox Jews, ten males) above age thirteen necessary for public services and certain other religious ceremonies.

miqvah. A communal bath for ritual immersion.

Mishnah. Lit. "teaching"; the digest of the recommended halakah as it existed at the end of the 2nd century.

mitnagdim. Lit. "the opposers"; opponents of the eighteenth-century Hasidim.

mitzvah (pl. **mitzvot**). Lit. "commandment," "obligation"; a ritual or ethical duty or act of obedience to God's will.

nabi (pl. *nebiim*). The "prophet" of ancient Israel.

nomos (pl. *nomoi*). A Greek term meaning "law" and referring to the Pentateuch, all of Jewish Scripture, and even proto-rabbinic halakah; an expert in *nomos* is termed a *nomikos.*

omer. Lit. "sheaf"; the sheaf of grain offering brought to the temple on Nisan 16; the name of the seven-week period between Pesah and Shabuot also known as the *Sephirah.*

Pentateuch. The Five Books of Moses: Genesis, Exodus, Leviticus, Numbers, and Deuteronomy; known in Jewish tradition as *Torat Mosheh* (the teaching of Moses), or simply Torah *(see Torah)*.

Perushim **(Pharisees).** Lit "separatists"; generally regarded as the founders of Rabbinism. However, I believe they were pietistic separatists, who were distinct from the proto-rabbis.

Pesach (Passover). Also known as *Hag Hamatzot* (Festival of Unleavened Bread). This festival commemorates the deliverance of the Hebrew people from Egypt (see Exod. 12–13).

Pharisees. An ancient group in Judaism whose origin and nature is unclear. Though many scholars define them as a party in Judaism identified with the ancient sages and rabbis who taught the oral and written law, I prefer to delineate them as a complex of pietistic, zealous, and separatistic sects.

phylacteries. *See tefillin.*

pilpul. Dialectical method of talmudic study.

piyyutim. Medieval hymns and poems added to standard prayers of the talmudic liturgy.

pogrom. From the Russian word for "devastation"; an unprovoked attack upon a Jewish community.

Proto-Judaism. The earliest form of the religion of Israel, which historically came to be called Judaism.

proto-rabbis. Pre-70 C.E. sages who set the foundations of post-70 C.E. Rabbinic Judaism before the ordination of rabbis.

Pseudepigrapha. From Greek *pseudos,* "deceit," "untruth," and *epigraphe,* "inscription"; the name given to a number of intertestamental apocryphal writings. The authors attributed their writings to an ancient worthy.

Qumran. The site near the northwest corner of the Dead Sea where a Jewish sect similar to the Essenes lived from the 3rd century B.C.E. to the 1st century C.E. They produced the Dead Sea Scrolls.

rebbe. The title of the spiritual leader of the Hasidim; *see zaddik.*

Rechabites. A dissenting movement in ancient Israel generally devoted to certain ascetic practices and a simple lifestyle.

redactor. An editor of books of the Jewish Bible.

responsa. Also called *teshubot,* from *sheelot uteshubot* (questions and answers); answers to questions on halakah and observances, given by scholars on topics addressed to them. They originated during the *geonic* period, and are still used as a means of modern updating and revision of halakah.

Rosh Hashanah. Lit. "beginning of the year"; Jewish New Year celebration.

Rosh Hodesh. Lit. "beginning of a lunar month"; the New Moon Festival.

Sabbatianism. A messianic movement begun in the 17th century by Shabbatai Zvi.

Sadducees. An ancient Jewish sect whose origin and ideas are uncertain. It probably arose early in the 2nd century B.C.E. and ceased to exist when the Temple was destroyed in 70 C.E. Sadducees supported priestly authority and rejected traditions not directly grounded in the Pentateuch, such as the concept of life after death.

Samaritans. Residents of the district of Samaria north of Jerusalem and Judah. One of numerous denominations in ancient Judaism that recognized only the Pentateuch as Scripture and Mt. Gerizim as the sacred center rather than Jerusalem. There was ongoing hostility between Samaritans and Judahites.

Sanhedrin. An ancient Jewish legislative and judicial body.

seder. Evening meal and service opening the celebration of Passover.

semikah. Rabbinic ordination.

Sephardim (adj. **Sephardic**). Primarily Jews of the Iberian peninsula (Spain and Portugal). After the Jewish expulsion from Spain in 1492, this term included those in general who resided in Islamic countries. *See Ashkenazim.*

Sephirah. Lit. "counting"; *see omer.*

Septuagint. The Greek translation of the Jewish Bible made during the reign of Ptolemy II, ca. 250 B.C.E.

Shabbat. Lit. "rest"; the Sabbath.

Shabuot (Pentecost). Lit. "weeks"; observed 50 days from the day the first sheaf of grain was offered to the priests; also known as Festival of First Fruits.

Shekinah. The Divine Presence; the Holy Spirit. In Kabalism it sometimes took on the aspect of the feminine element in deity.

Shema. Lit. "hear"; a prayer read every morning and evening based on Deut. 6:4-9; 11:13-21; Num. 15:37-41. Deut. 6:4 is the Jewish affirmation of the monotheistic creed.

Shemini Atzeret (the Eighth Day of Assembly). An eight-day festival that immediately follows the seven-day festival of Sukkot (Tabernacles).

shemoneh esreh. Lit. "eighteen"; the main section of prayers recited in a standing position. *See also amidah.*

shofar. Ram's horn sounded at Rosh Hashanah morning worship and at the conclusion of Yom Kippur.

Simhat Torah. Lit. "rejoicing with the Torah"; a festival which celebrates the conclusion of the annual reading cycle of the Torah.

sopher (pl. *sopherim*). Lit. "scribe"; used as a general designation for scholars and copyists in both talmudic and later literature; a "scholastic," a learned researcher whose vocation was the study and teaching of the tradition. In early times the *sopher* was the scholar. By the 1st century he was no longer a real scholar but a functionary and teacher of children.

Sukkot (Tabernacles). Lit. "booths" or "tabernacles"; seven-day festival beginning on Tishri 15 commemorating the *sukkot* where Israel lived in the wilderness after the Exodus; also known as *Hag Haasiph*, the Festival of Ingathering (of the harvest).

syncretism. Synthesis of variegated religious beliefs derived from more than one religion.

tallit. Prayer shawl; a four-cornered cloth with fringes.

Talmud. Lit. "study" or "learning"; the collection of rabbinic writings which comprise the commentary and discussion of the *amoraim* (teachers) on the Mishnah and Tosefta.

tanna (adj. *tannaitic,* pl. *tannaim*). A sage from the period of Hillel to the compilation of the Mishnah (20-200 C.E.), distinguished from later *amoraim. Tannaim* were primarily scholars and teachers. The Mishnah, Tosefta, and *Midreshey Halakah* were among their literary achievements.

Targum. Lit. "translation"; an Aramaic translation of Bible; also used for Aramaic portions of Bible.

tefillin. Usually translated as "phylacteries." Box-like appurtenances that accompany prayer; worn by Jewish adult males at the weekday morning services; one of each is placed on the head and left arm and held by a strap; they contain passages from the Pentateuch (Exod. 13:1-10, 11-16; Deut. 6:4-9; 11:13-21).

Torah, torah. Lit. "teaching, instruction"; hence torah refers to study of the whole gamut of Jewish tradition or some aspect of it. The Torah refers to the Five Books of Moses in the Hebrew Scriptures *(see Pentateuch).*

Tosefta (pl. **Tosafot**). Lit. "supplement"; supplements to the Mishnah. Termed *beraita* (extraneous material) in the Talmud.

typology. A form of biblical interpretation wherein a person, event, or institution is viewed as foreshadowing a later one.

305

yarmulke. *See kiphah.*

yeshivah (pl. **yeshivot**). An academy of higher rabbinic learning.

YHWH (Yahweh). The sacred name of God in the Bible; also known as the tetragrammaton. Since Hebrew was written without vowels in ancient times, the four consonants *YHWH* offer no clue to their original pronunciation. Though the pronunciation is uncertain, it is generally rendered "Yahweh." In most English versions of the Bible it is translated as "Lord."

Yiddish. The vernacular of Ashkenazic Jews; it is a combination of several languages, especially Hebrew and German, written in Hebrew script.

Yom Kippur. "Day of Atonement"; annual day of fasting and atonement, occurring on Tishri 10; the most important occasion of the Jewish religious year.

zaddik. Lit. "righteous one"; the spiritual leader of the modern Hasidim, popularly known as *rebbe*.

zizit. Lit. "fringes"; *see tallit.*

Zohar. "Book of Splendor"; the chief literary work of the kabalists. The author of the main part of the *Zohar* was Moses de Leon (12th century); however, it is pseudepigraphically ascribed to Simeon Bar Yohai (2nd century).

Bibliography

The following bibliography is by no means exhaustive. It includes only some of the works used in preparation of this work, and a reasonable selection of books useful for further study. Rather than group the books chapter by chapter, they are presented in a way that provides useful references for the study of the ancient period, the medieval period, and the modern-contemporary era. A bibliography for the appendix, "Images of Women in Judaism," has been added by the editor.

PRIMARY SOURCES

The student is well advised to peruse and study the primary sources: Jewish (Old) Testament, intertestamental literature, Dead Sea Scrolls, Christian Testament; and the rabbinic literature: Mishnah, Tosefta, Mekilta, Sifra, Sifre, Midrash Rabbah, and other midrashim, the Babylonian and Palestinian Talmuds. Many volumes of these Hebrew and Aramaic works are available in English, French, and German. So too the medieval responsa and halakic compilation should be used, especially that of Moses Maimonides, *Mishneh Torah*, available in the Yale Judaica Series in English. Biographies of many major figures are available and should be studied for the insights they provide for the development of Judaism. The works of Philo of Alexandria and Josephus should also be utilized.

PERIODICALS

Out of consideration of space, no articles (except for the author's and those in the appendix) are included in this bibliography. But a selection of appropriate relevant periodicals is here presented as a useful research aid: *Biblica*,

BIBLIOGRAPHY

Biblische Zeitschrift, Catholic Biblical Quarterly, Hebrew Union College Annual, Horizons in Biblical Theology, Jewish Quarterly Review, Journal of Biblical Literature, Journal of Jewish Studies, Journal for the Study of Judaism, New Testament Studies, Novum Testamentum, Vetus Testamentum, Zeitschrift für die alttestamentliche Wissenschaft.

GENERAL WORKS

Baron, Salo Wittmayer. *A Social and Religious History of the Jews.* 17 volumes. Philadelphia: Jewish Publication Society, 1952-1980.

Steinschneider, M. *Jewish Literature from the Eighth to the Eighteenth Century.* Repr. New York: Hermon, 1965.

Waxman, M. *A History of Jewish Literature.* 5 volumes. New York-London: Yoseloff, 1960.

Zinberg, Israel. *Toldot Sifrut Yisrael.* 6 volumes. Tel Aviv: Y. Shreberk, 1959-1960.

―――. *A History of Jewish Literature.* Ed. and trans. B. Martin. 12 volumes. New York: Ktav, 1974-1978.

CHAPTERS ONE-THREE

Aleck, Ch. *Mabo Lamishnah.* Jerusalem-Tel Aviv: 1959.

Alon, G. *Toledot Hayeludim Beeretz Yisrael Bitquphat Hamishnah wehatalmud.* 3rd ed. Tel Aviv: Hakkibutz Hameuchad, 1967.

Bacher, Wilhelm. *Tradition und Tradenten in den Schulen Palästinas und Babyloniens.* Repr. Berlin: 1966.

Bamberger, B. J. *Proselytism in the Talmudic Period.* New York: Ktav, 1966.

Black, M. *An Aramaic Approach to the Gospels and Acts.* 3rd ed. Oxford: Oxford University Press, 1967.

Cross, Frank M. *The Ancient Library of Qumran.* Rev. ed. Repr. Grand Rapids: Baker, 1980.

Daniélou, Jean. *The Theology of Jewish Christianity.* Trans. J. A. Baker. Chicago: Regnery, 1964.

Daube, David. *The New Testament and Rabbinic Judaism.* London: Athlone, 1956.

Davies, W. D. *Paul and Rabbinic Judaism.* London: SPCK, 1955.

De Vaux, Roland. *Ancient Israel.* Trans. J. McHugh. Repr. 2 vols. New York: McGraw-Hill, 1965.

Dupont-Sommer, André. *The Essene Writings from Qumran.* Trans. Geza Vermes. Repr. Gloucester, MA: Peter Smith, 1970.

Eissfeldt, Otto. *The Old Testament: An Introduction.* Trans. Peter R. Ackroyd. San Francisco-London: Harper & Row, 1965.

Elbogen, Ismar. *Der jüdische Gottesdienst in seiner geschichtlichen Entwicklung.* Frankfurt-am-Main: 1931.

Fitzmyer, J. A. *Essays on the Semitic Background of the New Testament.* London: Geoffrey Chapman, 1971.

Geiger, A. *Das Judentum und seine Geschichte bis zum Zerstörung des Zweiten Tempels.* 2nd ed. Breslau: 1865.

Ginzberg, L. *The Legends of the Jews.* 7 vols. Philadelphia: Jewish Publication Society, 1954.

Goodenough, E. R. *Jewish Symbols in the Greco-Roman Period.* 13 vols. Princeton: Princeton University Press, 1953-1968.

Gutman, Joseph, ed. *No Graven Images. Studies in Art and the Hebrew Bible.* New York: Ktav, 1971.

———. *The Synagogue: Studies in Origins, Archaeology and Architecture.* New York: Ktav, 1975.

Heinemann, Joseph. *Prayer in the Talmud.* Trans. Richard S. Sarason. Berlin-New York: de Gruyter, 1977.

Hengel, Martin. *Judaism and Hellenism.* Trans. John Bowden. 2 vols. Philadelphia: Fortress, 1974.

Henrix, Hans H., ed. *Jüdische Liturgie. Geschichte-Struktur-Wesen.* Freiburg-Basel-Vienna: 1979.

Herrmann, Siegfried. *A History of Israel in Old Testament Times.* Trans. John Bowden. Philadelphia: Fortress, 1975.

Herzog, Isaac. *The Main Institutions of Jewish Law.* 2 vols. 2nd ed. London-New York: Soncino, 1965.

Kaufmann, Yehezkel. *The Religion of Israel.* Abridged and trans. Moshe Greenberg. Chicago: University of Chicago Press, 1960.

———. *Toledot Haemunah Hayisraelit.* 4 vols. Tel-Aviv: Devir, 1952-1956.

Klausner, J. *From Jesus to Paul.* Trans. W. F. Stinespring. New York: Macmillan, 1943.

———. *The Messianic Idea in Israel.* Trans. W. F. Stinespring. New York: Macmillan, 1955.

Krauss, Samuel. *Synagogale Altertümer.* Berlin-Vienna: 1922.

Lieberman, Saul. *Greek in Jewish Palestine.* 2nd ed. New York: P. Feldheim, 1965.

———. *Hellenism in Jewish Palestine.* New York: P. Feldheim, 1962.

Montefiore, C. G. and H. Loewe, eds. *A Rabbinical Anthology.* Repr. New York: Schocken, 1974.

Moore, G. F. *Judaism in the First Centuries of the Christian Era.* 3 vols. Cambridge, MA: Harvard University Press, 1927-1930.

Neusner, Jacob. *The Rabbinic Traditions About the Pharisees Before 70.* 3 vols. Leiden: Brill, 1969.

Petuchowski, Jacob, ed. *Contributions to the Scientific Study of Jewish Liturgy.* New York: Ktav, 1970.

Sandmel, Samuel. *Judaism and Christian Beginnings.* New York: Oxford University Press, 1978.

Schechter, Solomon. *Aspects of Rabbinic Theology.* New York: Schocken, 1961.

Schoeps, H. J. *Jewish Christianity.* Philadelphia: Fortress, 1969.

Scholem, Gershom. *The Messianic Idea in Judaism.* New York: Schocken, 1971.

Schürer, Emil. *The History of the Jewish People in the Age of Jesus Christ.* 3 vols. Rev. ed. Trans. Geza Vermes, et al. Edinburgh: T. & T. Clark, 1973-1987.

Sellin, Ernst Fohrer Georg. *Introduction to the Old Testament.* Trans. David E. Green. Nashville: Abingdon, 1968.

Sigal, Phillip. *The Emergence of Contemporary Judaism.* Vol. I: *The Foundations of Judaism.* Part 1: *From the Origins to the Separation of Christianity.* Pittsburgh Theological Monograph Series, 29. Pittsburgh: Pickwick, 1980.

————. Vol. I, Part 2: *Rabbinic Judaism.* Pittsburgh Theological Monograph Series, 29a. Pittsburgh: Pickwick, 1980.

————. *The Halakah of Jesus of Nazareth According to the Gospel of Matthew.* Lanham, MD: University Press of America, 1986.

————. *New Dimensions in Judaism: A Creative Analysis of Rabbinic Concepts.* New York: Exposition Press, 1972.

————. "Early Christian and Rabbinic Liturgical Affinities: Exploring Liturgical Acculturation," *New Testament Studies* 30 (1984), 63-90.

————. "Elements of Male Chauvinism in Classical Halakhah," *Judaism* 24 (1975), 226-44.

————. "A Prolegomenon to Paul's Judaic Thought: The Death of Jesus and the Akedah." *Proceedings,* Eastern Great Lakes-Midwest Biblical Societies. Vol. 4 (1984), 222-36.

Simon, Marcel. *Versus Israel.* Paris: 1948.

Spiegel, Shalom. *The Last Trial.* Philadelphia: Jewish Publication Society, 1967.

Strack, Herman L. *Introduction to the Talmud and Midrash.* Repr. New York: Schocken, 1978.

Vermes, Geza. *Scripture and Tradition in Judaism.* Leiden: Brill, 1961.

CHAPTERS FOUR-SIX

Agus, I. A. *The Heroic Age of Franco-German Jewry*. New York: Bloch, 1969.

Altmann, Alexander. *Studies in Religious Philosophy and Mysticism*. Repr. New York: Arno, 1975.

————. *Jewish Medieval and Renaissance Studies*. Cambridge, MA: Harvard University Press, 1967.

Ashtour (Strauss), E. *Qorot Hayehudim Besepharad Hamuslemit*. 2nd ed. 2 vols. Jerusalem: 1966.

Baer, F. Y. "The Religious-Social Tendency of *Sefer Hasidim*" [Hebrew], *Zion* 3 (1938).

Baer, Yitzchak. *A History of the Jews in Christian Spain*. 2 vols. Philadelphia: Jewish Publication Society, 1961-1966.

Baron, Salo W. *The Jewish Community*. 3 volumes. Philadelphia: Jewish Publication Society, 1942.

Barzilay, I. *Yosek Shlomo Delmedigo*. Leiden: Brill, 1974.

Birnbaum, Philip, ed. *Karaite Studies*. Repr. New York: Hermon, 1971.

Dienstag, Jacob I., ed. *Eschatology in Maimonidean Thought*. New York: Ktav, 1983.

Ginzberg, Louis. *Genizah Studies*. New York: Hermon, 1929.

Goitein, S. D. *A Mediterranean Society: The Jewish Community of the Arab World as Portrayed in the Documents of the Cairo Genizah*. 3 vols. Los Angeles: University of California Press, 1970.

Guttmann, Julius. *Philosophies of Judaism*. Trans. David Silverman. Philadelphia: Jewish Publication Society, 1964.

Haberman, Jacob. *Maimonides and Aquinas*. New York: Ktav, 1979.

Hirschberg, H. Z. *Toledot Hayehudim Beaphrigah Hasephonit*. 2 vols. Jerusalem: 1965.

Husik I. *A History of Medieval Jewish Philosophy*. Philadelphia: Jewish Publication Society, 1966.

Katz, Jacob. *Exclusiveness and Tolerance*. New York: Schocken, 1962.

————. *Tradition and Crisis*. New York: Free Press of Glencoe, 1961.

Lasker, Daniel J. *Jewish Philosophical Polemics Against Christianity in the Middle Ages*. New York: Ktav, 1977.

Mann, Jacob. *Texts and Studies in Jewish History and Literature*. 2 vols. New York: Ktav, 1972.

Margaliot, M. *Hilkot aras Yisrael min Haggenizah*. Jerusalem: 1973.

Nemoy, Leon, ed. *Karaite Anthology*. New Haven: Yale University Press, 1952.

Neuman, Abraham. *The Jews in Spain*. Philadelphia: Jewish Publication Society, 1942.

BIBLIOGRAPHY

Neumark, D. *Geschichte der jüdischen Philosophie des Mittelalters nach Problemen dargestellt.* 3 vols. Berlin: 1907-1928. Hebrew translation: *Toledot Haphilosophiah Beyisrael.* 2 vols. New York: 1921.

Paul, André. *Ecrits de Qumran et sectes juives aux premiers siecles del l'Islam: Recherches sur l'origine du Qaratisme.* Paris: 1969.

Roth, Cecil. *History of the Jews in England.* Oxford: 1949.

—————. *The History of the Jews of Italy.* Philadelphia: Jewish Publication Society, 1946.

—————. *The Jews in the Renaissance.* Philadelphia: Jewish Publication Society, 1959.

Ruderman, David B. *The World of a Renaissance Jew.* New York: Ktav, 1981.

Scholem, Gershom. *Major Trends in Jewish Mysticism.* 3rd ed. New York: Schocken, 1965.

—————. *On the Kabbalah and its Symbolism.* New York: Schocken, 1965.

—————. *Sabbatai Sevi: The Mystical Messiah.* Princeton: Princeton University Press, 1973.

Shulvass, M. A. *The Jews in the World of the Renaissance.* Leiden: Brill, 1973.

Sigal, Phillip. *The Emergence of Contemporary Judaism.* Vol. II: *From the Seventh to the Seventeenth Century.* Pittsburgh Theological Monograph Series, 12. Pittsburgh: Pickwick, 1977.

—————. Vol. III: *From Medievalism to Proto-Modernity in the Sixteenth and Seventeenth Centuries.* Pittsburgh Theological Monograph Series, N.S. 17. Pittsburgh: Pickwick, 1987.

Stow, Kenneth R. *Catholic Thought and Papal Jewry Policy, 1555-1593.* New York: Ktav, 1977.

Tishbi, I. and P. Lahover, *Mishnat Hazohar.* 2 vols. Jerusalem: 1961.

Vajdo, Georges. *Recherches sur la philosophie et la kabbale dans la pensée juive du moyen age.* Paris: 1962.

Zunz, Leopold. *Die Gottesdienstlichen Vortrage der Juden.* Berlin: 1832. Hebrew translation: *Hadrashot B'Yisrael.* Trans. H. Albeck. Jerusalem: Mosad Bialik, 1954.

The student is advised to study the primary sources of medieval Jewish philosophy and mysticism, especially such works as those by Saadia, Judah Halevi, Moses Maimonides, Joseph Albo, and Samuel Usque, some of which are available in English, French, and German. The primary mystical works, *Sefer Yezirah* and *The Zohar,* are also available in English.

CHAPTERS SEVEN-EIGHT

Agus, Jacob. *Modern Philosophies of Judaism*. New York: Behrman, 1940.

Altmann, Alexander. *Moses Mendelssohn: A Biographical Study*. University: University of Alabama Press, 1973.

Berkovits, Eliezer. *Faith After the Holocaust*. New York: Ktav, 1973.

Chazan, Robert and Marc Lee Raphael, eds. *Modern Jewish History. A Source Reader*. New York: Schocken, 1975.

Cohen, Samuel S. *Jewish Theology*. Assen: Royal Vangorcum Ltd., 1971.

Davis, Moshe. *The Emergence of Conservative Judaism*. Philadelphia: Jewish Publication Society, 1965.

Fleischner, Eva, ed. *Auschwitz: Beginnning of a New Era?* New York: Ktav, 1977.

Goldberg, Hillel. *Israel Salanter: Text, Structure, Idea*. New York: Ktav, 1982.

Heschel, Abraham Joshua. *God in Search of Man: A Philosophy of Judaism*. Repr. Cleveland-New York: World, 1964.

Hirsch, Samson R. *Horeb: A Philosophy of Jewish Laws and Observances*. 2 vols. Trans. I. Grunfeld. London: Soncino, 1962.

Jacobs, Louis. *Principles of the Jewish Faith*. London: Vallentine Mitchell, 1964.

Kaplan, Mordecai M. *Judaism as a Civilization*. New York: Jewish Reconstructionist, 1957.

Katz, Jacob. *Out of the Ghetto. The Social Background of Jewish Emancipation, 1770-1870*. New York: Schocken, 1978.

Kayserling, Meier. *Moses Mendelssohn. Sein Leben und seine Werke*. Leipzig: 1862.

Kohler, Kaufmann. *Jewish Theology*. New York: Macmillan, 1918.

Kook, A. I. *Orot Ha-Qodesh*. 2 vols. Jerusalem: 1938.

Maimon, Solomon. *Autobiography of Solomon Maimon*. Trans. J. Clark Murray. London: East and West Library, 1954.

Mendelssohn, Moses. *Gesammelte Schriften*. Jubilaumsausgabe. Ed. Leo Strauss. Berlin: 1929-1932.

Meyer, Michael A. *The Origins of the Modern Jew*. Detroit: Wayne State University Press, 1967.

Petuchowski, Jacob J. *Prayerbook Reform in Europe*. New York: Union of American Hebrew Congregations, 1968.

Plaut, Gunther, ed. *The Growth of Reform Judaism*. New York: Union of American Hebrew Congregations, 1965.

————. *The Rise of Reform Judaism*. New York: Union of American Hebrew Congregations, 1963.

Rabinowitz, Harry M. *The World of Hasidism*. London: Hartford, Hartmore House, 1970.

Rosenbloom, Noah H. *Tradition in an Age of Reform: The Religious Philosophy of Samson Raphael Hirsch.* Philadelphia: Jewish Publication Society, 1976.

Rosenzweig, Franz. *The Star of Redemption.* Trans. William W. Hallo. Boston: Beacon Press, 1972.

Rotenstreich, Nathan. *Jewish Philosophy in Modern Times: From Mendelssohn to Rosenzweig.* New York: Holt, Rinehart and Winston, 1968.

Rudavsky, David. *Modern Jewish Religious Movements.* New York: Behrman, 1967.

Shohet, Azriel. *Beginnings of the Haskalah Among German Jewry in the First Half of the Eighteenth Century* [Hebrew]. Jerusalem: 1960.

Sigal, Phillip. "Aspects of an Inquiry into Dual Covenant Theology," *Horizons in Biblical Theology* 3 (1981), 181-209.

————. "*Halakhic* Reflections on the Pittsburgh Platform." In *The Changing World of Reform Judaism: The Pittsburgh Platform in Retrospect.* Ed. Walter Jacobs. Pittsburgh: Rodef Shalom Congregation, 1985, pp. 41-54.

————. "Halakhah Is Not Law," *Jewish Spectator* (February 1971), 15-18.

————. "The Organ and Jewish Worship," *Conservative Judaism* (Spring-Summer, 1963), 93-105.

————. "Reflections on Ethical Elements of Judaic Halakhah," *Duquesne Law Review* 23 (1985), 863-902.

————. "Women in a Prayer Quorum." In *Conservative Judaism and Jewish Law.* Ed. Seymour Siegel. New York: Rabbinical Assembly, 1977, pp. 281-92.

————. "Women in a Prayer Quorum," *Judaism* (Spring, 1974), 174-82.

Sigal, Phillip and Abraham J. Ehrlich. "A Responsum on Yom Tov Sheni Shel Galuyot," *Conservative Judaism* (Winter, 1970), 22-33.

Tama, Diogene. *Transactions of the Parisian Sanhedrin.* Trans. F. D. Kirwan. London: 1807.

Urbach, Ephraim E. *The Sages. Their Concepts and Beliefs* [Hebrew]. Jerusalem: 1969.

Wilhelm, Kurt, ed. *Wissenschaft des Judentums in deutschen Sprachbereich.* 2 vols. Tübingen: 1967.

Yerushalmi, Yosef H. *Zakhor: Jewish History and Jewish Memory.* Seattle: University of Washington Press, 1982.

IMAGES OF WOMEN IN JUDAISM

Aschkenasy, Nehama. "A Non-Sexist Reading of the Bible," *Midstream* (June/July 1981), 51-55.

Baum, Charlotte et al., eds. *The Jewish Woman in America*. New York: Dial, 1976.

Bird, Phyllis. "Images of Women in the Old Testament." In *Religion and Sexism*. Ed. Rosemary Ruether. New York: Simon & Schuster, 1974, pp. 41-88.

De Vaux, Roland. *Ancient Israel*, Vol. I. Trans. J. McHugh. Repr. New York: McGraw-Hill, 1965.

Dever, William G. "Asherah, Consort of Yahweh? New Evidence from Kuntillet of Ajrud," *Bulletin of the American Schools of Oriental Research* 255 (1984), 21-37.

Gendler, Mary. "The Restoration of Vashti." In *The Jewish Woman*. Ed. Elizabeth Koltun. New York: Schocken, 1976, pp. 241-47.

Ginzberg, Louis. *The Legends of the Jews*, Vol. I. Trans. Henrietta Szold. Philadelphia: Jewish Publication Society, 1954.

Greenburg, Blu. *On Women and Judaism: A View from Tradition*. Philadelphia: Jewish Publication Society, 1981.

Hallo, William. *The Exaltation of Inanna*. New Haven: Yale University Press, 1968.

Hauptman, Judith. "Images of Women in the Talmud." In *Religion and Sexism*. Ed. Rosemary R. Ruether. New York: Simon & Schuster, 1974, pp. 184-212.

———. "Women in the Rabbinate." In *Women in the Rabbinate, Priesthood, and Ministry*. Ed. Lillian Sigal. Grand Rapids: Ahavas Israel Congregation, 1987, pp. 1-10.

Hertzberg, Hans W., ed. *I & II Samuel*. Trans. J. S. Bowden. Old Testament Library. Philadelphia: Westminster, 1976.

Hyman, Paula. "The Jewish Woman in History and Literature." Sound Recording. New York: Jewish People's University of the Air, 1980.

Kramer, Samuel Noah. "Poets and Psalmists: Goddesses and Theologians," *Bibliotheca Mesopotamica* 4 (1976), 3-21.

Marcus, Jacob Rader. *The American Jewish Woman, 1654-1980*. New York: Ktav, 1981.

Meiselman, Moshe. *Jewish Woman in Jewish Law*. New York: Ktav, 1978.

Patai, Raphael. *The Hebrew Goddess*. New York: Ktav, 1967.

Rienstra, Marchiene. "Women in the Protestant Ministry." In *Women in the Rabbinate, Priesthood, and Ministry*. Ed. Lillian Sigal. Grand Rapids: Ahavas Israel Congregation, 1987, pp. 20-26.

Ruether, Rosemary R. *Womanguides*. Boston: Beacon, 1985.

Schneider, Susan Weidman. *Jewish and Female*. New York: Simon & Schuster, 1984.

Sigal, Phillip. "Divorce," *Jewish Spectator* (January, 1962).

————. "Elements of Male Chauvinism in Classical Halakhah," *Judaism* (Spring, 1975). (*See also* Appendix A in *Emergence*, II.)

————. *The Emergence of Contemporary Judaism*, Vols. I-III. Pittsburgh: Pickwick, 1977-1986.

————. "Halakhic Perspectives on the Matrilineal-Patrilineal Principles," *Judaism* (Winter, 1985).

————. *New Dimensions in Judaism*. New York: Exposition, 1972.

————. "Women in a Prayer Quorum," *Judaism* (Spring, 1974), 174-82.

Swidler, Leonard. *Women in Judaism: The Status of Women in Formative Judaism*. Metuchen, N.J.: Scarecrow, 1976.

Trible, Phyllis. "Eve and Adam: Genesis 2–3 Reread." In *Womanspirit Rising*. Eds. Carol Christ and Judith Plaskow. San Francisco: Harper & Row, 1979.

Umansky, Ellen M. "Women in Judaism: From the Reform Movement to Contemporary Jewish Religious Feminism." In *Women of Spirit*. New York: Simon & Schuster, 1979.

Index

INDEX

Ben Sira (Sirach), Joshua (Jesus), 33, 37, 41, 44, 48, 54, 90, 98, 103, 109
Benjamin of Tudela, 128
Beruriah, 282
Black Death, 132, 135
Blood libel, 120, 176
Boethusians, 40, 89, 94, 95
Booths (Sukkot), Festival of, 23-24, 25, 245-46
Buber, Martin, 236
Buxtorf, Johannes, 181

Calendar: and biblical holy days, 242; in Jubilees, 54; of Karaites, 118; promulgation of, 107; at Qumran, 61; of Samaritans, 65; solar vs. lunar, 23
Calvin, John, 129, 186-87
Canon (of Scripture), 36, 41, 98-99
Cantor, 121, 261. *See also* Hazan
Christian Jews, 40, 54, 59, 66, 67, 66n. 10, 77, 80, 80-84, 94
Christian Testament or Bible, 49, 50
Christiani, Pablo, 138
Christianity, 53, 65-84, 155-56
Church Fathers: Apostolic Fathers, 75; Clement of Alexandria, 47, 53; Clement of Rome, 82; Eusebius, 47, 53, 67, 169; Irenaeus, 75; John Chrysostom, 84; Justin Martyr, 53, 75, 79, 176; Origen, 53, 75
Circumcision: Abraham Geiger's view of, 200; in Ebionism, 83; and halakah, 2, 252-53; and Mosaic religion, 13
Cohen, Hermann, 152, 236
Confirmation, 197, 215, 253
Conservative movement: burial and mourning in, 255; dietary practices of, 51, 257; divorce in, 287; and halakah, 217; head covering in, 11, 260; language

of prayer in, 203, 288; Karaites and, 119; marriage in, 136, 287; minyan in, 288; in North America, 218-20; and science of Judaism, 197; and tefillin, 258; women cantors in, 288; women rabbis in, 288
Conversion (or proselytism), 5
Cordovero, Moses, 159, 160
Covenant: with Abraham, 8, 9, 10; and circumcision, 2, 252; and "concealment of presence [of God]," 234; and covenant community, 34; and Exodus from Egypt, 21; with Isaac, 10; and Israel, 7; with Jacob, 10; with Joshua, 13; as metaphor for marriage, 277-78; in Paul, 78, 79; in prophets, 29; and Sabbath, 20, 249-50
Covering the head. *See Kiphah*
Crescas, Hasdai, 149, 153
Cromwell, Oliver, 176
Crusades, 128, 134, 135, 136
Cyrus, 15, 16

Da Costa, Uriel, 170, 174
Da Modena, Leone, 171-73
David, 14, 15, 16, 249, 266
Day of Atonement (Yom Kippur), 22, 23, 25, 55, 240, 243, 244-45
De Lyra, Nicholas, 183, 187
Dead Sea Scrolls, 40, 54, 58-62, 59, 74, 95, 121. *See also* Qumran
Death, mourning, 254-55
Deborah, 269-70
Decalogue. *See* Ten Commandments
Delmedigo, Yosef Shelomo, 169, 170-71
Demonology (or satanism), 55, 157, 159, 169
Determinism, 151, 174
Dietary practices (kashrut), 51, 65; in Conservative Judaism, 218,